The *Annus Mirabilis* of Sir Isaac Newton
1666–1966

The *Annus Mirabilis* of Sir Isaac Newton 1666–1966

Edited by Robert Palter

THE M.I.T. PRESS
Cambridge, Massachusetts, and London, England

The articles in this symposium were originally published in *The Texas Quarterly*, Volume 10, Number 3 (Autumn 1967), © 1967 by the University of Texas, Austin, Texas.

"The Lad from Lincolnshire" by Frank E. Manuel is reprinted by permission of the publishers from Frank E. Manuel, *A Portrait of Isaac Newton*, Cambridge, Mass.: The Belknap Press of Harvard University Press, Copyright 1968 by the President and Fellows of Harvard College. "Reactions of Late Baroque Mechanics to Success, Conjecture, Error, and Failure in Newton's *Principia*" by C. Truesdell is reprinted by permission of the publishers from C. Truesdell, *Essays in the History of Mechanics*, New York: Springer-Verlag, Copyright 1968 by Springer-Verlag Berlin Heidelberg.

Comments and Introduction Copyright © 1970 by The Massachusetts Institute of Technology.

ISBN 0 262 16035 8 (hardcover)

Library of Congress catalog card number: 78–115762

Contents

An Ivory Portrait Medallion of Sir Isaac Newton, by David le Marchand. 7¾ in. by 5⅛ in.
From the collection of Mrs. T. D. Fryer. Reproduced with the kind permission of Sotheby
and Co., London.
"Mention was first made of this relief in the inventory taken of Newton's effects shortly after
his death in 1727; later it passed into the hands of Doctor Richard Mead, the Royal Physician,
was included in the sale of his remarkable collection of objet d'art in March 1755, and then
vanished into obscurity." Jane Spark, *Ivory Hammer 2* (1964), facing page 216.

Introduction

ALREADY IN THE EARLY 1960S IT HAD BECOME EVIDENT TO ALL STUDENTS of the history of science that an impressive revival of Newtonian studies was taking place. This revival had its quantitative side in the growing volume of interpretative writings and reprints of Newton's own works, but above all the revival was qualitative: scholars were learning to appreciate Newton's achievements in his own terms and the terms of his contemporaries instead of merely praising those achievements when they seemed to coincide with modern physical ideas (the wave-particle duality of light) and condemning them when they seemed outmoded (the mechanical conception of nature). Most important of all, vital new texts were becoming generally available as the rich mass of Newton's manuscripts and letters began to be exploited by a small but dedicated group of highly competent scholars.

With this situation in mind I approached my colleagues in the Philosophy Department of the University of Texas in early 1965 with a tentative scheme for a conference on Newtonian studies to commemorate the three hundredth anniversary of Newton's *annus mirabilis* of 1666. The response to my proposal was unanimously favorable. Under the enthusiastic leadership of Chairman (now Dean) John Silber, the Philosophy Department enlisted the support of the administration of the University of Texas, both Chancellor Harry Ransom and Vice-Chancellor (now President) Norman Hackerman taking a personal interest in the project. With the generous budget provided by the University of Texas supplemented by a grant from the National Science Foundation, it became possible to invite an international roster of distinguished Newtonian scholars to participate in the conference. I was fortunate in being able to rely at every stage of the planning on the sound advice of George Basalla (Assistant Professor of History at the University of Texas) and of the members of the Philosophy Department. From the start we had hoped that the papers might present a general conspectus of Newton's life, thought, and influence, as well as making available to a wide audience of interested scholars and laymen some of the significant findings of recent Newtonian scholarship. To stimulate discussion and to help in opening out wider perspectives, other scholars, often not themselves Newton specialists, were enlisted to read critical comments on most of the major papers. Finally, many historians, philosophers, and scientists were invited to attend and to participate in both the formal and the informal sessions of the conference. By thus bringing together a group of outstanding scholars from diverse disciplines for several days of intensive discussion, we wished to give fresh impetus and direction to Newtonian studies. Historians of physics, of biology, of philosophy, of art attempted to clarify both the sources and the consequences of Newton's thought, while philosophers of science and practicing scientists attempted to evaluate those parts of the Newtonian heritage which remain valid today.

The principal papers and commentaries presented in Austin, Texas, on November 10–12, 1966, are included in this volume; they speak for themselves, and it would be presumptuous and supererogatory for me to attempt at this point to summarize or criticize them. Perhaps, however, a word on Newton's *annus mirabilis* is in order. Not surprisingly, the very notion of the year 1666 as Newton's *annus mirabilis* was subjected to sharp questioning in some of the papers delivered at the conference: a few scholars felt that the wrong year (for the *annus mirabilis*, not for the conference!) had been selected; others opted for the two years, 1665–1666; and still others rejected the very attempt to periodize Newton's scientific development in this way. It might be well, therefore, to repeat here Newton's own testimony. At the beginning of the year 1665, when Newton was twenty-three, he retired for two years to his native village of Woolsthorpe to escape the plague which had closed down Cambridge University. In later life Newton recalled those years as his most creative period, when, as he put it, "I was in the prime of my age for invention and minded Mathematics and Philosophy more than at any time since" (Cambridge University Library, Add. MS. 3968, No. 2). In particular, Newton tells us that in 1666 he developed the fundamental principles of the integral calculus, verified the composite nature of sunlight, and satisfied himself by calculation that the earth's gravitation holds the moon in its orbit. Though, as I have remarked, recent scholarship may have effectively questioned the accuracy of Newton's memory, it will, I trust, still be considered acceptable to consider the "marvelous year" of 1666 symbolically as one of the decisive turning points in the history of modern science.

Robert Palter
July 1969

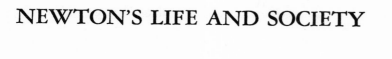

NEWTON'S LIFE AND SOCIETY

FRANK E. MANUEL

The Lad From Lincolnshire

EWTON'S LONG LIFE DIVIDES ITSELF NEATLY INTO THREE PARTS, EACH OF which is largely confined to a particular locality—the county of Lincolnshire, Cambridge, and London. He virtually never strayed outside this triangle. The first eighteen years, as well as part of the marvelously creative period we are celebrating, were spent in Lincolnshire, and he returned there for brief sojourns until he was a very old man. From his entry into Trinity in 1661 until he was elevated to the wardenship of the Mint in 1696 and moved away to the capital, thirty-five years passed. In London he lived for thirty-one years longer. On his personality and behavior during the Cambridge and London phases there are many documents in his own hand and the recorded testimony of numerous eyewitnesses, though some irksome questions remain unresolved. But Newton's underlying character structure was already shaped before he went up to Trinity, and for these early years the evidence is scanty and requires interpretation.

Before venturing upon a psychological analysis of the Lincolnshire lad, a few disclaimers. This treatment does not pretend to interpret Newton's genius or its mysterious energy. It merely purports to describe one aspect of the emotional context in which his genius worked itself out. There have doubtless been other men with similar psychic configurations who have never been heard of since. In his studies of great men, Freud forthrightly disavowed any intention of explaining their extraordinary powers. He was examining their characters, searching out the origins of their neuroses perhaps, but not establishing a relationship between the passions and fixations that sometimes drove them to distraction and their creativity. At most, he would point out signs of struggle with destructive force in their natures, clues left behind, proof that a battle had been waged. But he could not account for the victory. Sometimes we stand in awe before genius precisely because its works are achieved in the face of crippling odds which have crushed lesser men. Let nothing I shall have to say be construed as denigration because it departs from the eighteenth-century hagiographical image of Newton.

There is, moreover, no implication that the personality of the young man delineated in the first part of this paper had to develop by some ineluctable destiny into the Cambridge recluse, the psychically disturbed middle-aged man of the black year 1693, the authoritarian Master of the Mint, the dictatorial president of the Royal Society, and the fierce, often ruthless combatant in six or seven great wars of truth. Such psychological determinism is alien to me. But while life experiences may modify and alter a basic structure, the earliest impressions and traumas are the most powerful and pervasive—a rather old notion, to be sure, already part of the wisdom of Descartes and Locke, not to speak of Plato. Of course, it is only an acquaintance with the mature Newton that leads one to raise basic queries about origins, to seek, in the junior part of his life, for the roots of the consuming passions of the mature man.

Finally, Newton embodied attitudes and beliefs common to many men of his time and place, his professional status, religion, and social class. Through the educational process that began in early infancy, these forces were internalized and became a part of his being. The interplay of his own personality, that which was uniquely Newton, with what the society fostered, repressed, or tolerated in some fashion, is the essential drama of this story.

One might of course ask: Why bother with this tale? What is its purpose if it does not help to set Newton's achievement in some sequence in the history of science or thought, and if it eschews any attempt to explain his genius? My prime justification is that it brings the humanity of genius closer to us. A further reason is, as Hume would have said, "exposed to some more difficulty": it presumes that science in a given culture has a psychological envelopment, and hence the character components of its great, form-imprinting practitioners are, from one perspective, by no means a matter of indifference in understanding the nature of Western science itself.

Contemporary observations on Newton's personality in his later years are not always in consonance with one another. His countryman Dr. William Stukeley writes of his "natural dignity and politeness in his manner in common life"; Stukeley adds, "A spirit of beneficence and philanthropy was, as it were, the basis of his composition." His friend Locke said that he was "a nice man to deal with" (meaning touchy, hypersensitive), "a little too apt to raise in himself suspicions where there is no ground," and he therefore advised his kinsman not to approach him too directly lest he give offense. Hooke in his secret diary called him the "veryest Knave in all the Ho:." To "clippers and coyners," prisoners in Newgate who had witnessed Newton's rage during interrogations in the Tower, he was a "rogue," and they threatened to shoot him if King James returned. His successor in the Lucasian Chair at Cambridge, William Whiston, and Flamsteed, the first royal astronomer, paint almost identical unflattering portraits: they depict him as irascible, brooking no criticism, quick with sharp retorts, tolerant only of the darlings who praised him, "fearful, cautious, and suspicious." Jervas painted him as a pompous Royal Society president, a bird with ruffled feathers about to fly into a rage. There is family anecdotage about his tantrums. In his last years Leibniz considered him underhanded, capable of wicked chicanery, and he harped on his reputation for quarrelsomeness. For the astronomer John Keill, on the other hand, he was the divine Newton; and so he remained for Halley, not to speak of the lesser favorites in his entourage who owed their advancement to him. Fatio de Duillier worshiped him like a god, and so did John Conduitt, the man to whom Newton married off the daughter of his half sister. Great bishops of the realm spoke of Newton's piety with reverence. By the time of his death, a composite official portrait had been created—the calm, majestic genius who was above worldly concerns, a paragon of all the virtues of both Christianity and the Enlightenment.

THE MELANCHOLY COUNTENANCE

The original mold of the man, which survived through years of suffering, magnificent creativity, and final apotheosis, had been forged by the morality of seventeenth-century puritanism and an intricate family constellation that cut him off from much sensate pleasure.

Newton's first eighteen years were those of the Civil War, the Commonwealth, and the Protectorate. When he was six, a king of England was beheaded. Lincolnshire was an active theatre of operations, and a youthful notebook shows that he was aware of the military presence and familiar with contemporary theological and political controversies. We know nothing about the terrors that events of the war may have aroused either in him or in his mother. Neither his stepfather nor his maternal uncle, who were divines, seem to have been religious militants on either side. They were not removed during the Commonwealth, nor was his uncle ejected with the Restoration. A number of divines connected with the church at Grantham and with the grammar school, however, were dismissed as Dissenters, the only indication of a possible sectarian religious influence in Newton's youth.

Concealing his anti-Trinitarianism, Newton belonged to the Church of England all his life, and he was carried to his grave in Westminster Abbey by the foremost prelates in the kingdom. Though most of his university career spans the lax years of the Restoration and he rose to great prominence under a rather licentious Whig hegemony, the values he absorbed at an early age were what we must call puritan in the broad, loose, yet generally understandable, sense of that nettlesome term. Irrespective of the shifting religious alignments during this period, the temper of the countryside in the middling world to which Newton belonged was puritanical, in Christopher Hill's sense. When he arrived in Cambridge and confronted the gaming, hard-drinking, lecherous society that went wild during Stourbridge Fair, he withdrew into himself. He found solace in the company of Bible-loving John Wickins, who had been equally repelled by his carousing fellow students. Newton cut himself off from evil—though not without a few visits to the tavern, a wee bit of drinking, a small loss at cards, and sundry other such "useless expenditures," all meticulously recorded in the money accounts of his first years at Trinity, along with the price of his shoestrings and laundry bills. In later years Henry More, the Cambridge Platonist who also came from Lincolnshire, remarked on Newton's habitually melancholy countenance. Newton's university assistant, Humphrey Newton (no relation), heard him laugh but once. He has left a vivid portrait of the absent-minded, self-absorbed professor, "meek," "humble," "never seemingly angry," who "aimed at something beyond yᵉ Reach of humane art & industry," neglectful of food

FRANK E. MANUEL

and dress, but strict and precise in his experiments, and distressed if he saw a weed in his lawn.

The scrupulosity, punitiveness, austerity, discipline, and fear associated with the repressive morality of puritanism Newton accepted without overt rebellion. He had a built-in puritan censor, and lived ever under the Taskmaster's eye, as the divines had it. The decalogue he had learned in childhood became an exigent conscience that made deadly sins of lying, falsehood, Sabbath-breaking, egotistic ambition, as well as of any expressions of violence and breach of control. The Bible was both the general and the specific guide to conduct. Whatever was done by the virtuous characters in the Bible was allowable and whatever the Bible failed to mention or specifically interdicted was not. A prohibition against coveting was extended to cover all desires of the flesh, the admonition to honor father and mother made the most minor act of disobedience a religious transgression. The Sabbath was observed with almost rabbinic severity, and there is nothing casual about Newton's inclusion as sins in his confession of 1662 whittling and bathing in a kimnel on the Sabbath.

Though no correspondence has survived from the period of Newton's youth, we possess four notebooks in his hand from the last years in Lincolnshire and the first in Trinity—one each in the Morgan Library of New York, the Fitzwilliam Museum, Trinity College, and the University Library, in Cambridge. In addition, there is a Latin exercise book from a somewhat earlier period now in Los Angeles. These are perhaps the most telling sources for an understanding of his character formation—superior in many ways to the hero-worshiping memoirs of Stukeley and Conduitt pieced together immediately after his death because they are unconscious revelations—and have been the least exploited for the purpose. They afford us the basis for conjectures about his temper, his moods, and his emotions. They may even be a window into his fantasy world. Supplementing these materials are scattered marginalia in books that he owned as a boy, and a few stray sheets of his proposal for a new philosophical language. The notebooks can be interpreted on many levels. Students of the *Optics* and the *Principia* have found here his earliest scientific intuitions. But they are documents that also pose perplexing psychological questions and suggest some answers.

Of course, the notebooks constitute only a minor portion of Newton's total manuscript legacy covering correspondence; working notes and drafts of his mathematical discoveries, optics, dynamics, and alchemical experiments; shipbuilding blueprints; educational projects; ecclesiastical calendars; historical theology, interpretations of mythology and world geography; economic treatises; records of the Mint and of estates for which he acted as executor; chronological and historical studies of ancient kingdoms; commentaries on Daniel and the Apocalypse; medical abstracts and potions. These manuscripts, amounting to millions of words, especially those on chronology and theology, yield bits of psychological information, though mostly by indirection. He seems to have preserved a great many scraps not accidentally destroyed by fire. After one has scrutinized the twelfth version, with minor variants, of a reply to Des Maizeaux on the Leibniz controversy, or the twentieth copy of a world chronological table, the adjective "obsessive" does not seem too strong. The hoarding of pieces of paper, scribbled on all sides, from childhood exercise books and youthful expenditure accounts through six versions of his denunciation of the French chronologists before the Royal Society when he was eighty-three, bespeaks a certain parsimoniousness and obstinacy and, to say the least, retentiveness.

The early Latin exercise folios (written in the ornate "secretary" that Newton was taught at school and that we shall call "Old Barley" in honor of his Grantham writing master), the long word lists in the Morgan notebook written in the same script, word illustrations for the phonetic system he invented at the back of the same notebook but presumably of a later date because they are in a new, elegant, rather free hand which he acquired at the University and which we shall call "Trinity," as well as the universal language papers of about the same period, when considered along with the shorthand confession of 1662 in the Fitzwilliam notebook (deciphered by Professor Westfall), leave us with a consistent impression of the fear, anxiety, distrust, sadness, withdrawal, self-belittlement, and generally depressive state of the young Newton. Though some of the words and phrases in his lists are copied from Francis Gregory's *Nomenclatura*, many of the associations are random and free, and can serve as a rather primitive objective personality test, even though the data would hardly lend themselves to refined quantification techniques. While no single text in isolation is conclusive, in their total effect these records are compelling.

For example, in the Morgan notebook, under the subheading "Of Man, his Affections, & Senses," the word *Dreame* (from Gregory's *Nomenclatura*) is followed by *Doubting, Dispaire, Distrust, Desire, Dread, Displeasure, Discourtesie, Discredit.* A sequence that begins *Soule* is largely copied from a number of Gregory's sections, to which Newton added his own series: *Sorrow, Subtilness, Slumber, Sobing.* In the same notebook, under "Of Kindred, & Titles," the word *Orphan* precedes *Offender* —a self-accusation.

The three hundred and fifty-odd phrases of the Latin exercises, which Newton himself made up and translated, or adapted from common proverbs, or perhaps copied from *Sentences for Children*, are corroborative. While many are colorless, a great number are charged with affect. Among them are expressions of self-disparagement and a sense of insignificance: *A little fellow; My poore help; Hee is paile; There is noe roome for mee to sit.* Juxtaposition of phrases shows a sharp swing from affirmation to profound depression (*In the top of ye house* and *In ye bottome of hell*), from command to obedience (*He is ye Kings counsellor* and *He was thy footeman*). Doubts about his capacities and whether he was good for anything at all beset him: *What imployment is he fit for? What is hee good for?* This is the kind of sentence he composed or selected.

A general feeling tone of anxiety predominates. Things and persons are destroyed, disaster and catastrophe loom. *He is broken. This house of youres is like to fall. This pride of hers will come downe. Aboute to fall. The ship sinketh.* Words of fear are frequent: *Hee saith nothing for feare. I am sore affraide. There is a thing which trobelleth mee.* There is dread of punishment, and at the same time recognition of how enticing sin is. *Wee desire yose yings which hurt us most. Hee cannot forbeare doeing mischeife. The greatest allurement to sin is hope of spareing. Youe are sure to be punisht. Hee should have beene punished.*

Authoritarian commands of his elders ring in his ears and they push through his writing. *I will make thee to doe it. Take heede you dost it not. See you come backe. Thou maist be gone. Why rise you not? What hast you been doing? Speake out thy words. Show thyselfe a man.* A puritanical censorship of play and idleness, games, dancing, sport, thriftlessness is prominent: *The better gamester ye worse man. What else is it to dance but to play ye foole? Hee doth nothing but play. Soe much monie soe much credit. He is not able to pay. He is reported to be a spendthrift. He hath not where withall to buy a halten to hang himselve.*

Pronouncements of distrust and wariness are numerous: *I shall beware of him yt hee hurt mee not. You make a foole of mee. You are a foole to believe him. You know what account to make of him. You shall never make mee believe that taile.* There is a pervasive loneliness—*No man understands mee*—and utter despondency: *What will become of me. I will make an end. I cannot but weepe. I know not what to doe.*

In all these youthful scribblings there is an astonishing absence of positive feeling. The word *love* never appears, and expressions of gladness and desire are rare. A liking for roast meat is the only strong sensuous passion. Almost all the statements are negations, admonitions, prohibitions. The climate of life is hostile and punitive and Newton has made it his own. Competitiveness, orderliness, self-control—these are Puritan values that became part of his being.

The text of Newton's new phonetic system and stray leaves of the manuscript on a universal language tell the same story. He gave numerous examples to illustrate his new signs for vowels and semivowels and his symbols for a universal language. If we exclude the necessarily large number of neutral words, the rest principally connote inadequacy, pain, violence, and anger: *lament, taint, hit, folly, fall, fault, mourne, lust, hate, faile, feare, slew, quarrel, woe, yowle, wound, hang't, anguish, kill.*

Thomas Shelton's shorthand books published in the 1640s, which include brief word lists for practice in taking down sermons, vaguely resemble in spirit some of Newton's random associations, though they lack their intensity by far. Popular educational chapbooks, homilies, and moral treatises also have the same temper, on a different plane. Newton did not challenge the moral values of his puritan world, or its repression of instinctual desire. In him, puritan inhibitions were exaggerated with painful consequences. The censor was in full command.

Some remarks should be made on those sections of the Cambridge University

Library notebook that are virtually a commonplace book and cover all aspects of existence—Newton's earliest experiments and queries as well as philosophical, theological, and psychological reflections. They reveal a rich and complex inner life that is hidden from us in his later writings and rarely breaks through in his correspondence. He muses about the nature of dreams, fantasy, and the imagination, and at one point relates them to invention. Historians of his great physical theories should be interested in his passing references to Joseph Glanvill's report in *The Vanity of Dogmatizing* of an instance of psychic action at a distance, demonstrated experimentally by a former Oxford student to his fellows. In this same University Library notebook, along with cogitations on God, the soul, and creation, he gives utterance to a common belief that he seems to hold throughout his life: the idea, based on Scripture, that the world will be destroyed in a conflagration. In the *Observations on Daniel and the Apocalypse,* a work of his late years, though he refuses to date the end, as so many of his contemporaries were doing, he does indicate that it cannot be long in coming, for the full revelation of the true meaning of Scripture is now just about complete.

The destruction of worlds does not seem to alarm him. His moments of highest creativity occur during the plague and when God is visiting his rage upon wicked London in the fire of 1666. It has often been noticed that great neurotics are calm in the midst of catastrophe. Those who survive extraordinary disasters have experienced great surges of creative energy. Newton is, as we shall see, the prototype of the survivor.

HANNAH AND HER SON

While the melancholy temper of Newton's youth was in part a reflection of a general emotional climate, the genesis of his major neurosis is to be sought elsewhere, in the particular circumstances of his early life. The puritan censor merely aggravated his woes. Initially, they were inflicted by the one who loved him most.

The salient facts of Newton's childhood can be briefly summarized. He was born prematurely on Christmas Day 1642 in a small manor in Woolsthorpe, and was not expected to survive. Two women dispatched to Lady Pakenham to fetch some medicine entertained little hope of finding him alive upon their return. His mother told him that at birth he was so small he could fit into a quart pot. His survival was, on the psychological level, miraculous. Newton also remembered hearing that he was so weak he had to wear a halter around his neck, and that "he was very much below the usual size of children." Premature babies often have difficulty in breathing and in holding up their heads during the sucking of the breast. In the fear of suffocation, in the anger generated by insufficiencies in feeding, lie perhaps the first sources of Newton's anxiety. The fact that he recalled these stories of his infancy and recounted them to Conduitt is some measure of their significance.

As a boy he seems to have been frail, often preferring the company of girls, for whom he made toys, when he was a schoolboy in Grantham and lived in the home

FRANK E. MANUEL

of the apothecary, Dr. Clark. At some later date there occurred a school fight with the stereotype bully, whom he not only beat, but whose nose he rubbed against the wall. While he did not normally excel in sports, he used his understanding of wind currents to outstrip his fellows in a jumping game; knowledge was power.

His father, a yeoman who could not sign his name, had died three months before he was born, and his paternal grandfather, too, was dead. His mother, a gentlewoman, married again when he was three and went to live about a mile and a half away with her new husband, a man of sixty-three, the rich Barnabas Smith, Rector of North Witham. Isaac was left in his father's house at Woolsthorpe with his maternal grandmother under the legal guardianship of his maternal uncle. When he was about eleven, Reverend Smith died and Hannah Smith returned to live in Woolsthorpe with the children of her second marriage—Mary aged about four and a half, Benjamin aged two, and Hannah aged one. According to the records, Father Barnabas was still siring children when he was well over seventy. The anecdote about Newton's absorption with books and his reluctance to become a "grazier" on the lands he had inherited and those his mother had acquired is well known, and so is his early interest in mechanical instruments and popular works like John Wilkins' *Mathematical Magic* and John Bate's *Mysteryes of Nature and Art*—the Morgan notebook is full of excerpts from them.

Before her marriage to the Reverend Barnabas Smith, Hannah Ayscough Newton had arranged for the repair of the manor house at Woolsthorpe and had provided for land to increase Isaac's inheritance. Somebody, either her brother or a schoolmaster at Grantham, became aware of his genius and despite her reluctance got him to Cambridge as a subsizar. There were dangers that she would smother him, retain him by her side as son and elder brother-father to the children she brought from Barnabas. Hannah sacrificed her son to the University. (In 1665, when he returned home and was not busy discovering gravity, he still spent some time making out rent receipts for her tenants.)

Newton's mother is the central figure in his life. They were in union with each other during a critical period, and his fixation upon her was absolute. The trauma of her original departure, the denial of her love, generated fear, anxiety, and aggressiveness.

After the total possession—undisturbed by a rival, not even a father, almost as if his had been a virgin birth—he was cruelly abandoned. Not forever, but for long periods. She was there and yet not there. Hannah was in North Witham with Rector Smith. The elegant church steeple loomed high and could be seen piercing the sky for miles around. There was blind fury, and a desire was born to destroy both of them. This murderous obsession of the period before eleven remained alive in his memory long after the Reverend Smith lay dead, at least until Newton's twentieth year, when he recorded his guilt as sin number thirteen in the shorthand confession of 1662 in the Fitzwilliam notebook: "Threatning my father and mother Smith to burne them and the house over them." Sin number fourteen, "Wishing death and hoping it to some," a rather obscure sentence which might be interpreted as a suicidal wish as well as an expression of violence, indicates how generalized were his destructive fantasies. These cardinal sins are introduced surreptitiously, so to speak, in the midst of a total of forty-nine, mostly trivial, committed before Whitsunday 1662.

The return of his mother just before puberty accentuated Newton's fixation and made genital love for any other person virtually impossible. Yet the traditional version of his unalloyed adoration must be qualified. When she finally returned to Woolsthorpe after her second husband's death, she brought with her the hated brood of a new wedlock. Hannah Newton's motives in taking another husband had doubtless been protective of her son—it was a marriage of convenience; but for young Newton her act was a betrayal. On one level of his consciousness, the widowed mother who rewed was a wicked woman. In his fantasy he punished Father and Mother Smith for their sin of a polluted marriage by burning them in the hell of the Puritan sermons. And this wish must have induced terror, because of the fear that it would be punished by human or divine agency.

Nowhere does Newton's ambivalent relationship to his mother emerge with greater clarity than in a group of words written in random association under the letters of the alphabet from A through Y under the general rubric "Of Kindred, & Titles" in the Morgan notebook. It does not require a trained analyst to notice that M, which starts with *Marriage* and *Mother,* copied from Gregory's *Nomenclatura,* continues with Newton's own choices—a word of idealization, *Marquesse,* and then *Manslayer. Wife, Wedlock, Wooer, Widdow, Widdower,* from Gregory, Newton completes with *Whoore.* This ambivalence toward his mother will characterize his whole style of life. The letter F begins with *Father,* followed by *Fornicator, Flatterer,* and then two geographic proper nouns with overtones of sin and sensuality to the young puritan, *Frenchman* and *Florentine.* At the end, under Y, *Yeoman* stands alone—the status of his real, true father, who died before he was born.

Of the intensity of Hannah Newton's love for her first-born we have only two bits of evidence: the smidgen of a letter sent to the University in 1665, in which her love is repeated twice in a few lines, and her will, in which she made him her sole male heir, Benjamin having been provided for by his father, Barnabas Smith. She commended her soul to God and she left her body to be buried as Isaac "shall think fit," and he wrapped it in white wool.

The fixation upon his mother may have crippled Newton sexually, but there was also a great source of power, strength, and energy in the early, close relationship. It was in their garden in Woolsthorpe that he noticed the apple drawn to the earth—a story to which he frequently adverted in his last years; and a burst of creativity occurred when, during the plague, he returned to the bosom of his mother from the University. Newton referred to his knowledge and inventions as his "Garden" in the letter to Halley where he accused Hooke of pilfering from it.

The narcissistic element in Newton's affection for Fatio de Duillier may well be related to his early fixation upon his mother. In the orthodox Freudian manner,

　　　　　　　　　　　　　　　　　　　　　　　　　FRANK E. MANUEL

Newton first identifies himself with his mother and takes himself as the sexual object; then he finds young men resembling himself and loves them as he would have had his mother love him.

It is highly improbable that Newton ever had active homosexual relationships. This assumption seems justified not only on the basis of his own testimony to a relative that he had never violated chastity and Voltaire's report from Dr. Mead, Newton's physician and friend, that he died a virgin. The particular character of his neurosis almost precludes inversion, though not the development of tenderness toward a succession of younger scientists and philosophers. In the case of that aristocratic Swiss genius Fatio de Duillier, aged twenty-five, who appeared in England when Newton was in his mid-forties, these feelings reached an unwonted intensity, and the threat they posed and the demand for their repression may have played a role in Newton's breakdown in 1693. At one point the close friendship and scientific collaboration of Fatio and Newton drew frequent comment in international scientific correspondence, and Hooke in his diaries often notes their comings and goings together in the Royal Society. Fatio is one of the rare persons Newton ever asks after with concern—his inquiry is made in a letter to Locke. Fatio was a sort of replica of the young Newton, with the same universal scientific and theological interests. They even shared a love of apples, hypochondria, and a disposition to rely on homemade remedies when they fell ill. Fatio, however, lacked Newton's intellectual balance and control, and Newton even twitted him about his "mystical fancies." When Fatio was stranded in England without funds, Newton offered to give him a temporary allowance. And when Fatio announced that he believed himself to be dying, Newton replied with unaccustomed emotion. Among the private letters of Fatio, now in Geneva, is one alluding to a secret reason why he will never be able to marry, and marked homosexual fantasies are prominent in sheets of dreams he recorded with amazing lucidity and a wealth of detail, albeit at a later date. Fatio was one of the agents who kindled the Leibniz controversy, and to the end he considered himself the only true disciple. When he became involved with the wild French prophets from the Cévennes in 1707 and acted as their secretary, Newton dropped him, and seems never to have raised a finger to save him when he was condemned to stand in pillory for prophesying the doom of London. That Fatio sought his own abasement, refusing to cooperate with the diplomatic envoy who offered to get him freed on condition that he quit England, underscores his masochistic tendencies. But when Newton forsook him in his hour of trial, going about his business with routine meetings at the Treasury, was he re-enacting an earlier abandonment in his own life?

After Newton's psychic crisis, Hannah was reincarnated in the person of the famous Bartica, Newton's half niece Catherine, daughter of his half sister Hannah Barton. Born in 1679, the year his mother died, she was brought to London by her uncle in the bloom of her youth, and she lived in his house for twenty years. At her arrival she was, then, about the same age as his mother had been when he was born. A beautiful, brilliant, witty woman, she was the antithesis of her uncle in character and behavior. Swift, Dryden, and above all the great Whig Chancellor of the Exchequer, Halifax, were her friends. She told Swift risqué stories in a tête-à-tête in Newton's house, and made Stella jealous. A considerable literature exists on her relationship with Halifax. Gossip writers and authors of *romans à clef* depict Halifax as a drunk and as a roué; some have him ugly. The sources are Tory hirelings like the notorious Mary de la Rivière Manley, who openly refers to a liaison with La Bartica. Was Newton blind and deaf, a sixty-year-old man who saw and heard no scandal, totally engrossed in his battles with Flamsteed and Leibniz? By this time Newton surely knew the facts of life—what he never himself experienced he had certainly encountered at the Mint, in the personal interrogation of hundreds of criminal clippers, counterfeiters, and their molls.

I have nothing to add to the ambiguities of a relationship which so intrigued Augustus de Morgan. Though he could conceive of Newton's stacking a committee of the Royal Society against Leibniz, he could not, as a good Victorian, endure the idea of a sexual relationship with Newton's acquiescence and he concocted the theory of a secret marriage between Catherine and Halifax. There are moments when, despite the scandalmongers of the age, I opt for Catherine's virtue. But at other times I am tempted to hazard a bold hypothesis. Halifax, then Charles Montagu, was one of the younger scholars whom Newton was fond of at the University. The admiration was mutual. Newton on occasion had shifts of feeling common in such relationships, and it is not hard to conceive of an identification of his suppressed sensual nature with this brilliant, worldly man of the realm. Such an identification is suggested by the fact that Newton affects the same sort of easy, vernacular phraseology that Halifax used in corresponding with him. For example, when the mastership of the Charter-House is proposed, he refuses to be a candidate: "The competition is hazardous and I am loathe to sing a new song to ye tune of King's College." This is jaunty language for Newton, quite out of keeping with his official posture. Now Halifax has "conversation," as he expressed it in his will, with none other than the image of Newton's own young mother, with the charming Bartica. Was Newton living out an infantile desire when he countenanced this irregular relationship? But if one rejects the idea that Newton saw his child-fantasy of desire for his mother consummated through the agency of Halifax's making love to Hannah's incarnation in Catherine, then an alternative theory might apply. Emphasis can be shifted to Newton's affection for Montagu. Did this make possible the love-offering of his half niece, to the neglect of his puritan conscience?

Despite the resentful anger that was an element in Newton's feeling for his mother, the bond between Hannah and her son was never broken. Eventually his mother's wish was fulfilled and he did in fact become the father-master-elder brother of the whole Ayscough-Smith brood. He made settlements on his half sisters when they married, and when their husbands died he supported them and their sons and daughters. Eight of them, including Benjamin Smith's son, became his heirs. In this relationship he had finally supplanted his hated stepfather.

FRANK E. MANUEL

Though Newton was befriended by many older men who recognized his genius, there is not the slightest indication that he responded by making father surrogates of them—neither his uncles, nor his maternal grandfather, nor the schoolmasters of Grantham, nor his tutor at Cambridge, nor Henry More, nor Boyle, nor John Collins, nor even Isaac Barrow ever filled this role. He needed none of them.

When the child Newton was taught his prayers, his own father had long been in heaven—since almost three months before he was born. The image of his real father, the yeoman Isaac Newton who could not write, soon fused with the vision of God the Father, and a special relationship was thus early established between the son and his father. There is a widely held folk belief among many peoples that a male child born after his father's death is endowed with supernatural healing powers, and a present-day rector of Colsterworth has been able to attest its survival in an attenuated form in his own locality, where it is held that such a son is destined to good fortune. Newton's deep sense of being a chosen one was further reinforced by the date of his birth, Christmas Day. Dr. Stukeley reported it as an omen of future greatness in popular opinion.

Throughout his life Newton arrived at his conclusions, whether in physical science or world chronology, through the agency of the Holy Spirit, by intuition. He was in direct relationship with his father, and things were revealed to him as they had once been to the Hebrew prophets and the apostles and the legendary scientists of the ancient world who were identified with each other. Though Newton could speak freely in praise of Moses and Toth, Thales, Pythagoras, Prometheus, Chiron, and Apollonius, he only rarely had good words to say about either contemporary scientists or his immediate predecessors—and then not without equivocation. Among contemporaries he and he alone had access to the significant truths about God-his-Father's world. God revealed himself to only one prophet in each generation, and this made parallel discoveries improbable. Despite Newton's lip service to the common promotion of knowledge, he often felt that the findings of his fellow scientists were of no consequence, or only ancillary to his system, or else outright thefts from his "Garden." There was no aspect of creation that would be hidden from him—the inventions of mathematics, the nature of light, the movement of the planets, the elements of chemistry, the history of antiquity, the nature of God, the true meaning of God's word in Scripture. Newton's occasional denial of his mission, self-disparaging references to his discoveries in natural philosophy and in world history as "divertissements," are only the other side of the coin. Prophets have often tried to escape their destiny.

There was only one Father and one Son. Unitarianism was not too rare a religious position in the seventeenth century, though it was a punishable offense. But irrespective of the rational and historical basis of Newton's anti-Trinitarianism, there was an intensity to his secret belief that goes far beyond theological argument and criticism of the proof-texts in John, which he elaborated with such scholarly virtuosity. He was

The Lad from Lincolnshire

the only son of God and could not endure even the rivalry of Christ. Megalomaniac elements in Newton are not too far below the surface.

The taunts that fatherless children sometimes endure are known. When the child is told of the death of his father before he was born, an almost metaphysical anguish can be generated. Often the fantasy quest for his father continues in a thousand guises through his life. Where did he really come from? In Newton's case the search was rendered even more poignant by the absence of a paternal grandfather, who had died in 1641. Newton was absorbed in his genealogy long before he was knighted and had to prepare documents for the College of Heralds. He gave himself strange ancestors —at one time, if we are to believe James Gregory, he claimed that he was descended from a Scottish lord. In the word lists of the Morgan notebook, under the letter T in "Of Kindred, & Titles," *Twins* is followed by *Theife*. Is this an echo of the ancient myth of the abducted child of royalty, of the twin who was humbly reared while his brother inherited the throne? Fantasies of royal and noble birth are frequent among children who have no father. There are among Newton's euhemeristic historical and chronological papers in Oxford literally scores of genealogies of the gods and of the kings of all nations. In addition to their pragmatic use in revising world chronology, on the psychological plane these mask his own search for a line of ancestors.

Simultaneous with a sense that it was *his* father who occupied the heavenly throne were doubt and apprehension about his legitimacy. Was his birth tainted? His parents were married in April 1642 and he was prematurely born in December, which is possibly within the limits of virtue. But in drawing up his genealogy for the College of Heralds at the time of his knighthood (the manuscript, in his own hand, is in Wellesley, Massachusetts), he made a peculiar error, pushing back his parents' marriage to 1639. The 1639 date was not selected at random. This was the year when Newton's grandfather presented the manor in Woolsthorpe to his son and Hannah Ayscough, apparently in view of their forthcoming marriage. Reasons for the long betrothal are unclear. The actual union, however, did not take place for three years. Perhaps Newton was trying to establish the legitimacy of his birth beyond any question. There is no record of the precise date of the marriage in any parish register, and antedating the marriage removed the need for explaining the facts of a premature birth in a heraldic genealogy.

The many psychological ambivalences in Newton's character that have been hinted at were reinforced by the ambiguity of his social status. His father Isaac Newton was a yeoman and so were the other Newtons of the area. The Ayscoughs were gentlemen and rectors, apothecaries and architects. From the very beginning one has a feeling that there was some misalliance here: on the mother's side, a "very ancient family," once wealthy but now apparently on the downgrade, while the Newtons were yeomen coming up. Newton's father, who left about five hundred pounds in "goods and chattles" in addition to property, still called himself yeoman in his will, though the grandfather had already bought a manor, and Newton was born lord of the manor —a little one to be sure. The final marriage settlement was made more palatable to the Ayscoughs by the fact that another branch of the Newton family had a baronetcy to which Isaac Newton might have been an heir—or so his grandmother told him. He entered the University as a poor scholar, a subsizar performing menial tasks. Coming back from the University, at the Lincoln visitation in 1666 he described himself as a gentleman. All his life there was an element of the social climber about him, even after he was knighted. He fawned upon that worldly Venetian aristocrat Abate Conti. He admitted more noble nonentities into the Royal Society than any of his predecessors. On occasion he asked to have the official experimenter of the Royal Society perform in his house before archbishops and lords for their amusement. He seemed uncomfortable in the presence of the great of the realm and yet he always needed their recognition, legitimation.

What manner of man was the other father, Newton's stepfather, Barnabas Smith? He had matriculated at Lincoln College, Oxford, in December 1597 at the age of fifteen, and was a man of some learning. The diocesan record of the Bishop of Lincoln's visitation back in 1611 is laconic but pointed. It called Smith a person of "good behaviour, nonresident, and not hospitable." He certainly was not hospitable to little Isaac. That Newton hated Barnabas Smith seems a reasonable deduction, even from the sparse evidence in the notebooks. Whatever other factors made it impossible for Newton to take orders during his long years in Cambridge, the image of his stepfather, the "opulent divine," a scornful phrase from his Latin exercise book, was inhibitory.

Barnabas was not, however, a total loss for his stepson. He left Isaac nothing in his will, but his library of two hundred-odd works, mostly editions of the Church Fathers and ecclesiastical controversy, was transferred to the study at Woolsthorpe. Newton's learning in ecclesiastical history and in general history, the documentation for his unitarianism, was nourished by these works. He may have repudiated Father Smith, but he did not disdain his collection of patristic literature. He also fell heir to his stepfather's large commonplace book of more than a thousand folios, rich with the pompous moral citations of a humanist divine. And it was in this book that Newton wrote notes for many of his mathematical inventions, as John Herivel has shown.

Newton rediscovered the image of Barnabas in many faces; and others paid dearly for his abduction of Newton's mother.

When father Barnabas died, his son Benjamin was not yet three, and he came with his mother to live in Woolsthorpe Manor. In Newton's Latin exercise book there are first intimations of his antagonism to this rival: *I have my brother to entreate.* The word associations in the Morgan notebook under the letter B of subheading "Of Kindred, & Titles" are explicit enough. *Brother* is followed by *Bastard,* as in Gregory's *Nomenclatura*—a curious coincidence; to which Newton joins *Barron, Blaspheimer,*

Brawler, Babler, Babylonian, Bishop, Brittaine, Bedlam, Beggar, Brownist, and finally *Benjamite.*

There is no recorded emotive reaction to the fact that Newton's mother contracted the fever from which she died in 1679 while tending the sick Benjamin. In the end, a Ben Smith, the son of Benjamin, fell to Newton's care. By all accounts Ben was a wild character, a reprobate, a dilettante, an aesthete who hobnobbed with artists and traveled in Italy. For a time he lived in Newton's London house; later, one of his noble acquaintances got him a miserable living in a country parish where he referred to his flock as "baptized brutes," a contempt which they reciprocated. At one point Newton wrote him letters upbraiding him for his immoral conduct in language apparently so vivid that the parson into whose hands the documents eventually fell after Ben Smith's death destroyed them as a blemish on the name of England's most shining genius. Thus Newton finally vented his wrath upon the rival sibling in the person of his son; but it was a redress of grievances long delayed, and in the course of his life Newton had to appease himself with the slaughter of other rivals, a long and illustrious list. Perhaps the ironic climax to this relationship came when Newton's *Observations upon the Prophecies of Daniel and the Apocalypse of Saint John* was introduced to the world of letters by this same Ben Smith in a posthumous edition of 1733.

THE WARS OF TRUTH

A child's abandonment by its mother can give rise to a great rage. Let us not minimize the additional frustrations of a premature baby that cannot hold its mother's breast. Nor forget the rivals, Barnabas and his Benjamin. A mighty wrath smoldered within Newton all his life, eternally seeking outlets.

Of the colossal force of this anger Newton was early aware, and he made heroic attempts to repress it. He protests that he shuns controversies and confrontations. His censor was commensurate with his other great powers, but many were the times when it was overwhelmed and the rage could not be contained. In his adult years, with one known exception—his wishing Locke dead as he had Mother and Father Smith—the anger was directed into permissible channels. When the enemy was very powerful, as in the case of Hooke, he tended to withdraw, to avoid, to hide away, to bide his time. When in office, he used virtually every means at his disposal to defeat an antagonist, and he required total submission, public humiliation, annihilation. The inherited morality of the Puritan world, like all Christian morality, prescribed love of God and fellows; these were the two principles to which Newton reduced all religion in one of his manuscripts. But Puritanism also ordained the eradication of evil. To love and to destroy—an ambivalent message for a neurotic.

It is a commonplace that the scientific disputations of the seventeenth century were rough. These bitter contests had not yet been divested either of religious zealotry or the character of the aristocratic *duello.* Enmities in the English scientific world were frequent. Flamsteed and Halley, successive royal astronomers, Hooke and Oldenburg, officials of the Royal Society, Woodward and Mead, eminent doctors, conducted heroic battles that were not limited to mutual accusations of plagiarism, atheism, ignorance, stupidity, and downright fakery, but on occasion assumed the form of physical acts such as making faces at each other during meetings of the Royal Society and drawing swords on the street outside of Gresham College. Written protestations of esteem often concealed barbs manufactured with such consummate skill that only the recipient was aware of the virulence of the poison in which they had been dipped.

In international scientific rivalries, the participants charged one another with partisanship in favor of their countrymen. On the continent, the preëminence of English science was often resented, and there is smug satisfaction in Leibniz' prognosis of its decline in the eighteenth century. During Newton's quarrel with French chronologists, his friends reported with delight that Halley had worsted the *monsieurs*. Priority battles were violent. Was a hint a suggestion or a hypothesis a discovery? It usually depended upon who dropped the idea. Scientists protected their wares by writing in shorthand and cryptograms.

In the light of this prevailing combative temper, there might be a tendency to discount the import of the many acrimonious quarrels that engaged Newton during his lifetime. But even if allowances are made for the general turbulence of the intellectual atmosphere, Newton remains one of the more ferocious practitioners of the art of scientific controversy. Genteel concepts of fair play are conspicuously absent, and he never gave any quarter.

A fierce independence, a secret conviction that he was the chosen intermediary between the Creator and mankind, a sense of omnipotence, a neurotic swing between feelings of grandeur and masochistic self-depreciation (which some eighteenth-century and Victorian writers labeled modesty and humility), along with the acute capacity to remain on the lookout for minor weaknesses in an enemy's ramparts, conspired to make of him a formidable adversary. Anger and suspicion were his constant companions.

Newton may have experienced a number of psychic disturbances, but to our knowledge he sank into delusion only once, during the grave crisis of 1693 when he had passed his fiftieth birthday. Then the great man behaved as might any mortal who is struck down; he withdrew into a corner, broke off relationships with his friends, accused his intimates of plotting against him, and reported conversations that never took place. He retained some awareness of his condition, however: "I am extremely troubled at the embroilment I am in, and have neither ate nor slept well this twelve month, nor have my former consistency of mind." Newton stands naked before us only at this moment. "Your unfortunate servant," he signs himself in a letter to Locke begging forgiveness for having wished his friend dead.

What was oppressing Newton during the black year preceding the crisis? In addition, perhaps, to a regression associated with the male climacteric, a number of things may have upset his tenuous balance, maintained through rigid control. He had written a vehement anti-Trinitarian tract and had made a step to get it published by having Locke transmit it to Le Clerc in Holland. Then he took fright lest its author be revealed. The whole question of the unity of God was troubling him. Secondly, clearly in quest of a place, he had allowed himself to be pushed into Lord Monmouth's presence and he felt ashamed. He was surrendering his independence, putting himself in the power of others. He was seeking money and honor and neglecting God's work—a sin he had already felt a need to confess in 1662: *Setting my heart on money learning pleasure more than Thee.* Finally, the affective relationship to his friend and disciple Fatio seems to have approached a dangerous climax.

When the actual breakdown occurred in September 1693 and Newton struck out in letters with mad accusations, he chose friends as the objects of his hostility, Locke and Pepys, and he attacked them for evils with which he was possessed. If the nature of God was troubling him, Locke was called a Hobbist, which meant a materialist and an atheist "who struck at ye root of morality." If Newton was place-seeking, he denounced Pepys for trying to involve him in obligations to the idolatrous Catholic party. If he was conscious of a crisis in his emotional life, he charged Locke with trying to "embroil" him with "woemen."

The malady subsided, and a salvation which made it possible for him to cope successfully with existence for more than three decades came with the exercise of power. The scientific recluse became an administrator. The aggression was turned outward. In 1696 Charles Montagu finally secured for him the wardenship of the Mint, and soon he became its Master. There he could defend his and the realm's pot of gold. At the Mint Newton was engaged on the king's business and this provided a permissible release for his wrath. He could ride herd on coiners and clippers, lose his temper at them, prosecute them, pursue to the gallows a rascal like Chaloner, a Macheath type out of the *Beggar's Opera*. After his breakdown, instead of suffering prolonged depression, he was able to reconstitute his existence by shifting its center.

When Hooke died and Newton became president and "perpetual dictator" of the Royal Society—a title which one of his adulators actually wanted to bestow upon him —he moved on to a more elevated plane. He ruled world science: anyone who would not do his bidding was excommunicated. Egged on by his young ones, Newton destroyed Leibniz. The timing is of some interest. The two quarrels with Hooke and Leibniz spanned virtually the whole of Newton's mature life. The counterattack on the continentals who had criticized his theory of colors was a sort of side show though it had involved an extraordinary expenditure of psychic energy. No sooner had the archvillain Hooke died than the hitherto muted antagonism to Leibniz assumed vast proportions. This was the decisive battle of Newton's life, and he ungallantly pursued his enemy beyond the grave in an amplified edition of the *Commercium Epistolicum* in 1722. No sooner was Leibniz gone than another quarrel erupted, one between Newton and the French Academicians over Newton's revision of world chronology, which led to denunciations of Fréret, Souciet, and Conti from the presidency of the Royal Society.

FRANK E. MANUEL

Almost everybody in his circle felt at least an occasional flick of the whip. Favorites were dropped; the thwarting of his will in the slightest matter was punished with exclusion. He had no charitableness—one fault and a friend was rejected. He had a mission to extirpate evil, and he sat in constant judgment upon his fellow men. The fonts of love had been all but dammed up. At the University he dismissed the chemist Vigani from his presence for cracking a joke about a nun. He would not speak with Richard Bentley for a year over differences in the interpretation of Daniel. At one time he had a falling out with Charles Montagu over some unspecified "grudge." He fought with Flamsteed about the publication of the star catalogue, drafting in his own hand the order that wrested the royal astronomer's lifework from him. He censured Hans Sloane over the administration of the Royal Society, and Woodward over his dispute with Sloane. He broke with William Whiston after he was ejected from the University and because he dared criticize Newton's chronology. He was cold to Dr. Stukeley for a number of years because he stood as a candidate for office without Newton's permission. He went to law with one of his old tenants over an ill-repaired hut. Even Halley was in disfavor for a while because of his levity in religious matters.

The pros and cons of the scientific quarrels that punctuated Newton's career have been debated *ad nauseam*. There were *agents provocateurs* in this republic of science who relished the combat of the titans—Oldenburg, Fatio de Duillier, John Keill, Abate Conti—and they kept replenishing the weapons in the arsenal. In a number of instances Newton's conduct must be judged unhandsome by any standards. Because he was not satisfied with the pace at which Flamsteed sent him his unpublished astronomical observations, Newton told him in so many words that his fame depended not on his own contribution to science, but on his service to Newton. He called him a puppy before others. However one looks at the Leibniz controversy, Newton's activities were certainly not beyond reproach. He appointed his hangers-on as judges, and he himself wrote a good part of the decision. He even modified texts in the holy cause. The insecure social status of this self-made man, son of a Lincolnshire yeoman, doubtless exacerbated his violent response to any intimation that he and he alone might not be the creator of all his magnificent inventions. To destroy any stone of the edifice risked the whole structure.

The enemies on whom Newton vented his rage were not confined to the living; they included historical figures and institutions. Here again, commendable devotion to religious truth or chronological fact hid the genesis and real quality of Newton's intemperate anger, resentment, and unrelenting vengefulness. There had been priestly liars in antiquity: Manetho of Egypt, Berossus of Babylon. They had inflated pagan claims to antiquity and he, Newton, was the defender of the image of Israel—Puritan Israel—against them. Alexandrian chronologists, Eratosthenes and Apollodorus, had lied, too. And then there was a whole set of Christian liars, beginning with Athanasius, who falsified the true apostolic tradition and introduced Trinitarianism. Jerome was the next great adulterer of truth. When the accusation encompassed the Papists in general, Newton's fury can be matched, but not often surpassed, among his contemporaries. Writing on the Whore of Babylon— identified with the Papacy in his commentaries on *Prophecies,* now in King's College—he worked himself into a veritable paroxysm of rage. The catalogue of legitimate, permissible enemies of the Lord and Newton whom it was right to smite—as Saul had been ordered to kill the Amalek—was long. Living and dead, they were all liars, falsifiers, prevaricators, diversionists, impostors, corrupters of the truth—the same phrases occur again and again.

Newton's letters readily reveal a cunning, structure-making capacity. It exercised itself in building for others a schema of motives from minute details and suppositions which then became certainties. Hooke had accused him of plagiarizing his theory of gravitation. In fact, Newton maintains, it is Hooke who was the plagiarist, and Newton suggested to Halley how it *might* have happened: after Oldenburg's death, Hooke had possession of the letters of the Royal Society, and since he knew Newton's handwriting he *may* have read the letters in which Newton first hinted at the theory. Leibniz *could* have seen the cryptic letter on the calculus and therefore he plagiarized Newton's method. There is a subtle letter to Locke in which Newton tries to worm out of his friend whether shortly before his death Boyle had in fact, as he had told Newton, given him *all* the elements of a supposed discovery of the philosopher's stone or whether he had not betrayed him, lied to him, and, as he had begun to suspect, actually reserved more information for certain other "gentlemen." What was Flamsteed up to? Was he not trying to discredit Newton with questions about the moon, by showing that he was dabbling in the mathematics and not paying attention to the King's business at the Mint?

Newton is always analyzing and conjecturing and structuring the motives of others. And often as not he casts into them the devils that are harassing *him.* He of course understood the process of projection well enough—in his enemies. During the Leibniz controversy he assailed his rival with the characteristic accusation: "He himself is guilty of what he claims in others." A long letter to Des Maizeaux reaches its climax with: "It is he who is the aggressor."

The violence, acerbity, and uncontrolled passion of Newton's attacks, albeit directed into socially approved channels, are almost always out of all proportion with the warranted facts and character of the situations. One could, after all, have criticized Manetho's dynastic list without hurling epithets at an Egyptian who had been dead a few thousand years. The case in the Leibniz controversy could have been stated in a much more judicial manner, as indeed Newton did at one time. Normally, the wardenship of the Mint was a sinecure and did not call for the actual pursuit of criminals into their hangouts and the establishment of a network of informers. All this gives weight to the hypothesis that the source of the rage lies elsewhere, that it accumulated in personal historical situations, that it was the onerous heritage of childhood traumas. The rage carried over because it could not be effectively or fully discharged, or it was re-evoked and triggered off by life situations which seemed to reproduce the emotional climate of his boyhood. The lad Newton could not harm his half brother Benjamin or his stepfather Barnabas with impunity, but the great scientist Newton could destroy his rivals and his "enemies" living and dead. So deep is the hurt and so boundless the rage, however, that he cannot be appeased as long as he lives. His victories do not assuage; his anger grows by what it feeds upon.

But it would be false to end on this note. The mystic flights of Newton's religious imagination and the leaps of his scientific inventiveness remain enigmas. Each individual element may be identified in terms of contemporary theological, historical, and scientific preoccupations, but the nature of the whole eludes us. He was a great confabulator, putting together ideas from different areas in a novel manner, one of the most common characteristics of the paranoid; but in this case the structures assumed universal significance. This analysis cannot avoid concluding with that well-known self image that—if Conduitt is to be believed—Newton in his declining years would have liked to see preserved for posterity. For this, too, is a great truth about him, and one upon which I have not dwelt in this paper. It is the other side of his polar personality. Toward the very end of his life he may have regained, if only for a brief moment, that naïve wonderment and engaging simplicity which graced the early reports of his experiments with light, as he reflected wistfully:

> I do not know what I may appear to the world; but to myself I seem to have been only like a boy, playing on the seashore, and diverting myself, in now and then finding a smoother pebble or a prettier shell than ordinary, whilst the great ocean of truth lay all undiscovered before me.

DAVID T. HAKES

Comment

Professor Manuel has presented us with a fascinating account of some of the more personal facets of Newton's life. He has brought out some little-known data about Newton's early life and upon them has based some intriguing speculations about what *may* have been some of the early sources of Newton's character as an adult. As a result, I feel that some things about Newton make sense to me now that did not earlier.

Rather than commenting in any detail on the facts or speculations that Professor Manuel has presented, I would like to consider the general nature of the task he has undertaken. As I said a moment ago, his paper left me feeling that I understood Newton better than I had before. And the question I wish to raise is, simply, when should one trust his feelings? When, that is, should one be confident that he really does understand rather than merely feeling that he does?

I think the task Professor Manuel has set himself is not unlike the one the clinical psychologist undertakes in performing a psychological assessment of an individual. It might best be characterized as an attempt to develop a theory of an individual personality—a theory that in some sense permits us to understand that personality more deeply and more fully. I think it is clear that the feeling of understanding does not depend solely on the data, on the facts about the individual that are presented. More importantly, it comes from the way in which those data are organized and from the implications of that organization. But providing an organization for such data is just providing a theory about the personality involved. In short, Professor Manuel has presented us with a theory about the development and functioning of Newton's personality. So another way of phrasing the question is, what must such a theory be like to warrant serious consideration?

The first requirement is that such a theory of an individual *must* be based on a general theory—that it is really nothing more than the application of a general theory of personality to the special case of an individual. To be sure, a number of people have claimed that a general theory is not necessary—that the individuals can be characterized in their own right without reference to any general theory. But this is extremely misleading. It is not clear that this claim is true even for simple description. And it certainly is not true for any interpretative statements. What such people do is assume a general theory—usually a very vague and ill-formed one—and then refuse to admit their own assumptions. If one examines what such people *do* rather than what they *say* they do, the emptiness of their claim becomes obvious.

There are overwhelming reasons why a theory about an individual must be based on a general theory, and I do not wish to detail them here. The one point I wish to make is that the truth of the individual theory is closely tied to the truth of the general theory. If we have reason to doubt the general theory, any interpretation of the individual must also be doubted. Say, for example, that I hold a personality theory asserting that if a pregnant woman watches horror movies on TV between the 4th and 6th months her child will be highly anxious. Now, all the evidence of which I am aware argues that such a theory is false, pure and simple. But say that little Johnny is brought to me in a highly anxious state, and I discover in the course of my investigations that his mother watches

DAVID T. HAKES

a great many horror movies, more particularly that she watched them nearly every night while she was pregnant. Surely, no one should take me very seriously if I propose that Johnny is anxious *because* of his mother's TV viewing habits.

The general theory that Professor Manuel has assumed is one version of psycho-analytic theory of personality. And for any number of good reasons, this theory does not inspire much confidence. I wish I could suggest that Professor Manuel would have been on firmer footing had he chosen a different theory. But the state of the art is such that I cannot even make that suggestion—there exists *no* personality theory that can make a reasonable claim to truth. So, at the outset, there is a very severe restriction on the claims that this or any such theory about an individual can make.

But even if there existed a sound general theory there are other requirements the individual theory would have to meet. For one, the proposed theory would have to be consistent with the presented data. Any theory of any sort that cannot meet even this condition hardly warrants serious consideration. But although consistency with existing data is a necessary condition it is certainly not a sufficient condition for consideration.

The difficulty is, of course, that the existing data are necessarily finite. And for any finite data set there is an indefinitely large number of theories that can explain, account for, or be consistent with those data. So how are we to know that the proposed theory is one of the more reasonable members of this indefinitely large set? The answer is extremely simple, at least in principle. The proposed theory must successfully pass the most severe tests we can devise. It must yield up hypotheses about new data; and only if it correctly predicts these data have we any real basis for entertaining it.

(Let me note in passing that when I refer to *new* data I obviously do not mean data concerning events that had not occurred at the time the theory was formulated. If these were the only data that counted, then any sort of historical theorizing would be literally impossible, as would any theorizing about archeology, paleontology, and so forth. The requirement on the data is, rather, that they not be taken into account when the theory is formulated. The theorist may not have known about the data, or he may simply not have seen them as relevant. But he cannot have designed the theory to account for them.)

Honest attempts to test any theory are, of course, extremely difficult, so difficult that the proper evaluation of a theory is likely to be minimized and sometimes ignored completely. The general reasons for this are well known, and I need not belabor them here. What I do wish to indicate is some of the additional difficulties that arise in testing a theory when that theory is about an individual.

One difficulty is simply that the available data are scanty. This is particularly true when the individual in question is no longer with us. And the fewer the data, the greater number and variety of theories that are consistent with those data.

But far more crucial than the paucity of data is the fact that the data are typically of the wrong sort. In Newton's case, for example, we have comments by his contemporaries, we have his copy books and some of his correspondence, and we have miscellaneous other data. We do not have, and have no possibility of getting, the results of diagnostic interviews, the results of projective tests, or the results of objective tests. In short, we are hampered not only by a general lack of data but also by a lack of the kinds of data that, given the task and the kind of theory proposed, should be the most relevant.

(Please let me make clear that I am *not* saying that removing the data problems would solve anything. Even a cursory examination of the successes and failures of clinical psychologists makes clear that this is far from being the case.)

But the problems do not end here. For say we develop a theory of an historical personage and set out to test it. Let us even assume that the theory is sufficiently explicit and well-formed that it makes a number of clear predictions. We have no opportunity to systematically collect data relevant to those predictions but are, rather, forced to settle for those data that happen to be preserved somewhere. And bear in mind that for the test to be legitimate we cannot know in advance what these data are. As a result of all this, it would be an extremely lucky accident if any of the data that came to light were in any way relevant to the predictions. Worse yet, the more explicit the predictions are, the less likely it becomes that relevant data exist.

And finally, in such cases we are necessarily deprived of one of the scientist's most powerful tools: we have no way in which we can apply the method of differences. Since we have no opportunity to manipulate conditions we cannot tell if the predicted behavior occurs under the relevant conditions and *only* under those conditions.

If all this sounds rather discouraging, it should. We started with the question of what a theory of an historical individual would have to be like to inspire confidence. And we seem to have ended in the position of suggesting that it may not even be possible to do history this way. I cannot provide any neat proof that the task is literally impossible. But I think the arguments are quite sufficient to indicate that it is at least the very next thing to being impossible.

It would be tempting at this point to conclude that we ought simply to ignore the problems. And certainly many have done just that. But ignoring the problems buys us nothing worth having. For whether we like it or not we are necessarily theorizing. And ignoring the problems means simply that we are willing to settle for a theory that may be easy to construct but that is also impossible to test. Having such a theory is far worse than having no theory at all. For while it may give an intuitive impression of explaining something, the impression is at best false and misleading.

Up to this point I have been trying to suggest what a theory about an individual personality ought to be like. Obviously, this is a very harsh light in which to evaluate any theory. And just as obviously, Professor Manuel's theory about Newton does not show up very well in this light. There is, of course, another, more lenient sort of evaluation we could undertake—how does Professor Manuel's effort compare with those of others who have undertaken similar tasks? I have in mind here such cases as Freud's classic study of Leonardo da Vinci, Ernest Jones' analysis of Shakespeare through Hamlet, and numerous other such "psychological biographies."

Perhaps the most striking impression one gets from reading such studies is the extent to which fantasy runs rampant. Typically, one finds an extraordinarily large number of interpretative statements based on a very small number of data statements. Interpretations are mutually inconsistent. The theory is modified for each new case, usually rather capriciously. Where facts are missing, they are constructed—"X *must* have been the case"—even where there is no evidence that it even *might* have been the case and often when there is considerable evidence that it *could not* have been the case.

Compared with such studies I believe Professor Manuel's "Lad from Lincolnshire" fares creditably. It is not that he has been immune to overinterpretation; rather it is that he has resisted the temptation better than most. Much that he has suggested is not transparently implausible. And there are many hypotheses implicit in the paper that may prove to be testable. Whether they will ultimately prove to be of merit is, of course, an open question.

But, having said this in general, let me close by trying to suggest a few of the points at which I have the greatest doubts about Professor Manuel's effort. The section dealing with Newton's relationship with and reactions to his nonfather I find particularly bothersome. Manuel suggests that Newton fused his father with God the Father and, for this

DAVID T. HAKES

reason, regarded himself as standing in a very special relationship to God. The data are far too scanty to support such a contention. It may be true, but I for one am unconvinced.

Again, Professor Manuel argues that Newton's extraordinary attachment to his mother stemmed from the nature of their relationship during his early life, owing in large part to the fact that his father was absent. The nature of the attachment, he asserts, resulted from the fact that "They were in union with each other during a critical period. . . ."

Incidentally, I find the phrase "in union with each other" a particularly nice choice of words for describing a psychosexual relationship, but perhaps I overinterpret. In any event, I do not believe the facts are consistent with the psychoanalytic theory Professor Manuel has assumed. The theory suggests that the attachment of son to mother, in any of the usual senses of a psychosexual attachment, occurs *late* in the period of infantile psychosexual development—around the age of four or five. It is this attachment that under more normal circumstances is prevented by the Oedipal conflict between son and father. Now, in Newton's case, what is presumably important is that there was no father, hence no Oedipal conflict, and so the relationship with the mother developed. But we know that Newton's mother also was not present at the critical time—that she left him before his third birthday. Thus it is a bit difficult to see how the attachment could have developed in the way Professor Manuel claims. I suppose one could assume that Newton was psychosexually precocious. But I know of no evidence to support such an assumption.

Finally, a methodological comment. Professor Manuel has treated the word lists in Newton's copybooks as free associations. While I find this interesting and possibly illuminating, I am a bit dubious about how much interpretation can be placed on such data. First, we have no normative data with which to compare Newton's word lists. And without some idea of what others of the same period, age, education, and so forth were producing, it is difficult to tell to what extent the lists represent projections of Newton's personal idiosyncrasies as opposed to common associations. In all fairness, I should note that Professor Manuel holds this same reservation. But I do not think he holds it as strongly as I do.

Secondly, the fact that they are lists raises some problems, for it is well known that the items in a list are not independent. Having come up with a word of a given type may well trigger a whole series of words of the same type, whereas if the first word had been different the others would have been much less likely to occur. It is for this reason that most studies of word association limit themselves to dealing with only the first response to any word—and Lord knows even these are difficult enough to interpret.

More points of this general sort could be raised. But little further purpose would be served by doing so. Suffice it to say in conclusion that Professor Manuel has undertaken a task of rather extraordinary difficulty. It certainly cannot be said that he has succeeded. But in comparison with other such efforts, it must be judged a good try.

CHRISTOPHER HILL

Newton and His Society

I.

ONE WAY FOR ME TO APPROACH THE SUBJECT OF NEWTON AND HIS SOCIETY
would be to quote Professor Alexandre Koyré: "The social structure of
England in the 17th century cannot explain Newton."[1] Then I could sit
down. But of course we must gloss Koyré by emphasizing the word "explain." A
complete explanation of Newton cannot be given in social terms. The historian, however, *qua* historian, is not interested in single causal explanations. The questions he
asks are "Why here?", "Why now?" If science were a self-evolving chain of intellectual development, then it would be irrelevant that it was Newton, living in postrevolutionary England, who won international fame by following up Galileo, a perse-
cuted Italian, and Descartes, a Frenchman living in exile in the Dutch republic. But
for the historian the where, when, and why questions are vital. It is no more possible
to treat the history of science as something uncontaminated by the world in which
the scientists lived than it is to write the history of, say, philosophy or literature or
the English constitution in isolation from the societies which gave birth to them.[2]

Often the important thing for scientific advance is asking new questions, approaching a given body of material from a fresh angle.[3] All the factors which precede and
make possible such a breakthrough are therefore relevant. The real problem often
is not How do men come to look at familiar facts in a fresh way? but How do they
liberate themselves from looking at them in the old way? And here the history of the
society in which the scientist lived, as well as the facts of his personal biography, may
frequently be suggestive, if rarely conclusive. Newton shared much of the outlook of
his scientific contemporaries, their limitations as well as their strengths. But I want to
suggest that his Puritan upbringing, combined with the postrevolutionary environment of Cambridge, and possibly certain psychological factors which are both personal and social, may have helped him to ask fresh questions and so to break through
to his new synthesis.

II

Newton was born in 1642, the year in which the English civil war broke out.
The first twenty-four years of his life saw a great revolution, culminating in the
execution of Charles I and the proclamation of a republic. They saw the abolition
of episcopacy, the execution of the Archbishop of Canterbury, and fifteen years
of greater religious and political liberty than were to be seen again in England
until the nineteenth century. The censorship broke down, church courts ceased to
persecute. Hitherto proscribed sects preached and proselytized in public, and re-

CHRISTOPHER HILL

ligious speculation ran riot, culminating in the democratic theories of the Levellers, the communism of Gerrard Winstanley and the Diggers, the scientific materialism of Hobbes and the economic determinism of Harrington. Books and pamphlets were published on a scale hitherto unprecedented on all subjects, including science, mathematics, and medicine; for the natural sciences, too, benefited from Parliament's victory. Oldenburg rightly said in 1659 that science got more encouragement in England than in France.[4] Bacon was popular among the Parliamentarians, and from 1640 onwards began that climb to fame which soon caused him to be hailed as "the dictator of philosophy"—an ascent which the Royal Society materially assisted.

The first two decades of Newton's life, then, saw a political revolution which was also a religious and intellectual revolution, the climax in England of a transformation in ways of thought which had been proceeding for a century and a half, and of which Renaissance, Reformation and the scientific revolution were all part. Protestantism, by its hostility to magic and ceremonial, its emphasis on experience against authority, on simplicity in theology, helped to prepare an intellectual climate receptive to science—not least in the covenant theology, so popular in Newton's Cambridge, with its rejection of arbitrary interference with law, its insistence that God normally works through second causes, not by miracles.[5] In England transubstantiation was publicly ridiculed from the pulpit; in Roman Catholic Europe the miracle of the mass was believed to be a daily event, to be treated with awe and reverence. In the sixteen sixties Sprat was arguing, in defence of the Royal Society, that it was only doing for philosophy what the Reformation had done for religion. Samuel Butler, an enemy of the Society, was arguing at the same time that Protestantism led to atheism.[6] Both saw connections between protestant and scientific revolutions.

But the years immediately before 1666 had seen a reaction. In 1660 Charles II, the House of Lords, and the bishops came back to England. An ecclesiastical censorship was restored. Oxford and Cambridge were purged again. The scientists regrouped in London around Gresham College, and succeeded in winning the patronage of Charles II. But it was not all plain sailing. In the early years of its existence the Royal Society had continually to defend itself against the accusation that science led to atheism and social subversion—the latter charge made plausible by the Parliamentarian past of the leading scientists. "The Act of Indemnity and Oblivion," the renegade Henry Stubbe sourly reminded his readers in 1670, had been "necessary to many of the Royal Society."[7] Next year Stubbe denounced Bacon's philosophy as the root cause of "contempt of the ancient ecclesiastical and civil jurisdiction and the old government, as well as the governors of the realm."[8] The fact that John Wilkins, the Society's secretary, conformed to the episcopal church in 1660 seemed less important to contemporaries than that he had been Oliver Cromwell's brother-in-law and that he had been intruded by the Parliamentary Commissioners as Warden of Wadham, where he gathered around him the group which later formed the nucleus of the Royal Society. In 1667 his fellow Secretary, Henry Oldenburg, was arrested on suspicion of treasonable correspondence. Conservatives and turncoats in the universities and among the bishops attacked both science and the Royal Society.

III

The mechanical philosophy suffered from its very name. The word *mechanic* was ambiguous. In one sense it meant "like a machine": the mechanic philosophy was what we should call the mechanistic philosophy. In this sense Oldenburg spoke of "the mechanical or Cartesian philosophy."[9] But not all Englishmen were Cartesians, and this meaning crystallized only in the later seventeenth century. When Dudley North in 1691 said "Knowledge in great measure is become mechanical" he thought it necessary to add a definition: "built upon clear and evident truths."[10] Long before Descartes wrote Bacon had been urging Englishmen to learn from mechanics, from artisans, and to draw a philosophy from their fumbling and un-co–ordinated but successful practice. "The most acute and ingenious part of men being by custom and education engaged in empty speculations, the improvement of useful arts was left to the meaner sort of people, who had weaker parts and less opportunity to do it, and were therefore branded with the disgraceful name of mechanics." But chance or well-designed experiments led them on. (I quote not from Bacon but from Thomas Sydenham, who like Sprat learnt his Baconianism at Wadham in the sixteen fifties under Wilkins.[11])

Bacon too was only summing up a pre-existent ideology which held up to admiration "expert artisans, or any sensible industrious practitioners, howsoever unlectured in schools or unlettered in books" (Gabriel Harvey, 1593). John Dee referred to himself as "this mechanician." Marlowe expressed this ideology in heightened form in *Doctor Faustus*:

> O what a world of profit and delight,
> Of power, of honor and omnipotence,
> Is promised to the studious artisan!

Here the artisan was also a magician. But then so too was Dee; so, Lord Keynes would persuade us, was Newton.[12] We recall John Wilkins' *Mathematical Magick, or the Wonders that may be performed by Mechanical Geometry* (1648). Fulke Greville spoke of "the grace and disgrace of . . . arithmetic, geometry, astronomy" as resting "in the artisans' industry or vein." We recall also Wallis' reference to mathematics in the sixteen thirties as a "mechanical" study, meaning by that "the business of traders, merchants, seamen, carpenters, surveyors of lands and the like."

This ideology was shared by many of the early Fellows of the Royal Society, and expressed most forcibly by Boyle—no magician, but anxious to learn from alchemists. Boyle insisted that scientists must "converse with practitioners in their workhouses and shops," "carry philosophic materials from the shops to the schools"; it was "childish and unworthy of a philosopher" to refuse to learn from mechanics. Professor M. B. Hall is right to stress Boyle's good fortune in having not been subjected to the sort of academic education he would have got at a university before the Parliamentarian purges.[13] Hooke too consistently took counsel with skilled craftsmen. Cowley, in his *Ode to the Royal Society,* rejoiced that Bacon had directed our study "the mechanic way," to things not words. Newton himself was a skilled craftsman, who had already constructed a water clock, sundials, and a windmill while still a boy. Later he ground his own lenses, made his own grinding and polishing machines and his own telescopes, and conducted his own alchemical experiments. As late as the eighteenth century he was issuing specific and detailed instructions to Royal Society experimenters.

Yet the word "mechanic" was not neutral. It had other overtones. It conveyed the idea of social vulgarity, and also sometimes of atheism. The Copernican theory, said an archdeacon in 1618, "may go current in a mechanical tradesman's shop," but not with scholars and Christians. During the interregnum the word came into new prominence when applied as a pejorative adjective to "mechanic preachers," those doctrinally heretical and socially subversive laymen of the lower classes who took advantage of religious toleration to air their own disturbing views. Such men appealed to their own experience, and the experiences of their auditors, to confute authority, just as the scientists appealed to experiment. ("Faithfulness to experiment is not so different a discipline from faithfulness to experience," wrote Professor Longuet-Higgins recently.[14] "This I knew experimentally," said George Fox of his spiritual experiences in 1647.[15]) There is no need to labor the importance of the mechanic preachers, nor the consternation which they caused to their betters: this has been demonstrated in Professor Tyndall's admirable *John Bunyan, Mechanick Preacher,* analyzing both the genus and its supreme exemplar, who was safely in jail from 1660 to 1672, with many of his fellows. From 1641 onwards it had been a familiar royalist sneer that Parliament's supporters were "turbulent spirits, backed by rude and tumultuous mechanic persons," who "would have the total subversion of the government of the state"; "those whom many of our nation, in a contemptuous folly, term mechanics," wrote Marchamont Nedham defensively.[16] Many of the educational reforms proposed in the revolutionary decades were aimed at benefiting this class. Thus Petty proposed "colleges of tradesmen," where able mechanicians should be subsidized while performing experiments; William Dell wanted better educational opportunities for "townsmen's children."

So there were dangerous ambiguities in the word "mechanic," of which the Royal Society was painfully aware. (If its members ever forgot, Henry Stubbe was ready to remind them by denouncing them as "pitiful Mechanicks!")[17] Sprat in his *History,* in Baconian vein, spoke of "mechanics and artificers (for whom the true natural philosophy should be primarily intended)," and defined the Society's ideal of prose style as "the language of artisans, countrymen and merchants." But—consistently with his propagandist purpose—he was careful to insist that the technological problems of industry must be approached by "men of freer lives," gentlemen, unencumbered by "dull and unavoidable employments." "If mechanics alone were to make a philosophy, they would bring it all into their shops; and force it wholly to consist of springs and wheels and weights." This was part of a campaign to make the Royal Society respectable. The atheist Hobbes and the radical Parliamentarian Samuel Hartlib were kept out. Anyone of the rank of baron or over was automatically eligible for a Fellowship. A number of courtiers and gentlemen were made Fellows, some of whom were genuinely interested in science, but many of whom were not. The Society prepared pretty tricks for Charles II, Newton had to pretend that James II could be interested in the *Principia,* and that epoch-making work was issued over the imprimatur of Samuel Pepys as president of the Royal Society—an estimable man, but hardly Newton's peer.

In the long run, this had of course deplorable consequences for science. Despite Boyle's insistence, a gentleman dilettante like Evelyn could not lower himself to "conversing with mechanical, capricious persons."[18] Even Seth Ward, intruded professor of astronomy at Oxford during the interregnum, thought that "mechanic chemistry" was an unsuitable subject for the sons of the nobility and gentry to study at universities. But in the short run it was essential to free the scientists from the "mechanic atheism" which Cudworth scented in Cartesianism,[19] and from the stigma of sedition which clung around the word "mechanical." "Plebeians and mechanics," said a Restoration bishop, "have philosophized themselves into principles of impiety, and read their lectures of atheism in the streets and highways." Glanvill in his dedication to the Royal Society of *Scepsis Scientifica* in 1664 emphasized the Society's role in "securing the foundations of religion against all attempts of mechanical atheism"; "the mechanic philosophy yields no security to irreligion."

But there was a narrow tightrope here. Boyle, the "restorer of the mechanical philosophy," was opposed to occult qualities, wanted to expel mystery from the universe as far as was compatible with the retention of God. Wren had told a London audience in 1657: "Neither need we fear to diminish a miracle by explaining it."[20] "What cannot be understood is no object of belief," Newton said. "A man may imagine things that are false, but he can only understand things that are true."[21] But there were still many who held the view denounced by Bacon "in men of a devout policy"—"an inclination to have the people depend upon God the more, when they are less acquainted with second causes; and to have no stirring in philosophy, lest it may lead to an innovation in divinity, or else should discover matter of further contradiction to divinity." Experience of the interregnum had strengthened the prejudices of those who thought like that. And there were very real intellectual problems in combining scientific atomism with Christianity—problems which Boyle, the defenders of the Royal Society and Newton himself spent their lives trying to solve. Newton once referred, revealingly, to "this notion of bodies having as it were a complete, absolute and independent reality in themselves, such as almost all of us, through negligence, are accustomed to have in our minds from childhood." This was a main reason for atheism: we do not think of matter as created or dependent on the continuous action of the divine will.[22]

30

Professor Westfall has plausibly suggested that the violence of the scientists' attacks on atheism may spring from the fact that "the virtuosi nourished the atheists within their own minds."[23] Given the general social anxiety of the Restoration period, how were men to frame a theory of the universe which would accommodate both God and the new science? The problem was acute, "the vulgar opinion of the unity of the world being now exploded" (the words are those of Henry Oldenburg) "and that doctrine thought absurd which teacheth the sun and all the heavenly host, which are so many times bigger than our earth, to be made only to enlighten us."[24] Mechanic philosophy, purged of the atheism and enthusiasm of the rude mechanicals, offered the best hope. Newton ultimately supplied the acceptable answer; but he was only one of many trying to find it. The question would have been asked if Newton had never lived.

IV

We do not know how far Newton was aware of the great revolution which was going on while he was growing up, but it is difficult to think that it left him untouched. His county, Lincolnshire, was a center of strong pro-Parliamentarian feeling. His mother was an Ayscough, and Edward Ayscough was M. P. for Lincolnshire in the Long Parliament, a staunch Parliamentarian. Newton's maternal uncle became rector of Burton Coggles in 1642; the stepfather whom his mother married was rector of another Lincolnshire parish.[25] Both apparently remained on good terms with the Parliamentary ecclesiastical authorities. Newton lived for many years at Grantham while attending its grammar school. Until 1655 the leading ecclesiastical figure in Grantham was its lecturer, John Angell, a noted Puritan.[26] After his death, the tone was set by two more Puritans, both ejected for nonconformity at the Restoration, both praised by Richard Baxter. Over the church porch was a library given to the town fifty years earlier by Francis Trigge, another eminent Puritan, who wrote a treatise on the Apocalypse.[27] Newton almost certainly used this library; he may even have acquired his interest in the mysteries of the Book of Revelation from it.

I emphasize these points because there used to be a mistaken impression, based on a poem which he was believed to have written, that Newton was in some sense a royalist. Even L. T. More, Newton's best biographer, repeats this error. But this poem was not Newton's; he copied it from *Eikon Basilike* for his girl friend, Miss Storey. There is no evidence that Newton sympathized with the sentiments expressed in the poem. Even if he did regard Charles I as a martyr, this would not make him a royalist in any technical sense. Most of those who fought against Charles I in the civil war deplored his execution. The Army had first to purge the Presbyterians from Parliament. Indeed the author of *Eikon Basilike* was himself a Presbyterian divine, a popular preacher before Parliament during the civil war. It was only after the Restoration that he (like Wilkins and so many other Puritans) conformed to the episcopal church and took his reward in a bishopric.

Newton's whole education, then, was in the radical Protestant tradition, and we may assume that his outlook was Puritan when he went up to Cambridge in 1661. This helps to make sense of his later beliefs and interests; he did not take to theology after a mental breakdown in the sixteen nineties. Before 1661 he was learning Hebrew. In 1664–65, if not earlier, he was keeping notebooks on theology and on the ecclesiastical calendar.[28] He later argued that bishops and presbyters should be of equal status, and that elders should be elected by the people.[29] Newton conformed indeed to the restored episcopal church—as he had to do if he wanted an academic career. But he abandoned belief in the Trinity very early in life and resisted all pressure to be ordained. He seldom attended Trinity College chapel. He had a typically Puritan dislike of oaths, shared with Boyle and Ray. In Newton's scheme for tuition at Trinity he went out of his way to insist "No oaths of office to be imposed on the lecturers. I do not know a greater abuse of religion than that sort of oaths." In later life he was alleged to be "hearty for the Baptists."[30]

If Newton went up to Cambridge with Puritan inclinations, he can hardly have been happy in his first two years. John Wilkins had just been expelled from the mastership of Newton's College, despite the wishes of the fellows. We do not know how many fellows were ejected or forced to resign; the number may be of the order of twenty.[31] They included John Ray, who resigned in 1662, perhaps not before Newton had heard him preach sermons in the college chapel which were later written up as *The Wisdom of God manifested in the Works of the Creation* and *Miscellaneous Discourses concerning the Dissolution and Changes of the World*. (Those ejected also included John Davis, Fellow, Librarian and Hebrew Lecturer, and William Disney from Newton's county of Lincolnshire.) Ray had originally preached his sermons as a layman, but after 1660 ordination was insisted on for all fellows after their first seven years.[32]

As early as 1660 Ray had deplored the lack of interest in experimental philosophy and mathematics at Cambridge,[33] and the expulsion and withdrawal of men like himself and Wilkins did not help. By 1669, when the university entertained Cosimo de' Medici with a Latin disputation, the subject was "an examination of the experimental philosophy and a condemnation of the Copernican system." Newton can hardly have found this a congenial atmosphere.

Nevertheless, the interregnum left its mark on Cambridge. Isaac Barrow, who came up to Trinity in 1647, spoke of mathematics as then "neglected and all but unknown, even on the outward surface by most." A decade earlier Wallis and Seth Ward had both left Cambridge in order to learn mathematics from William Oughtred, a country parson. "The study of mathematics," Wallis said in an oft-quoted phrase, "was at that time more cultivated in London than in the universities." Wallis did not hear of the new philosophy till years after he went down. Barrow claimed to have introduced it to Cambridge, and in the sixteen fifties there was rapid progress there, as in Oxford. By 1654 or 1655 we find Barrow congratulating his university on escaping from traditional servility to scholasticism. "You have very

CHRISTOPHER HILL

recently begun to cultivate the mathematical sciences"; and natural philosophy (anatomy, medicine, chemistry) had lately started to be studied seriously. Barrow was one of the strongest early influences on Newton.[34]

Above all Cambridge had become interested in the Cartesian philosophy, and was the scene of the most elaborate attempt to adapt traditional Puritan covenant theology to accommodate the findings of the new science. This was the school misleadingly known as the Cambridge Platonists, which derived from Joseph Mede, whom we shall meet again when we discuss Newton's interest in the Apocalypse. Its members included Ralph Cudworth, Puritan and Parliamentarian, who had links with Newton; like Newton, he was accused of being unsound on the Trinity. The outstanding figure among the Cambridge Platonists when Newton came up to Trinity was Henry More, old boy of Newton's school at Grantham and tutor to two of his teachers there. More—later a Fellow of the Royal Society, like Cudworth—was strongly influenced by Descartes. But in 1659 More published *The Immortality of the Soul,* in which, he said, "I have demonstrated with evidence no less than mathematical, that there are substances incorporeal."[35] He hoped to become the Galileo of a new science of the spirit world. Newton was an intimate associate of More's, became an adherent of the atomic philosophy in his undergraduate days, and was influenced by Descartes. But in the sixties More came to reject the Cartesian mechanical philosophy because it led to atheism[36]; and Newton followed suit.

v.

If we try to think ourselves back into the position of men living in this postrevolutionary world, we can see that there were various intellectual possibilities.

(1) The older generation of revolutionaries, who had seen their hopes of building God's kingdom betrayed, necessarily withdrew from politics. Most of them, like George Fox and the Quakers, decided that it had been a mistake to try to build God's kingdom on earth. They turned pacifist, their religion became a religion of personal morality, not of social reform. They accepted the position of minority sects, asking only for freedom from persecution. Bunyan, writing in jail, saw his pilgrim oppressed by the burden of sin, and concerned only to get rid of it; even wife and children are secondary to that consideration. The toughest of all the revolutionaries, Milton, still wrestled with God and history to justify God's ways to men. He completed *Paradise Lost* in 1665, published it in 1667; even he looked for "a Paradise within thee, happier far."

(2) The more intellectual among the returned royalists, their high hopes equally disappointed, found consolation in a cynical and mocking materialist atheism, which was probably only skin deep. Many, like Rochester, abandoned it when they believed they were on their deathbeds. But at court, and among the court dramatists, sceptical Hobbism was fashionable, if only to *épater* the bourgeois and the Puritans. "There is nothing," wrote Samuel Butler, whose *Hudibras* was a best seller in 1662–63, "that

can prevail more to persuade a man to be an atheist as to see such unreasonable beasts pretend to religion."[37] His reference was probably to mechanic preachers. Oldham in 1682 wrote:

> There are, who disavow all Providence
> And think the world is only steered by chance;
> Make God at best an idle looker-on,
> A lazy monarch lolling on his throne.[38]

(3) Others among the returned royalists found that their authoritarian leanings could best be expressed by a return to Catholicism. Laudianism was dead in Restoration England, despite the apparent importance of some former Laudians in 1660. The revolution had made impossible any revival of the independent economic or political power of either church or crown. Henceforth both were subject to the ruling class in Parliament. Charles II and James II had to look for support from Catholic and absolutist France—or, still more desperately, from papist Ireland. Many men of authoritarian temperament were impressed by the achievements, military and cultural, of Louis XIV's France. Some ultimately were converted to Catholicism, like the former Trinity undergraduate Dryden; others, like Archbishop Sheldon, had abandoned the traditional Anglican doctrine that the Pope was Antichrist. Such men were in a dilemma in Restoration England, since most Englishmen regarded France as the national enemy. After 1688 this dilemma could be resolved by rallying to the Protestant William and Mary. But there was a time earlier when Catholicism was both intellectually and politically attractive, to the horror of traditional Protestant patriots. It was in this intellectual climate that Nell Gwyn claimed that, if she was a whore, at least she was a Protestant whore—unlike her French rival, the Duchess of Portsmouth. Newton would have applauded the theological part of her claim.

(4) The main group of middle of the road Parliamentarians adhered to a lay, secularized Puritanism. They accepted restored episcopacy in the Church, purged of Laudianism. They had no difficulty in joining hands with moderate and patriotic ex-Cavaliers. Both were enemies of enthusiasm (remembering the mechanic preachers) and of Hobbist atheism; but they were even more opposed to the much more real danger of popery. Atheism had no respectable support; it was a fashion, a whim. It was perhaps more important as a charge to hurl at the Royal Society and the scientists than in itself; and even here Henry Stubbe thought it necessary to accuse the Society of opening the door to popery as well as to atheism.[39]

Newton was of the postrevolutionary generation, and so had not known the former enthusiasm and present guilt of the revolutionaries. His Puritan upbringing ensured that by and large he shared the outlook of my last group—Puritans with the temperature reduced.

Caution was a natural result of the shock of the Restoration. Pepys was afraid someone might remember that after Charles I's execution in 1649 he had said that

34

the right text to preach from would be "The memory of the wicked shall rot."[40] Men like Dryden, Waller, Cudworth, Henry More, no less than scientists like Wilkins, Wallis, Seth Ward, Goddard, and Petty, had complied with the revolutionary régimes far enough to be worried after 1660. Anyone with Puritan sympathies plus a reasonable desire to get on in the world would learn in the early sixties not to talk too much. Newton did want to get on, and he was cautious; yet there were limits beyond which he would not compromise. He refused to be ordained, and I think we must reasonably refer back to this period the very strong antipapist feelings which he always showed. On principle he was very tolerant, but he would never extend toleration to papists or atheists—any more than Milton or Locke would.

This is something which Newton's liberal biographers have found rather shocking and have tended to underestimate. I have already stressed the patriotic reasons for opposing popery. In view of the crypto-popery in high places under Charles and James II, Newton's attitude was also anti-court. In one of his manuscripts he declared that idolatry (i.e., popery) was even more dangerous than atheism "because apt by the authority of kings and under very specious pretences to insinuate itself into mankind." He added, prudently, that he referred to pre-Christian kings who enjoined ancestor worship, but the application to Charles and James was clear enough.[41] "Was it the interest of the people to cheat themselves into slavery . . . or was it not rather the business of the court to do it?" Newton asked in a passage about Assyria which Professor Manuel very properly relates to the conflict with James II.[42]

I should like to emphasize Newton's behavior in 1687, when in his first overt political action he led the antipapal party in Cambridge in opposition to James II's measures, at a time when such action needed a great deal of courage. It is in this light too I think that we should see his acceptance of public service after 1688. It need not have resulted merely from political or social ambition. Perhaps Newton really did think something important was at stake in the wars of the sixteen nineties. If England had been defeated, Catholicism and absolutism might have triumphed on a world scale. Newton believed that the Pope was Antichrist, for which he had sound Anglican backing; and all the best interpreters of the Biblical prophecies agreed that the sixteen nineties would be a climacteric decade: I return to this later. The Mint was not just a reward—or only in the sense that the reward of service is more service. We should think of Newton in the same terms as of Milton, sacrificing his eyes in the service of the English republic, or of Locke, going into exile with Shaftesbury—and also taking office after 1688; or of the gentle John Ray, who like Newton seldom referred to politics, which makes his paean on 1688 all the more noteworthy: "the yoke of slavery has been broken. . . . If only God grants us peace, we can rely upon prosperity and a real age of gold."[43] In 1714 Newton tried to get an act of Parliament passed declaring that Rome was a false church.[44] It must have been with considerable pleasure that in 1717 he used—to support a telescope—a maypole which had just been taken down from the Strand. For its erection in 1661 had been a symbol of the victory of those "popish elements" in church and state whose final defeat in 1714–15 must have delighted Newton.

VI.

Nor was antipopery irrelevant to Newton's science. Copernicus' treatise was still on the papal Index; so were the writings of Descartes. Newton's dislike of mysteries and superstition is in the Protestant as well as the scientific tradition. And it also relates to his anti-Trinitarianism. In his *Quaeries regarding the word* ὁμοῶσιος his object was just as much to draw attention to papal corruptions as to argue a positive case. Anti-Trinitarianism seemed to Newton the logical consequence of Protestantism. He referred to Luther, Bullinger, Grotius, and others when discussing papal corruptions of Scripture. But like so many others of Protestantism's logical consequences, this one had been drawn mainly by the most radical and socially subversive lower-class sects.[45] In England from 1583 to 1612 a number of anti-Trinitarians were burnt, including (1589) Francis Kett, grandson of the leader of the Norfolk rebels in 1549 and Christopher Marlowe's friend; and in 1612 Bartholomew Legate, cloth merchant, the last Englishman burnt for religious heresy.

Anti-Trinitarianism seems to have been endemic in England, despite this persecution. One of the abortive Laudian canons of 1640 was directed against its prevalence among the "younger or unsettled sort of people," and undergraduates were forbidden to own or read Socinian books. Like so many other heresies, anti-Trinitarianism flourished during the interregnum. In 1644 there was a Unitarian group in Coleman Street, that nest of heretics. In 1652 the first English translation of the Racovian catechism was published; next year a life of Socinus appeared in English translation.[46] The most notorious anti-Trinitarian was John Bidle, son of a Gloucestershire tailor, who was in prison more often than not from 1645 onwards, and was the cause of a storm in the Parliament of 1654–55. Bidle was saved from savage punishment only by Cromwell's sending him, quite illegally, to the Scilly Isles. Released in 1658, he was arrested again after the Restoration and in 1662 died in prison at the age of 46.[47]

One reason for the virulent persecution was the notorious fact that denial of the divinity of Christ had often been associated with social heresies. At the trial of Servetus in 1553 the subversive consequences of his heresy were strongly emphasized. The doctrines of Socinianism, thought an Oxford don in 1636, "are repugnant to our state and government"; he referred specifically to the pacifism and anarchism of its adherents.[48] "The fear of Socinianism," wrote Sir John Suckling in 1641, "renders every man that offers to give an account of religion by reason, suspected to have none at all."[49] In 1651 John Pordage was accused both of anti-Trinitarianism and of saying there would soon be no government in England; the saints would take over the property of the wicked. Pordage had connections with William Everard the Digger.[50] Socinus was a Mortalist, Mede warned Hartlib; the chief English Mortalist was the Leveller leader, Richard Overton.[51]

CHRISTOPHER HILL

Conservatives were alarmed by the spread of anti-Trinitarianism. Bishop Joseph Hall in 1648 thought that Socinians should be exempted from the toleration he was prepared to extend to all other Christians (now that he was no longer in a position to do so). Twelve years later the London Baptists were equally intolerant of Socinianism.[52] Nevertheless, anti-Trinitarians continued to exist, if only in small groups. But they were outlaws, specifically excluded from such toleration as was granted in 1689; in 1698 those who wrote or spoke against the Trinity were disabled from any office or employment. A Unitarian was executed in 1697, another imprisoned in 1703. In 1711 Newton's friend Whiston was expelled from Cambridge for Arianism. There was every reason for not proclaiming anti-Trinitarian sentiments. Milton and Locke shared Newton's caution in this respect.

VI.

Newton's theology thus had radical associations. So had his studies of the Hebrew prophecies. Thanks to the work of Professor Manuel it is now recognized that this was a serious scholarly subject, occupying the best minds of the sixteenth and seventeenth centuries. Once grant, indeed, that the whole of the Bible is an inspired book and to be taken literally, it is difficult to see how a Christian could fail to be interesed in trying to date the end of the world and the last judgment. Servetus had expected the end of the world to come soon. An official declaration of Elizabeth's government in 1589 spoke of "this declining age of the world."[53] Leading British mathematicians, from Napier through Oughtred to Newton, worked on the problem. (Napier's *Plaine Discovery of the Whole Revelation of St. John* ran to twenty-one editions between 1593 and 1700.)

The quest received especial stimulus and a new twist from the revolution of the sixteen forties: eighty tracts are said to have been published on the subject by 1649. "The Second Coming is each day and hour to be expected," said one published in 1647.[54] "Though men be of divers minds as to the precise time," claimed another of 1653, "yet all concur in the nighness and swiftness of its coming upon us."[55] The *raison d'être* of the sect of Muggletonians, the last witnesses, was that the end of the world was at hand. And many excited radicals thought it their duty to expedite the Second Coming of Christ by political action. "Men variously impoverished by the long troubles," observed the mathematician John Pell, "full of discontents and tried by long expectation of amendment, must needs have great propensions to hearken to those that proclaim times of refreshing—a golden age—at hand."[56] There were two not very significant military risings in London, in 1657 and 1661. Militant Fifth Monarchists were an embarrassment to the scholarly interpreters of the prophecies, just as plebeian atheists were an embarrassment to mechanic philosophers; but the two activities were quite distinct in each case.

In England the best known scholarly interpreters were Thomas Brightman and Joseph Mede. Brightman, a supporter of the Presbyterian discipline, published his

Revelation of St. John Illustrated in 1615; it was in its fourth English edition by 1644. He thought that the saints' reign of a thousand years had begun in 1300, that the Reformation had been a great turning point, and that now "truth doth get ground and strengthens every day more."[57] The abomination would be set up in 1650, and the year 1695 should see the utter destruction of Turkish power by the conversion of the Jews. "Then shall be indeed that golden age."[58]

Mede was a botanist, an anatomist, a mathematician, and an astronomer, as well as a precursor of the Cambridge Platonists.[59] He too saw the years since about 1300 as a continuous upward movement whose phases were (1) the Albigensian and Waldensian heresies; (2) the Lutheran Reformation; (3) the reign of Elizabeth; (4) the Thirty Years' War; (5) would be the destruction of Rome—the Pope being of course Antichrist; (6) the destruction of the Turkish Empire and the conversion of the Jews; (7) the final judgment and the millennium.[60] Mede was a Fellow of Christ's College, Cambridge, the college of the great Puritan William Perkins. At the time of his election (1602, the year of "our Mr. Perkins's" death) Mede was "thought to look too much to Geneva," and he was wary of publishing in the Laudian thirties; but he seems to have been a middle-of-the-road man.[61] In 1642 Mede's *Key of the Revelation* was published in English translation by order of the Long Parliament. The translator was Richard More, himself an M. P. and a Puritan writer, and the official character of the publication was enhanced by the inclusion of a preface by William Twisse, the Presbyterian divine who was Prolocutor of Parliament's Assembly of Divines gathered at Westminster, and who was so much of a Parliamentarian that in 1661 his remains were dug up from Westminster Abbey by royal command and thrown with others into a common pit. In 1635 William Twisse had said in a letter to his friend Mede "This old world of ours is almost at an end."[62] In his Preface Twisse, in Baconian vein, observed that the opening of the world by navigation and commerce met at one and the same time with an increase of scientific and Biblical knowledge.

So though the Long Parliament encouraged this belief for its own propagandist purposes, perfectly sane and respectable scholars were taking the prophecies very seriously, and were concluding that they would soon be fulfilled. Milton spoke of Christ as "shortly-expected king"; Henry More thought the ruin of Antichrist was near.[63] In 1651 a scholarly friend of Brian Duppa, future bishop, expected the end of the world within a year;[64] in 1655 the great mathematician William Oughtred, a royalist, had "strong apprehensions of some extraordinary event to happen the following year, from the calculation of coincidence with the diluvian period." Perhaps Jesus Christ would appear to judge the world.[65]

On dating testimony converged. Napier was believed to have predicted 1639 as the year of the destruction of the enemies of the church[66]—a prophecy which must have been noted when episcopacy was overthrown in his native Scotland in that year. Vavasor Powell thought "1650 . . . is to be the saints' year of jubilee."[67] In Sweden and Germany the downfall of the Beast was widely expected in 1654

CHRISTOPHER HILL

or 1655.[68] Not only Brightman and Mede had foretold great events in the sixteen fifties; so too had Christopher Columbus, George Wither, Samuel Hartlib, Sir Henry Vane, and Lady Eleanor Davies (though this volatile lady had predicted catastrophe for many earlier dates).[69]

Once the sixteen fifties had passed, the next crucial period appeared likely to be the nineties. Brightman and Mede had both plumped for them. So did Nicholas of Cusa, Napier, Alsted, Henry Archer, Hanserd Knollys, Thomas Goodwin, Thomas Beverly the Behmenist, and John Mason.[70] The sixteen nineties saw Newton in the service of an English state now resolutely antipopish. The French Huguenot Jurieu thought that the destruction of Antichrist would occur between 1710 and 1715, following the defeat and protestantization of France.[71] Mede and Whiston expected the world to end in 1715.

It is thus not so odd as it used to be thought that Newton's theological manuscripts are as bulky as his mathematical and scientific writings. Perry Miller was perhaps a little bold to conclude positively that, from about 1693, Newton wanted to find out exactly how close he was to the end of the world.[72] Newton held, cautiously, that the prophecies would not be fully understood "before the last age of the world." But "amongst the interpreters of the last age," amongst whom he included Mede, "there is scarce one of note who hath not made some discovery worth knowing." "The great successes of late interpreters" suggested to Newton that "the last age, the age of opening these things," is "now approaching"; that God is about opening these mysteries." This gave him "more encouragement than ever to look into" them.[73] The point to emphasize is that this was an area of investigation which had traditionally attracted mathematical chronologists; Newton would have been in good company if he wished to throw light on the end of the world as well as on its beginning. And a number of serious scholars whom Newton respected, including Mede, had thought that great events might begin in the nineties. But again it was a subject which had radical associations and overtones; caution was needed.

VIII

By 1665–66 the Restoration honeymoon, such as it was, was over. Charles II's genuine attempt to continue Cromwell's policy of religious toleration had been defeated by Parliament. Between 1660 and 1662, 1760 ministers were driven out of the church. The Conventicle Act of 1664 and the Five Mile Act of 1665 expelled them from the towns which were the main centers of opposition. In 1665 England was involved in an aggressive commercial war with the Dutch ("What matters this or that reason? What we want is more of the trade the Dutch now have," said the Duke of Albermarle, with soldierly frankness[74]). This war was such a fiasco that men began to look back to the days when Oliver Cromwell had led England to victory. The city turned against Charles II as Dutch ships sailed up the Medway. Even Dryden, even in "Annus Mirabilis," said of the king

He grieved the land he freed should be oppressed,
And he less for it than usurpers do.

(Dryden no doubt recalled his fulsome praise of Cromwell seven years earlier, in "Heroic Stanzas to the Glorious Memory of Cromwell.") Samuel Pepys, another former Cromwellian who now looked back nostalgically, recorded in February 1666 that his old patron the Earl of Sandwich feared there would be some very great revolutions in the coming months. Pepys himself was full of forebodings, and was getting money in against a foul day.[75] Fifteen years earlier the famous William Lilly had quoted a prophecy that "in 1666 there will be no king here or pretending to the crown of England." The Plague in 1665 and the Great Fire of London in 1666, together with the comets of 1664 and 1665, again made men think that the end of the world was at hand. Lilly was in trouble for having predicted the Fire.[76]

In these troubled years 1665–66, Newton, in his retirement at Woolsthorpe, was discovering the calculus, the nature of white light, and universal gravitation. He made another discovery when the Heralds visited Lincolnshire in 1666: that whereas his father had never claimed to be more than a yeoman, he, Isaac, was a gentleman.

I tread warily in discussing Newton's elusive personality. There are some aspects of genius which it is futile to try to explain. But if we recall that Shakespeare abandoned the theatre just as soon as he could afford to, and set himself up as a gentleman in his native Warwickshire, we shall perhaps be the less surprised by the young Newton's improvement on his illiterate father's social aspirations in 1666, or by Newton's apparent abandonment of science for more gentlemanly activities from the nineties.

By 1666, too, or soon afterwards, Newton had decided not to marry Miss Storey. Why? "Her portion being not considerable," Stukeley tells us, "and he being a fellow of a college, it was incompatible with his fortunes to marry."[77] The reasoning is ungallant and unromantic, but it makes sense. Marriage would either have necessitated ordination and taking a living (to which we know Newton's objections); or else would have condemned him to the kind of vagabond life, dependent on the charity of others, which a man like John Ray led for twenty years after 1660.

I feign no Freudian hypotheses. But the fact that Newton, a posthumous child, never had a father, is surely relevant. He saw little enough of his mother after he was two years old, living first with his grandmother and then with an apothecary at Grantham. Only for a couple of years between the ages of sixteen and eighteen did he live with his mother, now widowed for the second time. So the decision not to marry Miss Storey would seem finally to have cut love out of Newton's life. Newton's later complaisance to his niece's affair with Halifax, which so bothered nineteenth-century biographers, may have been simply due to his not noticing.

Newton's theology denied the sonship of Christ, and though the Father exists he is a *deus absconditus,* in no close personal relation with his creatures. He is the first cause of a universe lacking all secondary qualities, all warmth and light and

CHRISTOPHER HILL

color. The eternal silence of those infinite spaces seems never to have frightened Newton. Professor Manuel comments on his history: "Newton never wrote a history of men. . . . The individuals mentioned in his histories . . . have no distinctive human qualities. . . . Nations are . . . neutral as astronomical bodies; they invade and they are in their turn conquered. . . An interest in man's creations for their own sake, the aesthetic and the sensuous, is totally absent in his writings."[78]

It would be naïve to suppose that these things would have been different if Newton had married Miss Storey. But the decision not to, apparently so easily taken and accepted, on prudential economic grounds, fits in with all we know of Newton's personality—his careful and minute keeping of accounts from boyhood until he became a very rich man indeed. Fontenelle in his *Eloge* rightly singled out Newton's frugality and carefulness for very special mention.[79]

This leads on to consideration of Newton's caution. Again a little history dispels some of the legends that have grown up around it. Many men—like Pepys—had reason to be cautious in the Restoration period. Newton's reluctance to publish, moreover, was no more than was expected of someone who had aspirations to be thought a gentleman. The part played by Halley in getting the *Principia* published repeats almost verbatim Ent's description of his role in persuading Harvey to allow his *De Generatione Animalium* to be printed in 1651. One may suspect that both accounts are highly stylized, remembering how many seventeenth-century poets claimed to publish only under great pressure or after alleged attempts to pirate their poems. There were parallels among the scientists. Ralph Bathurst, physician, F.R.S., and president of Trinity College, Oxford, had a wife who "scorns that he should be in print."[80] Francis Willughby died reluctant to publish his *Ornithology,* which Ray issued posthumously.[81]

And of course in Newton's case there were very special reasons for caution. His anti-Trinitarian writings would have been dangerous to publish. For the same reason Milton, not normally averse to seeing himself in print, held back the *De Doctrina Christiana*; and Locke showed a similar reticence. Hobbes thought the bishops would like to burn him; Waller dared not praise Hobbes publicly. After 1688 Newton did once consider publishing his *Historical Account of Two Notable Corruptions of Scripture,* anonymously, in French, and on the continent; but he thought better even of that. His theological heresies had other consequences. Newton was firm enough in his convictions to refuse to be ordained; but not to risk leaving Cambridge. In 1675 the Royal Society induced Charles II to issue letters patent authorizing Newton to retain his fellowship although not a clergyman. By accepting this quite exceptional use of the dispensing power Newton gave hostages to fortune. Any scandal attaching to his name would certainly be made the occasion for drawing attention to his anomalous position, and might call the retention of his fellowship in question. This did not prevent Newton taking serious political risks in 1687, and all credit to him; but on that occasion his deepest convictions were stirred. On any lesser issue he would be likely to play safe. This, combined with a natural furtiveness of temperament, seems an entirely adequate explanation of his early reluctance to publish. By 1694 he was uninhibitedly discussing with David Gregory a whole range of projects for mathematical publications.[82]

IX

Many of Newton's attitudes can, I suggest, be related to the post-Restoration desire for order, an order which should be as uncomplicated as possible. Puritanism and Baconian science had for many years been preparing for this ordered simplicity which Newton triumphantly achieved in the *Principia,* where the watchmaker God, "very well skilled in mechanics and geometry," presided over an abstract mathematical universe.[83] Similarly, Newton thought, there is a natural religion, "one law for all nations, dictated . . . to all mankind by the light of reason."[84] The same simplification informs Newton's anti-Trinitarianism, with its denial of the mystery of the Incarnation. Newton thought he found in the writings of Joseph Mede a single key which would likewise dispel the apparent mystery of the Biblical prophecies. "The prophets," Newton believed, "wrote in a language as certain and definite in its significance as any vulgar language." The heavens, the sun and moon, signify kings and rulers; the earth signifies inferior people; hades or hell "the lowest and most miserable of the people."[85] ("In Newton's pragmatization of myth and reduction of prophecy to plain history," said Professor Manuel, we can see "a reflection of the new realities of middle-class society"—the society which triumphed in England after the revolution of the mid–century.)[86] Similarly Mr. Forbes and Mr. Sherwood Taylor have suggested that in Newton's alchemical experiments he may have hoped to find a key to the presumed common language of the alchemical writings, and a synthesis of the micro-structure of matter which would have been the counterpart to his celestial and terrestrial mechanics.[87] In his concern with spelling reform, which goes back to his pre-Cambridge days, Newton wanted to find a "real character" which should replace Latin and be truly international because as abstract as mathematics. This was an interest he shared with Wallis, Evelyn, Wilkins, and many other Fellows of the Royal Society.[88] The quest for a simplified order in all intellectual spheres was very topical.

It is not unreasonable to compare Hobbes's simplification of the universe to matter and motion, of political science to individuals accepting sovereign power in the interests of order; or the literary classicism which was invented by the defeated royalists during the interregnum, yearning for decorum and order, and which became fashionable in the Restoration years of French influence, with the order-loving Dryden as its high priest.[89]

And yet—and yet. As has often been pointed out, Newton was not wholly a Newtonian. Though he stripped the universe of secondary qualities, his experiments with colors enabled eighteenth-century landscape painters and poets to paint far more brightly than before. Contradictions lurk in the heart of his universe. In his desire to refute the Cartesian mechanism, Newton, like Pascal, postulated an irrational God

42   **CHRISTOPHER HILL**

behind the irrational force of gravity, a *Deus absconditus* but very real. "A continual miracle is needed to prevent the sun and the fixed stars from rushing together through gravity."[90] "A Being eternal, infinite, all-wise and most perfect, *without dominion,* is not God but only Nature," Newton wrote.[91] Newton's God is as arbitrary as Hobbes's sovereign. Newton brought back into physics the notion of "attraction" which Boyle had devoted so much energy to expelling.[92] (It is ironical that the lectures in which Bentley used Newton's new "occult qualities" to confute atheism should have been endowed by Boyle; and not untypical of the difficulties in which seventeenth-century scientists found themselves in their determination to have both God and science.)

"Those things which men understand by improper and contradictious phrases," Newton assured the too impetuous Dr. Bentley, "may be sometimes really in nature without any contradiction at all."[93] Newton accepted, dogmatically, experimental science and Biblical revelation as equally self-validating. "Religion and philosophy are to be preserved distinct. We are not to introduce divine revelations into philosophy, nor philosophical opinions into religion."[94] Science deals with second causes. The experimental method itself assumes that there is an intelligible order in nature which is law-abiding, "simple and always consonant to itself."[95] The first cause is a matter of revelation. Perhaps one day, when the Baconian program has been completed, science and revelation can be linked. Newton never doubted that there was an ultimate mechanical cause of gravitation, though he could not discover it experimentally. But he had realized that this was a far longer-term program than Bacon had ever dreamed. "The great ocean of truth lay all undiscovered" before the "boy playing on the sea-shore . . . now and then finding a smoother pebble or a prettier shell than ordinary."[96] Newton may have worried lest the ocean itself might be annihilated before it was fully explored; but in fact the hope of linking science and revelation was abandoned before the explorers were out of sight of land.

NOTES

[1] Ed. M. Claggett, *Critical Problems in the History of Science* (Madison, 1959), p. 855.

[2] For an example of the egregious misunderstanding into which ignorance of the historical context has led commentators on Thomas Hobbes, see Quentin Skinner, "The Ideological Context of Hobbes's Political Thought," *Historical Journal,* IX (1966), esp. pp. 313–17.

[3] A. R. Hall, "Merton Revisited," *History of Science,* II (1963), *passim.*

[4] Ed. A. R. and M. B. Hall, *The Correspondence of Henry Oldenburg* (University of Wisconsin Press, 1965–   ), I, p. 278.

[5] Perry Miller, "The Marrow of Puritan Divinity," *Publications of the Colonial Society of Massachusetts,* XXXII (1935), p. 266.

[6] T. Sprat, *History of the Royal Society* (1667), pp. 371–2; S. Butler, *Characters and Passages from Notebooks* (ed. A. R. Waller, Cambridge University Press, 1908), p. 458. Sprat's comparison was pretty trite by this date: see my *Intellectual Origins of the English Revolution* (Oxford University Press, 1965), pp. 25–6, which gives sources for quotations unidentified above.

[7] H. Stubbe, *Legends no Histories* (1670), Sig. +2.

[8] H. Stubbe, *The Lord Bacons Relation of the Sweating-sickness examined* (1671), Preface.

[9] Oldenburg, *Correspondence*, II, p. 630.

[10] North, *Discourses upon Trade* (1691), in J. R. McCulloch, *Early English Tracts on Commerce* (1952), p. 511.

[11] Sydenham, *De Arte Medica* (1669), in K. Dewhurst, *Dr. Thomas Sydenham* (Wellcome Historical Medical Library, 1966), p. 82.

[12] Lord Keynes, "Newton the Man," in the Royal Society's *Newton Tercentenary Celebrations* (Cambridge University Press, 1947), p. 27.

[13] M. Boas, "The Establishment of the Mechanical Philosophy," *Osiris*, X (1952), p. 418.

[14] The *Times Literary Supplement*, 25 October, 1963.

[15] G. Fox, *Journal* (1901), I, p. 11.

[16] Sir John Coniers, quoted by B. Manning, "The Nobles, the People and the Constitution," *Past and Present*, No. 9, p. 61; *Mercurius Britannicus*, No. 107, November 24—December 1, 1645. I owe this reference to the kindness of Mr. Ian McCalman.

[17] Stubbe, *Legends no Histories*, Sig. + lv.

[18] R. Boyle, *Works* (1772), V, p. 397.

[19] J. Tulloch, *Rational Theology and Christian Philosophy in England in the 17th century* (1874), II, pp. 278–9.

[20] C. Wren, *Parentalia* (1700), p. 201.

[21] Ed. H. McLachlan, *Sir Isaac Newton's Theological Manuscripts* (Liverpool University Press, 1950), p. 17.

[22] Ed. A. R. and M. B. Hall, *Unpublished Scientific Papers of Isaac Newton* (Cambridge University Press, 1961), p. 197.

[23] R. S. Westfall, *Science and Religion in 17th century England* (Yale University Press, 1958), pp. 107–11, 205–6, 219–20.

[24] Oldenburg to Samuel Hartlib, in *The Correspondence of Henry Oldenburg*, I, p. 277.

[25] See C. W. Foster, "Sir Isaac Newton's Family," *Associated Architectural Societies' Reports and Papers*, XXXIX (1928), pp. 1–62.

[26] See Joan Simon, "The Two John Angels," *Transactions of the Leicestershire Archaeological and Historical Society*, XXXI (1955), pp. 38–41.

[27] H. McLachlan, *The Religious Opinions of Milton, Locke and Newton* (Manchester University Press, 1941), p. 119.

[28] Sir D. Brewster, *Memoirs of the Life, Writings and Discoveries of Sir Isaac Newton* (Edinburgh, 1855), II, p. 318; F. E. Manuel, *Isaac Newton, Historian* (Cambridge University Press, 1963), pp. 16, 268.

[29] H. McLachlan, *Sir Isaac Newton's Theological Manuscripts*, pp. 55, 137.

[30] W. W. Rouse Ball, *Cambridge Notes* (Cambridge, 1921), p. 258; Brewster, *op. cit.*, II, p. 338. The source for the last quotation (Whiston) is not of the most reliable.

[31] H. M. Innes, *Fellows of Trinity College* (Cambridge University Press, 1941).

[32] C. E. Raven, *John Ray* (2nd ed., 1950), pp. 57–8, 441, 461, 457. Ray reluctantly agreed to be ordained in December 1660, when he still hoped for a reasonable religious settlement.

[33] *Ibid.*, p. 28 and *passim*.

[34] I. Barrow, *Theological Works* (ed. A. Napier, 1859), IX, pp. 41–7; cf. R. H. Kargon, *Atomism in England from Hariot to Newton* (Oxford, 1966), pp. 78–9 and Chapter XI, *passim*.

[35] H. More, *The Immortality of the Soul* (1659), *passim*; *Collection of Several Philosophical Writings* (1662), p. xv.

[36] Hall and Hall, *Unpublished Scientific Papers of Isaac Newton*, pp. 75, 187; A. R. Hall, "Sir Isaac Newton's Note-Book, 1661–5," *Cambridge Historical Journal*, IX (1948), pp. 243–4; Boas, "The Establishment of the Mechanical Philosophy," p. 505.

[37] Butler, *Characters and Passages from Notebooks*, p. 466.

[38] J. Oldham, *Poems* (Centaur Press, 1960), p. 178.

[39] Stubbe, *Legends no Histories*, Sig.*

[40] Pepys, *Diary* (ed. H. B. Wheatley, 1946), I, p. 253.

[41] McLachlan, *Sir Isaac Newton's Theological Manuscripts*, pp. 49–51, 131–2. Cf. Pepys's fear of Catholicism in the early sixties—all the more significant in a man who was later himself to be accused of papist leanings.

[42] Manuel, *Isaac Newton, Historian*, p. 116.

[43] Raven, *John Ray*, pp. 251–2.

[44] Brewster, *op. cit.*, II, pp. 351–2.

[45] E. M. Wilbur, *A History of Unitarianism* (Harvard University Press, 1946), chapter 2 and *passim*.

[46] [Anon.], *The Life of that Incomparable man Faustus Socinus* (1653).

[47] J. Bidle, *The Apostolical and True Opinion concerning the Holy Trinity* (1653), *passim*. I have used the 1691 edition, which contains a *Life of Bidle*.

[48] Ed. F. S. Boas, *The Diary of Thomas Crosfield* (1935), pp. 85–6.

[49] Sir J. Suckling, *An Account of Religion by Reason* (1641), The Preface. Cf. F. Osborn, *Advice to a Son* (1656): the Socinians are "looked upon as the most chemical and rational part of our many divisions" (in *Miscellaneous Works*, 11th ed., 1722, p. 91).

[50] J. Pordage, *Innocence appearing through the dark Mists of Pretended Guilt* (1655), *passim*; cf. G. P. Gooch, *The History of English Democratic Ideas in the 17th century* (1927), p. 266. Pordage denied the accusations.

[51] J. Mede, *Works* (ed. J. Worthington, 1664), II, p. 1082; [Richard Overton], *Mans Mortallitie* (Amsterdam, 1644), *passim*.

[52] J. Hall, *Pax Terris* (1648); J. Waddington, *Congregational History, 1567–1700* (1874), p. 559.

[53] H. S. Bennett, *English Books and Readers, 1558 to 1603* (Cambridge University Press, 1965), p .225.

[54] [Anon.], *Doomes-Day* (1647), p. 6.

[55] J. Rogers, *Sagrir* (1653). By 1666 the Fifth Monarchy, Rogers predicted, "must be visible in all the earth."

[56] John Pell to Secretary Thurloe, March 1655, in *The Protectorate of Oliver Cromwell* (ed. R. Vaughan, 1839), I, p. 156.

[57] T. Brightman, *The Revelation of St. John Illustrated* (4th ed., 1644), pp. 378–81, 520, 824; cf. pp. 109–12, 124–5, 136–7, 157 and *passim*.

[58] Brightman. *A most Comfortable Exposition of the last and most difficult pages of the Prophecies of Daniel* (1644), pp. 966–7; *A Commentary on Canticles* (1644), p. 1077 (pagination of these last two is continuous with Brightman's *Revelation*, with which they are bound).

[59] Mede, *Works*, I, p. lxv.

[60] Mede, *The Key of The Revelation* (2nd ed., 1656), pp. 114–25; *Works*, I, pp. xlviii–li.

[61] Mede, *Works*, I, pp. lxv, xxxiv; II, pp. 978, 995.

[62] Mede, *Works, II*, p. 979; cf. pp. 1006–7.

[63] H. More, *Theological Works* (1708), p. 633.

[64] Ed. Sir Gyles Isham, *The Correspondence of Bishop Brian Duppa and Sir Justinian Isham, 1650–60* (Northamptonshire Record Society, 1955), p. 37.

[65] Ed. E. S. de Beer, *The Diary of John Evelyn* (Oxford University Press, 1955), III, p. 158.

[66] [Anon.], *The Popes Spectacles* (1623), p. 1083.

[67] V. Powell, *Saving Faith* (1651), p. 92.

[68] M. Roberts, review in *Journal of Ecclesiastical History*, VIII (1957), pp. 112–15.

[69] Brightman, *Daniel*, p. 967; Mede, *Remaines on some Passages in Revelation* (1650), p. 33; J. Merrien, *Christopher Columbus* (1958), p. 223; Wither, *Campo-Musae* (1643); Hartlib, *Clavis Apocalyptica* (1651); my *Puritanism and Revolution* (1958), p. 327; I owe Lady Eleanor Davies to the kindness of Professor Ivan Roots.

[70] J. Trapp, *Commentary of the New Testament* (1958—first published 1647), pp. 250, 420; my *Puritanism and Revolution*, p. 329; G. F. Nuttall, *The Holy Spirit in Puritan Faith and Experience* (1946), p. 109; D. P. Walker, *The Decline of Hell* (Chicago University Press, 1964), p. 245.

Newton and His Society

[71] G. H. Dodge, *The Political Theory of the Huguenots of the Dispersion* (Columbia University Press, 1947), pp. 35–8.

[72] P. Miller, *Errand into the Wilderness* (Harvard University Press, 1956), p. 228.

[73] Newton, *Opera Quae Exstant Omnia* (ed. S. Horsley, 1775), V. pp. 448, 450, 474.

[74] A. T. Mahan, *The Influence of Sea Power upon History, 1660–1783* (1890), p. 107.

[75] Pepys, *Diary,* IV, p. 366, V, pp. 218, 283–4, 328, VI, p. 113.

[76] W. Lilly, *The Lord Merlins Prophecy Concerning the King of Scots* (1651), p. 4; *Monarchy or no Monarchy in England* (1651), *passim.*

[77] E. Turnor, *Collections for the History of the Town and Soke of Grantham* (1806), p. 179.

[78] Manuel, *op. cit.,* pp. 137–8, 193.

[79] *The Elogium of Sir Isaac Newton, by Monsieur Fontenelle* (1728), p. 32.

[80] A. Wood, *Athenae Oxonienses,* I, *Life of Wood* (Ecclesiastical History Society, Oxford, 1848), p. 188.

[81] *Op. cit.,* Preface.

[82] Ed. H. W. Turnbull, *Correspondence of Sir Isaac Newton,* (1959–), III, pp. 335–6, 338.

[83] *Opera Quae Exstant Omnia,* V, p. 432.

[84] McLachlan, *Sir Isaac Newton's Theological Manuscripts,* p. 52. Wilkins has been described as "the English godfather of natural or moral religion" (G. McColley, "The Ross-Wilkins Controversy," *Annals of Science,* III, pp. 155, 186).

[85] McLachlan, *Sir Isaac Newton's Theological Manuscripts,* pp. 119–21; Newton, *Opera Quae Exstant Omnia.* V, pp. 306–10; cf. T. Brightman, *The Revelation of St. John Illustrated,* pp. 232–3, 273–92; J. Mede, *Works,* I, Sig.* xxx 4; J. Mede, *The Key of the Revelation* (1656), Sig. A4.

[86] Manuel, *op. cit.,* p. 121.

[87] R. J. Forbes, "Was Newton an Alchemist?," *Chymia,* II (1949), pp. 35–6; F. Sherwood Taylor, "An Alchemical Work of Sir Isaac Newton," *Ambix,* V (1956), p. 64; cf. I. B. Cohen, "Newton in the Light of Recent Scholarship," *Isis,* LI (1960), pp. 503–4.

[88] R. W. V. Elliott, "Isaac Newton's 'Of an Universall Language,'" *Modern Language Review,* LII (1957), pp. 1–18; cf. Elliott, "Isaac Newton as Phonetician," *ibid.,* XLIX (1954), pp. 5–12.

[89] P. W. Thomas, "John Berkenhead in Literature and Politics, 1640–1663" (unpublished Oxford D.Phil. Thesis, 1962), *passim.*

[90] *Correspondence of Sir Isaac Newton,* III, pp. 334, 336, 355; cf. A. J. Snow, *Matter and Gravity in Newton's Physical Philosophy* (Oxford University Press, 1926), *passim.*

[91] Hall and Hall, *Unpublished Scientific Papers of Isaac Newton,* p. 363 (my italics).

[92] Boas, "The Establishment of the Mechanical Philosophy," pp. 420–2, 479, 489 and *passim;* cf. Turnor, *Collections for the History of the Town and Soke of Grantham,* pp. 172–3.

[93] *Opera Quae Exstant Omnia,* IV, p. 439.

[94] McLachlan, *Sir Isaac Newton's Theological Manuscripts,* p. 58.

[95] Newton, *Mathematical Principles of Natural Philosophy* (transl. A. Motte, ed. F. Cajori, University of California Press, 1934), pp. 398–9.

[96] L. T. More, *Isaac Newton: A Biography* (New York, 1962), p. 664. The famous phrase curiously recalls one of Donne's sermons: "Divers men may walk by the sea-side and, the same beams of the sun giving light to them all, one gathereth by the benefit of that light pebbles or speckled shells for curious vanity, and another gathers precious pearl or medicinal amber by the same light. So the common light of reason illumines us all; but one employs this light upon the searching of impertinent vanities, another by a better use of the same light finds out the mysteries of religion; and when he hath found them, loves them not for the light's sake, but for the natural and true worth of the thing itself . . . . But . . . if thou attend the light of natural reason, and cherish that and exalt that, so that that bring thee to a love of the Scriptures, and that love to a belief of the truth thereof . . . thou shalt see that thou by thy small light hast gathered pearl and amber, and they [worldly men] by their great lights nothing but shells and pebbles; they have determined the light of nature upon the book of nature, this world;

CHRISTOPHER HILL

and thou hast carried the light of nature higher" (ed. G. R. Potter and E. M. Simpson, *The Sermons of John Donne,* California University Press, III, 1957, pp. 359, 361). It is too dreadful to think of Newton reading Donne, even Donne's sermons; but the passage was so relevant to the problems of the scientists that it was no doubt borrowed by many preachers in the Cambridge of Newton's youth.

LAWRENCE STONE

Comment

When asked to write a paper on the subject of "Newton: the Historical Background," Mr. Hill could have done one of several things. He could have prepared a study in pure intellectual history, and traced the strands of thought which finally came together in Newton's mind to produce the theory of gravity. He could, to be short, have expanded upon Professor Herbert Butterfield's remark that by 1665 "most of the ingredients of Newton's gravitational theory were in existence, though scattered in the writings of different scientists in such a way that no man held them in combination." So much work has been done on this problem by professional historians of science in recent years that it is very unlikely that a mere historian would have anything very valuable to contribute, and Mr. Hill has wisely left this question severely alone.

Alternatively Mr. Hill could have taken up again what is now generally known as "the Merton thesis," and given us a recapitulation of his views, which he has recently set out at some length elsewhere, of the relationship of the rise of the scientific spirit in late seventeenth century England to the rise of Puritanism and of a middle class of enterprising merchants and industrious artisans. Again it is difficult to see how he could have told us anything which has not already been said before, by himself, or by Professor Robert Merton, and he has therefore contented himself with a brief, dogmatic, statement of his position about Protestantism and a rather longer excursus on the artisan and the changing values built into the word "mechanic."

The main thrust of this sensitive and original paper is directed elsewhere, towards explaining the intellectual background of a Cambridge theologian called Isaac Newton. Ever since the publication of his writings sixteen years ago, this theologian has been a great embarrassment to historians of science, who have been uneasily aware that he is one and the same person as their Isaac Newton, the scientist. The speculations and calculations about the imminence of the Last Judgment were the product of the same assemblage of nerves and brain cells which produced the Law of Gravity and the research into optics. What Mr. Hill has done is to drag out into the open this other Newton— Newton the theologian—and have a good hard look at him. He shows us his background amid the moderately Puritan clergy of remote and rural Lincolnshire, growing up at a time of disillusionment with the great Puritan experiment of the Interregnum. As a result of this background, and of the prevailing religious mode at Cambridge when he arrived, Newton became what might be called a Low-Temperature Theologian. He abhorred enthusiasm in any form, but was particularly hostile to what he regarded as two specific forms of it, namely atheism and Roman Catholicism. Though in other ways a liberal and tolerant man, Newton shared what Mr. Hill shows to be the general prejudices of his age, and was prepared actively to oppose, and even persecute, the holders of these two positions. On the other hand, although a Cambridge don and therefore a member of a highly orthodox Anglican establishment, Newton was, as Mr. Hill shows, very far from orthodox in his religious beliefs. He resolutely refused to take orders and appears to have held clear anti-Trinitarian views. Perhaps the most interesting part of Mr. Hill's paper is that in which he sets Newton's preoccupation with the Last

Judgment in the context of the age, showing that it was a common preoccupation of influential Cambridge academics and indeed of English mathematicians since the days of Napier.

The question that interests a symposium on the history of science, however, is what is the relation of Newton's theology to Newton's science. To my mind, none at all. The concept of the fully integrated personality whose views on all subjects are in rational harmony one with another is surely one which has long ago been exploded. Culture, in the anthropological sense of the word, may be a coherent unity, attributable to any given society—though even here the relationship between the parts is far from uniform, and archaic, vestigial institutions abound if one cares to look for them. But the mind of man is a set of compartments: between some compartments there are broad open doors, between others tiny cracks and pinholes, between others no connection at all. We shoot rockets at the moon, and avoid walking under ladders; we may be liberal in national politics, and reactionary in campus politics; believe in the universal brotherhood of man, and still think it reasonable to slaughter large numbers of another society, if it is thought to threaten our values or our interests; and so on. Logically incompatible *attitudes* can evidently be held simultaneously without noticeable discomfort, although psychologists tell us that the presence of incompatible *moral* imperatives is at the root of much mental disorder.

It is obvious that a general philosophical belief about the nature of the universe and of man's role within it is likely to affect the strategy and style of scientific research. It did matter in the seventeenth century whether one was a Hobbesian or a Deist, as Newton's hostility to Descartes suggests. But on the other hand, hundreds of scientists from Newton's day to this have had no difficulty in accepting revealed religion on the one hand and the experimental findings of scientific inquiry on the other. Newton himself put the position very clearly: "We are not to introduce divine revelation into philosophy, nor philosophical opinion into religion." This being so, it seems to me that what Mr. Hill has left unexplained is just how Newton's anti-Trinitarian beliefs, and his obsession with the Apocalypse, affected his scientific activities. Until this is done, I am forced to conclude that an understanding of Newton's theological beliefs, an understanding which Mr. Hill has done much to advance in his paper, goes a long way to improve our understanding of Newton as a man, but very little to improve our understanding of him as a scientist.

It is on the psychological level, rather than on the level of content and method, that Newton's studies of science and of theology interlock. If ever a great thinker cries out for professional psychological analysis, it is surely Newton. Brought up as a fatherless and loveless child, Newton lived a fatherless and loveless intellectual existence. As Mr. Hill goes out of his way to emphasize, Newton's theology denied the sonship of Christ, his spelling reform projects tried to put order and reason into a disorderly and illogical system, his science conjured up the terrifying voids of space, his historical writings were utterly impersonal, swept clean of the mess and muddle and passion of human beings. Everywhere he was the Great Simplifier, or rather the Great Tidier. The life of his mind was surely a reflection of his calculating, economizing, meticulously neat, withdrawn and frigid personality. As for his famous caution, I see no need to drag in the political mood of the Restoration to explain a trait he held in common with the philosopher Thomas Hobbes, 54 years his senior.

Finally, since Mr. Hill himself raises the subject in his opening pages, I feel obliged to say a word or two about the Merton thesis, although I am only too well aware that this complex and controversial subject cannot be dealt with satisfactorily in a few min-

Comment

utes. First, the association of Protestantism with science: Mr. Hill sums up the argument in a sentence (p. 27): "Protestantism, by its hostility to magic and ceremonial, its emphasis on experience against authority, on simplicity in theology, helped to prepare an intellectual climate receptive to science." To this the objections are that the Puritans were just as much prey to superstition and magic as the rest of us, and were devout believers in witches and broomsticks; that a pedantic and obsessive insistence on the literal truth of the Bible accords ill with a faith in experience against authority; and that the connection of science with "simplicity in theology"—whatever that may mean—is very far from obvious. The only plausible link is a product of the Protestant rejection of the medieval Catholic pantheon of saints and angels who could intercede directly in the workings of Nature. Such demolition probably helped to clear the way for Newton's clockmaker God working through second causes, although it must be remembered that this intellectual position does not differ as much from that of the more moderate Catholics as is often assumed, and that Puritans were even readier than Catholics to see the direct intervention of God in the workings of Nature. Newton's Bostonian contemporary, Michael Wigglesworth, for example, ascribed to God the provision of a favorable wind for a voyage, and the supply of money to pay his debts.[1] If by the early seventeenth century the Catholic hierarchy was growing more suspicious of the pursuit of second causes by scientific methods, this was because it was more acutely aware of the truth of Hobbes' dictum: "in these foure things, Opinion of Ghosts, *Ignorance of second causes* [my italics], Devotion towards what men fear, and Taking of things Casuall for Prognostiques, consisteth the Naturall Seed of Religion."[2] In the light of the subsequent concurrent rise of science and decline of religion it looks as if Hobbes, and the Papacy, were right: the preservation of ignorance of second causes *is* a factor in the preservation of religion.

The second element in the Merton thesis is the influence of a rising middle class, by which is meant merchants and artisans, the former being the patrons of scientific education at Gresham College, and the latter the inventors of the practical tools needed for scientific advance. Mr. Hill devotes several fascinating pages to an elucidation of the word *mechanic* but I am puzzled to see its relevance to Newton, who until the 1690s lived the life of a remote and ineffectual don, and who probably hardly ever spoke to an artisan or mechanic in his life, except to instruct technicians to carry out experiments under his direction. He certainly profited in his research from the expertise of the instrument makers, but it is difficult to regard this anxious social climber as in any way bourgeois in his value system. The precise social role of a late seventeenth century scientist like Newton and the way it differs from that of a late sixteenth century alchemist like Dr. Dee, has yet to be elucidated, but there is prima facie no very obvious distinction. If Newton was knighted for his labors, so had been Sir Edward Kelly, while both moved in the most exalted circles. If there is such a thing as the social rise of the scientist in the seventeenth century, it must be ascribed more to the creation of a secure professional institution, the Royal Society, than to any change in the role of the individual.

To sum up, I believe that the most important elements in Mr. Hill's paper are firstly the suggestive hints he throws out about the psychological behavior pattern which underlies both Newton's personal life and his intellectual forays into every field; and secondly the scholarly and wholly convincing account of the intellectual background to his calculations about the Last Judgment. These are important contributions to our understanding of Sir Isaac Newton.

LAWRENCE STONE

NOTES

[1] E. S. Morgan, ed., *The Diary of Michael Wigglesworth 1653–57,* New York, 1965, pp. 19, 36.

[2] T. Hobbes, *Leviathan,* Everyman's Library edition, p. 54.

NEWTON'S SCIENTIFIC ACHIEVEMENTS

A. RUPERT HALL AND MARIE BOAS HALL

Newton and the Theory of Matter

THE ANALYSIS OF NEWTON'S THEORY OF MATTER IS A SUBJECT OF PERENNIAL interest to everyone familiar with his writings, for Newton wrote virtually nothing, except in the field of pure mathematics, that did not either explicitly or tacitly reveal his commitment to some version or other of the seventeenth century's constant preoccupation, the mechanical philosophy. And whereas the mechanical philosophy in the hands of those predecessors who were in some sense Newton's masters (Descartes and Boyle especially) was relatively simple and clear cut, Newton's theory is both complex and unsettled, and his exact meaning has presented and continues to present a fascinating puzzle to scholars, a puzzle important for the understanding of both Newton and the Newtonians.

We ourselves have long been concerned with this aspect of Newton's achievement, and indeed our edition of *Unpublished Scientific Papers of Isaac Newton*[1] was largely constructed out of extracts which we found of particular interest for Newton's theory of matter. We there stated our views of Newton's opinion of the structure of matter and his attitude towards aetherial and atomic explanations at some length. But for the benefit of those who have not been involved in this aspect of Newtonian scholarship, and as a general introduction to the more particular points we wish specifically to discuss in this paper, it seems desirable here to summarize very briefly the general position we have taken in the past.

It is, surely, fair to state that all Newtonian scholars now agree that a particulate theory of matter underlies all Newton's thinking about natural philosophy. Whether this is explicit, as in the 31st Query of *Opticks* ("it seems probable to me, that God in the Beginning form'd Matter in solid, massy, hard, impenetrable, moveable Particles," etc.) or relegated to prefatory hints, as in the *Principia,* it is nevertheless plain to be seen as a necessary mechanism, and as one which served Newton well in the interpretation and explanation of the laws of nature. Newton took particles virtually for granted; what for him deserved emphasis was the way in which these particles either possessed or were acted upon by the forces of attraction and repulsion. That the force of attraction existed between bodies, and by extension between particles was transparently evident from the one force which Newton could and did handle mathematically—gravity. Indeed the case of gravity showed explicitly that all forces acting between bodies could be reduced to forces acting between particles. Repulsion was a natural corollary to attraction: so he proclaimed in Query 31 "as in algebra, where affirmative quantities vanish and cease, there negative ones begin; so in mechanicks where attraction ceases, there a repulsive virtue ought to succeed." Of these things Newton had and could have no doubt, for it was to him obvious common sense; he could and did insist that he spoke in the most ordinary way. As he said in the suppressed "Conclusio," the unpublished ending to the *Principia* which should have, but did not, explain publicly his deepest thoughts on problems of matter,[2] "The force of whatever kind by which distant particles rush towards one another is usually, in popular speech, called an attraction. For I speak loosely when I call every force by which distant particles are impelled mutually towards one another, or come together by any means and cohere, an attraction."

This much was clear. There was a force of attraction, and its negative, a force of repulsion. But to say what this force was, this Newton regarded as quite a different matter. As he wrote agitatedly to Bentley in January 1692/3,[3] "The Cause of Gravity is what I do not pretend to know, and therefore would take more Time to consider of it." As we have tried to show by printing the relevant documents, Newton had been considering the cause of gravity (or, more generally, attraction) from very early days as he was to continue to do until the end of his life; yet never to his own satisfaction. We have in connection with these documents shown how Newton constantly balanced an action-at-a-distance concept of pure attraction against a quasi-Cartesian impulse mechanism. This latter he developed in various forms, from an aerial to an aetherial mechanism of ever increasing sophistication. Over and over again he juggled with the experimental facts as he knew them (rather a small range of experimental evidence: capillary attraction, the lack of adhesion in dry powder, the difficulty of pressing two surfaces together, the walking of flies on water, the anomalous suspension of mercury, the refraction of light, chemical activity, electrical attraction, only the last three being unused in the earliest discussions). Over and over again Newton tried to persuade himself that there was enough experimental evidence to provide a firm basis for a definitive theory, and over and over again there patently was not. Only thus can one explain why he continually tried to write his considered judgment on the problem for publication, and each time until *Opticks* never ventured more than a hint.

Other problems were deeply enmeshed with the problem of the cause of the forces of attraction and repulsion: the interpretation of forces, the value of hypotheses, the immediate role of God in the mechanism of the universe. This last we have discussed at considerable length in our introduction to the documents. The others we propose to consider here.

Let us begin with the obvious point that any theory of matter entertained by Newton was necessarily hypothetical, and that concerning hypotheses he had certain reservations that are very well known. Thus the historian seems to find in Newton himself firm injunctions to heed only his positive achievements in science and to disregard any "hypotheses" of a secondary order upon which they might appear to depend; yet the same historian must be uncomfortably aware that such positive achievements of Newton remain incomplete and intellectually indigestible if they are taken in isolation, divorced from his deeper views about the structure of things and about the causes of those phenomena which are susceptible of positive discussion. Moreover, as the historian extends his knowledge of the Newtonian *oeuvre,* he finds that Newton himself was so far incapable of remaining on the plane of icy positivism to which he found it convenient to retreat from time to time, that he openly showed how there were multiple leads that might be pursued at the fascinating level of hypothesis. So we have not only the question, "Did Newton himself have ideas about the deeper infrastructure of Nature?"—a question which nowadays we can hardly fail to answer in the affirmative, since we know that he wrote altogether at least fifty thousand words on the subject; there is also the question, "Did Newton attach particular probability to one set of ideas in preference to others?" And this question is one which is, to the historian, neither trivial nor merely descriptive, for we would expect some relationship between the preferred hypothesis and the positive achievement. Indeed, such a correlation has often been assumed in the past without critical examination.

Hence, we cannot by any means separate a consideration of Newton's ideas about matter from his epistemology, though we can effect one simplification not open to him. We are not now any longer concerned with the problem of *living,* rather than historical, science; with the question "Is this positive theory correct or not?" Obviously, when treating both optics and celestial mechanics, it was highly important to Newton not to have the fate of what he called a "doctrine" hang upon his reader's reaction to what he called a "hypothesis." This he stresses again and again: I am telling you, he says, that these properties of light are true properties, and that these equations apply to the motions of physical bodies, and that they do so *whatever* we think about gravity, or whatever we think about the nature of light. So he writes of Pardies,

> I do not take it amiss that the reverent father calls my theory an hypothesis, since he had not yet grasped it. But I had proposed it from a different point of view, in which it seemed to embrace nothing but certain properties of light, which I think can easily be demonstrated once they have been discovered, and which if I did not know them to be true, I would rather repudiate them as empty and idle speculations than acknowledge them as my own hypotheses.[4]

And, accordingly, Newton maintains more than once that the "properties" (same word again!) of light that he had discovered "were in some measure capable of being explicated not only by that [a corporeal hypothesis of light], but by many other mechanical hypotheses."[5] Now if we followed Popperian analysis we would deduce from this the emptiness of such mechanical hypotheses, from each of which the same phenomena (the properties) may be predicted; and it may be that Newton too had some such idea in mind. More to the point, however, is his contention: you must not think this property is only conformable to *my* view of light, for I can show that it is also consonant with *yours.*

We are not now concerned to examine Newton's usage of such words as "hypothesis" or "doctrine," nor to discuss the failure of his attempts to make his contem-

A. RUPERT HALL AND MARIE BOAS HALL

poraries judge his newly discovered properties or newly advanced doctrine as things in themselves, independently of hypotheses. Here we need only point the obvious moral, that scientists do find it very difficult to judge new "doctrines" without, at the same time, reflecting upon the deeper level of hypothesis about the structure of things. Nor do we have to evaluate the rationality or otherwise of the feeling of Newton's contemporaries, that along with his "doctrine" itself he was trying to smuggle into their minds something of his own way of interpreting that "doctrine." It is, at the very least, easy enough to see that in his early optical days Newton found it very difficult not to write of light as "body," just as later, when writing of gravitation, the word "attraction" would come naturally to his pen.

Having recognized that Newton fell over backwards in his effort, in the face of criticism, to do what we would all try to do—to get his principal idea across by sacrificing all inessentials—we then arrive at our first real difficulty: must we discount *all* Newton's reservations about hypotheses because we have discredited *hypotheses non fingo?* Because we have ceased to describe Newton as a Comtian positivist, must we *now,* falling over on our own faces, have to allow that whenever Newton suggested a mechanism appropriate to explain certain phenomena, he necessarily believed it to be the true and only mechanism? Obviously not. For sometimes we perceive Newton saying something which is open to question as an hypothesis without seeming to recognize the fact, in which case we may assume that he was not viewing that hypothesis critically; sometimes he is distinguishing between "my hypothesis" (always guardedly so qualified, of course) and yours, or Hooke's, or Lucas'; sometimes he is discussing directly contradictory hypotheses.

In fact, we return, with circumspection, to the point from which we might have set out with careless confidence: we must in the last analysis evaluate each of Newton's discussions of structural hypotheses on its own merits; there are no general grounds for endorsing one more or less than another. To this there is perhaps one exception: for throughout his life Newton constantly drew essentially the same distinction between "doctrine" and "hypothesis," and this to quite a large extent corresponds to a distinction between "experimental and mathematical" on the one hand, and Cartesian or first-order "mechanical explanation" on the other. (By first-order mechanical explanation we mean to distinguish the Cartesian or more generally aetherist view which makes mechanical *impact* the prime phenomenon of Nature. It is easy to overlook the continued elaboration of such explanations during the early years of Newton's maturity, without as well as within the strict Cartesian tradition. As examples of the former one may cite William Neile's philosophy of motion, the Hooke-Mayow theory of combustion, and Leibniz' *Hypothesis physica nova,* the first part of which was dedicated to the Royal Society. The aether was still the natural medium for all causal explanations. The term "second-order mechanical explanation" we apply to Newton's use of the concept of force which, unlike the former, proved in some special cases susceptible of a complete mathematical treatment.) It is perhaps hardly needful to add that Newton distinguished both mathematical and mechanical explanations from the qualitative explanations of the Peripatetics. In Newton's very first printed paper he wrote:

> to determine more absolutely, what Light is, after what manner refracted, and by what modes or actions it produceth in our minds the Phantasms of Colours, is not so easie. And I shall not mingle conjectures with certainties.[6]

(Certain ideas, certain forms of words even, seem to have crystallized in his mind at an early age; we need not wonder that this passage so exactly parallels the more famous one in the General Scholium.) It is not surprising to find that others before Newton drew the distinction; the logical issue is indeed an obvious one, and must surely have been expressed many times.

Clearly any ideas that Newton held about the structure of matter and the mechanical causes of phenomena must lie in the realm of "hypotheses." Unless one is to classify such ideas as merely derivative (as borrowed from Boyle and Gassendi, etc.), which we would be loathe to do, they can only be regarded as the products of something we might loosely call Newton's metaphysics of Nature, guided by more precise but always indefinite inference from the phenomena of physics, chemistry, and biology as they were known to him. To take an interesting example, Newton relates his aether hypothesis of 1675 to

> that puzzling problem, "By what means the muscles are contracted and dilated to cause animal motion," [which] may receive greater light from hence than from any means men have hitherto been thinking on.

And he goes on to explain his thought in the following sentence:

> For if there be any power in man to condense and dilate at will the aether that pervades the muscle, that condensation or dilation must vary the compression of the muscle made by the ambient aether, and cause it to swell or shrink accordingly.[7]

When Newton writes this, he is expressing his own modification of Cartesian nervous physiology—and incidentally providing in advance an explanation of a mysterious phrase in the *Scholium Generale* of forty years later. The problem, then, is to disentangle the various "hypotheses" that Newton entertained, and, further, even to allow for the various occasions when Newton appears to disdain hypotheses wholly. And we must first ask, was Newton always consistent?

Now palpably Newton's *utterances*—both those intended for public circulation and those not so intended[8]—are inconsistent. This assertion is generally granted, and it may be easily confirmed by setting side by side such a well-known passage as this from the *Principia's* Preface:

> I wish we could derive the rest of the phaenomena of Nature by the same kind of reasoning [the reasoning of mathematical physics] from mechanical principles, for I am induced by many reasons to suspect that they may all depend upon certain forces by which the particles of bodies, by some causes hitherto unknown,

A. RUPERT HALL AND MARIE BOAS HALL

are either mutually impelled towards one another, and cohere in regular figures, or are repelled and recede from one another . . .

with another passage, this from Book II (Section XI, Scholium)

In mathematics we are to investigate the quantities of forces with their proportions consequent upon any conditions supposed; then, when we enter upon physics, we compare these proportions with the phenomena of Nature that we may know what conditions of those forces answer to the several kinds of attractive bodies.

Here we see Newton setting out in unmistakable language the structure of second-order mechanical explanation, which is mathematical and vacuist.[9] To those, thirdly, we might add the already quoted proclamation of Newton's atomism in Query 31 of *Opticks*. And many other printed passages, not least the celebrated refutation of the Cartesian aether at the close of Book II of the *Principia*,[10] could be combined with the evidence we collected from manuscripts to show that Newton was (in his mature years at least) an upholder of second-order mechanism and had rejected the aether required for first-order mechanism.

On the other side must be cited many long passages in which Newton did compose first-order mechanical explanations. Anti-Cartesian in his metaphysics though Newton seems to have been from his early years, the term "aether" yet ran easily from his pen. Again, his first published paper is unguarded in this respect: for example, the hypothesis or, as he called it, "plausible ground of suspicion" that refracted rays of light are curved (which was refuted by measurements) rested on the possibility that "if the Rays of Light should possibly be globular bodies, and by their oblique passage out of one medium into another acquire a circulating motion, they ought to feel the greater resistance from the ambient Aether, on that side, where the motions conspire, and thence be continuously bowed to the other."[11] Again, when Newton insists in his letter to Pardies of 10 June 1672 that it is the randomness of *whatever* mechanical effect be hypothetically identified with "light" that causes true whiteness, he exemplifies these effects as "inaequales pressiones, motiones aut mota corpuscula per aethera quaquaversum trajiciantur" (that is, "inequalities in pressure, inequalities in motion, or inequalities between moved particles, that travel through the aether") .[12] It is clear that at this stage Newton was very far from supposing that an emission or corpuscular theory of light would liberate him from postulating an aether; hence his allusion to the aethero-emission theory (which was to become ultimately the theory of "Fits") in his reply to Hooke, and his development of it in the second optical paper, were quite in accord with his earliest view.[13] As for the aether concepts in the "Letter to Boyle," and in the "Queries" in *Opticks,* these are too well known to require repetition.

Faced with two bodies of evidence, some historians have simply turned a blind eye to Newton's second-order mechanical explanations (perhaps on the ground that these are merely mathematical, or products of a deliberate but misleading positivist posture), and accordingly have declared that Newton was always at heart an aetherist, as it were a super-Cartesian. Thus Professor Rosenfeld writes that there could be (in the common metaphysic of More and Newton) no "direct interaction of God and gross matter," and, he suggests, "could not a finer kind of substance provide the missing link? An aetherial fluid filling all space could, as Descartes wanted it, transmit various forces between the bodies by appropriate cyclic motions. . . ." And although he further states that after writing the *Principia* Newton was forced to restrict considerably the scope of his aether hypothesis, so that his "experimental philosophy" was a "position of retreat," it is clear that in Rosenfeld's eyes aetherism is Newton's preferred and indeed only logical position. In his view what we have called second-order mechanical explanations were very much a *pis–aller*.[14]

Now we have mentioned Professor Rosenfeld in this context only because his is a recent statement of this position; and we shall have occasion later to borrow a good point he has made. However, it must be noted that his conception of what Newton's first-order mechanical explanation did for him is open to question; most recent writers, following Koyré, Professor Guerlac among them[15] as well as we ourselves, have regarded Newton's views on the omnipresence of God as being antithetic to his aetherism. That issue is beside the point here, in any case; the main objection to wholehearted endorsement of the view that Newton was (at best) a discreet aetherist, is the obvious fact that it makes a nonsense of the *Principia* and of all that achievement in mechanics for which Newton has been venerated above all. For—if we may be forgiven here for reiterating an historical opinion we have often expressed before— *if* Newton meant what he said when he spoke of forces in physics (in the *Principia* texts as printed, and in so many manuscript passages), then he was indeed introducing a great new idea, analogous to and preparing the way for that of the field in nineteenth-century physics. This force concept introduced by Newton enabled him to transcend Cartesian, billiard-ball mechanism, the mechanism of impact. If particle A moves, it is not necessarily because it has been struck by particle B; it may be that a force (which is gravitational, magnetic, electrical, or chemical in nature) has acted upon it. It was this second-order mechanism that permitted Newton to extend the mathematization of physics so far, to construct celestial mechanics, and to reëstablish the void. In fact it enabled Newton to reëstablish atomism by returning to concepts closer to those of Epicuros than was the corpuscularian mechanism of the Cartesians; it was precisely the addition of the idea of force that made *mathematical* atomism feasible.

Here the Galileo-Descartes antithesis precisely parallels the Descartes-Newton antithesis. Descartes's criticism of Galileo's mathematical analysis of the fall of heavy bodies turned on Galileo's ignorance of the true cause of gravity, discovered by Descartes himself in the fabrication of the vortex. Descartes's hypothetical mechanism for gravity resisted mathematization; he could not devise the law $s = \frac{1}{2}gt^2$. The whole of Cartesian impact physics remained non-mathematical until after the appearance of the *Principia*—except, of course, insofar as Wren, Huygens, and Wallis

A. RUPERT HALL AND MARIE BOAS HALL

stated the laws of impact themselves. Then Newton, following Galileo, again mathematized physics by ignoring impact mechanisms and adopting second-order mechanical explanations that depended on the concept of force; that is, by confessing a limitation to knowledge comparable to that made by Galileo when the latter declined to discuss the *cause* of natural acceleration. Comparable to, not identical with, since Galileo possessed no concept of force, whereas Newton had a definite, though not sharp, idea of what it is that causes motion. Impressed forces arise from percussion, from pressure, from centripetal force. Centripetal force is exemplified by gravity and magnetism; considered as absolute, it is proportional to the magnitude of the generative body; considered as accelerative it is proportional to the acceleration it produces; and considered as motive it is proportional to the motion generated in a given time.[16] However, *force* is not the end of the chain; there is, Newton adds, a cause

> without which those motive forces would not be propagated through the spaces round about; whether that cause be of some central body (such as is the magnet in the center of the magnetic force, or the earth in the center of the gravitating force), or anything else that does not yet appear. For I here design only to give a mathematical notion of those forces, without considering their physical causes and seats.[17]

There we have it—not quite fairly, perhaps, in that a mathematical notion of forces (simply expressing the quantity *ma* by the symbol *f*) would not permit us to speak of magnetism or gravity, and would not indeed allow us to see the special interest of centripetal forces—a working if not a fully philosophical justification for a new concept in mechanics. Or rather, since the notion of *vis* is old enough, a justification for refusing to go beyond second-order mechanism to find the cause of *vis*, before we have got what we can out of the idea itself.

No one will deny that there are difficulties in the analysis of Newtonian mechanics in terms of second-order mechanism alone. But by contrast (it seems to us) if one holds that, for Newton, all the forces were mere pseudo concepts and that the reality was always in corpuscular aetherial impact, then one is really saying that the *Principia* is about pseudo science. This is the question of *De revolutionibus* and Osiander's preface all over again. Does the *Principia* contain a view of reality or is it just a convenient mathematical model—a way of computing the effects of the aether without actually introducing the aetherial mechanism? Either Newton in introducing into the first of his *Principia* prefaces phrases like "mechanical principles" and "certain forces by which particles are impelled" and so forth, was being his own Osiander, or (for that time at least) he meant what he said; that is, that the concept of force was what one needed for mathematical physics, and mathemaical physics gave a sufficient explanation of natural phenomena.

With this in mind, consider again Newton's notorious insistence on mathematical argument. We need hardly instance the *Principia*, though we might recall those passages in it where Newton discussed the transition from applied mathematics to the physics of nature. However, what we have particularly in mind is the sentence omitted for some reason from the printed version of the first optical letter (6 February 1672):

> I shall now proceed to acquaint you with another more notable difformity in its Rays, wherein the *Origin of Colours* is infolded. A naturalist would scarce expect to see ye science of those become mathematicall, & yet I dare affirm that there is as much certainty in it as in any other part of Opticks.[18]

To this Newton again referred in his reply to Hooke's observation (11 June 1672), in a passage similarly excised from the *Philosophical Transactions*:

> 12. That the Science of Colours is most properly a Mathematicall Science.
>
> In the last place I should take notice of a casuall expression wch intimates a greater certainty in these things then I ever promised, viz: The certainty of *Mathematicall Demonstrations*. I said indeed that the *Science of Colours was Mathematicall & as certain as any other part of Optiques*; but who knows not that Optiques & many other Mathematicall Sciences depend as well on Physicall Principles as on Mathematicall Demonstrations: And the absolute certainty of a Science cannot exceed the certainty of its Principles.[19]

No doubt both the original passage and the gloss upon it were struck out because Newton saw (from Hooke's criticism) that he had gone so far as to be liable to easy misunderstanding; nevertheless, in *Opticks* he was to declare again that color is a mathematically identifiable property of light:

> by consequence . . . all the Productions and Appearances of Colours in the World are derived, not from any physical Change caused in Light by Refraction or Reflexion, but only from the various Mixtures or Separations of Rays, by virtue of their different Refrangibility or Reflexibility. And in this respect the Science of Colours becomes a speculation as truly mathematical as any other part of Opticks.[20]

One cannot doubt that Newton was confident of the certainty of mathematical science and of its power to yield unique propositions—for if by the "mathematical way of reasoning" we derived multiple results—that a given planet could equally well move in any of three possible orbits for example—we should suspect our initial data or a mistake in the reasoning. Contrast this with Newton's attitude to first-order mechanical hypotheses: these are not unique, since it is possible to frame several, mutually equivalent, and they are uncertain because indemonstrable. On the other hand, second-order mechanical explanations in terms of forces are an integral part of the mathematization of physics; we cannot dispense with them, and by our very success in (for example) constructing celestial mechanics we find that our assumed force of gravitation is verified. There can be no doubt, then, that for Newton science moves to a new level of certainty when it moves from the nonmathematical state of multiple first-order hypotheses to the mathematical state of unique second-order explanations in terms of forces. Or, we need only employ the necessarily multiple and

A. RUPERT HALL AND MARIE BOAS HALL

equivalent hypotheses of aether until such time as they are succeeded by a mathematical physics in terms of forces. If, now, having done this we were to step back and seek to explain forces once more in terms of first-order aetherial hypotheses we should gain nothing: for once more it is possible to feign any hypothesis.

It seems to us that it is impossible to account for Newton's scientific epistemology except in one way, if any attempt is made to reconcile his utterances with the actual texture of his science. One need not suppose—indeed for our part we have never supposed—that Newton's thought on these matters was fully mature from the start. We are now learning that his recollection of achievement in the *annus mirabilis* of 1665–66 was by no means inflated, but we are also discovering more precisely how much he had to do in the next twenty years.[21] We would not now ask why Newton did not write the *Principia* in 1666; we know he could not have written it then. In mathematics, optics, astronomy and mechanics Newton's thought slowly ripened, his technical expertise widened, and his knowledge deepened. Now Professor Rosenfeld has already remarked that Newton's late discovery of the true power of the law of gravitation—after 1680—was a blow to his aetherial hypotheses; for a Cartesian aether was not only needless after this as a last-resort fund of explanation for unresolved problems in celestial kinematics, it was positively difficult to see how it could agree with the unresisted motion of the planets.[22] With the law came the interstellar vacuum. But this is by no means all that can be said. Remembering that "De motu corporum" was long Newton's simple title for the growing work, one may well doubt whether he was cognizant (before it began to take shape) of the extent to which Natural Philosophy was founded on mathematical principles. He had gone far in that direction in optics already, yet by no means so far as he was to go in 1704. In other words, before the *Principia* Newton (still under the influence of Descartes) perforce was content to leave a large role for first-order mechanical hypotheses. What he discovered—not in his brilliant youth but in his mature development of mechanics—was the success of the concept of force in rendering mathematical science possible; this was something he could not learn fully until he had raised celestial mechanics on the foundation of the force of gravitation.

If this explains the dominance of second-order mechanical explanations during Newton's mature years we are still left with the question: Why did Newton make fresh, oracular pronouncements about the aether and mysterious spirits in 1706, 1713, and 1717? And in the later "Queries" and so forth, without withdrawing anything of what he had said before. It must first be said that this new aether of Newton's is strange indeed. It is emphatically distinguished from the crude, dense "first matter" of the Cartesians since

> to make way for the regular and lasting Motions of the Planets and Comets, it's necessary to empty the Heavens of all matter, except perhaps some very thin Vapours, Steams, or Effluvia, arising from the Atmospheres of the Earth, Planets, and Comets, and from such an exceedingly rare Aetherial Medium as we described above.[23]

(The last twelve words were added in 1717 to the version of 1706. Newton was patching his text.) But to continue: the dense Cartesian aether "is of no use, and hinders the Operations of Nature . . . therefore it ought to be rejected." The new medium accordingly must be 49×10^{10} times more elastic than air in proportion to its density.[24] In fact it is so utterly unphysical that it does not infringe the metaphysical interaction between God and his universe sketched directly by Newton in his letters to Bentley, and indirectly in those of Samuel Clarke to Leibniz. Consistent with this we still read in the text of Query 28 (lightly patched from the Latin of 1706) that it was a mistake on the part of natural philosophers to explain all things mechanically without recognition of a First Cause which is nonmechanical; and that these philosophers should seek "not only to unfold the mechanism of the world, but chiefly to resolve these and such like questions," which, when set out, turn on the Great Architect's eye to the harmony of Creation. There is here only the minimum alteration required by consistency in favor of aetherist interpretations.[25]

The Queries remain enigmatic. Here are some new queries concerning them. Will any one explain how a particulate aether which is enormously less dense than air can have such force between its particles that it is more elastic than air? And whence does this force arise? Must it not be supposed that the divine intervention gives the aether these properties; and if so, why should God act thus deviously? How can the particles of aether press on material bodies to cause gravitation, yet not resist the motions of these bodies? How can the aether press on bodies not only to cause gravitation, but other forces also? And how can Newton, that great abstainer from hypotheses, not have seen how pressed with difficulties these hypotheses of his own are? Perhaps we must admit that Newton has, in the end, made the whole business of the relation between the universe, God, and mechanical hypotheses (or indeed, nonmechanical hypotheses) utterly incomprehensible.

This is perhaps a cry of despair. Some may continue to feel that the enigma of the Queries is adequately solved by simply stating that Newton abandoned forces in favor of his Mark II, God-powered aether. Professor Guerlac, for example, has lately drawn attention to the source of the fresh experimental evidence recited by Newton in the "Queries" and "Scholium Generale."[26] He suggests that this fresh evidence revived the vigor of aetherial explanations in Newton's mind, to the extent that he resuscitated *in print* notions that he had carefully refused to publish during more than half a lifetime:

> Le revirement de Newton—sa nouvelle disposition en faveur d'un éther—date des experiences de [Francis] Hauksbee et de la collaboration scientifique toute particulière entre les deux hommes.[27]

The point is well made. But it is still hard to understand why experiments on the electric fire should have invited Newton to revise his conception of the dynamics of Nature, and to recast his conceptions of light and gravitation, if this is really what happened. For note that Newton did not by any means revert to a simple, first-order

A. RUPERT HALL AND MARIE BOAS HALL

aetherial theory, nor did he withdraw anything that he had written earlier in second-order terms, during the extensive revisions of the *Principia* and *Opticks*. Even in the latter work he did not reinstate the full aetherial explanation of the theory of "Fits" that he had provided in 1675; though it is hinted at in Query 18, the text remains unaltered. Yet these revised aetherial hypotheses are not wholly dependent on Hauksbee's new work; in Query 18, just mentioned, for example, Newton refers to the (erroneous) observation that a thermometer placed *in vacuo* shows external temperature changes as swiftly as another open to the atmosphere. "Is not the heat of the warm room," he asks, "conveyed through the vacuum by the vibrations of a much subtiler medium than Air, which after the Air was drawn out remained in the Vacuum?" So we find Newton in the Queries reverting once again to the familiar phenomena of first-order mechanism, and drawing the same antivacuist lessons that others had drawn before him.

It cannot be simply the case, then, that the aging Newton was compelled to change his mind by fresh evidence. Something deeper was occurring, or some other necessity pressed him. Now it seems impossible to believe that, at this stage of his life, Newton revolted against all he had learned from Henry More, and that he sought to return, via a revived aether, to the logically complete mechanism of Descartes for which, indeed, an aether was essential. We know that at just this same time Newton was conspiring with Clarke to defend the spiritual agency within the physical universe against the complete mechanism of Leibniz. It would be strange if Newton were developing a secret partiality toward his opponent's philosophy! Nor, it seems, can we believe that Newton had really changed his mind about the irrelevance and possible evils of mechanical hypotheses. However, we do know that Newton had employed such hypotheses before, in order to refute those who held that his "doctrines" were mechanically incomprehensible, or led to mechanically unacceptable consequences. It seems not impossible that he saw occasion enough in Hauksbee's new results for choosing yet again the same aetherial escape route. If mechanical hypotheses alone could make his "doctrines" acceptable, then mechanical hypotheses Newton would provide—in the form of Queries.

However, the extent to which these represent a genuine shift in Newton's opinion is debatable. Unfortunately we have no "Letters to Bentley" from the last years of Newton's life; on the other hand, we do have a consistent testimony from Newton's friends and associates. The second and all subsequent editions of the *Principia* contain a preface written by Roger Cotes, the editor whom Newton admired the most, which begins with a severe attack upon mechanical hypotheses, producing a "Fabulem quidem elegantem forte et venustam, Fabulam tamen"; and ends with scorn for those who would postulate a medium that is indistinguishable from vacuity:

> So that we must conclude that the celestial fluid has no inertia, because it has no resisting force; that it has no force to communicate motion with, because it has no inertia; that it has no force to produce any change in one or more bodies, because it has no force wherewith to communicate motion; that it has no manner

of efficacy, because it has no faculty wherewith to produce any change of any kind. Therefore certainly this hypothesis may be justly called ridiculous and unworthy a philosopher, since it is altogether without foundation and does not in the least serve to explain the nature of things.[28]

This might almost be a critique of Query 21! And Cotes concludes (as one might expect) that those who deny the vacuum deny God for the sake of asserting Necessity.

Samuel Clarke, Newton's champion, translator and exponent, is no less clear, for he actually infers the vacuum from the fact of gravitation, in one of his notes to Rohault:

> But it is very evident from Gravity . . . that there must not only be a Vacuum in Nature, but that it is the far greatest Part . . . why should not the same quantity of matter, make the same Resistance, whether it be divided into a great many very small Parts [Clarke asks] or into a few large ones? . . . Since therefore the Essence of Matter does not consist in Extension, but in impenetrable solidity, we must say that the whole world is made up of solid bodies which move in a vacuum. . .[29]

Again, Henry Pemberton, last of Newton's editors, was equally emphatic that the phenomena of nature arise from the solid particles composing bodies, not from the interstices between them. He takes Newton as his authority for rejecting the plenitude of space:

> Sir Isaac Newton objects against the filling of space with such a subtle fluid, that all bodies in motion must be unmeasurably resisted by a fluid so dense, as absolutely to fill up all the space through which it is spread.

Like Clarke, Pemberton shows how (on Newtonian principles) resistance is proportional to density, unless the aether be supposed deprived of

> the same degree of inactivity as other matter. But if you deprive any substance of the property so universally belonging to all other matter, without impropriety of speech it can scarce be called by this name.[30]

Indeed, Pemberton comes close to the offense of declaring that gravity is inherent in matter, for, he says, this

> power in the great bodies of the universe, is derived from the same power being lodged in every particle of the matter which composes them: and consequently, that this property is no less than universal to all matter whatever, though the power be too minute to produce any visible effects on small bodies.[31]

These Newtonians all wrote in the last fifteen years of Newton's life; another, David Gregory, made a highly important record at a rather earlier date—21 December 1705 —when Newton had told him of the additions he intended to make to the Latin edition of *Opticks,* obviously showing him the passage that was to appear at the end of Query 28 in the later English versions of the Queries. It begins, "What is there in places almost empty of Matter, and whence is it that the Sun and Planets gravitate

A. RUPERT HALL AND MARIE BOAS HALL

towards one another, without dense Matter between them?" (The "almost" is an afterthought; Gregory calls it, "the space that is empty of body.") Gregory's comment is:

> The plain truth is, that he believes God to be omnipresent in the literal sense; And that we are sensible of Objects when their Images are brought home within the brain, so God must be sensible of every thing, being intimately present with every thing: for he supposes that as God is present in space where there is no body, he is present in space where a body is also present. But if this way of proposing this his notion be too bold, he thinks of doing it thus. *What cause did the Ancients assign of Gravity.* He believes that they reckoned God the Cause of it, nothing els, that is no body being the cause; since every body is heavy.[32]

Notice again the consistent Newtonian dual linkage between inertia and matter, God and absence of matter. We find it difficult to believe that Newton ever gave up these principles, upon any evidence whatsoever. Certainly if he did, he was the only early Newtonian so to do.

NOTES

[1] Cambridge, 1962; hereafter *Unpublished Papers* only.

[2] *Unpublished Papers*, p. 334.

[3] I. Bernard Cohen (ed.), *Isaac Newton's Papers & Letters on Natural Philosophy* (Cambridge, Mass., 1958), 298 (hereafter *Papers & Letters* only).

[4] Newton to Oldenburg, 13 April 1672 in H. W. Turnbull (ed.), *The Correspondence of Isaac Newton* (Cambridge, 1959), I, 142 (hereafter *Corr.* only); or in *Papers & Letters*, 85. Our translation.

[5] Newton to Oldenburg, 11 June 1672; see *Corr.*, I, 174; *Papers & Letters*, 118–19.

[6] *Corr.*, I, 100; *Papers & Letters*, 57.

[7] *Corr.*, I, 367; *Papers & Leters*, 182.

[8] It may be worth noting that in Newton's early years the reading of a letter or paper at a meeting of the Society followed by its subsequent registration (copying into the Register-book with, usually, retention of the original also) constituted effective publication. If he were anxious to secure complete privacy, the writer of a letter had to request (a) that it be not read or (b) that it be not registered. Hence we should certainly count Newton's optical papers as published in this sense.

[9] We attempted an analysis of some characteristics of "Newton's 'Mechanical Principles' " in the *Journal of the History of Ideas*, XX, 1959, 167–178.

[10] *Principia*, third edition, Props. 52, 53 and Scholia.

[11] *Corr.*, I, 94; *Papers & Letters*, 50.

[12] *Corr.*, I, 168; *Papers & Letters*, 102. This insistance on the random nature of the causal mechanism is interesting, for it arises from the belief that it would be unreasonable to postulate a single or double mode of vibration, emission, etc., in the source of light, as inference suggests if light itself is single (homogeneous) or double, etc., in its mechanical nature.

[13] *Corr.*, I, 174; *Papers & Letters*, 119.

[14] L. Rosenfeld, "Newton and the Law of Gravitation," *Archive for the History of Exact Sciences*, 2 (1965), 384–85.

[15] Henry Guerlac, *Newton et Epicure*, Conférence au Palais de la Decouverte, Paris, 1963 (D 91).

[16] *Principia*, Definitions IV to VII.

[17] *Ibid.*, Definition VIII. John Herivel (*The Background to Newton's Principia*, Oxford

1965, 5) also associates Newton's definition of force with the success of his mathematical theory.

18 *Corr.*, I, 96.

19 *Ibid.*, 187.

20 *Opticks*, Book II, Part II, end (Dover edn., 1952, 244).

21 See D. T. Whiteside, "Newton's marvellous year: 1666 and all that," *Notes and Records of the Royal Society*, 21 (1966), 32–41. Although Dr. Whiteside opens with some doubts concerning the traditional story of Newton's three-fold discoveries, he goes on to justify it (for the most part) as it relates to mathematics. Other studies have shown that it holds in outline (though not exactly) for optics and mechanics also.

22 *Loc. cit.* (note 14), 384.

23 Query 28 (*loc. cit.*, 368).

24 Query 21 (*ibid.*, 351).

25 See Alexandre Koyré: "Les Queries de l'Optique," *Archives Int. d'Hist. des Sciences*, 13, 1960, 22–23.

26 Henry Guerlac, "Francis Hauksbee: expérimentateur au profit de Newton," *Archives Int. d'Hist. des Sciences*, 16, 1963, 113–28.

27 *Ibid.*, 128.

28 *Principia*, second edition, Cambridge 1713, b2 verso, c4.

29 Samuel Clarke (ed.) *Rohault's System of Natural Philosophy* . . . (London, 1723), I, 27, note.

30 Henry Pemberton, *A View of Sir Newton's Philosophy* (London, 1728), 169–70.

31 *Ibid.*, 259.

32 W. G. Hiscock (ed.), *David Gregory, Isaac Newton and their Circle* (Oxford, 1937), 30.

Henry Guerlac's comment on the preceding paper has already been published in *Notes and Records of the Royal Society of London*, 22 (September, 1967), 45–57 [Ed.].

A. RUPERT HALL AND MARIE BOAS HALL

D. T. WHITESIDE

Sources and Strengths of Newton's Early Mathematical Thought

IN THIS TERCENTENARY YEAR WE CELEBRATE, IN SPIRIT IF PERHAPS NOT WITH full historical accuracy, the first maturing of Newton the exact scientist. Persuaded by a wealth of pleasant traditional anecdote and autobiographical reminiscence, our thoughts go back three hundred years to a young Cambridge student, at twenty-three scarcely on the brink of manhood, working away undisturbed in a cramped, roughhewn study set in a sunny corner of the small stone house where he was born, amidst the lazy, undulating fields of his native Lincolnshire countryside. The busy intellectual stir of the university at which he recently graduated and the daily excitements of student life at Trinity College are eighty miles distant to the south and a world away in mood. We are a little awed at the explosion of mental energy in a man in the prime of his age for invention, who in little more than a year transmuted the received theoretical bases of infinitesimal calculus, dynamics, and optics into their classical forms. But we live in a skeptical, hardheaded age and all this is for us uncomfortably close to heroic myth, if not to wonderland. What we praise and commemorate we now require to have had a real past existence and we seek the historical truth which underlies the tradition of Newton's *annus mirabilis*. What did happen in 1666? Where and how did it happen? What was its significance? What formative pattern did it create for the future development of Newton's scientific thought? The detailed illumination of the sequence and import of his discoveries in natural philosophy at a time when he minded it "more then at any time since" I leave in the capable hands of my colleagues. For almost ten years now I have been myself preoccupied with the study of Newton's mathematical achievement per se. Let me then, for my own part, discuss his preliminary researches in that field up to the end of his magical year of discovery and try to assess their role in the creation of Newton's mature mathematical method.

When we talk conventionally of Newton's mathematical achievement we refer, directly or obliquely, to the content of six small tracts of his authorship—precisely, the *De Analysi per Æquationes Numero Terminorum Infinitas* of 1669, the so-called *Methodus Fluxionum et Serierum Infinitarum* of 1671, the *Arithmetica Universalis* of 1683, the *De Quadratura Curvarum* of 1693, the *Enumeratio Linearum Tertij Ordinis* of 1695, and the *Methodus Differentialis*, which went into its final form as late as 1710.[1] We have also, perhaps, one eye on the relevant portions of his *Lectiones Opticæ* of 1672 and especially of his *Principia Mathematica* of 1686. (These dates, I would hasten to say, are rough terminal dates of composition, not those of their first publication.) In fact, however, a stream of mathematical researches poured forth from Newton's pen with scarcely a break between early 1664, when he was in his last undergraduate year, and the spring of 1696, when he forwent the sheltered, routine existence of a university mathematics professor with a bare minimum of teaching obligations for the demanding, sophisticated whirl of public life in London. Even thereafter his creative flame was not quenched but flared up again from time to time—not least, indeed, in his eightieth year when he personally edited the second edition of his *Universal Arithmetic* in correction of Whiston's unauthorized version of fifteen years before. In bulk, the extant record of the totality of that achievement covers something of the order of five thousand quarto and folio sheets crowded with Newton's small, distinctive writing and ranging in subject from elementary mensuration to sophisticated projective geometry, from analysis of fundamental algebraic operations and introductory number theory to finite differences and abstruse theory of equations, from the first principles of coordinate geometry and the tracing of curves to the detailed subclassification of cubics and the general theory of lines of higher order, from the finding *ad hoc* of tangents to simple curves and the "squaring" of their area to the complex ramifications of a mighty fluxional calculus which, in application, clarified geometrical dioptrics and revolutionized the study of celestial mechanics. In the first installment of what, I hope, will eventually be a comprehensive selection from this huge corpus of unpublished manuscript[2] I have recently, with the able secretaryship of Dr. Michael Hoskin, gathered within the confines of a single volume that portion composed during the period 1664–66 whose terminal year we now celebrate. In what follows let me use it as my bible.

For anyone who attempts to understand Newton's first mathematical years one question immediately arises: How and where did Newton receive his mathematical education and what was its content?[3]

Out of necessity, for our knowledge of Newton's preuniversity education we rely heavily on William Stukeley and John Conduitt,[4] only the latter of whom personally knew him well. We learn that he passed a couple of years at local dame schools as a child and then spent his boyhood and youth, except for a period in his late teens when his mother recalled him to manage the Woolsthorpe farm, at grammar school in the nearby market town of Grantham. At the first he would receive a bare introduction to the elements of reading, writing and reckoning, while we know enough of the latter's headmaster, John Stokes, to realize that he was progressive and would take pains to inculcate into his pupils something more than Ben Jonson's despised "small Latine and lesse Greeke." But we should be careful not to overestimate the mathematical content of the curriculum even of a go-ahead English school at this period. The comparison, tempting though it is to make, with that of a modern grammar or high school course in mathematics is wholly invalid and we should remember that the study of Euclid was at this time a university discipline while algebra and trigonometry were not even there taught formally—indeed, in contemporary English academic circles they were widely held to be essentially practical subjects which did not adequately exercise the mind and were therefore better left to the working mathematical practitioners of London and the main provincial centers of business and trade. Perhaps

D. T. WHITESIDE

the content of a small notebook, dated 1654, which is now in Grantham Public Library[5] affords a truer glimpse into Newton's preuniversity mathematical studies. If its worked examples are typical of those which he himself went through at school in Grantham he would there have acquired a passable facility with the basic arithmetical rules and a ready acquaintance with elementary weight and mensuration problems and the casting of accounts—otherwise, little. The few details we have of Newton's early life in effect confirm this impression, though we would very much like to know what he read among the miscellany of books parcelled up in the garret of the town apothecary, Mr. Clark, with whom he lodged for several years. From Stukeley we hear tales of an interest in constructing sundials and of a developed aptitude for mechanical invention and that the walls of the same Grantham garret "were full of the drawings he had made upon them, with charcole: . . . birds, beasts, men, ships, plants and mathematical figures as he took them, being circles and triangles"—perhaps these last were similar to the roughly incised sets of "intersecting lines and circles" scribbled, we presume, by the young Newton on the walls of his Woolsthorpe home.[6] Nowhere is there evidence of real mathematical (or indeed scientific) precociousness and we must accept that up to the time, June of 1661, when, in his nineteenth year, he entered Trinity College Newton had had no proper experience of mathematics as a deductive, structural discipline.

With Newton's admission to Cambridge we pass from loose hearsay knowledge backed with but little direct information to a factual world firmly defined by extant documentation. The content of an undergraduate notebook[7] which annotates texts by Aristotle and several contemporary standard commentaries upon him stresses the sound disciplining in the trivium of logic, ethics, and rhetoric which Newton received in his early university years under a system still essentially scholastic in structure, one laying emphasis both in formal lecture and informal disputation on the teaching of Aristotle and with its classical bias reinforced in Newton's own case by the interests of his tutor, Benjamin Pulleyn, soon to become Regius Professor of Greek. To his hard training at this time in the intricacies of syllogistic argument Newton's later vigorous clarity of logical exposition certainly owed much, but the mathematical content of such a medieval program of study was low, consisting almost entirely in the analysis of elementary portions of Euclid's *Elements* from a logical viewpoint. When Newton sought to evaluate the technical content which underlay the complicated formal logic by which Euclid's propositions were deduced he was, if we may trust Conduitt,[8] disillusioned, finding it so easy and self-evident that he wondered anybody would be at the pains of writing a demonstration of them and laid Euclid aside as a trifling book. Whether or not he paid for his early neglect of Euclid when later he was thwarted in his aspiration to be a Scholar of his college—a setback redeemed, we are told, only after he had satisfied Barrow of his knowledge of the *Elements*[9]—need not concern us, though we should remember that the many crowded margins of Newton's copy of Barrow's 1655 edition, now in his old college, Trinity,[10] reveal that no later than early 1664 he had made a close study of the more "arithmetical" books, V, VII, and X. In his later years, of course, he referred back frequently to a variety of Euclidean theorems in support of stages in his own mathematical arguments. Nonetheless we will not find in Euclid, or indeed any of the Greek masters, notably Archimedes, whom he later studied, the source of his first creative researches. Indeed, the true mathematical fount of the fertile discoveries of Newton's *annus mirabilis* is not to be located in anything he learned formally from his teachers during his undergraduate years in Cambridge, but rather may we trace it to the books he then read without official guidance or approval, whose content he mastered and then transmuted by his own unaided genius. Newton was an autodidact genius, not a gifted pupil.

The year 1664 I just now mentioned is a crucial period in Newton's development both as scientist and mathematician. Then it was he began to extend his reading beyond such conventional Aristotelian texts as Magirus' *Physiologia Peripatetica* to the modern mechanical philosophy expounded by Gassendi, Charleton, and Boyle and to the "new" Keplerian astronomy promoted by Ward and Streete.[11] In the same notebook in which he made his jottings on Magirus he began a new section of his own *Quæstiones quædam philosophicæ* whose tone, at first conventionally scholastic, changed rapidly to accommodate the bons mots of the new philosophers. Above all, Newton was one of Roger North's "brisk part of the university"[12] who in that year began to be stirred by the Cartesian ideas which, propagated by Rohault, were to dominate the Cambridge scene for over thirty years and to encourage such theses for disputation as that defended by Wharton in 1682: "Cartesiana Cometarum explicatio nec Physicis nec Astronomicis repugnat Principiis."[13] Within a few months it would appear that Newton read everything of Descartes's available in print, and certainly the *Dioptrique, Geometrie,* and *Principia Philosophiæ* whose themes recur again and again in his mature work. It was inevitable that to advance in these demanding scientific studies Newton would have to acquire a competency in existing mathematical techniques—without it whole stretches not only of Kepler, Descartes and Galileo but even of Streete's modest *Astronomia Carolina* were denied to him. In the event, according to De Moivre, the expatriate French intimate of Newton in his last years, the immediate impulse to begin a course of mathematical self-education was that, in skimming through a "book of Astrology" (perhaps Streete's *Astronomia?*) bought at Stourbridge fair, he was halted by "a figure of the heavens which he could not understand for want of being acquainted with Trigonometry," and when he bought an unnamed work on that topic he was at a loss for want of knowledge of Euclid's *Elements*. He therefore

> Got Euclid to fit himself for understanding the ground of Trigonometry. Read only the titles of the propositions, which he found so easy to understand that he wondered how any body would amuse themselves to write any demonstrations of them. Began to change his mind when he read that Parallelograms upon the same base and between the same Parallels are equal, and that other proposi-

D. T. WHITESIDE

tion that in a right angled Triangle the square of the Hypothenuse is equal to the squares of the two other sides. Began again to read Euclid with more attention than he had done before and went through it.

Read Oughtreds [*Clavis*] which he understood tho not entirely, he having some difficulties about what the Author called Scala secundi & tertii gradus, relating to the solution of quadratick [&] Cubick Equations. Took Descartes's *Geometry* in hand, tho he had been told it would be very difficult, read some ten pages in it, then stopt, began again, went a little further than the first time, stopt again, went back again to the beginning, read on till by degrees he made himself master of the whole, to that degree that he understood Descartes's Geometry better than he had done Euclid.

Read Euclid again & then Descartes's Geometry for a second time. Read next Dʳ Wallis's *Arithmetica Infinitorum*, & on the occasion of a certain interpolation for the quadrature of the circle, found that admirable Theorem for raising a Binomial to a power given. But before that time, a little after reading Descartes's Geometry, [he] wrote many things concerning the vertices Axes [&] diameters of curves, which afterwards gave rise to that excellent tract de Curvis secundi generis . . ..[14]

This has the ring of authenticity and is surely at least an accurate recounting of Newton's own version of his mathematical baptism. The order in which he read Oughtred and Descartes we cannot confirm but the former's *Clavis Mathematicæ*, especially in its latest 1652 edition (a copy of which Newton bought),[15] was widely studied as an introductory text in higher mathematics, while Descartes's *Geometrie* was in every sense an advanced monograph, made indeed, by its author's own testimony, deliberately obscure. Newton's unpublished investigations of the properties of curves by transforming their Cartesian equations to new axes, dated between September and December of 1664, still exist[16] and certainly precede by several months his researches in generalization of Wallis into the binomial expansion, which invariably in later life he delegated to the following winter. What we miss in De Moivre's account is a detailed list of Newton's early reading. Newton himself long afterward went some way towards widening our knowledge of this aspect, adding in parenthesis to his still extant early notes on Wallis' *Arithmetica* and Schooten's *Miscellanea*[17] that "By consulting an accompt of my expenses at Cambridge in the years 1663 & 1664 I find that in yᵉ year 1664 a little before Christmas . . . I bought Schooten's Miscellanies & Cartes's Geometry (having read this Geometry & Oughtred's Clavis above half a year before) & borrowed Wallis's works and by consequence made these annotations out of Schooten & Wallis in winter between the years 1664 & 1665."[18] If we add a few other names, especially those of Viète, Hudde, and Heuraet, we will have a tolerably complete list of the external sources of Newton's mathematical achievement during the two years preceding his *annus mirabilis*. These names we encounter time and again when we read through

Sources and Strengths of Newton's Early Mathematical Thought   73

the extant record of his mathematical researches during those two golden years of invention, investigations whose detailed elaboration was to occupy him with but brief intermission the remainder of his active life.

What I have tried to suggest is that up to the beginning of 1664 Newton's grounding in basic mathematics was not deep, that, though adequately competent in the techniques of arithmetic and elementary mensuration, he had but a sketchy knowledge of the fundaments of algebra and trigonometry, and that his appreciation of geometrical structure went little further than the opening propositions of the *Elements*. In a very real sense Oughtred's *Clavis Mathematicæ* was a mathematical key which unlocked for Newton the door to a realization of the potentialities of the algebraic free ("specious") variable in codifying not merely arithmetic but also geometry. It further directed him to the more profound investigations of Viète, conveniently collected in Schooten's 1646 Leyden edition.[19] In the opening pages of a small pocket book, now in the Fitzwilliam Museum in Cambridge, we may see Newton noting the Pythagorean theorem which relates the sides of right triangles— that which had halted him in his first progress through the *Elements*—stating it in algebraic form but hesitating between a reference to Caput XVIII (the "Penus analytica") of the *Clavis* and to Euclid I, 47, then ultimately settling for the latter. In a second notebook, now in Cambridge University Library, we find him shortly afterward annotating Viète's method for resolving numerical equations but making wide use of the simplified notation introduced by Oughtred in his appended *De Æquationum Affectarum Resolutione in numeris* in so doing.[20] From the two thick volumes of Wallis' *Opera Mathematica*[21] which he borrowed at the close of 1664 he gained his first insight into the naïve calculus of indivisibles, learning how to compound and interpolate integrals in mathematically significant ways and sharpening Wallis' methods of so doing. Out of his annotations of "Dr. Wallis his Arithmetica infinitorum,"[22] exactly as he told Leibniz twelve years later in his *epistola posterior*,[23] there of course developed his series expansion of the general binomial. But Schooten's bulky second Latin edition of Descartes's *Geometrie* was the work which, with some complements from Schooten's own fat *Exercitationes Mathematicæ* of 1657,[24] was overwhelmingly to direct the future course of Newton's mathematical development. The concept of the defining equation of a locus with respect to suitable coordinate line lengths, not necessarily "Cartesian" but perhaps bipolar (an alternative suggested by Descartes) or one of the variants proposed by Newton in a paper of October 1664, as the algebraic mirror of the geometrical curve which the locus represented was the essential idea which the *Geometrie* explored, though inexpertly and incoherently—to appreciate it fully, indeed, it was necessary to cut away much of the dross with which Descartes loaded his tract, not least his approach to curves by paired degrees. In his elaboration[25] Newton was for the first time to make the algebraic concept of degree fundamental in the subclassification of curves and to systematize the linear transformations of coordinates by which they are reduced to canonical forms (as Descartes had reduced

the conic locus to its three nondegenerate species). At a differential level the Cartesian algorithm for constructing the "subnormal" at a point on a curve was to be
of fundamental importance in clarifying his thoughts on differentiation and in suggesting to him that it is an exact converse to integration.[26] When in May 1665 Newton became interested in the geometrical construction of equations[27] the *Geometrie*
was once more his inspiration. It was, lastly, in tracts appended to the Latin *Geometrie* that Newton encountered the others I have mentioned: Hudde, whose al-
gorithmic improvement of Descartes's subnormal method[28] was highly cherished by
Newton, and Heuraet, whose rectification procedure[29] suggested to him a geometrical proof of the inverse nature of the methods of tangents and of quadratures.

In all this a strong bias to the analytical away from the purely geometrical is noticeable and that emphasis is clearly borne out by a reading of the documentary
record of Newton's early researches. What little of "Greek" geometry there is,
mostly derivative from Viète or Schooten, is usually approached in Cartesian fashion
by reduction to an algebraic equivalent. We are, too, perhaps a little disappointed
that Newton read so little of standard contemporary mathematical works, or if he
did has left no hint—nowhere in his early autograph papers do we find the names
of Napier, Briggs, Desargues, Fermat, Pascal, Kepler, Torricelli, or even Archimedes and Barrow. Nevertheless, we will readily admit that from his reading Newton fashioned all that a creative mathematician needs: a usable, flexible set of notations, a competent expertise with basic mathematical structures, an excellent technical grasp of the hard core of contemporary knowledge in his subject and, not
least, some sense of promising avenues for research. Nor should we think of the
period of Newton's annotations as a defined first stage in his mathematical development which can be set off as a period of submissive apprenticeship to his chosen
discipline. Already in his first notes on Schooten, Descartes and Wallis it is difficult
to separate mere annotation from creative reaction: a few months later, by the spring
of 1665, they had outlived their usefulness for him and it was time for Newton to
pursue his own independent researches.

Leaving aside further discussion of the sequence of external historical event, let
me now try and suggest to you something of the creative power and excitement
which a reading of the still extant manuscript record of those researches evokes. At
the same time let me attempt to draw certain inferences which I believe to be true
of Newton's mathematical development generally.

Not unexpectedly, his first researches in a mathematical field stemmed directly,
in the early autumn of 1664, from the *Geometrie* and its appended tracts. In the
Fitzwilliam notebook we see him slowly mastering the intricacies of the geometrical and analytical theory of conics and also, not always correctly, essaying certain
improvements of his own. He there shows himself to be fascinated by the mechanical descriptions of those curves which he found in Schooten and De Witt[30]—an
interest which a few years later was to lead him to consider their unified "organic"
construction and then develop their projective theory.[31] Elsewhere at this time, on

the verso of the first page of his Waste Book, he was hard at work seeking to perfect his understanding of the ovals which Descartes had, in his second book, introduced for their refractive property of transmitting all rays of white light emergent from one point through a second.[32] A few weeks later Newton approached one of the most difficult problems of elementary analytical geometry: given a coordinate system and some defining equation, to draw the "crooked Line" which that equation represents and evaluate its "propertys." The particular properties he chose to concentrate his attention upon were all generalizations of ones significant in a conic, namely "axes, vertices, diamiters, centers or asymptotes . . . supposeing it have them."[33] His technique was beautifully simple: try to reduce the given defining equation by permissible transformation to a form which evidently represents a curve possessed of the required property. In example, his criterion for a curve to have a diameter was that its equation be reducible by linear transform to a second in which odd powers of one of the coordinate variables were not present. The technical implementation of this insight was, of course, less easy. In reducing the second degree equation to its three nondegenerate canonical species Descartes had made use, but only implicitly, of a simple change of coordinates: the general theory of such transformations from one oblique pair to another had nowhere yet been worked out. Over the three months October to December of 1664 Newton did just that, developing the theory of such transforms in complete generality and indeed, for easier manipulation in their practical application, constructing lengthy, complicated tables of coefficients.

Let me briefly illustrate Newton's approach. In November 1664 he set himself, on one of the pages of his Waste Book,[34] to trace the cubic curve represented in a perpendicular Cartesian system by $(x - y)^3 = y^2(x - y + 2a)$. On considering the effect of the linear transform $x = X + AY$, $y = BY$ (with $A^2 + B^2 = 1$) to an oblique pair of coordinates inclined in direction at the angle $\tan^{-1} B/A$, he quickly realized that the simplest reduction was to be effected by taking $A = B = 1/\sqrt{2}$, so that the new coordinates X, Y, would be inclined at 45°. In this new system the cubic's equation assumes the form $2X^3 = Y^2(X + 2a)$ and so, in immediate corol-

bc $= x$, cd $= y$; bh $= X$, hd $= Y$:
  $(x - y)^3 = y^2(x - y + 2a)$.
x $= X + AY$, y $= BY$; $A = B = 1/\sqrt{2}$:
  $2X^3 = Y^2(X + 2a)$.
bhc $(Y = 0)$ is a diameter.

lary, the line $Y = 0$ is a diameter of the curve with regard to ordinates inclined to it at $45°$. I reproduce his tracing of the cubic, in which $bc = x$, $cd = y$, $bh = X$, and $hd = -hn = Y$. You will see that he has missed two out of the three infinite branches and has inserted one of the three real asymptotes possessed by the curve: a gentle reminder that Newton was not always omniscient.

These researches into curve properties and coordinate transformation were not, however, to receive their true reward till some years later when he first attacked— and brilliantly if not quite completely resolved—the problem of subclassifying the general cubic on the analogy of the three subspecies of conic. After applying a general linear transform to the ten terms of the cubic's defining equation he was faced with simplifying a derived equation of eighty-four terms. It is a tribute to his mental stamina and concentration no less than to his genius that he did so, and then proceeded to enumerate almost all of the seventy-eight species into which the cubic subdivides on Newton's terms. The complexity bothered him somewhat, so he thereupon gave the more manageable Eulerian division into sixteen species differentiated only by the nature of their infinite branches![35]

But what above all we celebrate in this tercentenary year is Newton's creation of his calculus of fluxions and his first insights into infinite series. From his own autobiographical reminiscence in old age and from certain other documents published, or at least circulated, at the time of his priority dispute with the Leibnizians, it has long been known that his early researches in these topics were considerable.[36] No one, however, who has not worked through the still extant manuscript of those researches can begin to appreciate their massive complexity. In my edition of those papers, indeed, I have found it helpful to incorporate a guide map to the ramifications of their highways and byways.[37] I do not need to say that I cannot here begin to summarize their detail.

On Newton's celebrated discovery of the general binomial expansion in the winter of 1664/5 let me be brief.[38] Exactly as he later admitted, Newton's inspiration derived from his careful study of Wallis' interpolation of the "circle" integral $1/\int_0^1 (1 - x^2)^p.dx$, $p = \frac{1}{2}$, in the integral sequence defined as p varies between zero and infinity. (This fruitful integral, may I interject, was the source both of Wallis' infinite-product and Brouncker's continued-fraction development of $4/\pi$.)[39] In hindsight it will be obvious that the numerical upper bound, unity, to Wallis' integral sequence was the main reason why he himself failed to detect the crucial binomial pattern of coefficients implicit in its expansion, but we will at the same time appreciate the brilliance which led Newton to make it algebraically free and consider the binomial pattern as it emerges from a suitable spectrum of values of p. The remaining generalization,

$$\int_0^X (1 - x^2)^p.dx = X - \binom{p}{1}.\frac{1}{3}X^3 + \binom{p}{2}.\frac{1}{5}X^5 - \ldots.$$

and its more usual derivative form, is all but trivial to formulate. (Its proof is, of course, something else and Newton nowhere attempted it.[40]) I should not forget to recall that he was for a period highly delighted with his result, from the expansion for $p = \frac{1}{2}$ deriving the inverse sine series in various ways and from that for $p = -1$ computing the logarithmic series with which, at Boothby in the summer of 1665, he spent many a happy hour calculating natural logarithms to "two and fifty" and more places—numerically correct, however, to scarcely half that number.[41] Nor that within a few years of Newton's discovery, which he did not circulate, infinite series (such as Mercator's for the logarithm and Leibniz' for the inverse tangent) which made implicit use of particular binomial expansions were common. It is hard to resist the impression that the binomial expansion was going to be discovered, come what may, and that Newton was chosen to do so by historical accident. I have myself, indeed, elsewhere shown that the expansion for index $\frac{1}{2}$ is implicit in Chapter 8 of Briggs's preface to his 1624 *Arithmetica Logarithmica*, while since 1939 we know that James Gregory rediscovered the general expansion in 1670 as a corollary to his finite-difference researches.[42] Even more startling perhaps, as J. A. Lohne will no doubt soon show us, are the anticipations to be found in the still unpublished manuscripts of Thomas Harriot, penned around 1605.

The fluxional calculus, however, is Newton's undivided glory. Beginning in the early autumn of 1664 with Descartes's double-root algorithm for constructing the subnormal to an algebraic curve—the projection of the normal at any point upon the curve's base—Newton swiftly appreciated the computational facility of Hudde's multipliers for finding maxima and minima (expounded in a tract of his[43] appended by Schooten to the Latin *Geometrie*) and straightaway applied it to the construction of the subtangent—the similar projection of the tangent—and circle of curvature at a general point on a curve. Within a few months, by the spring of 1665, he had unified his several methods of resolving normal, tangent, and curvature problems into a general differentiation procedure founded upon the concept of an indefinitely small and ultimately vanishing increment of a variable, whether algebraic or a general geometrical line-segment.[44]

Essentially, Newton found the derivative of the function $y = f(x)$ (and so, in geometrical terms, the slope at a point on the curve represented by that equation in some oblique Cartesian co–ordinate system) by positing the small increment o of its base variable x and then considering the limit of $z = f(x + o)$ as o tends to zero. (This "little zero" notation for an increment, an unconscious echo of Beaugrand's usage of thirty years before,[45] first appears in Newton's rough notes, in September 1664 or a little after, on the Cartesian-inspired problem of two refractions[46] but was at once taken over into his more narrowly mathematical researches.) Supposing for simplicity that the angle of coordinates is right and making some

$ac = x$, $ch = y = f(x)$, subnormal $ce = v = ydy/dx$;

$cd = o$, $(ad = x + o)$, $ds = z = f(x + o) = y + o\dfrac{v}{y}$;

subnormal $df = w = v + o\dfrac{dv}{dx}$.

m is the meet of the normals at h and s; $pc = c$.

Slope at h is $\quad \lim\limits_{o \to zero} \left(\dfrac{z - y}{o} \right) = \dfrac{v}{y} = \dfrac{dy}{dx}$.

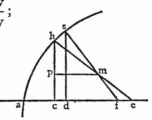

use of an equivalent modern notation, I may expound the essence of Newton's approach to elementary differential geometry in the following way. Let the perpendicular coordinates $ac = x$, $ch = y$ determine the point h on the curve ahs represented by some given defining equation, say $y = f(x)$, and let the increment $cd = o$ determine a corresponding incremented ordinate $ds = z$: likewise, the subnormal $df = w$ will be the incremented form of the subnormal $ce = v$ (or ydy/dx in modern Leibnizian notation). First, since the segment hs of the given curve is very nearly the tangent at h — and will be exactly so when the increment $cd = o$ vanishes —, it is perpendicular to the normal he and we deduce straightforwardly that, to $0(o^2)$, $ds = z = y + ov/y$. Hence in the limit as o vanishes $\dfrac{v}{y} = \dfrac{z - y}{o}$ is the slope of the curve at h[47]: in modern equivalent, $\dfrac{dy}{dx} = \lim\limits_{o \to zero} \left(\dfrac{1}{o}[f(x + o) - f(x)] \right)$, where of course the right hand side is the derivative of $f(x)$, to be calculated by expanding $f(x + o)$ as $f(x) + of'(x) + 0(o^2)$. In later standardized notation (first introduced in late 1691) Newton represented this derivative as the ratio of "fluxions" $\dfrac{\dot{y}}{\dot{x}}$, where $\dot{x}$ and $\dot{y}$ are instantaneous limit "speeds" of increase of the variables x and y with respect to some third, conventional variable of "time." During his early life, however, he made use of a variety of notations, in part literal (p and q for $\dot{x}$ and $\dot{y}$) but elsewhere—particularly in his 1665 manuscripts—using somewhat fussy combinations of superscript dots. (In denoting the reverse procedure of taking the "fluent" of a fluxion—"integrating" as we now say following Bernoulli—Newton widely used the pictograph of a small square in one of several positions, but there he had been anticipated by Mengoli's use of "O"—for "omnes" —in his 1659 *Geometria Speciosa*.) For exposition's sake, let me anachronistically employ the standard Newtonian dot-notation and, for further simplicity, suppose that x itself is the time variable (so that $\dot{x}$ is unity). Immediately we may set $v = y\dot{y}$, so that $z = y + o\dot{y}$ and $w = v + o\dot{v}$, to $0(o^2)$.

Consider now the second normal sf to the curve at s and suppose that it meets the first, he, in m at the distance $pc = c$ from the base ae. In the limit as the increment $cd = o$ vanishes, this meet m will be the centre of curvature of the curve ahs at the point h and we have consequently a way of calculating the curvature radius hm: in fact, since

$$pm = o + \frac{w}{z}(z-c) = \frac{v}{y}(y-c),$$

we easily deduce that

$$hm = hp \times \frac{he}{hc} = (y-c)\sqrt{1+\frac{v^2}{y^2}} = \sqrt{1+\frac{v^2}{y^2}} \cdot \lim_{o \to zero} \left(\frac{1 + \frac{v}{y} \times \frac{w}{z}}{\frac{1}{o}\left(\frac{w}{z} - \frac{v}{y}\right)} \right).$$

In a somewhat more verbalized equivalent this formula was the basis for Newton's extensive researches into curvature in November and December 1664,[48] during which time he traced (independently of Huygens[49] if five years after him) the three conic evolutes, and subsequently, in May 1665, when he less successfully tried to probe the concept of extremes of curvature. On the twentieth and twenty-first of the latter month, however, he generalized his previous methods in a magnificent way.[50]

To cut through the camouflage of his partly verbalized argument I will again use a somewhat anachronistic notation to convey the pattern of his argument. Consider a general two-variable function $f \equiv \sum_i p_i y^i = 0$, in which the various p_i are functions of x alone, and define

$$f_x = \sum_i \dot{p_i} y^i, \quad f_y = \sum_i i p_i y^{i-1}.$$

Evidently the incremented function is also zero; consequently

$$\sum_i (p_i + o\dot{p_i})(y + o\dot{y})^i = \sum_i (p_i + o\dot{p_i})(y + o\frac{v}{y})^i$$

$$= \sum_i p_i y^i + o\sum_i (\dot{p_i} y^i + \frac{v}{y} i p_i y^{i-1}) = 0,$$

or $f_x + \frac{v}{y} f_y = 0$ and so $\frac{v}{y} = -\frac{f_x}{f_y}$. This is the general rule "of tangents" which Newton recorded in his Waste Book on May 20, and of which he was later so proud when he communicated it to Collins in December 1672. On the following day—a Sunday!—he further developed this approach, extending it to treat of the curvature problem. Since $\frac{w}{z}$ is the incremented form of the slope $\frac{v}{y}$, therefore to $0(o^2)$

$$\frac{w}{z} = - \frac{\sum_i (\dot{p_i} + o\ddot{p_i})(y + o\frac{v}{y})^i}{\sum_i i(p_i + o\dot{p_i})(y + o\frac{v}{y})^{i-1}} = - \frac{f_x + o[f_{xx} - (f_x/f_y)f_{xy}]}{f_y + o[f_{xy} - (f_x/f_y)f_{yy}]};$$

in which

$$f_{xx} = \sum_i \ddot{p}_i y^i, \quad f_{xy} = \sum_i i\dot{p}_i y^{i-1} \text{ and } f_{yy} = \sum_i i(i-1)p_i y^{i-2}.$$

If lastly, we substitute these values for $\dfrac{v}{y}$ and $\dfrac{w}{z}$ into the above-found formula for the curvature radius and then take the limit as o vanishes, we have Newton's final result:

$$hm = \frac{(f_x + f_y)^{3/2}}{f_y^2 f_{xx} - 2f_x f_y f_{xy} + f_x^2 f_{yy}}.$$

It will be obvious to you that the various f's are the five first and second order partial derivatives of $f(x,y)$, the first time these appear in mathematical history and thirty years before Leibniz and L'Hospital.[51] Charles Hayes in his *Fluxions* of 1704[52] was, I believe, the first to hint in print at this general curvature formula. I should perhaps observe that Newton himself used a more complicated, homogenized notation, denoting f by the large cursive capital χ and taking $\cdot\chi = xf_x$, $\chi\cdot = yf_y$, $\therefore\chi = x^2 f_{xx}$, $\cdot\chi\cdot = xyf_{xy}$ and $\chi\therefore = y^2 f_{yy}$, but I have not otherwise essentially departed from his scheme. The previous May Newton had not yet read Descartes's *Geometrie*.

Over his other early achievements in calculus I must, for want of time, pass quickly. Making the Cartesian subnormal $v = y\dfrac{dy}{dx}$ his derivative basis (and using a superscript double-dot homogenized notation) Newton was able, about the same time or soon after, to state[53] the standard differential algorithms in full generality a decade before Leibniz (and nineteen years before they were published by him). A parallel stream of researches in integration, founded on Wallis' "arithmetick of infinites" and on Heuraet's rectification procedure, led to a firm grasp on Newton's part of the problem of quadrature and the geometrical insight that it is an exact inverse to that of tangents.[54] In the summer and early autumn of 1665, away in Lincolnshire with ample time for unhurried reassessment, he recast the theoretical basis of his newly acquired calculus techniques, making the change from the fundamental concept of the indefinitely small, discrete increment of a variable to that of its "moment," the product of its fluxion and the unit increment of the conventional variable of "time."[55] Whatever the logical satisfaction of the new basis, from a technical viewpoint, of course, the transition was without effect: in modern terms, it involved merely the replacing of each increment dx of a variable x by its equal ox, where o is the increment of time variable t and $\dot{x} = \dfrac{dx}{dt}$ is the "fluxion" of x. Also at this time he made a first attack on simple fluxional equations but with very limited success[56]—but it is startling that he should attempt their systematic resolution at all in 1665. Later, in the autumn of that year, Newton returned to the tangent problem, attacking it for a curve defined in an arbitrary co-ordinate system by evaluating and suitably compounding the limit-motions at a given point. After a crisis on October 29,[57] when he attempted to apply

Sources and Strengths of Newton's Early Mathematical Thought   81

the parallelogram of "forces" to the construction of the tangent to the quadratrix of Dinostratus (the meet of a uniformly translating line with a uniformly rotating radius vector), he discovered his howler and wrote up the correct construction in a paper on tangents to "mechanichall" curves ten days later.[58] The next May (1666), between the fourteenth and the sixteenth, he formulated a comprehensive general analysis of such limit-motions, extending its application in a novel way to the finding of a curve's points of inflexion.[59] (Hitherto his method had been to define such points as those at which the curvature was zero.) A few months later in the following October, in a grand finale to two crowded years of mathematical discovery Newton reworked his calculus discoveries and, together with a long list of integrals, began to enter them in condensed form in a small tract on fluxions and series methods.[60] Unfortunately, probably diverted by the growing demands of his optical researches, he never finished it and it was five years later to be merged into his 1671 fluxional treatise. Even so, the thirty crowded pages he did write—published in full for the first time only four years ago[61]—are irrefutable documentary proof of his achievement in mathematics by the close of his *annus mirabilis*.

Together, Newton's fluxional algorithms and infinite series expansions, successively unfolded in his *De Analysi* of 1669, the 1671 calculus tract, and the several versions of his *De Quadratura Curvarum,* were to be the keystone of his mature mathematical method, and his development of Descartes's "analytical" geometry was to be the means of applying it universally. In his *Lectiones Opticæ* he was to apply it to theoretical optics, making use of the first derivative in elementary refraction problems and progressing to the second in his consideration of diacaustics. Above all, in his *Principia Mathematica* he was to employ it time and again in expounding his quantitative theory of universal gravitation (whose action he defined to be second-order differential impulses of "force" and whose composition therefore, in orbital problems, required a double integration). But I will leave my colleagues the pleasure of listing the splendors of that mathematical treasure house, with its general solution of the two-body problem (and approximate resolution of that of three) and variety of sophisticated mathematical procedures and results.

Let me conclude. On looking back I see that I have said a great deal concerning the two preparatory years, 1664 and 1665, but only too little of the *annus mirabilis* we now celebrate. From a mathematical viewpoint the emphasis has, I think, not been misplaced. In calculus, particularly, the great creative period of discovery was the year and a half from mid-1664 on. The only two significant 1666 papers, that of May 14–16, and the uncompleted October 1666 tract, were essentially the securing of ground already won. The extensive researches into the theory of equations and the location of their real and complex roots,[62] his introduction of finite-difference techniques into the study of the factorization of polynomials,[63] his findings in the general theory of angle sections,[64] all belong to the spring and summer of 1665, while his codification of plane and spherical trigonometry,[65] contemporaneous with his investigations into the division of the musical octave,[66] belongs firmly to the following autumn. What we may rightly conclude is that by the end of 1666, having matured rapidly over two richly crowded years, Newton's genius was fully formed and had begun to express itself on the frontiers of current mathematical advance. Henceforth, in mathematics at least, a pattern for future discovery existed. Remembering, then, his parallel achievements at this time in optics and dynamics—however difficult it may now be for us to document them with precision—and allowing for his good fortune in being born at the right time and place to take full advantage of the work of his predecessors, we may justly celebrate, three hundred years on, if not one single magical year at least a *biennium mirabilissimum.*

NOTES

(Unless otherwise stated the manuscripts listed are in Cambridge University Library.)

[1] These six tracts have recently been reissued, in contemporary English versions, as *The Mathematical Works of Isaac Newton*, New York, 2 vols. 1964–7: in my editorial introductions I seek to place them in the totality of Newton's mathematical experience.

[2] *The Mathematical Papers of Isaac Newton, Volume I: 1664–1666*, Cambridge, 1967. *Volume II: 1667–1670*, 1968 and *Volume III: 1670–1673*, 1969 are now also published while *Volume IV: 1674–1684* is in press. Four more volumes will complete the set.

[3] See also my articles, "Isaac Newton: birth of a mathematician" and "Newton's marvellous year: 1666 and all that," *Notes and Records of the Royal Society of London 19*, 1964, 53–62; *21*, 1966, 32–41.

[4] Especially we are heavily in debt to Stukeley's letter to Richard Mead (King's College, Keynes MS 136, partially printed in Edmund Turnor's *Collections for the History of the Town and Soke of Grantham*, London, 1806, 174–80), which was the common basis for the early portions of Stukeley's own *Memoirs of Sir Isaac Newton (1752)* (ed. A. Hastings White), London, 1936 and of Conduitt's several accounts (especially King's College, Keynes MS 130.4).

[5] Grantham Public Library D/N 2267 (Hill 31).

[6] Stukeley's *Memoirs* (note 4), 42; H. W. Robinson, "Note on some recently discovered geometrical drawings in the stonework of Woolsthorpe Manor House," *Notes and Records of the Royal Society of London 5*, 1947/8, 35–6.

[7] Add 3996.

[8] King's College, Keynes MS 130.4, 5.

[9] This story, an interpolation by Conduitt in his composite of the accounts of Stukeley and De Moivre, seems highly disputable.

[10] *Euclidis Elementorum Libri XV. breviter demonstrati . . . Euclidis Data succinctè demonstrata*, Cambridge, 1655: Newton's copy is Trinity College, NQ.16.201.

[11] The main portion of his notes on these "philosophers" was entered in Add 3996: the following *Quæstiones* are ff.88^r–135^r of the same notebook.

[12] MS Baker 29, 163^r: see M. H. Curtis, *Oxford and Cambridge in Transition, 1558–1642*, Oxford, 1959, 257–8.

[13] Lambeth Palace (London), MS 592 (Cod. H. Wharton 592), 8 pp. (unpaginated).

[14] Add 4007, 706^r–707^r (Luard's nineteenth century copy of the "Memorandum relating to Sr Isaac Newton given me by Mr Demoivre in Novr 1727," the original of which was sold at Sotheby's in 1936).

[15] Trinity College, NQ.8.59 (partly manuscript copy).

[16] Add 4004, 6^v–27^v.

[17] Add 4000, 82^r–84^r/15^r–24^v; 12^r–14^r/90^r–92^r.

[18] Add 4000, 14^v.

[19] *Francisci Vietae Opera Mathematica, In unum Volumen congesta, ac recognita . . .*, Leyden, 1646. Newton seems never to have had a personal copy.

[20] Add 4000, 2^r–6^r/8^r–11^v.

21 *Operum Mathematicorum Pars Prima/Altera*, Oxford, 1657/1656. The *Arithmetica Infinitorum, sive Nova Methodus Inquirendi in Curvilineorum Quadraturam* . . . appears in the latter volume (published first).

22 Add 4000, 15^r–18^v.

23 Newton to Oldenburg for Leibniz, 24 October 1676 (*The Correspondence of Isaac Newton 2*, Cambridge, 1960, 110ff).

24 *Exercitationum Mathematicarum Libri Quinque*, Leyden, 1657, the fifth book of which contains "Sectiones trigintas Miscellaneas." Newton's lightly annotated copy is now in Trinity College (NQ.16.184).

25 Especially Add 4004, 15^{v}ff.

26 Add 4000, 93^v–116^r.

27 Add 4004, 67^v–69^r.

28 *Johannis Huddenii Epistola Secunda, de Maximis et Minimis* (*Geometria*, 1659, 507–16).

29 *Henrici van Heuraet Epistola de Transmutatione Curvarum Linearum in Rectas* (*Geometria*, 1659, 517–20).

30 *Johannis De Witt Elementa Curvarum Linearum* (*Geometria*, Tom.2, 1661, 153–340).

31 The autograph manuscript of these projective researches (in the decade from *ca.* 1667), mostly in private possession, is reproduced in the second and fourth volumes of my edition of Newton's *Mathematical Papers* (note 2).

32 Add 4004, 1–^{v}4^v.

33 Add 4004, 15^v–16^r.

34 Add 4004, 24^r.

35 Add 3961.1, *passim:* these researches are reproduced in the second volume of my edition of his *Mathematical Papers* (note 2).

36 See especially his anonymous review, "An Account of the Book entituled *Commercium Epistolicum* . . ." (*Philosophical Transactions 29*. No. 342 [for January/February 1714/15], 173–224) of his own *Commercium Epistolicum D. Johannis Collins, et Aliorum de Analysi Promota*, London, 1712; and his equally anonymous appendix (pp. 97–123) to Joseph Raphson's *Historia Fluxionum*, London, 1715 [–16].

37 *Mathematical Papers* (note 2) I, 154.

38 I have discussed this topic in "Newton's Discovery of the General Binomial Theorem," *Mathematical Gazette 45*, 1961, 175–80.

39 See my "Patterns of Mathematical Thought in the later Seventeenth Century," *Archive for History of Exact Sciences 1*, 1961, 179–388, especially 210–13, 236–41.

40 Roger Cotes, in still unpublished researches of about 1709 (Trinity College, R.16.38, 362^{r}ff), was, I believe, the first to attempt any proof.

41 Compare Add 4000, 14^v and 19^{r}ff.

42 See my "Henry Briggs: The Binomial Theorem Anticipated," *Mathematical Gazette 45*, 1961, 9–12; and H. W. Turnbull, *James Gregory Tercentenary Memorial Volume*, London, 1939, 132ff, 370ff.

43 See note 28.

44 Add 4004, 30^v–33^v, 47^r–50^r.

45 *De la Manière de trouver les Tangentes des Lignes Courbes par l'Algebre* . . . . (first published by C. de Waard in his *Supplement* to the *Œuvres de Fermat*, Paris, 1922, 98–114, especially 106ff).

46 Add 4004, 2^r.

47 Add 4004, 8^v (revised on 47^r).

48 Add 4004, 6^r and 30^{v}ff.

49 See his *Œuvres complètes 14*, The Hague, 1920, 387–406, especially 391–6.

50 Add 4004, 47^r–50^r.

51 See their correspondence in late 1694 and March 1695 in (ed.) C. I. Gerhardt, *Leibnizens Mathematische Schriften 2*, Berlin, 1850, 261ff.

52 Newton's curvature algorithm is developed implicitly by Hayes on p. 190 (§ 239) of his *A Treatise of Fluxions: Or, An Introduction to Mathematical Philosophy*, London, 1704. This

D. T. WHITESIDE

book was the first English work to make systematic use of the Leibnizian "S" sign for integration.

[53] Add 4000, 120^{r}ff; Add 3960.12, 206 and 199–202.

[54] Add 4000, 120^r–122^r/134^v–136^r.

[55] Add 4000, 152^r; Add 4004, 57^r/57^v.

[56] Add 3958.2, 30^r/30^v.

[57] Add 3958.2, 34^r/37^v.

[58] Add 4004, 50^v/51^r (dated 8 November 1665).

[59] Add 4004, 51^r/51^v.

[60] Add 3958.3, 48^v–63^v.

[61] In A. Rupert Hall and Marie Boas Hall, *Unpublished Scientific Papers of Isaac Newton*, Cambridge, 1962, 15–64 (though substantial excerpts from it appeared in James Wilson's edition of the *Mathematical Tracts of the late Benjamin Robins*, London, 1761, 2, Appendix: 351–6).

[62] Add 4004, 55^r–56^v and 85^r–86^v.

[63] Add 4004, 87^r–89^r.

[64] Add 4000, 80^v–82^v.

[65] Add 3958.2, 31^r/31^v (revised as ff 23^r–25^v of a notebook now in the Pierpont Morgan Library, New York).

[66] Add 3958.2, 34^v/35^r/37^r; Add 4000, 104^r–113^r and 137^v–143^r.

ASGER AABOE

Comment

I am not going to tell you what Dr. Whiteside was trying to say, for that is precisely what he has just done himself very admirably, and to take issue with him would be rather stupid, first, because he is very clever indeed and second, because he is the only person, with the exception of the learned Dr. Hoskin of Cambridge and some learned printers in the Cambridge University Press, who has been through the material upon which much of his lecture is based. Instead I shall make a few vague remarks on his methodology, what it is and what it is not.

To treat the latter point first, it may seem absurd to talk about what a man does not do; to take a parallel from the history of science, a great many words, and some effort, have been devoted to "explaining" why Greek science did not achieve this, that, or the other thing. I agree that these endeavours have, on the whole, been idle; if it is hard to account for what went on, how much harder must it be to take care of what did not, for so many more things did not happen than did. But like most parallels, this parallel is misleading. The temptation for a young scholar to follow prevalent routes of investigation is great, and to describe those he did not take may serve to set his chosen path in relief.

There is, of course, a long and great tradition for work of the highest quality in the history of the sciences, and particularly of the exact sciences. It takes no effort to make an impressive list of historians from the nineteenth and early twentieth centuries— even without worry about completeness—men like Delambre, Todhunter, Woepcke, Hankel, Dreyer, Heiberg, Manitius, Zeuthen, Tannery, Kugler, Heath, Nallino, Suter, Steinschneider, and here we even ignore earlier historians from Eudemus to Montucla.

These were all scholars of quality with highest competence in at least one field.

During the first half of this century there came then upon us the era of promotion of the history of science, and with it, as a natural consequence of widened scope and increased demand, a drastic lowering of minimal standards of work. One saw the appearance of histories of such breadth that it has been said that the title pages of first editions —which were reproduced in them in great number—well illustrated the level of penetration into the scientific works described. After such histories of scientific title pages we have had histories of scientific prefaces and with them much concern with the philosophical envelopes of scientific presentations. May I here insert the remark that the latter form contains, I believe, a danger if it, as it often does, proceeds from the tacit axiom that if one has said something about a scientist's professed philosophical tenets, one has automatically said something about his scientific work. If one reads beyond the prefaces it becomes amply clear that this is not at all a viable axiom but rather a theorem to be proved or disproved in each case.

Interest began to spread out and embrace anything and everything associated with scientists and science. We have seen evidence of interest in scientific institutions, in stamps and coins bearing the graven images of scientists, in the psychology, normal or hopefully otherwise, of scientists, in the fiscal matters of science, and so on. Though much of this, when well done, can be very useful, I still miss some of the true, distinctive flavour of history of science, as I understand it, naïvely and literally.

But wherefore, historians will and do ask, is this history different from all other histories? I believe the answer is that because of the limitation of our subject and because of its very nature, we can in the history of science, and particularly in the history of the exact sciences, achieve a level of understanding and control far beyond what, for example, a political historian in his right mind may dream of; in doing so we can supply the more general historian with good hard bricks which he may and, I hope, will use to strengthen his edifice. And since such levels of understanding can be reached, it seems a pity not to try .

Unfortunately, not all do try. There are too many examples of historians of science who copy the errors of other historians of science, adding a few of their own, and of whom it may be said, what al-Biruni said of a certain class of astrologers:

> They babble proudly about things they barely hear, without verifying them, and they are satisfied by associating fancies with them.[1]

That it is possible to gain such understanding and control does not mean that it is always easy, and Newton's mathematics and mechanics have always been singularly inaccessible; this is why we owe a particularly great debt to Derek Whiteside. Placing himself squarely in the great old tradition of scholarship in the history of science, he is with penetrating techniques and apparently boundless energy making available to us the massive material in Newton's mathematical notes. I have had the good fortune to get a glimpse of the wretched scratchings he has to work from—I cannot even begin to give you a feeling for the bulk of the manuscripts—and to see what he makes of it. We are lucky that it was he who got access to these notes, for he brings to the task of publishing them not only an uncanny gift for entering into Newton's manner of thought, but also a thorough familiarity with the mathematical modes of the seventeenth century so that he can consider Newton's mathematical work in its proper framework, which is mathematics in the seventeenth century rather than, say, the history of Interregnum and Restoration England.

We shall then have the unique opportunity of following in detail, as we have just heard, the genesis of Newton's work, and I do not hesitate to say that Whiteside's edition of the mathematical papers is in my estimation the greatest single contribution to the recent history of the exact sciences. It is projected to run to 8 volumes of which the first will appear in the spring. The first proof of this volume is on display outside this room, and I advise you strongly to take a look at it. I am sure that I speak for all of us when I say that we are exceedingly grateful to him for having come over here to give us this glimpse of what is to come.

NOTE

[1] *Al-Biruni on Transits,* edited by Saffouri, Ifram, and E. S. Kennedy, Beirut, 1959, p. 71.

RICHARD S. WESTFALL

Uneasily Fitful Reflections on Fits of Easy Transmission

F ITS OF EASY TRANSMISSION, NOT TO MENTION THEIR TWIN BROTHERS, FITS
of easy reflection, those strange notions inserted near the end of Book II in Newon's *Opticks*, have been the occasion of more fits of uneasy comprehension than
anything else in the work. Unexpected and unwanted, disagreeably reminiscent of an
age supposed to be dead, they emerge with unsettling abruptness in a setting hardly
calculated to display them to advantage—like prehistoric beasts grazing on a well-
kept suburban lawn. For the rest of the *Opticks* is not like them. The rest of the
Opticks is filled with observations and concepts that the science of light in its development has made familiar and comprehensible to the reader of the twentieth century.
Almost no one finds the fits of easy transmission and of easy reflection familiar and
comprehensible. The famous experiment with a lens pressed hard against a flat piece
of glass revealed a series of rings—"Newton's rings" as we still call them—in the
thin film of air thus produced. If a bright ring appeared in reflected sunlight at a
thickness x, others appeared at 3x, 5x, 7x and so on for about six or seven rings
whereas dark rings appeared between them at thicknesses of 2x, 4x, 6x and so on.
"Every Ray of Light in its passage through any refracting Surface," Newton concluded, "is put into a certain transient Constitution or State, which in the progress of
the Ray returns at equal Intervals, and disposes the Ray at every return to be easily
transmitted through the next refracting Surface, and between the returns to be easily
reflected by it. . . . The returns of the disposition of any Ray to be reflected I will call
its *Fits of easy Reflection*, and those of its disposition to be transmitted its *Fits of easy
Transmission*, and the space it passes between every return and the next return, the
Interval of its Fits."[1]

Certainly historians have not been reticent to comment on the bizarre appearance
of the assertion. Even Ferdinand Rosenberger, devoted to the Newtonian tradition
though he is and inclined to seek a favorable interpretation of Newton's declarations,
pulls up short when he faces the theory of fits.

> Newton had wanted to exclude all hypotheses from his work and yet found him-
> self compelled in this case to admit properties of light rays which are hypotheti-
> cal in the fullest sense. The fact is only that rays which pass the first surface of a
> thin film either emerge freely through the back surface or are reflected there ac-
> cording to the thickness of the film. It is a bald assumption, however, and one
> indeed with very dubious physical credentials, when this behavior of light is ex-
> plained by an inclination or a disposition of the individual ray, deriving from its
> very nature, to be easily transmitted or reflected.[2]

Vasco Ronchi, who shares neither Rosenberger's deference to Newton nor his Germanic caution, simply throws up his hands in a disceptically disarming display of Italian irritation. Disposition of rays to be transmitted? What can Newton possibly mean except a voluntary intention on the part of rays?—"those which wish pass; those which do not wish do not pass."

> In all these pages one feels a certain reticence and dissatisfaction on the part of the author himself. If he had been consistent, he ought to have limited himself to saying: The rings necessitate a periodicity; partial reflection of light at transparent surfaces exists; experience tells us as much; but the corpuscular theory is unable to explain all this by actions that are rationally comprehensible between matter and the corpuscles of light. On the contrary Newton wished to start building the theory by giving a name to the phenomenon and to some of its elements; thus he defined the fits and "the interval of the fits."[3]

I wish to suggest that the theory of fits is not all that difficult and obscure. Seen against the background of Newton's intellectual development, it appears as a deposit formed by the interaction of his philosophical speculations on his optical studies. Seen against the background of his statements on method, it appears as a consistent expression of his outlook on the scientific enterprise. The function of historical research is not solely to understand in order to forgive, however, and there is a third perspective on the theory of fits which must not be omitted. Seen against the background of optical science at the end of the seventeenth century, it reveals a crisis in the study of light more profound than we have been ready to acknowledge.

First, we must examine the theory against the background of Newton's intellectual development, and to do this we must return briefly to Newton's first consideration of light and colors as recorded in 1664 or '65 in a student notebook. The context of his notes is familiar but not for that uninteresting or unimportant. Newton had been converted to the mechanical philosophy of nature, and within its framework of thought he was speculating on the mechanical origin of sensations of color. Already an adherent of the corpuscular conception of light, Newton considered specifically how the motion of corpuscles might be modified in various circumstances so as to produce different impulses on the eye. And in the midst of these thoughts he chanced to consider that maybe the modification of rays is not what happens at all. Perhaps the rays of light are ultimately heterogeneous, and perhaps the sensations of different colors are caused by the different rays when they are separated from each other.[4] The very heart of Newton's contribution to optics was contained in that idea.

Not too much later, perhaps early in 1666, Newton had clarified his initial insight to the point that he could expound it coherently in an essay recorded in another notebook.[5] The essential ideas that were expanded into the *Lectiones Opticae*, into the paper of 1672, and ultimately into Book One of the *Opticks* were there set forth, and to support them the basic experiments with the prism. What were known as "emphatic" or "apparent" colors, phenomena such as the rainbow and the prismatic spectrum, were shown to derive, not from the modification of light, but from its

Uneasily Fitful Reflections on Fits of Easy Transmission 89

analysis by means of refraction. Newton's intention went much further, however. An adequate theory must explain the permanent colors of solid bodies as well, and in extending his theory to include them, Newton took his first step toward the doctrine of fits.

The direction of the step was indicated by the colors of thin films, as reported by Robert Hooke in his *Micrographia*.[6] In the brief essay of 1666, Newton recorded a few experiments with the film of air between two prisms pressed together. By using a lens of known curvature and measuring the diameter of the rings, he did what Hooke had not known how to do; that is, he determined (rather inaccurately in this case) the thickness of the film. Already his speculations extended beyond his experiments, and he indicated that the permanent colors of bodies are similar phenomena. Thin films were exactly the means Newton needed to extend his theory. Although the colors of thin films are the products of reflection instead of refraction, nevertheless they manifest a similar process of analysis. A film of given thickness, now able to be measured, reflects light of one sort while it transmits the rest. Book Two of the *Opticks* is no more than an elaboration of that theme.

The elaboration, mostly completed during the first half of the 1670s and recorded in the "Discourse of Observations" dated 1675, required experiments more sophisticated than those of 1666. In the early essay, Newton followed Hooke's lead to a considerable degree as far as the phenomena of thin films were concerned. He indicated how the films could be measured in principle, but the one measurement he made was crude, yielding a calculated thickness 25 per cent too large. What concerns us most, he accepted the suggestion—Hooke's suggestion, let me repeat, however fiercely Newton's ghost may scowl—that the phenomena are periodic, and he indicated how their periodicity could be demonstrated by the same experiment, although he did not carry the demonstration through. Sometime before he composed the first version of the "Discourse of Observations" in 1672, Newton did carry it through. The paper recording his experimental investigation has survived, a magnificent specimen of experimental acumen.[7] Using a lens of much greater radius of curvature than he had used before to increase the size of the rings, measuring the rings with extreme care so that he confidently recorded their diameters, not merely in hundredths of an inch, but in fractions of hundredths, squaring the diameters to show that the thickness of the film increases in arithmetic proportion with each successive ring, Newton moved the concept of periodicity in one gigantic step from the realm of speculation to the realm of fact.

Once again, the comprehensibility of Newton's procedure to us depends upon our seizing the intellectual context in which the experiments were performed, just as the comprehensibility of the results to Newton depended on his ability to explain them. To be brief, the mechanical philosophy of nature remains the key to understanding. However ironic it may appear to us, it seems clear that Newton originally expected his experiments to furnish support for the corpuscular conception of light. Earlier he had observed that the rings grow in size as they are viewed at increasing obliquity.

RICHARD S. WESTFALL

Careful measurement now established that the thickness of the film varies inversely as the sine of the angle of "obliquity," which is to say inversely as the component of the corpuscle's motion perpendicular to the film "or reciprocally as ye force it strikes ye refracting surface wth all."[8] A similar point lay behind the substitution of water for air. The thickness of the film should depend not only on the momentum of the corpuscle, but also on the density and resistance to the medium, and Newton established that the ratio of thicknesses in air and in water is identical to the ratio of indices of refraction in the two media, a ratio deriving in his estimation from the respective resistances of the media. By 1672 most of this speculation had dropped away, probably because it contained internal contradictions. Whereas the weakness of the blow in the case above was related to a greater thickness of film, rings also appeared in red light at greater thicknesses than they appeared in blue, and the corpuscles of red had been established as bigger and stronger on other grounds. The importance of the speculations for us lies in the view they provide of Newton's mechanical conception of optical phenomena.

His understanding of periodicity rested on the same foundation. The paper recording the investigation did not attempt to explain the phenomena. It implied an explanation, however, in its use of the word "pulse" in relation to the thickness of the film. In the earlier essay, he had defined the calculated thickness of the film as "ye space of a pulse of ye vibrating medium."[9] By "medium" in turn he clearly referred to the aether which pervaded the essay as freely as, in theory, it pervaded the universe. That Newton postulated the existence of an aether was hardly strange, for an aether was the *sine qua non* of a successful mechanical philosophy of nature. The basic premise of such a philosophy was the assertion that all the phenomena of nature are produced by particles of matter which are in motion and which are able to interact only by impact. Thus for every phenomenon that does not obviously display its mechanism—examples are legion, but the optical phenomena under consideration here will do as well as any—the mechanical philosopher had to invent an invisible mechanism usually in a subtle and invisible fluid. Newton's aether served the same function in his early optical writings. Already clearly implied in 1666, the hypothesis of the aether had been systematized by 1672 and was sent to the Royal Society in 1675.[10]

The "Hypothesis of Light" was Newton's attempt to develop a general mechanical system which would account, among other things, for all of the known properties and phenomena of light. Based on the corpuscular conception of light and positing the existence of an omnipresent aether varying in density, it set about deriving optical phenomena from the changes in direction that such an aether must impose on corpuscles moving through it. Since the aether was held to stand rarer in the pores of bodies than in free space, a corpuscle of light incident on a sheet of glass, for example, would be refracted toward the normal, and emerging from the glass into air would be deflected a second time in the opposite direction. In the latter case—a corpuscle within a dense transparent medium and incident on its surface—if the angle of incidence were sufficiently great, the corpuscle would not succeed in emerging at all but would be reflected internally. Since the zone of lesser density was extended a small distance beyond the surface of a body, a corpuscle passing near a body's edge must also suffer a deflection. The hypothesis had several advantages from Newton's point of view. The regularity of the aether's variations, in comparison to the supposed irregularity of the constituent particles of bodies, would explain the regularity of reflection and refraction, whereas light could hardly be turned uniformly in the same direction if it had to strike on the parts of bodies, as the prevailing mechanical philosophies held. The hypothesis offered an explanation of internal reflection as well, even in the apparently difficult case of light incident on a surface beyond which lies a vacuum. No previous hypothesis had been able to touch this phenomenon.

Not the least of its advantages was the explanation the hypothesis offered of thin films. Every film of transparent material was a film of aether as well, a film distinguished from the surrounding aether by its specific density. In striking the surface of such a film, a corpuscle of light would set up vibrations, just as a stone falling into water causes waves. Just as the surface of water continues to oscillate for some time after the stone hits it, so the surface of the film of aether would continue to vibrate; and because the vibrations were held to travel faster than the velocity of light, the corpuscle must arrive at the farther surface of the film simultaneously with some part of a vibration. What part of the vibration arrived with the corpuscle would depend on the thickness of the film. The vibrations, of course, were conceived as what we call longitudinal waves, pulses of condensation and rarefaction. After all, the entire hypothesis depended on variations in the aether's density acting upon the motion of corpuscles. At the farther side of the film the corpuscle would encounter a surface dense enough to reflect it or rare enough to permit its passage, and because a periodic wave determined the state of the second surface, the phenomena of thin films must likewise be periodic. When the reference in 1666 to pulses in a vibrating medium is considered, it becomes evident that Newton associated periodicity with wave motion from the first moment he accepted Hooke's suggestion, even before his own measurements had confirmed it. The wave motion did not belong to light as such, of course. Since the ultimate source of the corpuscular conception lay in the apparent identity of rectilinear propagation with inertial motion, corpuscles could not move with oscillations. An hypothesis based on the interaction of corpuscles with an aether could locate the waves with equal facility in the aether, and this Newton did. The "Hypothesis of Light" contains the clearest discussion of wave motion as we understand it to be found in seventeenth–century optical literature.[11]

Such the explanation was in 1675. Such, at least in rudimentary form, it had been for about ten years. Such it continued to be in the letter to Boyle of 1679. Soon thereafter it ceased to be a possible explanation for Newton because he abandoned belief in an aether's existence sometime after the letter to Boyle. The permanence of planetary motion was by no means the only or the original factor leading Newton toward this conclusion, although it finally became the argument of overwhelming impor-

RICHARD S. WESTFALL

tance. An experiment with a pendulum had already demonstrated the nonexistence of an aether. The fact that pendulums come to rest in a vacuum almost as quickly as they do in air had once appeared to Newton as evidence for the existence of an aether.[12] Now he saw that the experiment demanded closer control. A carefully suspended pendulum eleven feet long, the bob of which was a wooden box, was displaced about six feet and set free to swing, not in a vacuum but in the open air. The places to which it returned on the first four swings were marked. The box was now filled with metal so that its weight filled, plus the weight of one half the thread, was seventy-eight times the weight of the empty box plus the calculated weight of the air it contained and half the weight of the thread. Since the weight stretched the thread, its length was adjusted to make the period isochronous with that of the first trial. According to the mechanical explanation of gravity, the bob was now heavier because the aether penetrated the box and pressed upon the metal within. If this were so, the aether ought equally to resist its motion of oscillation. Far from coming to rest more quickly, the heavier pendulum required more time for its motion to decay to the points marked on the first four swings of the lighter pendulum. To be exact, it took almost seventy-eight swings to reach the first mark, almost seventy-eight more to reach the second, and so on. Which is to say, there can be no aether.[13] The experiment itself, performed at some undated time several years before the publication of the *Principia*, appears to have been the result of a growing tension which we can trace within Newton's speculations on nature. Although his speculations, as embodied in the "Hypothesis of Light" and the letter to Boyle, were couched in the conventional terms of mechanical philosophies, they concentrated heavily on phenomena difficult to explain in mechanical terms, even with an aether, the wild card of mechanical speculations which could take any trick. When he discussed the same phenomena in speculations associated with the composition of the *Principia*, he did not mention the aether.[14] The wild card was no longer in the deck, and attractions between particles were now declared trumps. In mechanical philosophies of nature attractions were only phenomenal; they were so defined, one might say, by the rules of the game. Since reality held only particles of matter in motion, apparent attractions had to be explained away. Sometime after 1679, Newton stopped playing the game by the conventional rules. Instead of using the wild card to cover every attraction, if I may inflict my figure one last time, he discarded it. In plain terms, he denied the existence of an aether and asserted the reality of forces between particles.

Seventeen years later, the *Opticks* applied the same conclusion to its range of phenomena. "Do not Bodies act upon Light at a distance, and by their action bend its Rays; and is not this action (*caeteris paribus*) strongest at the least distance?" Newton asked—or perhaps declared—in Query 1.[15] In the body of the work attractions replaced aethereal pressures, just as gravitational attraction had replaced aethereal pressure on the cosmic scale. Thus a corpuscle incident on a transparent body would receive an acceleration normal to the surface and be refracted; when it emerged from the other side, the attraction of the body, producing an equal effect, would refract it again into a path parallel to its original one. Indeed, Newton was able to demonstrate from the principles of mechanics that the sine law of refraction must follow.[16] A corpuscle within a dense transparent medium and incident on its surface at an angle sufficiently great would be prevented by the attraction from emerging and would suffer an internal reflection. The same force would deflect corpuscles passing very near the surface of bodies—what Newton called "inflection" and we call "diffraction." "Bodies reflect and refract Light," he declared, "by one and the same power, variously exercised in various Circumstances."[17] In a word, the new explanation covered the same phenomena as the old. It had the same advantages, moreover, accounting for the regularity of reflection and refraction—which are caused, Newton said, "not by a single point of the . . . Body, but by some power of the Body which is evenly diffused all over its Surface, and by which it acts upon the Ray without immediate Contact."[18]

There was one thing, however, which the new hypothesis of forces could not be made to do. Forces would not vibrate periodically as the aether had done. That is to say, Newton had worked himself into a considerable dilemma. His contributions to optics consisted primarily of the discovery of two new properties, the heterogeneity of light and the periodicity of some optical phenomena.[19] The first proved to be as easily reconciled to the hypothesis of forces as it had been to the hypothesis of an aether, and the whole of the *Opticks* may be looked upon as a series of changes rung on the theme of heterogeneity. Periodicity, on the other hand, required an aether, and the aether now had been abolished. The *Opticks* itself provides ample proof that periodicity was only intelligible to Newton in terms of wave motion. The one effort he made to explain it made use of waves, located now, for want of a better subject, in the transparent medium itself.

> Those that are averse from assenting to any new Discoveries, but such as they can explain by an Hypothesis, may for the present suppose, that as Stones by falling upon Water put the Water into an undulating Motion, and all Bodies by percussion excite vibrations in the Air; so the Rays of Light, by impinging on any refracting or reflecting Surface, excite vibrations in the refracting or reflecting Medium or Substance, and by exciting them agitate the solid parts of the refracting or reflecting Body, and by agitating them cause the Body to grow warm or hot; that the vibrations thus excited are propagated in the refracting or reflecting Medium or Substance, much after the manner that vibrations are propagated in the Air for causing Sound, and move faster than the Rays so as to overtake them; and that when any Ray is in that part of the vibration which conspires with its Motion, it easily breaks through a refracting Surface, but when it is in the contrary part of the vibration which impedes its Motion, it is easily reflected; and, by consequence, that every Ray is successively disposed to be easily reflected, or easily transmitted, by every vibration which overtakes it.[20]

If he could not explain the property adequately, why not simply ignore it? Christiaan

RICHARD S. WESTFALL

Huygens had been impressed by the same suggestion of Hooke that had started Newton's investigation; he had even thought of the same device to measure the film and had observed what I shall call Huygens' rings, which he treated as periodic.[21] Later on, when periodicity presented an obstacle to his theory of light, he simply forgot that he had ever accepted it. Newton could not forget. Whereas Huygens' experiments had been brief and superficial, Newton's had been long and convincing, and their conclusion was too deeply printed on his mind to be erased. I shall pause to remark that if he had sought, and found, the means to serve his immediate interest in consistency by eliminating all mention of periodicity, he would have sacrificed unknowingly the much greater credit due him as the discoverer of periodicity. One cynic, at least, has been surprised to note that in one instance, at least, virtue had its own reward. In fact, however, Newton could not have eliminated mention of periodicity had he tried. It was thoroughly entwined with the heterogeneity of light, his other major discovery in optics. If the question of periodicity is logically distinct from the observed property of specific films to reflect light of one color and to transmit that of others, the experiments establishing the latter, and measuring the films, established the former as well. And Newton could not eliminate the treatment of thin films from the *Opticks*. Without it, his theory of colors would have been hopelessly incomplete.

What alternative was left? None, I suggest, except the one he took. The theory of fits, that is to say, appears to be a bald statement, in terms consonant with the corpuscular conception of light, of the empirical fact that some optical phenomena are periodic. A comparison of Book II of the *Opticks* with the original investigation from which it grew supports such an interpretation. To be sure, the early paper was a record of experiments, not an exposition of the conclusions drawn from them. Nevertheless, one cannot miss the fact that periodicity (plus the corpuscularity of light, as I mentioned before) was the very goal of the investigation. In Book II, on the other hand, the same experiments, now considerably elaborated, were directed with singleness of purpose toward the theory of colors. "In the former Book," he stated in the opening paragraph, "I forbore to treat of these Colours [in thin transparent films], because they seemed of a more difficult Consideration, and were not necessary for establishing the Properties of Light there discoursed of. But because they may conduce to farther Discoveries for compleating the Theory of Light, especially as to the constitution of the parts of natural Bodies, on which their Colours or Transparency depend; I have here set down an account of them."[22] An exposition of some complexity and length follows, occupying eighty pages in the first edition. Then, at the end of Part III, nine propositions crammed into nine pages announce the theory of fits. Staccato, brief statements, shorn almost entirely of discussion and justified merely by reference back to the experimental evidence that requires their statement, the propositions announce by the form in which they are cast the interpretation to be placed upon them. Should the form not be enough, Newton added his explicit words partially quoted above. "Those that are averse from assenting to any new Discoveries, but such as they can explain by an Hypothesis, may for the present suppose . . ." and he proceeded to suggest vibrations in the substance of the thin plates—an obviously lame attempt to transfer the vibrations of the late departed aether to a medium obviously unsuited, in the context of Newton's idea of nature, to receive them. "But whether this Hypothesis be true or false," he concluded, "I do not here consider. I content my self with the bare Discovery, that the Rays of Light are by some cause or other alternately disposed to be reflected or refracted for many vicissitudes."[23] If we grant that Newton intended the theory of fits as a statement of empirical fact, one question still remains. Why should he have chosen such peculiar phraseology to describe periodicity? The phrase does appear peculiar, but the reasons for its peculiarity appear to belong more to us than to Newton. First, Newton borrowed a word from current medical usage, meaning one of the recurrent attacks of a periodic or constitutional ailment, which is not ordinarily used in the same sense today. Second, we do not adequately think ourselves back into Newton's specific context with his specific assumptions. If we should start where Newton started, with the conviction both that light is corpuscular and that an aether capable of supplying periodic vibrations does not exist, we might find it rather difficult to provide a better expression for periodicity.

Historians have not been hesitant to point out that Newton's position was fraught with irony. Sometimes indeed the story of fits appears as nothing more than a long chain of irony. The man who discovered periodicity in optical phenomena discovered equally that periodicity was a wholly anomalous property in his own conception of light. The leading champion of the corpuscular view of light established the property which ultimately confirmed the opposite view. The man who rejected the wave conception of light provided his opponents with what they had not yet known how to provide themselves, an exposition of wave motion without which their conception was crudity itself. As Ronchi remarks, with a touch too much of drama perhaps, and smacking his lips a bit too obviously in satisfaction, Newton himself "had sharpened the weapon that would slay his theory."[24]

We must not allow historical research to conclude only in the stating of irony, however, and we must not permit the irony of Newton's dilemma to obscure the importance of the distinction he drew. "But whether this Hypothesis be true or false I do not here consider. I content my self with the bare Discovery, that the Rays of Light are by some cause or other alternately disposed to be reflected or refracted for many vicissitudes." The statement only repeats the very sentence with which Newton chose to begin the *Opticks*. "My Design in this Book is not to explain the Properties of Light by Hypotheses, but to propose and prove them by Reason and Experiments."[25] How familiar the words sound in Newton's mouth. Over thirty years earlier, Father Pardies referred to Newton's theory of colors as his "hypothesis." "I am content," Newton replied with manifest discontent, "that the Reverend Father calls my theory an hypothesis if it has not yet been proved to his satisfaction. But my design was quite different, and it seems to contain nothing else than certain

RICHARD S. WESTFALL

properties of light which, now discovered, I think are not difficult to prove, and which if I did not know to be true, I should prefer to reject as vain and empty speculation, than to acknowledge as my hypothesis."[26] Three years after the paper referred to by Pardies, the paper which demonstrated his theory of colors, Newton sent what he called the "Hypothesis of Light" to the Royal Society—to make his experiments and conclusions on thin films more intelligible, he said. "I shall not assume either this or any other Hypothesis," he stated, "not thinking it necessary to concerne my selfe whether the properties of Light, discovered by me, be explained by this or Mr Hook's or any other Hypothesis capable of explaining them."[27] Ten years after the *Opticks*, he expressed the same point of view in a context directed not to light but to gravity, in its definitive form—"*hypotheses non fingo.*"[28]

As everyone knows, the statement is simply not true if words retain their ordinary meaning. Newton did feign hypotheses and pretty bold ones at that. If pygmies be allowed to trifle with giants, let me venture to rephrase the famous statement to say what I understand Newton to have meant. *Hypotheses fingere nil opus est*—I do not need to feign hypotheses. I can construct hypotheses. I do construct hypotheses. I do not need to construct hypotheses. I do not need to construct hypotheses because the description of order in nature is in itself a valid aim of science. Student of Gassendi, ultimate heir of the skeptical crisis, Newton had explicitly denied the possibility of Descartes's confident dream, that reason might probe the farthest corners of nature, that wonder might be abolished in understanding and obscurity be bathed in light. Newton was convinced, on the contrary, that nature, as the product of an omniscient God, was in its ultimate reaches unknowable to finite man. The goal of science, then, could not be knowledge of the nature of things. Rather, knowledge of phenomena was the business of science, and an adequate description of phenomena was a valid conclusion of scientific research whether the cause of the order described were known or not. The fact that Newton had framed explanatory hypotheses, both in the case of the heterogeneity of light and in the case of gravity, does not compromise his distinction in the least in my opinion. The certainty of the description of phenomena, concluding in the heterogeneity of light in the one case, and in the law of universal gravitation in the other, was one thing; the speculative nature of hypotheses framed to explain the conclusions was another. Newton appears wholly justified in his insistence that the two not be confounded and treated as one.

The theory of fits occupies a unique position in regard to Newton's methodological statements. Periodicity was the most important discovery in the entire corpus of his scientific work for which in the end he had no explanatory hypothesis.[29] The history of optics since his day makes one long commentary on the validity of his describing periodicity whether or not he could explain it. Indeed, if I may be allowed to add one last irony to the earlier list, let me call attention to the historians of science whose enthusiastic applause for Newton's positivism applied to gravity has dissolved into pained bewilderment when they face exactly the same distinction applied to the fits of easy transmission.

There must be some reason, however, why a distinction which appears so just in one context should have been ignored so generally in another. I suggest that the reason is found in the different states of the sciences of celestial mechanics and optics at the end of the seventeenth century. The law of universal gravitation was a generalization of sweeping range, binding together all of the known phenomena of celestial motions and correlating them to the acceleration of gravity measured on the surface of the earth. Whatever the cause of gravity, be it known or unknown, here was a conclusion powerful beyond any other yet formulated in its ability quantitatively to correlate diverse phenomena. One might be hard pressed to describe periodicity as it appears in Newton's *Opticks* in similar terms. We must wait for Fresnel to find in optics a generalization analogous in scope to the law of universal gravity in mechanics. Newton had demonstrated periodicity in a limited number of phenomena. As yet he had not correlated it with anything else; it remained an anomaly in optics, a described phenomenon but not a coordinate part of a unified theory. As Ronchi clearly shows, the same can be said for polarity and for the phenomenon of diffraction. The essence of Ronchi's complaint then is Newton's failure to achieve a unified point of view embracing all of the known phenomena of light. Thoroughgoing champion of the wave conception of light that he is, Ronchi does not make it equally clear that the same and more can be said of Huygens. If it can be said of the two leaders, surely it can be said of optics as a whole at the end of the seventeenth century. I wish to argue that the theory of fits is symptomatic of the state of optics at the end of the seventeenth century, symptomatic, that is to say, of a state of chaos.

When Descartes took up the study of light early in the seventeenth century, the properties he had to consider were exactly those which had been known to optics for two thousand years. Beyond the phenomena immediately associated with sight—rectilinear propagation, reflection, refraction, color—only the capacity of light to heat bodies was known. Such were the phenomena for which Descartes had to account if he were successfully to include the most nonmechanical of appearances in his mechanical philosophy of nature. At the end of the seventeenth century, the publication of Huygens' *Treatise of Light* constituted one of the climactic achievements of the century's science of optics. It comes as something of a shock to list the range of phenomena for which Huygens attempted to account—rectilinear propagation, reflection, refraction, the capacity to heat, with the anisotropic refraction of iceland crystal added as a sort of cherry on top of the pudding. It is Descartes's list plus one and minus one. We might be inclined to say in Newton's favor that at least he undertook a more ambitious program, but in all fairness to Huygens if we examine, not what Newton undertook, but what he handled successfully, the list turns out to be identical to Huygens' with the addition of the interrelated issues of color and the heterogeneity of light.

Shall we then conclude that the science of optics stood still during the seventeenth century? Such a conclusion has all the normal attraction of the apparently outrageous with only the disadvantage of being untrue. On the latter point, alas, the evidence

RICHARD S. WESTFALL

appears conclusive—during the seventeenth century optics did not stand still. Perhaps however, its line of progress was somewhat other than we have believed. A century of vigorous experimentation discovered four new properties of light wholly unsuspected before—the heterogeneity of light, the polarity of light, the periodicity of some phenomena, and the capacity of light to be diffracted.[30] In 1700 knowledge of the properties of light was immeasurably deeper and broader than it had been in 1600. With one exception, the properties of light known at the beginning of the century were the properties associated with physiological optics; the properties discovered during the century became the foundation of physical optics. When we compare the state of optical knowledge to the state of optical theory, however, we are apt to conclude that during the seventeenth century optics had indulged in a game of intellectual serendipity. As in so much else, students of light in the seventeenth century began with the assumption that the phenomena were known. The problem was to lay bare the nature of light and to show its conformity to the principles laid down by the mechanical philosophy of nature. Experimenting with this goal in view, they discovered instead a clutch of properties they had not suspected, properties with which they were unable to deal, properties, one is tempted to say, they would have preferred not to discover. In his *Treatise of Light*, Huygens chose to ignore all four.[31] Newton successfully incorporated the heterogeneity of light into optics as the basis of a new theory of colors, and this aspect of his work has survived successive revolutions in optics substantially unchanged. For the other three he was unable to do much more than acknowledge them as empirical facts, except in so far as he saw in all further evidence of the heterogeneity of light—in which again optics has continued to follow him. But the heterogeneity of light was itself a principal obstacle to his assimilation of the other discoveries. From his earliest perception of it, apparently, heterogeneity had confirmed Newton's conviction of the corpuscular nature of light. In his paper of 1672, he allowed himself to forget the limits he intended to impose on his own discussion. "These things being so," he declared, referring to his conclusion that colors arise from the separation of rays, not from the modification of light, "it can be no longer disputed . . . whether Light be a Body. For, since Colours are the *qualities* of Light, having its Rays for their intire and immediate subject, how can we think those Rays *qualities* also, unless one quality may be the subject of and sustain another; which in effect is to call it *substance*."[32] Thirty years later in the 29th Query he asked: "Are not the Rays of Light very small Bodies emitted from shining Substances? For such Bodies will . . . be capable of several Properties, and be able to conserve their Properties unchanged in passing through several Mediums, which is another Condition of the Rays of Light."[33] In a passage of derisive condescension, Newton himself explained to Hooke how the heterogeneity of light could be reconciled with the wave conception.[34] Obviously he never took his own suggestion seriously, and with one exception the supporters of "wave" conceptions in the seventeenth century never picked it up. Suppose that they had and that with the idea of frequency they had reconciled the heterogeneity of light to the wave conception.

As the example of Malebranche demonstrates, the crisis in optics would not have been solved to any degree, for other problems beyond their capacity remained. The phenomenon of color in thin films was one; without a concept of interference wave motion was unable to explain it. Newton's dilemma, as expressed in the theory of fits, then, was the dilemma of optics as a whole, the embarrassment of riches perhaps, but riches all too analogous to Midas' gold, the dilemma of a science which knew more than its age allowed it to understand.

NOTES

[1] *Opticks,* based on 4th ed., (New York, 1952), Proposition XII, Book II, pp. 278–81. Proposition XIII (pp. 281–2) extends the theory of fits to explain partial reflection at refracting surfaces. "The reason why the Surfaces of all thick transparent Bodies reflect part of the Light incident on them, and refract the rest, is, that some Rays at their Incidence are in Fits of easy Reflexion, and others in Fits of easy Transmission." In his brief discussion Newton referred to Observation 24 of Book II, which was really a phenomenon of thin films, not of partial reflection. "And hence Light is in Fits of easy Reflexion and easy Transmission," he concluded, "before its Incidence on transparent Bodies. And probably it is put into such fits at its first emission from luminous Bodies, and continues in them during all its progress. For these Fits are of a lasting nature, as will appear by the next part of this Book."

[2] *Isaac Newton und seine physikalischen Principien,* (Leipzig, 1895), p. 296.

[3] *Storia della luce* (Bologna, 1939), pp. 138–9.

[4] Cambridge University Library, *Add. MS. 3996,* ff. 105v, 122–4. *Cf.* A. R. Hall, "Sir Isaac Newton's Note-book, 1661–65," *Cambridge Historical Journal,* 9 (1948), 239–50, and my article, "The Development of Newton's Theory of Colors," *Isis,* 53 (1962), 339–58.

[5] Cambridge University Library, *Add. MS. 3975,* pp. 1–20. *Cf.* A. R. Hall, "Further Optical Experiments of Isaac Newton," *Annals of Science,* 11 (1955), 27–43; and my article, "Development of Newton's Theory."

[6] See Newton's notes from the Micrographia in *Unpublished Scientific Papers of Isaac Newton,* eds. A. R. and M. B. Hall, (Cambridge, 1962), pp. 400–13.

[7] Cambridge University Library, *Add. MS. 3970.3,* ff. 350–53v. *Cf.* my article, "Isaac Newton's Coloured Circles Twixt Two Contiguous Glasses," *Archive for History of Exact Sciences,* 2, (1965), 181–96.

[8] Cambridge University Library, *Add. MS. 3970.3,* f. 350.

[9] Cambridge University Library, *Add. MS. 3975,* p. 10.

[10] *Cf.* my article, "Newton's Reply to Hooke and the Theory of Colors," *Isis,* 54 (1963), 82–96.

[11] In the *Principia* (Section VIII of Book II) the qualitative discussion of wave motion found in the "Hypothesis" was transformed into a quantitative analysis, the pioneering investigation of simple harmonic motion.

[12] *Cf.* "Hypothesis of Light." *The Correspondence of Isaac Newton,* ed. H. W. Turnbull, 3 vols. (Cambridge, 1959 continuing), *1,* 364; "De Aere et Aethere," *Unpublished Scientific Papers,* pp. 227–8.

[13] *Mathematical Principles of Natural Philosophy,* trans. Andrew Motte, ed. Florian Cajori (Berkeley, 1960), General Scholium to Section VI, Book II, pp. 325–6. I am taking the liberty of adding at this point an explanatory note that was not in the original version of the paper. Newton's interpretation of his experiment is to be judged against the background of his earlier statements on the aether. Thus in *De Aere et Aethere* he argued that the behavior of a pendulum in a vacuum proves the existence of an aether. "And that in a glass empty of air a pendulum preserves its oscillatory motion not much longer than in the open air, although that motion ought not to cease unless, when the air is exhausted, there remains in the glass something much more subtle which damps the motion of the bob." [*sic*] (*Unpublished Scientific Papers,* 227–8.) That is, the aether Newton had conceived was not a nineteenth century sort of aether, but an

aether offering resistance apparently much greater than that of the air, since the presence of air does not substantially reduce the time it takes a pendulum to come to rest. The English translation of the *Principia* is based on the later editions; the first edition must be held to give the closest approximation to Newton's interpretation of the experiment at the time he performed it. In the first edition the experiment was placed at the end, not of Section VI of Book II (The Motion and Resistance of Pendulous Bodies), but at the end of Section VII (The Motion of Fluids, and the Resistance Made to Projected Bodies). In the original version, what became the penultimate paragraph in the English translation had three sentences beyond the final one in the translation. The final sentence in the translation (differing slightly from the original version) says that the reasoning (that the resistance of the empty box in its internal parts is more than five thousand times less than the resistance on its external surface) depends on the supposition that the greater resistance of the full box arises from the action of some subtle fluid upon the included metal. "At causam longe aliam esse opinor. Nam tempora oscillationum pyxidis plenae minora sunt quam tempora oscillationum pyxidis vacuae, & propterea resistentia pyxidis plenae in externa superficie major est, pro ipsius velocitate & longitudine spatii oscillando descripti, quam ea pyxidis vacuae. Quod cum ita sit, resistentia pyxidum in partibus internis aut nulla erit aut plane insensibilis." (p. 353) The final sentence could hardly be more definite. Newton considered that the experiment disproved the existence of an aether.

[14] *Cf.* Partial draft of Preface and "Conclusio," *Unpublished Scientific Papers,* pp. 302–5, 321–33.

[15] *Opticks,* p. 339. *Cf.* Observation 1 of Book III, on diffraction: because a hair in a narrow beam of light casts a shadow broader than it would be if the light passed by on both sides without being deflected, "it follows that the Hair acts upon the Rays of Light at a good distance in their passing by it." (p. 319.) Book II of the *Opticks* is mostly identical to the "Discourse of Observations" sent to the Royal Society in 1675. Since the "Hypothesis of Light" accompanied the "Discourse," Newton tried to confine discussion of the aether to the "Hypothesis." Some references to it did creep in, however, and the scarcely noticeable changes that Newton introduced in the following passage when the *Opticks* was published suggest the shift in his point of view. What became Proposition III of Part III, Book II, contained this sentence in 1675: "Between the parts of opake or coloured bodies are many interstices, replenished with mediums of other densities, as water between the tinging corpuscles, wherewith any liquor is impregnated; air between the aqueous globules that constitute clouds or mists; and for the most part spaces void of both air and water; but yet perhaps replenished with some subtiler medium between the parts of hard bodies." (*Isaac Newton's Papers & Letters on Natural Philosophy,* ed. I. Bernard Cohen, Cambridge, Mass., 1958, p. 228.) In the *Opticks* the sentence was slightly altered: "Between the parts of opake and colour'd Bodies are many Spaces, either empty, or replenish'd with Mediums of other Densities; as Water between the tinging Corpuscles wherewith any Liquor is impregnated, Air between the aqueous Globules that constitute Clouds or Mists; and for the most part Spaces void of both Air and Water, but yet perhaps not wholly void of all Substance, between the parts of hard Bodies." (p. 249) The changes are interesting in their revelation of conflict in Newton's own attitude. On the one hand, he felt obliged to modify the direct reference to the aether and to admit the possibility that the spaces are wholly empty. On the other hand, he apparently found it difficult boldly to eliminate the aether altogether, at least in an optical context, and he referred vaguely to the possible presence of some "substance." At least two other passages in the "Discourse" of 1675 vaguely referring to the aether remained unchanged in the *Opticks—cf.* pp. 207–8, 262.

[16] *Ibid.,* Proposition X, Part III, Book II, pp. 270–1. The rigorous demonstration of the sine law is to be found in the *Principia,* Proposition XCIV, Book I, pp. 226–7.

[17] *Opticks,* Proposition IX, Part III, Book II, p. 269.

[18] *Ibid.,* Proposition VIII, p. 266. Proposition VIII contains a fairly long discussion of internal reflection (pp. 262–6) that cannot fail to remind the reader of the similar discussion in the "Hypothesis." In both discussions Newton stressed the impossibility of reflection being caused by the particles of reflecting bodies. The only significant difference in the two discussions lies in the reflecting mechanism assigned—the aether in 1675, forces in 1704.

Uneasily Fitful Reflections on Fits of Easy Transmission

[19] Obviously I use the word "discovery" to mean, not a speculative suggestion, but a demonstration that can be said to establish the property as fact. Hooke first suggested the periodicity of light, apparently basing his suggestion on an intuitive comprehension of the phenomena of thin films. Newton's careful measurements of the rings demonstrated the periodicity, not of light, but of the rings, and by implication of similar phenomena of thin films.

[20] *Opticks,* Proposition XII, Part III, Book II, pp. 280–1. Two passages in the queries added to the Latin edition of the *Opticks* in 1706 and therefore from substantially the same time as the first English edition demonstrate further the connection of periodicity with wave motion in Newton's mind. In what became Query 28 in later English editions he listed the arguments against wave conceptions of light. Among his arguments was the difficulty such conceptions have in explaining fits of easy reflection and transmission "unless perhaps one might suppose that there are in all Space two Aethereal vibrating Mediums, and that the Vibrations of one of them constitute Light, and the Vibrations of the other are swifter, and as often as they overtake the Vibrations of the first, put them into those Fits." (*Ibid.,* p. 364.) He went on of course to say that the simultaneous existence of two aethers was impossible. In what became Query 29, he argued in favor of the corpuscular conception. "Nothing more is requisite for putting the Rays of Light into Fits of easy Reflexion and easy Transmission," he suggested as part of the argument, "than that they be small Bodies which by their attractive Powers, or some other Force, stir up Vibrations in what they act upon, which Vibrations being swifter than the Rays, overtake them successively, and agitate them so by turns to increase and decrease their Velocities, and thereby put them into those Fits." (*Ibid.,* pp. 372–3.)

It is always assumed that Newton inserted the set of further queries, restoring an aether to his picture of nature, in the second English edition of the *Opticks* in order to provide a mechanical explanation of gravity. His continental opponents had raised the cry of "occult qualities"; the aether replied by explaining gravity in terms that were acceptable to mechanical philosophers—at least to those who did not read too closely. Newton's reasons may well have been such, but it is worth recalling also that the first new query, Query 17, applied the aether to the explanation of fits of easy reflection and easy transmission. What is more, the new aether was composed of particles mutually repelling each other and therefore subject to the mathematical analysis, given in the *Principia,* of wave motion in such fluids. In the "Hypothesis of Light" the waves had only been crudely imagined. Mathematical analysis then had shown that periodic waves might be transmitted through a fluid composed of particles mutually repelling each other. The new aether was exactly of that sort.

[21] *Oeuvres complètes,* pub. Société hollandaise des sciences, 22 vols., (La Haye, 1888–1950), 17, 341–8. The MS is dated November 1665. Huygens did not measure successive rings to demonstrate the fact of periodicity. He simply accepted periodicity, and having determined the thickness at the inner and outer rings, he divided the difference by the number of rings to arrive at the increment of thickness necessary for one ring to succeed another.

[22] *Opticks,* pp. 193–4. Near the end of Part II in Book II Newton included a general discussion of the phenomena of thin plates in relation to his theory of colors. Several of the experiments confirm the conclusion of Book I; from them it appears necessary "that every Ray have its proper and constant degree of Refrangibility connate with it, according to which its refraction is ever justly and regularly perform'd; and that several Rays have several of these degrees. And what is said of their Refrangibility may be also understood of their Reflexibility, that is, of their Dispositions to be reflected, some at a greater, and others at a less thickness of thin Plates or Bubbles; namely, that those Dispositions are also connate with the Rays, and immutable. . . ." As there is a "constant relation between Colours and Refrangibility . . ." so also "there appears to be the same constant relation between Colour and Reflexibility . . . Whence it follows, that the colorifick Dispositions of Rays are also connate with them, and immutable; and by consequence, that all the Productions and Appearances of Colours in the World are derived, not from any physical Change caused in Light by Refraction or Reflexion, but only from the various Mixtures or Separations of Rays, by virtue of their different Refrangibility or Reflexibility." (pp. 242–4.)

[23] *Ibid.,* pp. 280–1.

RICHARD S. WESTFALL

[24] *Storia*, p. 140.

[25] *Opticks*, p. 1.

[26] Newton to Oldenburg, 13 April 1672; *Correspondence, 1,* 142.

[27] Newton to Oldenburg, 7 December 1675; *Ibid., 1,* 363.

[28] *Principia*, General Scholium, p. 547. Two passages on method which first appeared in the queries added to the Latin edition of the *Opticks* in 1706 are relevant to my argument. In what became Query 28 in later English editions, Newton listed the arguments against the existence of an aether and noted that the authority of the ancient atomists supported its rejection since they tacitly attributed the gravity of atoms to some other cause than an aether. "Later Philosophers banish the Consideration of such a Cause out of natural Philosophy, feigning Hypotheses for explaining all things mechanically, and referring other Causes to Metaphysicks: Whereas the main Business of natural Philosophy is to argue from Phaenomena without feigning Hypotheses, and to deduce Causes from Effects, till we come to the very first Cause, which certainly is not mechanical . . ." (p. 369) In Query 31 he included a famous passage on method: "As in Mathematicks, so in Natural Philosophy, the Investigation of difficult Things by the Method of Analysis, ought ever to precede the Method of Composition. This Analysis consists in making Experiments and Observations, and in drawing general Conclusions from them by Induction, and admitting of no Objections against the Conclusions, but such as are taken from Experiments, or other certain Truths. For Hypotheses are not to be regarded in experimental Philosophy. . . . By this way of Analysis we may proceed from Compounds to Ingredients, and from Motions to the Forces producing them; and in general, from Effects to their Causes, and from particular Causes to more general ones, till the Argument end in the most general. This is the Method of Analysis: And the Synthesis consists in assuming the Causes discover'd, and establish'd as Principles, and by them explaining the Phaenomena proceeding from them, and proving the Explanations. In the two first Books of these Opticks, I proceeded by this Analysis to discover and prove the original Differences of the Rays of Light in respect of Refrangibility, Reflexibility, and Colour, and their alternate Fits of easy Reflexion and easy Transmission, and the Properties of Bodies, both opake and pellucid, on which their Reflexions and Colours depend. And these discoveries being proved, may be assumed in the Method of Composition for explaining the Phaenomena arising from them: An Instance of which Method I gave in the End of the first Book." (pp. 404–5.) Thus Newton specifically limited the fits of easy reflection and transmission to the realm of analytic discoveries.

[29] A tone of mathematical formalism pervades the section of the *Opticks* in which the theory of fits was announced. Newton attempted to find mathematical rules which correspond to the phenomena he had described, but rules which seem to defy any attempt to place a rational construction on them. Thus Propositions XV and XVI: "In any one and the same sort of Rays, emerging in any Angle out of any refracting Surface into one and the same Medium, the Interval of the following Fits of easy Reflexion and Transmission are either accurately or very nearly, as the Rectangle of the Secant of the Angle of Refraction, and of the Secant of another Angle, whose Sine is the first of 106 arithmetical mean Proportionals, between the Sines of Incidence and Refraction, counted from the Sine of Refraction." "In several sorts of Rays emerging in equal Angles out of any refracting Surface into the same Medium, the Intervals of the following Fits of easy Reflexion and easy Transmission are either accurately, or very nearly, as the Cube-Roots of the Squares of the lengths of a Chord, which sound the notes of an Eight, sol, la, fa, sol, la, mi, fa, sol, with all their intermediate degrees answering to the Colours of those Rays, according to the Analogy described in the seventh Experiment of the second Part of the first Book." (pp. 283–4) *Cf.* Observations 7 and 14 (pp. 203–5, 210–12) in which these relations were originally derived. In the corresponding passages of the "Discourse of Observations" in 1675, Newton gave the same experimental data but refrained from drawing such "laws." *Cf.* Observation 4 of Book III (p. 325) where he followed a similar procedure in regard to the diffraction patterns he had observed. The three cases cited in this note all seem deliberately to limit themselves to mathematical descriptions of empirical facts. According to my interpretation, the theory of fits pursued the same goal.

[30] Since no one in the seventeenth century recognized the dependence of diffraction on

periodicity, I have listed the two separately. Perhaps a fifth discovery of the seventeenth century ought to be included—the finite velocity of light as measured by Roemer. Although the great majority of opinion before Roemer supported the infinite velocity of light, finite velocity, as one of two alternatives which between them exhaust the range of possibilities, had not failed to be considered. It was implied in the treatment of light by the ancient atomists, for example. At any rate, the finite velocity of light met no serious opposition. In fact, it appears to have been more easily brought into harmony with the mechanical philosophy of the seventeenth century than infinite velocity; to Newton it was necessary, and to Huygens welcome.

   31 As I commented above, he had earlier accepted Hooke's suggestion of periodicity and had observed a pattern of rings strongly implying it, but his *Treatise of Light* explicitly rejected periodicity as a property of light. What we refer to as Huygens' wave theory was in reality a theory of nonperiodic pulses. Letters by Huygens discussing aberrations in lenses (to Mr. Smethwick, 9 October 1675; to Leibniz, 11 January 1680; to B. Fullenius, 12 December 1683 and 31 August 1684; *Oeuvres, 7, 512; 8, 257, 478, 534*) reveal that he accepted Newton's demonstration of heterogeneity. The preface to the *Treatise,* however, specifically excluded colors from the subjects to be treated, and heterogeneity was not mentioned in the *Treatise* itself. Likewise diffraction was not mentioned, despite its seeming relevance to Newton's assertion that a wave theory was impossible because of rectilinear propagation. As to polarity, Huygens' famous solution of the double refraction of iceland crystal dealt only with the anisotropic refraction. When the observed fact of polarity came up, Huygens acknowledged its difficulty and refused to deal with it.

   32 Newton to Oldenburg, 6 February 1672; *Correspondence, 1, 100.*

   33 *Opticks,* p. 370.

   34 Newton to Oldenburg, 11 June 1672; *Correspondence, 1, 174.* Perhaps the immutability of the heterogeneous properties appeared as a further obstacle to Newton; after all, motions are always changing, and it may have been difficult to see why waves should not change their lengths also. Be that as it may, Newton's discussion of polarity in the *Opticks* exudes his satisfaction in having found another original property of light and one that could not be reduced to wave motion. Query 25 deals with anisotropic refraction. "The unusual Refraction," it concludes, "is therefore perform'd by an original property of the Rays." (p. 358) Query 26 discusses what we call polarity, concluding that the sides of the rays of light are endued with original properties. "To explain the unusual Refraction of Island Crystal by Pression or Motion propagated, has not hitherto been attempted (to my knowledge) except by *Huygens,* who for that end supposed two several vibrating Mediums within that Crystal. But when he tried the Refractions in two successive pieces of that Crystal, and found them such as is mention'd above; he confessed himself at a loss for explaining them. For Pressions or Motions, propagated from a shining Body through an uniform Medium, must be on all sides alike; whereas by those Experiments it appears, that the Rays of Light have different Properties in their different Sides. He suspected that the Pulses of Æther in passing through the first Crystal might receive certain new Modifications, which might determine them to be propagated in this or that Medium within the second Crystal, according to the Position of that Crystal. But what Modifications those might be he could not say, nor think of any thing satisfactory in that Point. And if he had known that the unusual Refraction depends not on new Modifications, but on the original and unchangeable Dispositions of the Rays, he would have found it as difficult to explain how those Dispositions which he supposed to be impress'd on the Rays by the first Crystal, could be in them before their Incidence on that Crystal, and in general, how all Rays emitted by shining Bodies, can have those Dispositions in them from the beginning. To me, at least, this seems inexplicable, if Light be nothing else than Pression or Motion propagated through Æther." (pp. 363–4). Too bad for Newton; Fresnel handled that objection as well.

RICHARD S. WESTFALL

THOMAS KUHN

Comment

The invitation to comment on Professor Westfall's paper has given me great pleasure. Partly that is because I am a long-standing admirer of his work on Newton. Equally it is because the invitation has taken me back to a period and subject matter closely associated with my entry into the history of science almost two decades ago but with which I have had nothing at all to do since. The return has provided an opportunity to discover something of what has happened to this part of the field since my own attention turned elsewhere. Anyone doubtful about the rapid rate at which the profession has been maturing would profit from a similar experience. No conference at this level of scholarship and sophistication could have been imagined twenty or even ten years ago. The change is another part of what we are here gathered to celebrate.

Turning now to my assigned task, Dr. Westfall's challenging analysis of a famous passage in Newton's *Opticks*, I take it that his paper develops three major themes which I shall consider in order of decreasing centrality. First is an explanation of what Newton meant to convey when introducing the phrases "fits of easy reflection" and "fits of easy transmission"; second is an analysis of Newton's reasons for introducing that special phraseology; and third is a discussion of the state of optics at the end of the seventeenth century.

About the first and most central of these themes I can do little more than express complete and enthusiastic agreement. On this subject my remarks will be correspondingly brief but brevity should not disguise my sense of the importance of what Dr. Westfall is saying. He argues that there is nothing strange, or odd, or inconsistent about Newton's resort to the terminology of "fits." On the contrary, Newton was here doing what he had repeatedly done elsewhere in the course of his scientific career. He was substituting what he took to be a mere description, derivable in its entirety from experiment, for a hypothetical explanation in terms of corpuscular or aethereal mechanism. If I understood it correctly, this is the distinction between "doctrine" and "hypothesis" introduced earlier in this conference by Professor and Mrs. Hall.

The most relevant parallel in Newton's career is, of course, his abandonment, both in his first optical paper of 1672 and in Book I of the *Opticks*, of his corpuscular view of light and its replacement by a description couched entirely in terms of rays. That substitution is what enabled him—somewhat disingenuously, I think—to insist during controversy with Hooke and others that he had advanced no hypothesis but was merely describing the outcome of experiment. To that parallel should be added Newton's treatment of gravity and other intercorpuscular forces during the years before the preparation of the *Principia* and again after 1710. On the one hand, the behavior of forces between particles was directly deducible from observation. To supply a name and a force law was not, Newton insisted, to indulge in hypotheses. On the other hand, having discovered the existence and behavior of such forces from experiment, one could still hope to explain their cause, a subject on which Newton did invent hypotheses relating sometimes to his thoughts about the aether and at others to the omnipresence of God. Dr. Westfall urges that we set Newton's "fits" into this context, recognizing that the term itself may be borrowed from standard medical literature. The suggestion is most illuminating. It facilitates understanding of Newton's optical writings, and it shows once again the considerable consistency of his career.

Professor Westfall also argues, however, that Newton resorted to the terminology of "fits" because he was forced to abandon aether mechanisms by a direct confrontation with nature in the ingenious pendulum experiment reported in Book II of the *Principia*. About this part of his argument I am extremely uneasy. Clearly Newton did fall silent about, and may well have abandoned, aether mechanisms for a time which included the preparation of the first, but not the second, edition of the *Principia*. His own experimentation may have provided some of his reasons for doing so, though I have yet to be entirely convinced. But I am very doubtful that experiments with pendulums spoke against the aether at all and am quite certain they provided no categorical evidence. For this large divergence between our views, two differences in textual analysis are responsible. Dr. Westfall and I read Newton's discussion of the pendulum experiment quite differently. In addition, we are at odds about the construction to be placed on the three extra sentences deleted from that discussion between the first and the second editions. [1]

Since the texts are easily accessible and interested readers will need to examine them in any case, I shall somewhat condense the technical argument. Newton constructed a special pendulum whose bob was a box, and he compared the rate at which its oscillations were damped when the box was empty and when it was filled with heavy metal. If there were an aether, he indicated, it should offer more resistance to the full than to the empty box, for the latter would be far more porous to the aether. Dr. Westfall tells us that, since Newton found the full box requiring almost 78 swings to decay as much as the empty box did in one, he was forced to conclude that there could be no aether. Thereafter, until about 1710, he had no recourse to the aether.

But this analysis of the experiment is not Newton's. He tells us that the full box is just 78 times as heavy as the empty one and that the inertia (with which it overcomes both air and aether resistance) is therefore also 78 times as great. It follows, according to Newton, that in the absence of an increase in aether resistance the heavy box must take just 78 times as long to decay as the light one. In practice it takes only 77 swings to descend to the mark reached by the empty box after one. That difference between 77 and 78 measures the effect of the aether. Or at least it does, says Newton, if we suppose that the effect is due to the action of the aether on the interior of the box. On this supposition Newton computes what he describes as the ratio of the resistance due to the outside of the empty box to that due to the inside. His result is 5928:1, a very large ratio, but not surprisingly so. The planets do not spiral down out of their orbits, and a feather falls as fast as a coin in an evacuated receiver. [2] Aether resistance must be a very small effect.

In the second and subsequent editions Newton's argument ends at this point. Clearly it does not necessitate the existence of an aether—we shall shortly discover a means of evading it. But it does make the aether more likely, which is presumably why Newton left it in this form for those editions of the *Principia* in which he did make reference to aether mechanisms. In this form it can only be an argument, though surely not a very forceful one, in favor of the aether.

That being so, it is not surprising that Newton added to the conclusion of his argument in the first edition where he made no reference to the aether mechanisms he had apparently abandoned for the time. After reminding his readers that his reasoning depended upon the supposition that the greater resistance of the full box arises from the action of some subtle fluid upon the included metal, Newton continued: "But I suppose that the cause [of the slower damping of the heavy bob] is very different. For the times of oscillation of the full box are less than those of the empty one, and therefore the resistance to the external surface of the full box is greater, by virtue of its velocity and the length of its oscillations, than to the empty box. From which it follows that the resistance [due] to the internal parts of the box is either zero or entirely insensible." [3] These sentences surely do show, if further demonstration is needed, that Newton was making no use of aether mechanisms when he wrote the first edition of the *Principia*. They do not, however, even hint that Newton had derived an argument against such mechanisms from the experiment. On the contrary, Newton is here simply explaining away a phenomenon which, in the absence of some alternate explanation, would have provided an argument for the aether. No argument of the sort he gives can, in principle, prove a null result. In practice, Newton, who was elsewhere circumstantial in his experimental reporting, does not say that or how he actually measured the relative periods of oscillation of the two pendulums or give the results of such measurement. Nor does he indicate how those measurements would be used in computation to reduce (perhaps to nothing) the previously observed difference between 77 and 78 oscillations. He has certainly shown that some or all of the small observed discrepancy may be due to a nonaetheral factor, but he has not used the pendulum to disprove the aether. [4] I conclude that the pendulum experiment Dr. Westfall cites cannot have played the key role in which he casts it. As for the more general question of the role of pendulums in Newton's thought about aether mechanisms, I ask for a verdict of not proven. After all, we have already noted that no special considerations are needed to explain Newton's resort to "fits."

This brings me to my last point, the one with which Professor Westfall's paper begins and ends. Early in his presentation Dr. Westfall suggests that the problem of "fits" is symptomatic of a deep crisis in optics at the end of the seventeenth century. In concluding he expands that theme. During the seventeenth century, he suggests, progress in optics was predominantly experimental, and its result was, through a process like serendipity, to disclose a large variety of new optical phenomena many of which could not be assimilated to existing theory. It is this failure to fit which Dr. Westfall believes caused a crisis.

About the failure to fit, he is, of course, entirely right. Given the advantage of hindsight, knowing the work of Young and Fresnel a century later, it is clear to us that a crisis could (some would say, should) have resulted from the progress of optical experimentation during the seventeenth century. But crisis is, I take it, always in the eye of the beholder, and I am not aware that the men who actually worked in optics at the end of the seventeenth century saw one at all. There was a crisis in optics, and it arose for precisely the reasons Dr. Westfall specifies, but not for almost another hundred years. The clearest sign of its recognition is the prize offered by the French Academy at the start of the nineteenth century for a paper on polarization effects, a prize which Malus won and which was closely associated with Fresnel's decision to undertake optical research. Recognizing, with Dr. Westfall, that the problems which evoked this crisis had been accessible since the late seventeenth century, one may well wonder how he can possibly be wrong. Why was the crisis so long in coming?

If that question demands an explanation of the timing of the actual crisis, then I think we are insufficiently informed about eighteenth century optical research to provide even an intelligent guess. It is, however, possible to suggest why the crisis was postponed beyond the end of the seventeenth century and the early decades of the eighteenth. As Dr. Westfall implies, optics in the seventeenth century was a very old science with a great many traditional concerns. Among them were the problems of refraction, of prismatic colors, of the rainbow, and of vision. Most of these topics accrued to the optical tradition in antiquity and were much discussed both in the Middle Ages and the Renaissance. Some progress had been made with them, but not vast amounts. It was only in the seventeenth century that this constellation of concerns responded rapidly and together to the work of men like Kepler, Snel, Descartes, and Newton himself. Viewed in terms of these problems, which for many practitioners virtually defined the field, seventeenth-century progress in optics was not purely experimental. On the contrary, the progress was in the understanding of optical phenomena, in optical theory, and it was quite comparable in kind, though not in extent, to the progress made in mechanics.

If that is so, then we need not be surprised to find that the men who worked in optics at the end of the century were little concerned about their inability to fit into their theories all the details of the new experiments which the century had also produced. They could have—and I suspect they did—believe that success would continue as it had begun, that closer scrutiny both of theory and of experiment would suffice to bring the two into line. Why, or even whether, that attitude lasted for a hundred years, I do not know. But that no crisis should have been felt—which is the same as saying that there was no crisis—at the end of the seventeenth century seems to me only normal scientific behavior.

NOTES

[1] When these remarks were delivered orally, I had not yet compared editions of the *Principia,* for Dr. Westfall's paper, before the instructive revisions in note 13, referred only to the Motte-Cajori translation. I am very grateful to Professor Guerlac for calling to my attention the probable importance of such a comparison.

[2] These observations, well known to the seventeenth century, make me skeptical of Dr. Westfall's suggestion, in his revised note 13, that Newton conceived of "an aether offering resistance much greater than that of the air." The sentence he quotes does suggest this view indirectly, but it does not enforce it, and I doubt that it will, in isolation, bear the weight. That point, however, is not the one mainly at issue here. My argument relies only on the assumption that aether resistance, if measurable at all, is very small.

[3] My translation. The original is quoted in Dr. Westfall's note 13.

[4] There is a further oddity here, and it suggests a speculative reconstruction. The additional sentences which appear only in the first edition reads like an afterthought appended to a text like that given in the second and subsequent editions. It is hard to see why Newton should have cast the main argument as he did if he were ultimately going to deny its significance. Just possibly these sentences were an afterthought. Newton mentions that he no longer has his original notes on the experiment and is proceeding from memory. He might have performed the experiment and written up a description like that in the later editions of the *Principia* at a time when he still believed in aether mechanisms and thought the experiment made them more likely.

Since this manuscript was prepared, a more fundamental way of eliminating this difficulty and others has been suggested to me by Mr. R. S. Turner. He believes that Dr. Westfall and I may be misunderstanding Newton's intent in the pendulum experiment. It is not, he thinks, the aether itself which is at stake but rather the question of whether the aether, if it does exist, is able freely to pervade the interiors of dense bodies. That is, I now realize, all Newton says the experiment deals with, and the point would concern him since he had previously speculated that aether density must be greatly attenuated inside gross bodies. This interpretation, which I now find very plausible, has the considerable merit of explaining why Newton computes, not aether resistance itself, but only the ratio of internal to external resistance (and for the empty box, at that). He is concerned to show only that all, or virtually all, resistance is external, whether due to the air or to the aether. If that is right, then the differences between the first and subsequent editions of the *Principia* are relatively minor, which explains what is otherwise rather odd behavior of Newton's.

THOMAS KUHN

PIERRE COSTABEL

Newton's and Leibniz' Dynamics

Translated by J. M. Briggs, Jr.

ANOVER IS PREPARING TO CELEBRATE THE 250TH ANNIVERSARY OF THE death of Leibniz, but one need not here consult the calendar to remind us of the commemorations of 1966. One could not speak for very long about Newton without mentioning his great rival, and this has already been done. Perhaps it would be fitting, however, to devote this communication more specifically to an attempt at a systematic comparison that would go beyond mere casual observations.

It can be only an attempt, because any other pretension would be vain and ridiculous on our part. That I have written on Leibniz and dynamics has determined the choice of subject proposed to me. But everything considered, the limitations imposed by the subject are neither troublesome nor artificial.

We have good reason to think that the state of the history of mathematics does not yet permit the last word to be said about the quarrel over the infinitesimal calculus; and in the development of the thought of these two great rival thinkers the science of motion has been of such importance that it would not be profitable to judge them on the basis of that quarrel.

We are, moreover, entering upon a domain which has been the object of recent research and we must make clear immediately that our aim is less to consider the enormous amount of scholarship which is at present being undertaken than to attempt to define some general perspectives. The history of science admits of diverse levels and the study of manuscript sources which have been misunderstood or badly exploited is very important. But according to the old adage, sometimes one cannot see the forest for the trees. And as far as the proposed subject is concerned, it seems to us that it would not be a bad idea to undertake once more a comparison of Newton and Leibniz based on the most accessible and best known sources.

The very name dynamics is original with Leibniz. That is something that cannot be taken from the Hanoverian philosopher. One can speak of Newtonian dynamics only because the vocabulary has undergone an evolution during three centuries in accordance with the wear and tear experienced by words in general use.

Without doubt Newton declared in the preface to the first edition of the *Principia* that he was interested in the study of motion resulting from any forces whatever, but the demonstrative science which he thought he was founding he called *Mechanica rationalis*. One should not hasten to change the name on the pretext that people today no longer use the name rational mechanics although everybody still uses the term dynamics to designate in a general sense the aspect taken on by the science of motion when it is organized around the idea of force. The insistence with which Leibniz, the inventor of "dynamics," claimed for himself recognition as founder of an *entirely new* science, warns us that it would be good to take a close look at what is involved.

Leibniz' new science was born between 1686 and 1692, while he was militantly engaged in the anti–Cartesian movement, and also discussing the possibility of ecumenism with his theological friends. These two concerns intersect at a particularly important point. It is difficult to be sure where polemics leave off and science begins. But whatever Leibniz' profound position with respect to eucharistic dogma, his declarations leave no doubt about the help he thought he was bringing to Catholic orthodoxy. The heretic is not the one people think, and the Cartesian philosophy of extension as the essence of matter is not capable of taking into account a real presence which remains intact even when matter is broken apart and dispersed. In 1691–92 Leibniz' offensive, which was aimed at conquering Paris, developed simultaneously on several fronts, but dynamics was a key element and Bossuet himself was informed of these arguments in the middle of debates relating to the Council of Trent. Bossuet was informed, and agreed, that a sound natural philosophy consists in making of matter something more than extension, of putting in it an active principle, a *dynamis*. So there was no doubt about it. The thing that gave Leibniz his awareness of launching something novel was not the fact of introducing a new word but of being the first to recognize a *reality* until then unknown.

In this regard he expressed himself with all the clarity one could desire, distinguishing carefully between the language and the coherence of the ideas he wished to link together. His criticism of Descartes is not based on the formal definition of force as quantity of motion, for each man is free to call force whatever he wishes on condition that the body of definitions be clear and unambiguous. But contrary to Descartes's belief, the quantity of absolute motion never enters into a law of conservation and the corresponding definition of force loses for this reason all theoretical or practical utility. The definition does not go beyond words. In order to avoid such a blunder, it is necessary to begin with a good metaphysics, that is to say, by the negation of all creation *ex nihilo* in the phenomenal world. And that is why Leibniz' living force, the diminution or loss of which is accounted for during each instant of actual or potential motion, is something quite different from a mere word. Without doubt the formal definition of it says nothing about how it is coordinated with the other notions of the science of motion, mass and velocity, but one can be sure beforehand that whatever be nature's response on the form of this coordination, the new idea is independently meaningful. And that is also why Leibniz can declare that he knows nothing more real than force.

Leibniz' dynamics is therefore not a neutral elaboration with regard to its primary constitutive ideas. Dynamics is so named only because its author claims in the name of metaphysics to enter the field by making the *dynamis* the primary idea.

There is nothing of the kind in Newton's *Principia,* which had proposed to the intellectual world a "natural philosophy" stripped of the very metaphysics which

Leibniz was at the time pursuing. It has been said that insofar as the *Principia* publicly propounds a deliberately didactic discussion, it is not capable of taking into account the genesis of the author's doctrine; and it is not our intention to slight the patient research which can reconstruct the long chain of development culminating in this masterly work. From the point of view we have chosen to take here, we should like simply to remark that the form in which an author's ideas are expressed means more to us than the history of his doubts or his meandering steps. And when it comes to judging the orientation that Newton gives mechanics, it would be strange indeed to take exception to our reliance on his most basic writing.

Now the preface to the first edition, already cited, concedes nothing in clarity to Leibniz' work. The whole difficulty of (natural) philosophy, we are told, consists in investigating natural forces, *vires naturales*, through the phenomena of motion; one can then "demonstrate" by the same forces other phenomena. This means that the science of motion occupies a chief place in the scheme of knowledge just as it means that the essential character of the science lies in the homogeneity of its subject matter. At the level of phenomena, motion has the privilege of revealing, thanks to mathematical analysis, a universally transposable structure.

In this "method of philosophy," *huic philosophandi modo,* the question of knowing if force is real or not, if it is a primary notion or not, is not formally posed nor does it emerge. The question is one of "deriving" a way of arguing from mechanical phenomena translated into mathematical terms, and in which the "demonstrative" scheme should be applicable throughout. The mechanics of Newton is truly a *Mechanica rationalis,* but it is not dynamics in the sense of Leibniz.

This is not a subtle or uninteresting distinction. For the stake underlying the debate is nothing less than the unity of science, surely a very old problem, but one that undeniably still dogged opinion in the middle of the seventeenth century. Descartes testifies to this, particularly in his lengthy response to Morin's objections of 13 July 1638. Descartes testifies to this, clearly, at the same time that he is promulgating a method. His critic tried to convict him of "circular logic" and for Descartes it is an occasion to express himself as he has not done earlier. First, to explain effects by a cause and then to prove the cause by the effects is not circular logic because there is a great difference between *explaining* and *proving*. Further, to fit the same cause to several effects is not as easy as it would seem. To succeed in doing so leads to a strong presumption that this cause is certainly the true one. Finally, to use this result to prove *several other* effects is to increase the certainty of the cause. Thus, far from going in circles, Descartes knows that he has on the contrary redrawn the map of research. All that has been done until then in physics, he says, is to *try to imagine several causes* to explain phenomena, but men have succeeded only in piling up a bric-a-brac of real qualities, substantial forms, of elements and like things, *of which the number is nearly infinite.* The *Monde* of Descartes on the other hand is prepared with a great economy of principles, following rational steps to which the *Regulae* alone hold the key. But many in Descartes's circle—Renaudot, for example, in his *2ème Centurie du Bureau d'Adresse* (1634)—debated the question. Is science a *compendium,* or is there rather a fundamental unity in its diverse chapters? The great majority of those who cannot accept a negative answer to this question are divided as to the mode of the unity and many are inclined to look for this mode at the summit, that is to say, in metaphysics. Leibniz, putting to good use a half century of intense scientific activity, is the fundamental champion of this way of thinking. Newton prolongs, clarifies, and completes the Cartesian movement for which "mathematical demonstrations teach more how to discover truth than to disguise it."

At our present level of discussion, this affirmation should not cause any dismay. In whatever way Newton knew and understood Cartesian thought, he came into a world where the general way of thinking was being transformed with respect to the problem that we have just stated, and he furthered the transformation by drawing up some characteristic guides. For example, he placed the law of inertia, completely explicated, at the beginning of his mechanics. For another example, he gave a logical status to the idea of the composition or resolution of motion which permitted making this idea a solid instrument of mathematical analysis. Now if that is something new, certainly it is in the sense that he completed the sketch of something already sufficiently clear in certain parts of Descartes's works. However severely Alexandre Koyré may have criticized Descartes's particular formulation of the law of inertia, the fact remains that Descartes recognized this as the great law of nature; that Descartes's *Dioptrique* gave rise to so many contradictory commentaries from then until now does not mean that the book does not illustrate the masterly manner of the analogical method of *Regula* VIII. Descartes accords a central role to the laws of inertia and composition of motion in defining the isomorphisms that permit one to pass from mechanical phenomena to the other *natural powers.* From Descartes to Newton the same fundamental climate of rationality at the level of phenomena was affirmed, and the same role of the revelation of formal structure was assigned to the science of motion. .

Not so Leibniz. What he retains from Descartes to criticize and transform is the law of the conservation of motion. He is not interested in the law of inertia and the composition of motion is for him only a corollary of a theorem on the conservation of the *quantity of progress* of the center of mass of a body. He looks beyond phenomena for the fundamentals of his science, and if he is also a brilliant mathematician who could exhibit the rationality implicit in the interrelations of the principles, he has a predilection for the idea of conservation because it is the most appropriate for explaining the stability of invisible realities.

Will it be said that this way of looking at things is too remote and insufficiently attentive to details? It is quite certain that a desire to compare Newton's mechanics with Leibniz' requires a more precise study of specific points.

Is not the law of inertia truly a conservation law, and is not the opposition we have underlined purely artificial? The question cannot fail to be asked. The permanence of the state of rest or of uniform rectilinear motion of which Newton says, in Definition III, that it is the underlying fact of the inertia of matter, seems to refer to a conserved reality since there is also mentioned a "power of resistance to change" and a *vis insita* which resides in matter. But the author takes care to assure us that these are only other ways of "conceiving," and one must ask if it is not also a question of more suggestive ways of expressing oneself at the pedagogical level. Definition III actually concludes on the affirmation of the relativity of motion as well as of rest, and shows a clear awareness, which is possibly confused but certainly there, of the nature of the difficulty. A relative state varies according to the point of view from which one considers it. How can this be explained? To say that the states of rest and uniform rectilinear motion need no cause to persist thus corresponds to a requirement following from the definition of an equivalence-class with regard to the relative states. That is merely reason and logic, certainly not metaphysics.

Is this way of reading Newton too modern to be true? No doubt the best way to determine this is to pursue the reading of Newton. Definition IV in fact considers the *vis impressa,* the instantaneous and ephemeral action capable of changing the state of relative motion. After the fleeting instant of its intervention, the rule of perseverance again takes over. The *vis impressa* acts by a sudden mutation which gives rise to a new velocity, *combining* with the old to form a new inertial motion. Up to this point we have only followed the text, step by step. But now a question cannot be side-stepped. We clearly understand the precautions taken to distinguish the *vis insita* from the *vis impressa,* yet the former in some way absorbs the change by composition with the latter. The former is inertia, a plasticity which yields to the latter as wax yields to a metal pressed into it, or as one power resists another power. The language of force used by Newton for the law of inertia does not therefore correspond to the conception of a thing which truly exists. It is a language which is useful for didactic expression and for the linking of propositions, but it is only a language.

Does the *vis impressa,* moreover, fit into a realistic philosophy? We have already described a characteristic tone that would scarcely lead to a positive answer to this question. The *vis impressa* is, let us repeat, instantaneous and ephemeral. Its effect is manifested and destroyed at the same time. Certainly, even though the fact is not mentioned but is used in what follows, the *vis* can be in some way renewed at each instant and thus persist in time. The fact remains that the fundamental attribute of its existence is lacking. It is only a clever fiction. For, if the states of rest and of uniform rectilinear motion constitute an equivalence-class whose members require no cause for their persistence, nevertheless these states are distinguishable when one refers them to the same reference point; more generally, under these circumstances, the state of relative motion can be infinitely varied. Thus considered, a cause is needed to explain the passage from one state to another, but since the states of the equivalence-class need no cause to persist, it is also necessary that this cause be without duration and take on the aspect of a sudden mutation.

This mutation is made manifest by a velocity, that is to say, a direction, a sense, and a magnitude. Is this not enough to give the body something real, however fleeting it is? In this regard the law of composition must certainly make clear to us what is in Newton's mind. It is useful to note that in Corollary I of the three primary laws of motion (*axiomata sive leges*), the composition deals only with the *vis impressae*. When one carefully reads the development of the elegant justification of the rule of the parallelogram, one notices that the crux of the reasoning is as follows: a *vis impressa* does not alter the motion in the direction parallel to that which it could impress [even] when the motion takes place along a different route; this is so whether the body to which the force is applied already has an inertial motion, whether it be acted on simultaneously by another force, or both. Thus, on the one hand it would be incorrect to conclude that Corollary I refers only to composition of rectilinear and uniform motions, a purely kinematic rule. The notion of force is a major factor linked to parallel motion [i.e., to a motion in a given direction whatever the other influences on the body]. On the other hand it would be wrong to say that the *vis impressa* truly has a direction and a sense. It does not disturb a direction and a sense [already present] and this is not entirely the same thing.

As for the magnitude of the velocity impressed by the *vis impressa,* it is remarkable that at no point does the author feel the need to be more precise about it. Without a doubt this is a relative magnitude, depending essentially on the reference frame brought to bear, and Newton needs no lesson from anyone in this respect. But one would nonetheless expect Newton to say that the above–mentioned impressed velocity is very small, if not infinitely small, with respect to the velocities of the inertial motions. One would expect this because one knows the subsequent role assigned by Newton to acceleration and the progressive deviation from uniform motion. But Newton does not say it. And if he does not say it, it is because he thinks it unnecessary to say, not because it goes without saying but because it has no relevance. Whatever the common standard adopted for the motions in question, the propositions advanced have their own independent and mathematical consistency.

There is certainly lacking in our opinion a clear awareness of the commutative and associative axioms required to justify the invariance of the composition of *vis impressae* with respect to the fundamental equivalence-class, but what is undeniable is that this composition cannot be thought of as a simultaneous conjoining of the motions because it [i.e., the composition of *vis impressae*] is distinguishable from the compound motion itself and because *vis impressa* by definition does not possess the independent reality of a body.

There can be no question here of following the applications that Newton made of the law of composition of *vis impressae.* One must simply remember that he found in it the key to the mathematical treatment of numerous mechanical problems which he investigated. For he did in fact investigate numerous problems, and, for those who are commemorating the present tricentennial, primarily the problems of

PIERRE COSTABEL

the moon and the planets. And it is in these laborious investigations, pursued at such length, that he succeeded in giving a mechanical meaning to the curvature of a trajectory. This result, it seems to us, is the most significant.

The story has often been told of his spontaneous answer to Halley in August 1684, concerning the trajectory of the planets according to the hypothesis of solar attraction inversely proportional to the square of the distance. "An ellipse."—"And how do you know?"—"Why, I calculated it." And the story adds that Newton could not put his hands on his calculation, but that he began over again a little time later. It is permissible to doubt the interpretation which Newtonian hagiography gives this episode. What one cannot doubt, because Book I of the *Principia* is very explicit in this regard, is the calculation of the central acceleration of motion along a conic with respect to the focus; but Corollary I of Propositions XI, XII, and XIII, which formulates the converse problem, does not admit of any calculation. This corollary consists in linking together two new propositions. The first is purely geometric in nature: given a focus, the tangent at a given point, and the curvature at that point, a conic section is completely determined. The second is mechanical in nature: two orbits which touch one another and are traversed with equal velocities and equal centripetal forces must be identical. In the two cases it is more a question of intuition than of demonstration and one would be wrong in thinking that Newton knew at that time how to formulate and resolve problems through the integration of differential equations. But two comments are in order. On the one hand, Corollary I defines precisely the structure of a mathematical demonstration and a program which is capable of being eventually carried out; on the other hand, it is clear that the language of centripetal force has only a pragmatic value. What is important is the curvature of the trajectory as a function of the velocity and the acceleration.

Pragmatic value, however, should not be minimized. If Newton is led to "suspect" that universal attraction can be the basis of fruitful analogies and make it possible to realize the construction of a mechanics capable of unifying the science of nature, it is because he tested the fidelity of the language of force. He attempted to settle everything possible concerning the different types of "non-manual powers" that the ancients did not know of or neglected and which were being discussed by those around him, in particular the *"vis elastica"* that the Marquise du Châtelet was so happily inspired to translate as "electric force," thus committing a curious and instructive error. Everywhere Newton made sure that the formal scheme derived from his laws was eminently comprehensive, and therefore worthy of forming part of the framework of Natural Philosophy.

But what Newton did in this fashion is precisely what Leibniz did not believe himself obliged to do. Leibniz solved several problems, notably that of the curve of most rapid descent, and he did so with a similar mathematical apparatus, making use also of the notion of acceleration. He did so by calling *force morte* what Newton called *vis impressa*. He did not, however, attempt to undertake a systematic investigation. And if the point of furthest advance reached in his *Essay de Dynamique,* of 1698, does open wide a fruitful path for mathematical analysis based on conservation principles, through the idea of minimum "action," this is no more than an essay oriented toward generalities and not toward the proof of applications. Leibniz doubted the laws of Kepler and he left to others, to Varignon and John Bernoulli, the task of applying his own calculus, the differential and integral calculus, to centrally accelerated motions; to the demonstration in 1710-11 of the converse envisaged in the Newtonian corollary we have referred to above.

In order to answer "M. le Chevalier Newton" he wrote on 9 April 1716 to the Abbe Conti: "As far as problems are concerned, I was careful not to propose any to Mr. Newton, for I would not have wished to be so busied when people proposed them to me; we can dispense with that at our age, but we have friends who can make up for us what we lack." The meaning of what he says is interesting; we limit ourselves simply to noting that Leibniz did not wait until the end of his life to assume an attitude that conformed to the awareness of himself and his role as a philosopher.

One would be quite wrong to imagine that Leibniz did not attempt to understand Newton. He declared further in his letters to Conti: "I do not fail to value highly the physicomathematical meditations of Mr. Newton . . . I strongly approve of his method of drawing from phenomena whatever one can without preconceiving anything. . . . I am very much for experimental philosophy . . . ," but he reproves Newton for going too far in his task. "Mr. Newton cites no experiment nor sufficient reason for the existence of atoms and void, or for mutual attraction generally." And because of the fact "that one still does not know perfectly and in detail how gravity or elastic force or magnetic force are produced . . ." one is then tempted to indulge in bad metaphysics. "I believe that the metaphysics used by these gentlemen is a *narrow one* [sic] and their mathematics easily *arrivable* [sic]."

According to Leibniz it is much better to begin by building a good metaphysics. The metaphysics which "relates to dynamics or the doctrine of forces" could not be "anything else but the conservation of the nature of things as created" which permits the "demonstration" of the fundamentals. That task is for great minds, and that in any case is what Leibniz recognizes as his own task. After this is done, others will be able to work more productively.

"I have been more fortunate in my disciples." At the moment when Leibniz expressed this self-satisfaction, he perhaps had some reason to think that his belief was well founded. Later history has judged otherwise, but the number of disciples and the weight of their influence are not the criteria of truth. Truth is nourished progressively in human conflicts, and both Newton and Leibniz were equally necessary, in a privileged age, to the positive science of motion.

PIERRE COSTABEL

J. M. BRIGGS, JR.

Comment

Pierre Costabel has aimed his essay at no small question. The unity of science, we are told, was the issue between Newton and Leibniz. Leibniz chose to unify science by making use of the concept of the *dynamis,* the physical manifestation of which accounted for order in the world. Newton developed a rational mechanics instead, using force only as a fictional device to allow the development of a mathematical formalism.

Costabel implies that the phrase "rational mechanics" is not used today and that the phrase "Newtonian dynamics" which is usually substituted is in fact a misnomer. Since so distinguished a scholar as Clifford Truesdell is present, a mild protest must be made. For Truesdell has written at length on the development of rational mechanics, particularly rational fluid mechanics, in the eighteenth century. He has done so with such verve that there can be no doubt that he considers the development of rational mechanics to be of paramount importance in the post-Newtonian world. The mild protest is therefore not trivial, particularly since the unity of science is at stake.

Dynamics, Costabel has said, is the general aspect taken by the science of motion when it is organized around the idea of force. Rational mechanics, presumably, is a study in which various forces or influences are put forth as hypotheses in order to allow mathematical analysis to carry the burden of the development; the results can then be checked against the world of phenomena. Dynamics in this sense depends on the success of the primary metaphysical assumptions which underlie it. Rational mechanics, on the other hand, leans toward positivistic science. It may not be totally arbitrary, for it must at least make a good match with the phenomenal world, but it is nonetheless neutral, or attempts to be neutral, with respect to metaphysical causality.

Now in judging Newton and Leibniz with regard to their sciences, there are, as Costabel notes, many possible criteria. Scholars are sure to disagree over the question of which criteria are the most significant. Probably the bulk of the disagreements one might have with Costabel would be for this reason. One can, for example, tend to judge in terms of historical development rather than philosophical accuracy or consistency. It can be argued that to dismiss the number of disciples as unimportant, as Costabel has done, is to miss the point. The men of the eighteenth century followed Newton, not Leibniz, and science for better or worse became Newtonian, no matter how Newton's thought might have been altered or transformed. Leibniz lost much of his potential support from the French *philosophes* precisely because of his insistence on metaphysics, something the *philosophes* saw as all too recently drummed out of science. They had to go to some lengths to show that mv^2 was either a derivative concept or else a primary concept for nonmetaphysical reasons. And those such as Maupertuis who fell into metaphysical ways of thinking were ridiculed.

On the other hand, it cannot be denied that many of Leibniz's ideas later proved to be fruitful. In spite of the effort to escape his metaphysics, mathematical physicists found that Leibniz's science was not to be shrugged off. That Leibniz's advocacy of the relativity of space and time was later justified in Einstein's work is well known. But even apart from that, modern science is in fact much closer to Leibniz than to Newton. The fundamental law today is the conservation of energy. And who today in the world of nuclear power is comfortable asserting that energy is purely a mathematical function with no body of reality?

Inevitably the question arises in one form or another: who is superior, Newton or Leibniz? Although we may argue that this is not the proper question to ask, it will not be totally put down. We may have some semantic quibbling about the word "superior", but we have few qualms in saying that Newton is superior to Robert Hooke. But how to judge Leibniz and Newton, whose philosophical positions were so diametrically opposed? Costabel has given some steps here, as we shall see.

Probably few would argue with Costabel's general characterization of Leibniz. It seems doubtful that even future research will alter the picture of him as a man devoted to placing physics subservient to metaphysics. The *dynamis,* and later the monad, were aimed at describing the manifestations of God's power. Leibniz not only openly announced his metaphysical bias, he hammered away at it time after time. His position is easy to gauge.

Newton is more difficult to judge in this respect, and some might argue that Costabel's picture of him is out of focus, or at least truncated. If we take the *Principia* at face value, we are in a different position than we were with Leibniz. For, as Newton tells us in the preface to the first edition, he has "cultivated mathematics as far as it relates to philosophy." Since the treatise is mathematical, the physical questions of force, matter and so on never do emerge, but lurk instead in the shadows. We are given, it might be said, operational definitions, not physical realities. Costabel is correct; force in the *Principia* is a fiction with pragmatic value. The *Principia* is indeed a *Mechanica rationalis*.

It is for this reason that the genesis of Newton's ideas is so much more important than the genesis of Leibniz's. Newton deliberately suppressed the means by which he formulated his ideas, thereby leaving a series of enigmas over which his later emulators were forced to scratch their heads. The very strength of the *Principia* is in its mathematical tone. And the fact that Leibniz never wrote a systematic treatise—or when he did it came out a *Theodicy*—makes it difficult to compare him to Newton in this regard. One suspects that Newton might have considered Leibniz to be in the same category (though at a much higher level) as Hooke: a man who claims credit for the ideas while letting others do the drudgery of computing.

Although Costabel is correct in saying that Newton used the language of force, that does not mean that Newton thought that all forces were fictitious. In fact Newton needed forces and spent a good deal of time thinking about them. The issue between Newton and Leibniz was indeed fundamental, as old as Greek science and as new as today. In Greek terms, the tension was between being and becoming; in modern terms between particles and fields; at any time the tension occurs between the concepts of what exists and how those things act on each other. Leibniz took action to be real and the body to be fictional; Newton invested bodies with reality and had to postulate hypothetical forces. Hence his preoccupation with his own brand of ether and its appearance later in the famous Queries to the *Opticks*.

One cannot, in other words, isolate the discussion from concepts of matter, space, and time. Newton's theory of matter has been the subject of research, and his notions of space and time were clearly given in the *Principia*. Newton was not a positivist; he had a keen sense of the physical. But absolute space and time were the sources of some of the troubles Newton experienced, troubles which Costabel has underlined.

Costabel is aware of course of many of these things, for they are commonplace. Why has he not discussed them? Partly, no doubt, for reasons of space. But his view is also

J. M. BRIGGS, JR.

sympathetic to Leibniz, and he reads Newton as one who is convinced of the reality of forces. And although I argue that this is a questionable procedure, it has led Costabel to the analysis of specific passages in Newton as they have not been analyzed before. Some of the results are, if not surprising, at least provoking. Newton, for example, is not often styled a Cartesian, and yet it is certainly true that the *philosophes* of the eighteenth century had little difficulty in adapting his thought to a Cartesian style. D'Alembert, who claimed to be Newtonian, refused to deal with forces at all, and cut them out of mechanics.

But more important is the emphasis that Costabel places on the means by which Newton linked his mathematical formalism to mechanical physics. That he was able to give a mechanical meaning to the curvature of a trajectory is to Costabel the most significant thing he did. The relationship of mathematics to the world is something Costabel has written about before now, and in Newton's work the relationship is important indeed.

On this point it seems to me that two complaints (for they are complaints rather than objections) must be made. First, I confess that some of Costabel's reasoning remains obscure to my mind. The trouble may be in my mind, of course, and to that extent I leave myself open to a countercomplaint. But Costabel's elucidation of Newton's law of composition, a very important law for Newton, is confusing. Further, I do not know why it is inescapable that the causes of change in velocity must "be without duration and take on the aspect of a sudden mutation." And I must also say that I do not understand the necessity for associative and commutative axioms as Costabel claims they are needed.

I think that all of these difficulties are related to the central argument that Costabel is putting forward, which I may instinctively be refusing to grant. And that argument deals with the forces, the *vis insita* and the *vis impressa*. Costabel, as we have seen, claims them to be fictional forces, mathematical entities which Newton introduces but does not give any substantial meaning. Since they are fictional, I believe that Costabel is arguing that there must be a complete set of axioms showing how such forces must be manipulated in mathematical operations. If they are not real, for example, how can they be directed? In what ways can they be added together? The parallelogram law deals with forces, not velocities, and yet somehow the two get muddled in Newton's treatment. Without sets of axioms dealing with the operations of forces, such laws as that of the parallelogram are at fault for confusing different sets of concepts. Costabel may be correct, but surely Newton thought that his second law, which defined both magnitudes and directions, sufficed for his purposes. And so I am confused about Costabel's objections.

And this leads to my second complaint, which is that Costabel devotes too much time to a general characterization that is not particularly new, while devoting too little time to specific analyses that do bring some new arguments into such a discussion. It is an old technique, of course, to criticize a person for writing the wrong paper; yet, in this case it seems to me that Costabel has let the general theme dominate the more important questions he has raised. He has raised these questions not by finding new sources, but by reading parts of the sources that have long been available. He has pushed beyond the prefaces, definitions, and scholia that have become so familiar to scholars that they can recite long passages by heart. And so if his analysis is confusing to me, the only way to resolve the confusion is to follow Costabel through the material he has considered.

It is at the very least in this sense that Costabel has performed a service. For, as it was stated earlier, if a judgment of the superiority of Newton or Leibniz is raised in any form, the answers will be found in the mathematics and the bearing of the mathematics on the set of concepts that make up theory.

JOHN HERIVEL

Newton's Achievement in Dynamics

THE *Philosophiae Naturalis Principia Mathematica*[1] CONTAINS THE CONSID-
ered expression of Newton's system of dynamics, and is the most impressive
and fitting monument to his achievement in that subject. It is, of course, much
else besides: it represents one of the most impressive monuments to Newton's many-
sided genius in applied mathematics, especially to that uncanny ability—shared in
equal measure perhaps only by Euler and Laplace—to circumvent obstacles and find
a path to solutions exact or approximate to the most intractable seeming problems: it
is a monument also to Newton's immense intellectual energy—matched only by a certain unwillingness to release this energy which is so often the accompaniment of
creativity whether in art, or literature, or science. Moreover, apart from the achievement of the *Principia*, there is also the question of its influence. From this point of
view it must be counted among a small number of works including Ptolemy's *Syn-
taxis*, Galileo's *Dialogue*, and Laplace's *System of the World* which have marked an
epoch in the history of the physical sciences. And the *Principia* was influential not
only because of its great merits—its dynamical system, and the many impressive applications of this system, above all to the age-old problem of the motion of the planets; it was, I suspect, also influential even by reason of its apparent demerits. For the
uncompromising closeness of the argument, the paucity of mathematical explanation,
and the highly intuitive method of treatment of orbital motion in Book I, would have
served to stimulate rather than to repel the attention of Newton's successors from
Clairaut to Laplace—*mathemata mathematicis scribuntur*!

But to return to the *dynamical* achievement of the *Principia*. Before we can hope to
judge this we must briefly examine the essential structure of the work from the dynamical point of view. First there is the formal dynamical system consisting of definition, axioms, and corollaries together with the famous philosophico-physical justification of the assumption of absolute space and time basic to the whole system. The
remainder of the work consists of three books. Book I may be divided into five distinct parts: Section I, on *Final and Ultimate Ratios* which is of purely mathematical
interest apart from Lemma X; Sections II–X which are concerned with the motion of
a single body under the action of a central force; Section XI, which deals with the
motion of a pair of mutually attracting bodies—especially the case of an inverse
square attraction; Sections XII–XIII which deal with the problem of extended bodies
all of whose smallest parts exert attractive forces, especially the problem of a uniform
sphere attracting according to the inverse square law; Section XIV which deals with
the motion of a particle through an attracting medium.

Book II is devoted to the problem of the motion of bodies in fluids resisting accord-

JOHN HERIVEL

ing to various laws, apart from Sections V and VIII which deal with hydrostatics and sound, respectively. The book ends (Scholium to Prop. 53, Theor. 40) with an attempted proof of the impossibility of an explanation of the observed motions of the planets in terms of a system of vortices. Though Newton is careful not to name Descartes, it is certain that this proof was chiefly aimed at the vortex system put forward in Part III of the latter's *Principia Philosophiae*.[2]

Book III, *Concerning the System of the World,* applies the results of Book I to establish the inverse square law of gravitation on the basis of Kepler's first two laws of planetary motion and the mean motion of the moon, and continues with a treatment of the problems of the moon, the tides, and comets.

Having outlined the essential structure of the whole of the First Edition of the *Principia*, I shall henceforth restrict attention to the initial dynamical system and to Book I. This restriction can be justified on purely dynamical grounds: for the parts of Book II which deal with the motion of bodies in resisting fluids consist almost entirely of applied mathematics, the dynamical content being restricted to an appeal to the formal dynamical system (second law of motion) in order to formulate the mathematical problems corresponding to the various laws of resistance assumed: while the two remaining sections (V and VIII) on hydrostatics and sound, though of great interest historically from the theoretical-physical point of view, especially the section on sound, fall outside the scope of the present paper. As to Book III, while the *implicit* dynamical content is far larger than in the case of Book II, nevertheless it is again largely a case of the *application* of the initial system and certain results from Book I.

While the restriction of attention to the initial dynamical system and to Book I certainly simplifies the problem of assessing Newton's dynamical achievement in the *Principia,* nevertheless this problem would necessarily remain an insoluble one *in terms of the evidence provided by the* Principia *alone.* There are at least two good reasons why this should be so: in the first place, we can form no sort of just estimate of Newton's achievement in dynamics unless we know the magnitude of his debt in dynamics to his predecessors and contemporaries. A curious example of the untrustworthiness of the *Principia* itself in this connection is provided by Newton's unjustified attribution of a knowledge of the second law of motion to Galileo.[3] In the second place, even if we could pick out the key dynamical propositions in Book I, it would still be difficult to assess the magnitude of the achievement involved if we had no inkling of the train of thought leading to their construction. It is clear, therefore, that our estimate of Newton's dynamical achievement in the *Principia* will be largely dependent on our knowledge of Newton's researches in dynamics prior to the composition of the *Principia*.

Judging by the available documentary evidence,[4] Newton's dynamical researches prior to the composition of the *Principia* seem to have been concentrated rather sharply into three distinct periods: the earliest researches covering the period around 1664 to 1666, the researches in the winter of 1679–80 following Hooke's intervention and culminating in the solution to the problem of Kepler-motion, and the researches beginning around May 1684 which led on to the composition of the *Principia* itself. It would be possible to start with a description of the earliest researches and follow through the development of Newton's dynamical thought up to the period of the composition of the *Principia*. This, however, would have the disadvantage that one would either have to describe all Newton's earliest dynamical researches regardless of their relevance for his achievement in the *Principia*, or else one would have to give reasons why a particular piece of research was not to be taken into account. Instead of considering Newton's researches in dynamics prior to the *Principia* in their natural, chronological order, I shall therefore commence with his solution to the problem of Kepler-motion. This was his most decisive achievement in dynamics, and one which by reason of its nature and importance dominated his whole position in the subject: on the one hand it pointed the way forward to the *Principia* which would itself never have been contemplated in the absence of a solution to this problem; on the other hand it pointed back to Newton's predecessors, and to his earliest researches in dynamics which in many ways prepared the ground for the *Principia*, and to which it represented the natural culmination and crown. A careful study of Newton's solution to the dynamical problems posed by Kepler's first two laws of planetary motion will therefore provide the best possible point of departure for a proper assessment of the nature of Newton's dynamical achievement in the *Principia*.

According to his own account,[5] Newton solved the problem of Kepler-motion in the winter of 1679–80, following Hooke's intervention. We have, however, no certain indication of the method first employed.[6] Newton himself at one point seems to imply that he first solved it by an analytical method based on the method of fluxions. We have no such proof either documentary or in the *Principia*. The nearest approach is the general method for "determining figures" given the law of variation of the central force.[7] This method is surprisingly *not* applied to the special case of an inverse square law. One possible reason, of course, is the fact that the inverse square law *by itself* does not discriminate between an hyperbola, an ellipse, or a parabola. On the other hand no analytical method is given in the *Principia* for deriving the law of central force given the nature of the orbit. As for "synthetic" proofs, although there is one such proof which may go back to 1679,[8] this is not generally accepted to be the case, and so we are forced to consider the solution contained in the first version of the so-called tract *de Motu*[9] which certainly dates from about the summer of 1684.

Since the solution in the tract *de Motu* is effectively identical with that given in the *Principia*, its examination is particularly relevant to our assessment of Newton's achievement in dynamics in that work. Whether or not it was discovered in 1679 as opposed to 1684 is then of little importance for this assessment, though personally I think that the many links between the earliest researches and the *de Motu* solution to the problem of Kepler-motion make it probable that *if Newton did achieve a synthetic solution in 1679,* then this solution did not deviate greatly from that found in the tract *de Motu*.

Let me remind you of the formulation of the first two of Kepler's laws of planetary motion: the first law states that a planet describes an ellipse with the sun at one focus, and the second that in its motion about the sun the planet sweeps out area at a constant rate. It is the second law whose meaning Newton first unravels in the tract *de Motu*. We follow the argument given in Proposition 1 of the first (and later) versions of that tract which is itself effectively identical with that found at Prop. 1 Theor. 1 of all editions of the *Principia*.

We have no indication how Newton first guessed the surprising inner, dynamical significance of this law—that the force on a planet is wholly directed to the sun—thus banishing forever the need of transverse, pushing forces of the kind imagined by Kepler.[10] What he actually proves in the tract *de Motu* is the converse of Kepler's second law, namely, that if a body moves under a force constantly directed to a point, then it will sweep out area about this point at a constant rate. In the *Principia* we also find the proposition corresponding directly to Kepler's second law.

Let us now examine in detail Newton's Proposition I of the tract *de Motu*. The first problem to be circumvented is the presence of a *continuous* force directed towards the centre O [Fig. 1]. He has no direct way of dealing with such a force.

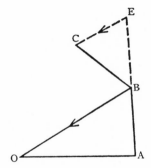

FIGURE I

Therefore he replaces it by a set of equally spaced, centrally directed, discrete *impulses* which in the limit of vanishingly small impulses and intervals (Δt) will tend ever more nearly to the given continuously acting force. As a result the actual, continuous path of the body becomes replaced by an inscribed polygon ABC . . . . . , since the principle of inertia requires that in the intervals between the action of the discrete impulses at A, B, C, ... , the body moves uniformly in straight lines AB, BC, ... The magnitude of the impulses at B, say, is unknown, only its direction along BO. But if we are told the new direction BC into which the motion is turned as a result of this impulse, then we can find the position of the body on BC at the end of the given interval of time Δt in the following ingenious manner: produce the original path AB to E so that AB = BE. Then by the parallelogram law for the combination of independent motions (given in primitive form in version 1 of the tract *de Motu* as Hypothesis 3, and in the *Principia* as Corollary 1 to the laws of motion) the actual position of the body will be found by drawing a line through E parallel to BO to meet the new line of motion at C. Since EC is parallel to OB,

$$\triangle OCB = \triangle OEB$$

But since $\triangle$s OEB and OBA have equal bases and the same height

$$\triangle OEB = \triangle OBA$$

therefore $\triangle OCB = \triangle OBA$

Similarly for all following positions, so that the areas swept out in equal intervals of time about O are always equal. The required result then immediately follows in the limit—provided, of course, like Newton and Leibniz, you are able to think in terms of limiting processes!

In all versions of the tract *de Motu* and in the *Principia* Newton proves the proposition corresponding to Kepler's first law—that motion in an ellipse implies an inverse square attraction to the focus—as a special case of a general result applicable to any motion under a central force. We need only consider the general result, as this contains all the dynamical arguments. Imagine, says Newton (Prop. 3 of tract *de Motu* = Prop. 6 Theor. 5 of Book I, *Principia*) a body moving in a curved path PQ [Fig. 2] under the action of a force constantly directed towards a fixed point S.

FIGURE 2

Suppose that in a small interval of time, Δt, the body moves from P to Q, and draw a line through Q parallel to SP cutting the tangent at P at R. Then if the central force had suddenly ceased acting as the body reached P, the latter would have moved steadily along the tangent PR with the velocity it had in the curve at P. The fact that the body actually traces out a curved path PQ deviating from the inertial path PR is due to the action of the central force. The following results then hold:

For a *given interval of time* Δt: QR $\propto$ Magnitude of force at P   (1)

For a given central force F_P: QR $\propto \Delta t^2$ (2)

Therefore in general: QR $\propto F_P(\Delta t)^2$

i.e. $F_P \propto \dfrac{QR}{(\Delta t)^2}$ (3)

As for Δt, by the previous proposition the areas swept out by the body between P and Q $\backsimeq \triangle SQP = \frac{1}{2}$ QT.SP $\propto \Delta t$

In the above formula (3) we may therefore replace Δt by QT.SP giving

$$F_P \propto \frac{QR}{(QT.SP)^2} \qquad (4)$$

This result is approximate only due to the actual variation of force between P and Q, but it becomes exact in the limit as Q $\to$ P and $\Delta t \to 0$.

Let us gather up the component parts of the two propositions.

First Proposition

Replacement of continuous force by a set of equally spaced impulses.

Replacement of continuous path by inscribed polygon.

Principle of inertia.

Parallelogram law for composition of independent motion.

Passage to limit.

Second Proposition

Assumption that deviation proportional to force.

Assumption that deviation proportional to Δt^2.

Passage to limit.

I propose now to trace these component parts back to their origins in the work of Newton's predecessors or in his own early researches in dynamics.

The simultaneous replacement of a continuous force by a sequence of equally spaced impulses, and that of a continuous path by an inscribed polygon, is found in Newton's earliest treatment of the problem of centrifugal force in the *Waste Book*,[11] probably dating from the year 1665. There he ingeniously considers the case not of a stone at the end of a string, but of a ball moving horizontally within a spherical surface, and finding himself unable to make any progress towards a *quantitative* treatment, he imagines[12] the actual circular path of the ball replaced by a regular inscribed polygon along the sides of which the ball can move interminably [Fig. 3],

FIGURE 3

the actual pressure of the surface on the ball (equal and opposite to the outward centrifugal force of the ball) being replaced by a series of equally spaced "forces of reflection" at the impacts of the ball with the surface at the corners of the polygon. In the limit, as the order of the polygon tends to infinity, the path traced out by the ball tends ever more closely to the actual circular path, and the sequence of forces of reflection tends ever more closely to the continuous force of the surface on the ball.

We find, therefore, in this early treatment of circular motion explicit use of three of the elements in the proof of Proposition 1. Of the remaining two elements, the principle of inertia is employed implicitly, and there is no occasion to use the parallelogram law for the composition of independent motion. This law, however, is found in another early manuscript,[13] probably composed a short time after the latest writings in the *Waste Book,* and in any case long before 1684.

As regards the second proposition, the assumption that the deviation between the actual, curved path and the inertial path along the tangent is proportional to the force acting should be compared with the same assumption in the immediately preceding proposition [2] in the tract *de Motu* in which Newton derives the dependence of *centripetal* force for uniform circular motion on the speed and the radius. This latter assumption should in turn be compared with that found in the treatment of circular motion in MS Add 3958[14] C.U.L. There the *centrifugal* force is said to be of such a magnitude that it would carry the body outwards *away* from the circumference through a distance equal to the deviation DB [Fig. 4] in the time for motion through

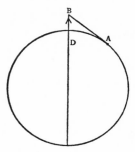

FIGURE 4

a small distance AD along the circle.

Replace the deviation DB *outwards* from the circumference to the tangent, by an equal and opposite deviation BD *inwards* from the tangent to the circumference, and replace the *centrifugal* force outwards by the *centripetal* force inwards, and one has the argument in the tract *de Motu*.

MS Add 3958 C.U.L. was said by Newton to have been composed before his election to the Lucasian Chair in 1669, and was in any case certainly composed before his letter of 23 June 1673 to Oldenburg for Huygens.

Notice that in MS 3958 Newton does not say that the centrifugal force is proportional to the deviation, only that it is of such a magnitude that . . . . But later in the same paper he compares the centrifugal force with the force of gravity through the respective distances covered by the body under the action of these two forces in a given finite interval of time.

In order to make this comparison he assumes that the distance moved by the body under the given centrifugal force acting in a constant direction will vary as the square of the time.

We find, therefore, in the early MS 3958 what would seem to be the genesis both

JOHN HERIVEL

of the assumption force proportional to deviation, and of the application of (Newton's generalization of) Galileo's t² law. I shall examine both these assumptions in more detail later. But having looked back from 1684 to the early researches with their exact analogies to all the basic elements in the *de Motu* solution to the problem of Kepler-motion, let us now look forward to the finished presentation of Newton's dynamics in the *Principia*.

The formal system preceding Book I is made up (following the traditional Euclidian—or, if you prefer, Archimedean—pattern on which Newton obviously modeled his work) of *Definitions,* and *Axioms* or *Laws of Motion.* The definitions are followed by the famous *scholium* containing Newton's *apologia pro spatio absoluto suo,* and the laws are followed by six corollaries and a succeeding *scholium* containing appropriate acknowledgments to Galileo and certain of Newton's contemporaries (but not to Descartes), together with certain experimental results in support of the law of conservation of momentum.

Definitions. I do not propose to spend much time on the Definitions. I doubt if any of the small band of readers of the *Principia* has ever paid much attention to them either. Definitions there must be, but only of things with which we are already familiar! Nor do they contribute much to Newton's achievement in dynamics. But notice, however, one very important point: nowhere in these Definitions does Newton refer to *centrifugal* as opposed to *centripetal* force: the realization by Newton that *as far as orbital motion is concerned*[15] centrifugal forces are not only unnecessary but nonexistent marked, I think, an important conceptual advance in his dynamical thought. I very much doubt if any of Newton's contemporaries appreciated the force of this distinction between centripetal and centrifugal force. For example, Leibniz had a proof of the necessity of an inverse square law for motion in an ellipse under the action of a force to one focus.[16] Disregarding the question of whether Leibniz really found this proof independently of a reading of the *Principia*—for it was certainly *published* after that work—his method of proof remains interesting from a mathematical point of view, and possibly important too for its influence on the long process of reformulation of Newton's dynamical method in the eighteenth century. But from the dynamical point of view it is, to say the least of it, obscure! This obscurity being largely due to Leibniz' unjustified use of *centrifugal* force. In the case of a uniform circular motion, of a stone in a sling, for example, we can (as engineers still do) *regard* the circular path of the stone as the outcome of a balance between the tension of the string inwards and the centrifugal force of the stone outwards. This was the attitude adopted by Descartes when he explained the stability of a (circular) planetary orbit as due to a balance between a vortex pressure inwards and the centrifugal force (*conatus*) of the planet outwards.[17] Newton was familiar with this view,[18] and it may well have been—probably was—the attitude he adopted on the occasion of his supposed first test of the inverse square law of gravitation against the moon's motion during the Plague Years.[19] On the other hand, when he came to consider the problem of uniform circular motion in the tract *de Motu* all trace of centrifugal force had disappeared: it was now an equal, but opposite, centripetal force which sufficed to explain the continued bending away of the body from its natural inertial path along the tangent.

Scholium to Definitions. As opposed to the Definitions proper, the succeeding *Scholium,* devoted to the distinction between absolute and relative space (and time), is of enormous interest and importance. One thinks of the Leibniz-Clarke[20] and succeeding controversies over the relative merits of the two kinds of space, controversies which continued right up to Einstein's Special Theory of Relativity—and beyond. Time does not permit an extended discussion of this aspect of Newton's dynamical system, and I must confine myself to the following remarks: in the first place, it should be noted that the genesis of Newton's views on space (and time) as we find them in the *Principia* can be followed in an earlier manuscript[21] which proves that they developed in direct reaction to Descartes's views of space and motion in his *Principia Philosophiae.* In the second place, when we compare Newton's outmoded view of absolute space unfavorably with the much more modern-looking relativistic views of space and motion put forward by Leibniz in his controversy with Clarke, we should remember two things: first, the cogency of Newton's argument for a fundamental difference between motions initiated by force and those resulting merely from a change of reference frame—an argument whose force was frankly admitted by Leibniz himself; secondly, given the obvious impossibility of a Special Theory of Relativity in the seventeenth (or eighteenth) centuries we should surely count it fortunate that Newton was able to find so solid a basis for his dynamics as his absolute theory of space and time—and, we may add, so good an approximation to the "truth." Finally, we should note that even if Newton's view of absolute space and time had certain philosophical weaknesses—as proved by Leibniz—nevertheless it reminds us that Newton was not merely a scientist, or a mathematician, but also a natural philosopher.

We say *Newton's* laws of motion, as if to contrast them with other laws, such as those of Aristotle. The appellation is partly just, partly unjust. The first law of motion, the principle of inertia, was certainly not discovered, or should I say *imagined,* by Newton. We find him enunciating this law explicitly in the earliest researches,[22] and then continually using it in an implicit manner. But by 1665 the principle of inertia had become generally accepted as a result of the writings of Galileo and his disciples, and of Gassendi and Descartes, and we find it reproduced in many works, for example in Hobbes's *de Corpore* or in Wallis' *Mechanica Sive de Motu.* As for Newton, there is good evidence that he was at least familiar with, if not influenced by, the first general formulation of the principle by Descartes in Part II of his *Principia Philosophiae.*[23] What is also probable, and certainly much more important, is that Newton took one of the basic ideas of his treatment of orbital motion from Descartes's application of the principle of inertia to circular motion: I refer to the notion that a body moving in a curved path is always, at every instant, endeavoring to follow its natural, inertial path along the tangent to the curve, being prevented

JOHN HERIVEL

from so doing only by the intervention of force. The importance of this notion—and hence of the principle of inertia—in Newton's treatment of orbital motion cannot be overemphasized. In this respect Newton's dynamical method was entirely different from the modern treatment of the same problem in which the principle of inertia plays no part, having been rendered superfluous by the reformulation of Newton's second law in terms of *accelerative* rather than *motive* forces.

If the first law of motion does not belong to Newton, the second undoubtedly does though, as we have seen,[24] Newton himself curiously attributes it to Galileo. There seems to be no evidence for this view. On the contrary, the law given by Newton in the *Prinicipia* seems to have been entirely original. Once again, as in so many other respects, we can trace this element of Newton's dynamics back to his earliest researches, for in the *Waste Book*[25] we find a number of results all equivalent to the formula force ∝ change in motion [= momentum]. Newton seems to have arrived at this formula from his early (and completely exhaustive) study of the problem of collisions.

The enormous influence of Newton's second law of motion on the development of dynamics *after* Newton is matched by the comparative unimportance of the law for Newton himself. This curious situation is due to the fact that the second law became the foundation-stone of post-Newtonian dynamics only when it had been modified to apply to *accelerative* rather than *motive* forces. That is, until it became changed from force ∝ change of motion—thus implying that the "forces" under consideration were really impulses—to force ∝ *rate* of change of motion. Once this had been done the principle of inertia could be forgotten—apart, that is, from idle dreamers like Mach and Einstein—and the whole of the theory of orbits, for example, based on the second law of motion alone. Not so for Newton, whose second law applied to motive forces, whereas the forces he was interested in physically—above all the force of gravity—were continuous, accelerative forces. It followed that all Newton's appeals to *his* second law of motion in Book I of the *Principia* were, strictly speaking, unjustified. On the other hand, when he applied his second law in Book II to the motion of bodies in resisting fluids in the differential form

dv (= small change in speed) ∝ resisting force = some function of speed,

he naturally reached the correct results, provided he assumed the corresponding intervals of time were all equal—as was the case. For

$$\frac{dv}{dt} = F(v) \text{ implies } \frac{dv_1}{F(v_1)} = \frac{dv_2}{F(v_2)} = \ldots \ldots (\Delta t)$$

As regards the third law of motion, once again we find its germ in the earliest dynamical researches in the *Waste Book*[26] where action and reaction are said to be equal and opposite both as regards magnitude and direction in the case of the oblique collision of two bodies.

The corollaries and *scholium* to the laws of motion call for no particular comment, nor does Section I of Book I apart from Lemma X which contains Newton's generalization of Galileo's t^2 law; these will be studied in detail later. As to the essential dynamical content of the remainder of Book I apart from Sections XI and XII, everything is contained within Prop. I Theor. I and Prop. 6 Theor. 5. These differ little from the two propositions of the *de Motu* corresponding to Kepler's first two laws of planetary motion which have already been described, and to which I shall return presently. There remain Sections XI and XII–XIV. The latter are a matter of integration rather than dynamics, though showing enormous ingenuity, and of great importance to Newton's system of the world, especially the famous Prop. LXXI Theor. XXXI in which it is proved that a uniform solid sphere made up of particles attracting according to the inverse square law will attract at points outside it as if all its matter were concentrated at its center. Section XI, treating of the motion of a pair of naturally attracting bodies, represents one of Newton's great achievements in dynamics, and leads ultimately to his modification of Kepler's Third Law and to his discussion of the effect of the mutual intersections of the planets. From the point of view of dynamical content, however, the only new elements are the use of the third law of motion, and of Corollary 4 to the laws of motion relating to the inertial nature of the motion of the center of gravity of a system of mutually attracting particles. An exhaustive investigation of this result in the case of two bodies is found already in the *Waste Book*.[27]

In the course of this survey of what is in my view the essential dynamical, as opposed to mathematical, content of the *Principia,* two things will have become evident. In the first place, in almost every case we have found a foreshadowing of the dynamics of the *Principia* in the earlier researches. Nor am I thinking here of the researches in the year 1684 which saw the composition of the tract *de Motu* and the beginning of the *Principia.* On the contrary, we have seen how the various component parts of the proofs of the two propositions corresponding to Kepler's first two laws of planetary motion could all be regarded as the application or development of concepts or methods used in the earlier researches.

In the second place, it will be clear that I have assigned a quite extraordinary significance and importance to the two propositions (Prop. I Theor. I and Prop. 6 Theor. 5) of Book I of the *Principia* corresponding to the first two of Kepler's laws. All the more so, as I have claimed that the second law of motion, which is always regarded as the most important of Newton's laws, plays no legitimate part in these (or any other) propositions in Book I of the *Principia.*

Let us now, in the light of this survey, attempt to estimate the magnitude of Newton's achievement in dynamics in the *Principia.*

As regards the formal, dynamical system this was undoubtedly an impressive achievement and a necessary part of the *Principia.* But I am not convinced that it represented a *creative* dynamical achievement of the first order. Put it another way, I find no great difficulty in imagining one or other of Newton's contemporaries such as Wallis or Huygens achieving an equally general formulation of dynamics, especially if they had had the same incentive as Newton to achieve such a formulation. For although even at the time of the earliest researches Newton seems to have had a

JOHN HERIVEL

natural *penchant* towards the drawing up of best-possible axiomatic systems, when he began to compose the *Principia* he would have had an *overwhelming* reason for doing so.

Two exceptions must be made, however, to this general judgment of the formal dynamical system: the second law of motion, and the justification of absolute space and time in the *Scholium* to the definition. These represented, in my opinion, the most original aspects of the formal system. The fact that Newton was able to make *his* formulation of the second law the basis of his treatment of motion in resisting fluids in Book II, in spite of the fact that his appeals to the same law in Book I were unjustified, provides one example, among many, of his total inability to put a foot wrong in dynamics, his consistent "good fortune" and uniform success in the subject. The justification of absolute space and time has already been touched on.

Given this attitude to the formal dynamical system, our estimate of Newton's achievement in dynamics must then largely depend on our estimate of his achievement in solving the problem of Kepler-motion. It is here, I think, that we see his creative powers in dynamics at their highest. And the two most original elements in his dynamical approach were undoubtedly his use of the *deviation* as a measure of the centripetal force, and the assumption that for small intervals of time, Δt, this deviation would vary as Δt².

Both these assumptions look intuitively plausible, but it will be as well to justify them first by "modern" methods.

Suppose, then, that a particle moves under some variable central force directed to a fixed point O which we take as origin. Let $\vec{r}(t)$ be the position vector of the particle with respect to O [Fig. 5] as a function of the time t, and suppose at time t = o the

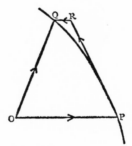

FIGURE 5

particle is at P. Then by Taylor's theorem

$$\vec{r}(\Delta t) = \vec{r}(o) + (\Delta t)\left(\frac{d\vec{r}}{dt}\right)_{t=o} + \tfrac{1}{2}(\Delta t)^2\left(\frac{d^2\vec{r}}{dt^2}\right)_{t=o} + O(\Delta t)^3$$

If, therefore, we neglect terms in Δt³

$$\vec{r}(\Delta t) = \vec{r}(o) + (\Delta t)\left(\frac{d\vec{r}}{dt}\right)_{t=o} + \tfrac{1}{2}(\Delta t)^2\left(\frac{d^2\vec{r}}{dt^2}\right)^2_{t=o}$$

But $\left(\dfrac{d\vec{r}}{dt}\right)_{t=o} = \vec{v}_P$ = velocity of particle at P — and in the direction PR of the

Newton's Achievement in Dynamics

tangent to the curve at that point. And by the *modern* formulation of Newton's second law

$$\left(\frac{d^2\vec{r}}{dt^2}\right)_{t=0} = \frac{\vec{F}_P}{m}$$

where $\vec{F}_P$ is the vector representing the force acting on the particle at P.

If then in the diagram we draw PR along the tangent at P, make $\vec{PR} = \vec{v}_P \Delta t$, and let Q be the position of the particle at time Δt, we have

$$\vec{r}(0) = \vec{OP}$$

$$\vec{r}(\Delta t) = \vec{OQ}$$

and
$$\vec{OQ} = \vec{OP} + \vec{PR} + \tfrac{1}{2}(\Delta t)^2\frac{\vec{F}_P}{m}$$

but
$$\vec{OQ} = \vec{OP} + \vec{PR} + \vec{RQ}$$

therefore
$$\vec{RQ} = \tfrac{1}{2}(\Delta t)^2\frac{\vec{F}_P}{m}$$

But the force $\vec{F}_P$ on the particle at P is along the direction PO,

therefore $\vec{RQ}$ will be parallel to PO, and its magnitude will equal $\tfrac{1}{2}(\Delta t)^2\frac{\vec{F}_P}{m}$

Now according to Newton's construction RQ will be the *deviation* at Q,

therefore deviation at $Q = \tfrac{1}{2}(\Delta t)^2\frac{\vec{F}_P}{m}$

therefore deviation at $Q \propto (\Delta t)^2$ and $\vec{F}_P$, as assumed by Newton.

Newton's formula is therefore (of course) correct. The great question from the point of view of our insight into his achievement in dynamics is his manner of reaching it. We have already noted his use of the negative deviation as a measure of the centrifugal force many years prior to 1684, and likewise, in the same paper, his application of Galileo's t^2 law. This opened the way to his derivation of the law of centrifugal force—certainly the greatest achievement of his early researches in dynamics. Here we happen to have a measure of Newton's achievement, for although the problem of centrifugal force had already been brought to the fore through its discussion by Descartes in his *Principia Philosophiae*,[28] and by its employment by Borelli[29] as an explanation of the stability of planetary orbits in terms of some kind of alternation between the dominance of the inward pull of the sun and the outward centrifugal force of the planet, Huygens was the one person apart from Newton able to derive the correct law of centrifugal force for the case of uniform circular motion.[30]

Given the evident magnitude of Newton's achievement in his earlier researches of this derivation of the law of centrifugal force, and given that his dynamical method in his treatment of Kepler-motion shows every sign of having grown naturally out of his method of treating centrifugal force in the earlier researches, what was the *additional* achievement involved in his solution to the problem of Kepler-motion?

Here we must notice that apart from the greater difficulty of the problem of Kepler-motion compared with that of uniform circular motion—as epitomized by the fact that this time Newton *alone* achieved a solution—there were certain fundamental differences between Newton's approaches to the two problems. First there was the surrender of the very notion of centrifugal force and the absolutely clear and definite realization that only the inward, centripetal force counted. This by itself represented a great conceptual achievement, one (to my knowledge) unmatched by any of Newton's contemporaries—and, as I have already remarked, an aspect of Newton's system which I suspect they did not properly understand.

In the second place, there was a different attitude to the relationship between the deviation and the force. In his early treatment of the problem of uniform circular motion Newton gives no indication that he regarded the deviation as proportional to the force. On the contrary, he simply says that the centrifugal force is *of such a magnitude* as to cause the deviation in the given small instant of time. If it were then to act on the body with the same force but in a constant direction (as in the case of the force of gravity) the distance moved in a finite time, say one second, could be calculated by application of the t^2 law of Galileo; and this distance could then be compared with that described under the action of some other constant force—such as the force of gravity—to give the ratio of the magnitudes of the two forces. In the case of Kepler-motion this approach was impossible. For now not only the *direction* but also the *magnitude* of the force on the body was changing from instant to instant. Hence the necessity of setting the deviation for a given small interval of time actually proportional to the force. Finally, there was the altogether different application of the t^2 law. In the case of circular motion this, as we have just seen, was used to calculate what would be the distance moved under the action of the given centrifugal force acting in a straight line for *a finite interval of time*; now it is used to give a measure of the actual deviation for a given centripetal force acting at a particular instant, an entirely different matter. This extension of Galileo's t^2 law is first referred to in Version I of the tract *de Motu* where it appears as an *hypothesis*, as if to emphasize that Newton was confident of its validity before he could prove its necessity: later, in Version III of the tract *de Motu*, and in the *Principia* (Lemma X, Section I, of Book I) he gives a proof of the result based on an appeal to the fact that the area under a velocity-time graph is proportional to the distance traversed.[31]

We may ask ourselves how Newton first *divined* this extension of Galileo's law. There is no indication of this, so that the following guess is as good as another. Newton must have been familiar with the *Discorsi* of Galileo at an early stage.[32] He would have been particularly struck with two things in that work: the discussion of uniformly accelerated motion corresponding to free fall downwards under gravity, and the derivation of the parabolic path of a projectile. We might expect, too, that it was the proof of the latter which above all impressed Newton, and that this was perhaps one of the things which drew him towards a study of dynamics.

Now you will remember that in his proof Galileo imagines the body first to be moving along a horizontal table until it reaches the edge at P [Fig. 6]. From that

FIGURE 6

point on, while preserving its original horizontal motion, it now has added to it an accelerated motion due to its weight, so that for any point Q on its trajectory the distance PR is *directly* proportional to the *square* of the time elapsed. In this case, however, RQ is a line drawn *parallel to the force acting* (vertically downwards) from any point Q on the curve to meet the line AP at R. But AP was the original (horizontal) line of motion of the body, and is obviously a tangent to the curve at P. In other words, for *all positions* Q, RQ is the *deviation* of the body from its original inertial path.

Could it have been that in thinking of the motion of a *planet* in an ellipse about the sun Newton was reminded of the trajectory of a stone at the surface of the earth, just as the falling of the stone had reminded him of that of the moon? If so his unerring dynamical common sense would have told him that the result, true *always* for the deviation of Galileo's projectile, would be true *in the limit* for the case of the planetary orbit.

If one recalls that Newton's attention may originally have been drawn to the notion of deviation by his study of Descartes's treatment of centrifugal force, we have then the possibility of the greater part of the dynamical method in his treatment of orbital motion being derived ultimately from Galileo and Descartes. If true, however, this would surely rather *increase* than *decrease* our admiration for Newton's central achievement in dynamics; for it would then serve only to emphasize the transforming power of his genius in the subject. Is this not, in fact, one of the most essential qualities of genius, at any rate in science, and at any rate in the past, to see significance and analogy where others, possibly quicker and more intelligent, but intellectually less humble and less discerning, see nothing? Was this perhaps what Newton had in mind when he talked of the "smoother pebbles" found on the vast shore of knowledge? The casual observer whose mind is fraught with the common anxieties and cares of life will as likely as not see no pebbles at all! Whereas your intellectual theorist will fit the pebbles somehow into his own dogmatic view of things. Only the genius who can allow the pebbles to speak to him in their own language, and as if for the first time, will be able to grasp their true message.

JOHN HERIVEL

NOTES

[1] References throughout will be to the first Latin edition.

[2] For a discussion of Newton's reaction to Descartes's dynamics including his vortex system, see A. Koyré, *Newtonian Studies* (London, 1965), Chapter 3.

[3] At the beginning of the *Scholium* to the laws of motion.

[4] See Chapter 6, Part I, of my *The Background to Newton's* Principia (Oxford, 1965), hereafter referred to as *Background,* for a discussion of the order of composition and dating of Newton dynamical MSS prior to the composition of the *Principia.*

[5] See especially the statement in his letter of 14 July 1686 to Halley: "This is true, that his [Hooke's] letters occasioned my finding the method of determining figures, which when I had tried in the ellipsis, I threw the calculation by, being upon other studies."

[6] For a discussion of this point see p. 17 Note 2, *Background.*

[7] See Prop. 41, Book I, *Principia.*

[8] See MS VIII, Part II, *Background.*

[9] Reproduced in MS IX, Part II, *Background.*

[10] For a discussion of Kepler's dynamical system see A. Koyré, *La Révolution Astronomique,* (Paris, 1961), Part II, Chapter 6.

[11] See Ax-Prop. 20 ff. MS IId, Part II, *Background.*

[12] See MS IIa, Part II, *Background.*

[13] See § 3, MS V, Part II, *Background.*

[14] Reproduced as MS IVa, Part II, *Background.*

[15] This qualification is necessary in the light of Newton's appeal to centrifugal force in his argument for absolute space based on his famous "bucket experiment." See *Scholium* to Definitions in *Principia.* For a discussion of Newton's concept of centrifugal endeavor or *conatus* see Chapter 3, Part I, *Background.*

[16] For a reproduction of part of this paper together with a commentary see E. J. Aiton, "The Celestial Mechanics of Leibniz," *Annals of Science 16* (1960) 65–82.

[17] See Art. 140, Part 3, *Principia Philosophiae.*

[18] See §2, MS VI, Part II, *Background.*

[19] For a discussion of this test see Chapter 4, Part I, *Background.*

[20] See for example H. G. Alexander, *The Leibniz-Clarke Controversy* (Manchester, 1956).

[21] MS Add 4003 C.U.L. reproduced in full in A. R. and M. B. Hall, *Unpublished Scientific Papers of Isaac Newton* (Cambridge, 1962). For extracts from this MS of particular interest for Newton's views on dynamics and space, see MS VI, Part II, *Background.*

[22] See, for example, Ax-Prop., 1, 2, MS IId, Part II, *Background.*

[23] For the influence of Descartes on Newton in Dynamics see Chapter 2 §2, Part I, *Background.*

[24] See Note 3 above.

[25] See Ax-Prop. 3–6, 23, MS IId, Part II, *Background.*

[26] See Ax. 119, 121, MS IIe, Part II, *Background.*

[27] See Prop. 27–32, MS IIf, Part II, *Background.*

[28] See especially Art. 38, Part II, Art. 57–59, Part III.

[29] In his *Theorica medicearum planetarum* . . . (Florence, 1666).

[30] In his *De Vi Centrifuga,* written by 1659, published posthumously in 1703 among the *Opuscula Posthuma.*

[31] See p. 34, Chapter I, Part I, *Background.*

[32] It was published in English translation in Tome II of Salusbury's *Mathematical Collection* (London, 1665). Most of these were destroyed by the Great Fire of London, but there were copies, for example that in the library of Newton's friend Richard Jones.

GERD BUCHDAHL

Comment*

Mr. Herivel has done an admirable job in concentrating on some of the *minutiae* of Newton's work in Book I of the *Principia,* thereby avoiding the temptation of easy generalizations. This has enabled him to stress an element difficult to characterize in a few words, what he calls "the transforming power" of Newton's genius (p. 134), by virtue of which Newton managed to absorb certain concepts and techniques found in the work of predecessors such as Galileo and Descartes, frequently only of marginal importance in their writings, and placing these concepts with a new-found clarity in the forefront of his own thinking in dynamics. One of the more interesting examples of this process Herivel traces in the development of Newton's thought where his "dynamical intuition" led him gradually to abandon the concept of "centrifugal force" in favor of "centripetal force"; this being apparently also one of the few cases where the early Newton had not yet achieved the requisite "clarity" to be found in his later writings; all of which illustrates Herivel's general contention that we need to study Newton's early writings in order to grasp the debt he owed to his predecessors as well as the magnitude of his own achievement. Of similar interest are some of the other items which Herivel singles out in his Newton "testimonial": the concept of composition of motions; the place of "force" in the laws of motion; the application of the concept of inertia to circular motion; the cracking of the problem of Kepler motion; the concept of conservation of motion in its application to the case of colliding bodies; although here it may be worth noting that conservation principles in their full generality did not form a part of Newton's vision, as distinct from his illustrious contemporary, Leibniz. Whether many of the other aspects which Mr. Herivel lists in his testimonial are of much help in *explaining* Newton's achievements I doubt. For instance, the reference to his "clarity of thought" *in general* is too much like describing his achievements rather than explaining them. And the same goes for the references to Newton's mathematical genius and to his dynamical intuition: these descriptions are rightly taken from the facts which Mr. Herivel has adduced in the first part of his paper; but they cannot necessarily be counted as "deep" factors that were responsible for Newton's achievements.

Herivel has shown very interestingly the difficulties that lay in the path of conceptual clarification of notions like centrifugal and centripetal force, as well as of force in general, and the way it enters into the second and third laws of motion. He puts rather less emphasis on an equally great achievement in dynamics, viz. Newton's contribution toward stabilizing the concept of mass. This is not the place to retell the story of Newton's separation of the various confused ingredients which history had handed to his period. Yet Newton's genius emerges here at its most brilliant, clarifying confused ideas, seeing the essential ingredient, stripping it of misleading adumbrations, and synthesizing a number of previously existing notions occurring in different contexts into a new concept and placing it at the center of the theory. I nearly said: "Into a new concept, precisely defined." But is it?

Of course, as Herivel reminds us (p. 129), Newton's second law of motion is framed by him in the form "change of motion is proportional to motive force." And the concept of motion here referred to does not make use of the concept of mass with the explicitness with which it is employed in the post-Newton formulation, "accelerative force is proportional to mass times acceleration." True, "motion," by definition II is measured by the product of velocity and quantity of matter. But it takes some searching and careful reading of definition III and Newton's comments thereon, to link "quantity of matter" with the "innate force of matter" referred to in the latter; that innate force which is used (for instance) explicitly in Book I, Prop. I which has the demonstration of Kepler's law of areal velocity.[1] Such considerations suggest that to appreciate the full import of Newton's thought at this point requires reference to the definitions.

Now this brings me to a remark of Herivel's on p. 127 which throws an interesting light on this question of what attitude as historians of science we should bring to a work like the *Principia*. For in the place referred to Herivel says that he does not propose to spend much time on the definitions which Newton prefixed to Book I of his work. He does not want to spend any time on them because he thinks hardly anyone has ever read or now bothers to read them. One wants to ask: Why did Newton choose to insert these definitions? A possible answer might be that he wished to follow closely the form of a geometrical treatise. There is, however, another reason. Mr. Herivel suggests that Newton's definitions of mass, momentum, inertia, force, were of "things with which we are already familiar" (p. 127). This was however clearly not Newton's opinion, since he expressly states that these definitions are of "words as are *less known*," and that they are meant to explain "the sense in which I would have them be understood in the following discourse" (Scholium to def. VIII).[2] This means that these definitions enshrine for the reader the result of those very conceptual changes to which Mr. Herivel has drawn our attention. They are therefore valuable pointers in our estimation of Newton's achievement in dynamics—more important in some respects than the study of the technical sections of the treatise. Anyone reading for instance the wording of definition III, together with Newton's comments, on "vis insita" or "inertial force," sees as in a mirror the turning point of two worlds. Inertia is still called a "force" which is "innate" or "in" the body. But Newton shrewdly remarks that it manifests itself only when another (external) force "endeavours to change" the state of uniform velocity (or rest) of the body. To mark this fact, he adds that the inertial force is a veritable "force of inactivity," and that it does not really differ from the "inactivity of the mass," thereby registering the relation between this force and the mass of the body, making mass a "dynamical" concept.[3]

Now this was a difficult notion to digest. And the term "force of inertia" did little to ease confusion. For it still suggested that there was a force in the body, acting even when not manifesting itself through interaction with other forces, thereby letting in by the back door the older view that this is a force which prevents the moving body from coming to rest. Anyone who doubts the insidious possibility of such confusions need only look at the writings of Leibniz and the early Kant that were published *after* the appearance of the *Principia,* to see that this is still how they understood the position.[4] In the case of Leibniz, this manifests itself in his contention that "matter in itself resists motion by a general passive force of resistance," requiring thus another "motive force" to maintain the motion;[5] though it ought to be added in fairness that these forces are not by Leibniz conceived as strictly belonging to the realm of phenomenal dynamics, but to "metaphysics." Rather, Leibniz tries to fit Newton's concept of force into a different conceptual framework from that which subsequently came to be termed "Newtonian"; resisting the idea that all forces are only "external," that all matter is only "inert," etc. In the case of the early Kant (*Estimation of Living Forces*), the confusions are more subtle; but it certainly seems that in paragraphs 15–16, 117–120 of this work there is a clear indication of that slipping back into the belief that a body would not maintain its uniform motion unless it were motivated by a special "living force" (Leibniz's *vis viva*); an even more confused transformation of Leibniz's already confused earlier views.

These remarks do of course technically no more than underline the point already made by Mr. Herivel that Newton had a clearer and more succinct view of mass and force than his predecessors, and, incidentally, of some of his spiritual successors. I only wish to add that in order to see this as an historical phenomenon we must consider the whole of Newton's work, and the spirit in which it is written; requiring that we should pay close attention also to those nonformal aspects of his work that are of less importance to the technical scientist, since the latter is already working within the Newtonian paradigm.

Similar comments go for the significance of definition IV, concerning the concept of "impressed force," and its relation to the First Law of Motion dealt with elsewhere in this volume by I. Bernard Cohen, to which I will only add one further distinction. In the definition Newton wants to emphasize the relationship of his conception of force to the phenomenon of inertia, *if such phenomenon there be*. The First Law states that there *is*; that bodies *do* move inertially. But in the definition Newton reminds us of older doctrines, according to which the impressed force, once imparted to the body, remained in that body; since without such an "innate force," or "impetus," no motion could maintain itself.

I am not unaware, of course, of the modern contention that the concepts of force, mass, time, etc. are really "defined implicitly" by the laws themselves, although be it noted that one needs for this to use all three laws jointly. But it is by no means certain yet whether this program of implicit definitions has ever been worked out satisfactorily and completely; and whether or not somewhere such "theoretical concepts" need linking with the language of the "vulgar" and with the preoccupations of "common sense." If this were the case, Newton's nonformal introductions of his technical concepts would receive new significance from the philosophical point of view.

Toward one set of definitions Mr. Herivel displays a more respectful attitude: those of absolute space, time, and motion, though here again I sense a slightly worried, even patronizing attitude generated by his knowledge that for the Newtonian and post-Newtonian scientist these concepts have not stood the test of time, have become "outmoded" (p. 128). But the triumph of modern relativistic views should not cause us to overestimate so-called "relativistic" theories like those of Leibniz in Newton's own time. When these are carefully studied, they betray as many if not more confusions—if confusions they be—than the views of Newton. Many critics have frequently felt that Newton's absolutist conceptions had little relation to the remainder of his dynamics. Mach for instance was inclined to locate the significant core of it in Corollary V, Book I, following the laws of motion, and which expresses the so-called "Principle of Newtonian Relativity." Anyway, I wish Mr. Herivel had indicated at least briefly why, as he says, Newton's own conceptions here support, despite "certain philosophical weaknesses," his claim to being a "natural philosopher" (p. 128).

Actually, I think Newton's case was rather stronger in this last respect than he is usually given credit for. First of all, it should be noted that Leibniz did not, perhaps, quite manage to banish space from the philosophical universe; his reference to "order of relations" is proverbially too nonspecific to deserve unquestioned acceptance. Besides (as Herivel hints also), Leibniz himself had to introduce his notion of "metaphysical force" in order to differentiate between "apparent" motion (due to mere change of reference system) and "real motion," though an objection to this move is that "real motion" is not the same as "absolute motion," as was implied by Berkeley already, and explicitly stated in Kant's *Metaphysical Foundations of Science* (IV: General Observation).[6] But then,

GERD BUCHDAHL

the same comment could be made on Newton's various arguments involving the experiment of the bucket, the two globes, and so on. Nevertheless, we can understand one of his intellectual motives: a demand for symmetry. If we grant his contention that *nonuniform* relative motion can be distinguished from nonuniform absolute motion by means of the resulting forces, it was an easy step to claim that the entailed concept of absolute space apply to uniform motion also. "But," as is sometimes remarked by modern exponents of general relativity, "Newton in that case did not apply his principle of symmetry far enough. He allows the action of space on matter; yet he forgets to let matter react on space," which is precisely what the modern theory does, with its concept of a modification of the spatio-temporal metric in the neighborhood of matter.[7]

Now I mention these points in order to say: If historians want to play the game of giving marks in terms of hindsight, then Newton deserves here more marks than are usually accorded to him. For if his treatment had one virtue, it was that it placed the concept of space in the forefront of the discussion. Nor should we make too much here of the distinction between the "scientist" and the "natural philosopher." From the point of view of creative science (as distinct from what T. Kuhn has called "normal science")[8] these are one and the same thing. But we, as philosophers and historians, may well see afterwards more clearly the significance of some of the moves.

This is not to answer the question, which there is no space to explore, what *technical* role these conceptions of absolute space, time, and motion play in Newton's treatise. No doubt, in part they are a response to Newton's need to speak of real or "true motions" (cf. last sentence of the scholium on space, time, and motion).[9] But here of course the charge is made—and Mr. Herivel repeats it—of *"philosophical* weaknesses." What were these? To answer this question and briefly develop it, I shall introduce comparisons with some of Newton's philosophical contemporaries or near contemporaries. Such a method, as much as the study of Newton's unpublished writings, can help us to arrive at significant interpretations by exploring some of the possibilities that may lie encapsuled in Newton's tentative suggestions. This implies that the critical historian cannot hope simply to uncover what "the real views" of the subject of his studies were unless he reveals them as an element in a dynamically developing intellectual situation. There perhaps never was *a* "real" view.[10]

What then were the "philosophical weaknesses" of Newton's conception of "absolute space and time"? That absolute space and time are unobservable? This is not very clear; what would it be like to make space and time observable? Space and time are "presuppositional entities"; a fact which Kant subsequently registered through his theory that these entities are transcendental presuppositions of the possibility of sensory apprehension. "But we are speaking of the concept of absolute space," so comes the retort. Here again, however, it is perhaps possible that a non-self-contradictory interpretation of such a notion can be given from the methodological point of view, of the kind Kant for instance proposed in his *Metaphysical Foundations of Natural Science*. There it is introduced simply as the "idea" of an "ultimate" but *"indeterminate"* physical coordinate system to which all movable empirical matter and space are referred. "Indeterminate" means that although "ultimate," it is only *relatively* speaking the "last" system to which everything is referred, such as that of the fixed stars in the case of the Newtonian system. But it is always possible to *seek* yet a further reference point, here: for the system of fixed stars, which will then in turn be regarded as "ultimate." Now this contradictory process, whereby we have to postulate an ultimate reference system, and yet are always driven to go beyond it to a further system, yields what Kant calls "the idea of absolute space"; an "idea" being something that is hypostasized as an ultimate and real entity, though this is at the same time really no more than the subject of a "regulative" process in which a merely *relatively* "ultimate" condition must always be regarded as capable of being referred to yet another condition. Since such an "idea" only expresses the scientist's "regulative demand" for contradictory intellectual operations, it is immune from the usual criticisms; and insofar as Newton's own concept obscurely feeds on such a situation—as it surely does—it is a perfectly intelligible construct.[11]

It may, however, be objected that this seems to go against Kant's own characterization of the Newtonian conceptions of absolute space and time as "nonentities" (*Undinge*). Here we must, however, distinguish between the reformulation of the *methodological* aspect of these concepts in terms of the "regulative process" just described, and the quite different problem of their *ontological status,* reminding us of the need to distinguish, in Newton's own complex reflections on space and time, between these aspects. For Newton himself clearly did not take his methodological treatment of absolute space and time as requiring him to underwrite the theory that these conceptions denoted certain independent and vacuous kinds of receptacles. If methodologically absolute space was needed as an abstract reference system, to give *meaning* for instance to his "hypothesis" that "the centre of the system of the world is immovable,"[12] ontologically Newton did not at all hold with the doctrine of the "independent empty receptacle." He felt as much as anyone in his time that these things had to be given an "ontological locus," if I may so label it. And such a locus was characterized for him through the conception of God's *sensorium.* Now such a move immediately brings out condescending reactions on the part of the hard-headed scientist, but this betrays his lack of understanding of philosophical method. Thus Howard Stein, in the contribution to this volume already referred to, rightly draws attention to Newton's *methodological* motives which made necessary for him the conception of absolute space, but then paradoxically goes on to say that Newton did not need for this his *theology;* whereas in fact, the theological model was employed by Newton in an attempt to characterize the *ontological* status of space— quite a different matter. What Newton seeks to do is to register his acknowledgment that space and time are neither substance, nor relation, nor accident, and yet something. He hence must fall back on a model. Such a model, as he explains at greater length in Queries 28 and 31 of the *Opticks,* is the human *"sensorium"*; something that is expressly called a "similitude" in Clarke's reply to Leibniz.[13] Now what is *our "sensorium"*? Careful reading of the relevant passages shows that Newton employs something like Locke's theory of perception, according to which our mind is in the direct presence of its "ideas," the latter corresponding to, and being prompted *via* a rather questionable causal process by those external things which our ideas "represent" in our minds. However, though the "ideas" are "in our minds," this is metaphor; more strictly, they are presented *to* our minds, and further, they are such that what is perceived, is perceived "in space." The important question now becomes: *is* there, and in what sense is there, such a space? Who can tell? In a sense there are just the ideas and ourselves (or our minds). But the idea (what is represented) as it were "appears" in space; the ideal thing (the object of perception) is *seen* in space.

As is well known, this theory gave immense trouble to Locke's successors, Berkeley and Hume, who both tried to "reduce" this idea of "outness" and to make it something "derivative"; for the story of the ideas had been so told as to make us imagine that they were "really in us," or "with us"; there could then be no place for space! Yet space there "seems to be"; some modern logicians (e.g. Russell) have labelled it "perceptual space"; and I think something like this is what Newton was driving at in respect of a theory of human perception.

Now it will be seen that such a theory supplies a meaning for space without either having to make it a thing or forcing it to become nothing. But, it may be said, this so far supplies us at most only with a *meaning,* and not the required universal reality, corresponding to the locution of "public space," let alone absolute, existing space. Before turning to Newton's response to this, i.e., his theory of space and time as *God's sensorium,* let us once more consider the whole logic of the situation in the light of the corresponding Kantian doctrine, in the hope that this will help us to see more clearly the significance of Newton's move. Kant solved this ontological problem (as already mentioned) by making space (and time) *universal presuppositions,* for the possibility of empirical cognition of "phenomena," or "appearances." Such an explication of the concept of space is specifically intended to restore the notion of "outness" as basic. Things, quâ "phenomena" are *directly* seen as "out there in space."[14] However, such a conception is highly sophisticated and does not easily answer the ontologist's worries. *What* is thus presupposed, was of course simply the space and time in which phenomena, quâ phenomena, i.e., "appearances," are "seen" ("intuited"), i.e., "appear." (This is part of the "definition" of the concept of "phenomenon." *Per contra,* whatever does not thus satisfy the definition, will for this reason be termed "noumenon.") With respect to phenomena, space and time are thus "empirically real." But *that* phenomena *have necessarily* to be "seen" as appearing in space and time is what (for Kant) provides the ontological sheet anchor, though it is an anchor that translates "ontological" into "transcendental" (something possessing "transcendental ideality"), i.e., into a *universal presupposition* of anything being a phenomenon.

Now it is this feature, and this feature alone, that Newton was still trying to catch with his model of God; where space is said to be "God's *sensorium.*" And I think Newton's intentions are vastly illuminated by contrasting them with Kant's scheme which offers us a different and more comprehensive model, more closely linked to the whole of the epistemological situation; but still only an alternative *model.* In the case of Newton, space, too, gets its *meaning* as that in which "things" are "seen" (*sc.* "things" quâ Lockean "ideas"); but its ontological support is pictured through the phrase "being seen by God," God being a locution through which Newton seeks to render the fact— as he expressly remarks—that things are thus seen (by God) "everywhere and always," thereby affirming the independence from any subjective reference of this model of space and time. The "human *sensorium,*" by becoming "God's *sensorium*" is universalized; space and time become "real," though "transcendentally *real*" (in Kantian locution) rather than "transcendentally *ideal,*" as in Kant's own theory.

The various theological, religious or psychological trappings in which this concept of God may have been encapsuled for Newton should therefore not conceal his real intention. Just as things are "outside" our minds, in the way in which "ideas" that are "formed in our brain" (as Clarke says) represent them, and are thus "outside" without there being more than mere "perceptual space" intended, so things created by God (*sc.* "real things," non-ideal) are "present to God" as "outside" without this notion of "outside" (and hence that of space) having a stronger sense (by analogy) than that of the analogon of our own "perceptual space." Space is (thus made) real, without having thereby become a thing.

Now I think that such wider vistas, buried in Newton's treatise, are a very important piece of evidence explaining the vast influence which his work had on subsequent generations. In other words, not just the solid achievements in dynamics,—which in any case become really solid only through their entrenchment in the history of dynamics which *might* perhaps have gone another way; but the open vistas, the half-tied knots, which

Newton left behind. "Idle dreamers" like Mach and Einstein owe a lot to these questions which Newton left unanswered. If we are to believe Mr. Kuhn, it is these intellectual "anomalies" which build up the pressures toward real advances in science, rather than the solved questions, the stable techniques, which are of importance to the applied scientists. It is for that reason that we must necessarily spend more time on the former, rather than on the technical perfection of which Newton's genius is such a supreme example.

NOTES

*The following discussion is based on an earlier and somewhat different version of the paper by John Herivel [Ed.].

[1] *Principia*, F. Cajori (ed.), Berkeley, 1946, p. 40; for the definitions, cf. pp. 1–2.

[2] *Ibid.*, p. 6, my italics.

[3] *Ibid.*, p. 2.

[4] But it should be noted that the late Kant, in his *Metaphysical Foundations of Science*, explicitly remarks that "the designation force of inertia (vis inertiae) must, in spite of the eminence of its founder's name, be entirely banished from natural science, not only because it carries with it a contradiction in expression, or because the law of inertia (lifelessness) might thereby be easily confounded with the law of reaction in every communicated motion, but principally because thereby the mistaken conception of those . . . would be maintained and strengthened according to which the reaction of bodies, to which they refer under the name force of inertia, is [confusedly believed to] consist in the motion thereby being swallowed up, diminished or destroyed, instead of mere communication of motion being thereby effected . . ." (iii, Prop. 4, Observation 2; E. B. Bax (transl.), *Kant's Prolegomena and Meta-Physical Foundations of Natural Science,* London, 1883, p. 229).

[5] Cf. Leibniz, *Philosophical Papers and Letters,* L. E. Loemker (ed.), Chicago, 1956, vol. ii, pp. 721, 839.

[6] Bax (transl.), *Metaphysical Foundations of Science,* p. 240.

[7] As H. G. Alexander (in *The Leibniz-Clarke Correspondence,* New York, 1956, p. IV), has pointed out, the "reality of space-time" often claimed, in these terms, by modern expositors of the general theory of relativity may be more in tune with Newton's conceptions than with those of Leibniz, whose relativistic notions at the level of "appearance" were coupled with a metaphysical theory according to which these conceptions were in any case "unreal," and reducible to the substantial being of his "monads." Newton's conception of the divine "sensorium," discussed in my remarks, is precisely intended as a move to prevent this metaphysical reduction from being effected.

[8] See, T. S. Kuhn, *The Structure of Scientific Revolutions,* Chicago, 1962.

[9] *Principia,* Cajori (ed.), p. 12. Cf. Howard Stein's development of this point elsewhere in this volume ("Newtonian Space-Time").

[10] And as Professor Kuhn intimated to me in a private comment, this goes also for the philosophical critic's attempted appraisals, for they in turn subtly transform what they believe to be the "historical case," and in this way act as intellectual transmuting forces.

[11] Bax (transl.), *Metaphysical Foundations of Science*, p. 239.

[12] *Principia,* Cajori (ed.), Bk. III, p. 419.

[13] Alexander, *Leibniz-Clarke Correspondence,* Clarke's First Reply, 3, p. 13. Cf. also Newton's *Opticks,* Queries 28 and 31. Dover edition, New York, pp. 368 and 405.

[14] For the connection between this sense of "outside" and "space," cf. Kant's *Critique of Pure Reason,* A23/B38: "Space is not an empirical concept . . . For in order that certain sensations be referred to something outside me (that is, to something in another region of space from that in which I find myself), and similarly in order that I may be able to represent them as outside and alongside one another, . . . the representation of space must be presupposed."

I. BERNARD COHEN

Newton's Second Law and the
Concept of Force in the *Principia*

INTRODUCTION[1]

EWTON'S *Principia* APPEARED IN 1687 IN THREE "BOOKS," PRECEDED BY
two preliminary sections: "Definitions" and "Axioms or Laws of Motion."
My assignment here is to discuss the Second Law of Motion in relation to
Newton's concept of force. In this presentation, I shall begin with the *Principia* as it
stood in 1687, and then turn for further illumination to certain revisions either
projected by Newton or actually incorporated in later editions.

Let me remind you that in the *Principia* there are three Axioms or Laws of Motion.
The third, which shall not concern us here, posits the equality of "action" and "reaction." The first is the Law of Inertia.

The Second Law specifies or quantifies how "motion" is produced, or altered,
either in magnitude or in direction or in both simultaneously. Since the main burden
of the *Principia* is to analyze the motions of bodies, and the changing motions of
bodies, in terms of the forces causing such actions, the Second Law of Motion in its
manifold applications lies at the very heart of the Newtonian system of physical
thought.

In the physics of gross bodies, Newton had to deal with three groups of "forces"
which may change "motion": percussion, pressure, and the varieties of centripetal
force. The first two of these are contact "forces," exerted when one body actually
touches another; but the third includes both contact "forces" and those that act at a
distance. (In the *Principia*, Newton's examples include (1) the whirling of a stone
in a sling [contact] and (2) gravity, the planetary force, and magnetism [action-at-
a-distance].) Another way of dividing these "forces" is in terms of the duration of
their action. Percussion alters the motion of a body in an instant, as when one billiard
ball strikes another or a racquet strikes a tennis ball. But pressure and centripetal
force act continuously during a finite time-interval. A third way of grouping these
"forces" is to note that percussion and pressure produce a change in "motion" in
which an act associated with the "force" may be independently observed; whereas in
the case of centripetal force acting at a distance, we are able to see only a change in
"motion" and from this observation alone deduce that a force has been acting.
Finally, pressure and certain types of centripetal force may be quantified independently of the alteration of motion; e.g., the downward "force" accelerating a stone
in free fall may be determined by weighing the stone. But the quantification of percussion comes from the observed change of "motion" and cannot ordinarily be
gained independently.

All these differences belie the commonality of a single concept of "force." We may well understand that Newton's predecessors and contemporaries did not have a simple and unified system of physics to encompass all these varieties of the alteration of the "motion" of bodies. Thus, we shall see below, it is a clear sign of Newton's genius that he was able to produce a physics of central forces upon the more generally acceptable base of the contact "forces" of impact or percussion.

In the presentation that follows, it will be seen how Newton made the transition from the physics of impulses or instantaneous "forces" to the physics of continuous forces. Some attention will be given to two forms of the Second Law of Motion,

$$(1.1) \quad \vec{F} = m\vec{A} \ or \ \vec{F} = m\frac{d\vec{V}}{dt} ,$$

which is the way we currently write the law, and yet another,

$$(1.2) \quad \text{"force"} = k \cdot \Delta(m\vec{V}) ,$$

which is closer to the way in which Newton enunciated the Second Law in the *Principia*, although of course Newton did not write the Law as an equation. We shall see that although equation (1.2) represents the Second Law as formally stated by Newton, he also knew and used the law in the more familiar version represented by equation (1.1).

THE SECOND LAW OF MOTION

The Second Law reads (in Whiston's literal translation, 1716) as follows: "The Mutation of Motion is proportional to the moving Force impress'd; and is according to the right Line in which that Force is impress'd." Newton is thus dealing with "mutatio motus," or "change in motion," or, to refer back to Definition II, a change in the "quantity of motion," a quantity measured by the product of mass and velocity: hence with the alteration of what we denote today by momentum. There is no ambiguity. Newton does not say here, "*rate of* change in quantity of motion" or "change in quantity of motion *per second*," despite the many scientists and historians who have alleged that this is what he meant. The "force" in this statement of the Second Law is clearly what we have come to know as an "impulse."

In the presentation which follows, I shall mean by impulse a "force" acting *for a very brief time* indeed, as when a steel ball at the end of a pendulum strikes another, or when a tennis racquet strikes a ball. I shall refer to such "forces" or impulses as *instantaneous*, in order to contrast them with continuous "forces" like gravity and other "centripetal forces." (But of course they are not absolutely instantaneous in the sense of requiring no time whatsoever for their action!) We may now restate Newton's Second Law: every change of momentum of a body is proportional to the impulse which produces it, and occurs in the direction of the line of action of the impulse.

A fundamental question that we must explore, therefore, is whether this impulse form of the law—however much it may appeal to us because it is both dimensionally sound and physically true—is a proper rendition of what Newton intended. Is it in this form that he applied the law? And if the answer to this question is "Yes," we must then ask how Newton ever got to the law as we know it:

$$\vec{F} = m\vec{A} \text{ or } \vec{F} = \Delta(m\vec{V})/\Delta t,$$

where $\vec{F}$ is force in our modern sense and is consequently a measure of (or measured by) the rate of change of momentum.

The answer to the first question is simple. We have only to examine the first instance in which the law is applied: in Corol. 1 to the Laws of Motion, immediately following the statement of the three Laws. Here it is Newton's intention to show how effects of two "forces" may be combined. The corollary reads:

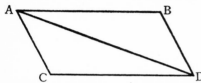

A body, acted on by two forces simultaneously, will describe the diagonal of a parallelogram in the same time as it would describe the sides by those forces separately.

The proof begins by considering the motion of a "body in a given time, by a force M impressed apart in the place A": it will, in this time, "with an uniform motion be carried from A to B." There is no doubt that in referring to the "force impressed," Newton has in mind an impulse; it cannot be a force acting continually while the body moves from A to B, since Newton says that after the force has acted the body will have a "uniform motion." Next Newton supposes that a wholly different "force" (an impulse, or a blow) N is "impressed apart in the same place," A; then in the above-mentioned time, the body "should be carried from A to C." Now, "by both forces acting together," the body will subsequently move in this given time along the diagonal of the parallelogram ABDC from A to D.

In the paragraph following the enunciation of Law III, Newton gives the following example: "If a body impinge upon another, and by its force change the motion of the other, that body also (because of the equality of the mutual pressure) will undergo an equal change, in its own motion, towards the contrary part [i.e., in the opposite direction]." Here is a case of impact, where a body, "by its force," produces a change in the quantity of motion or momentum of another body. Yet another example of Newton's direct use of impact to illustrate force in the Second Law occurs in Prop. I, Book I, of the *Principia*, and is discussed below.

TWO LAWS OF MOTION RATHER THAN ONE[2]

In the *Principia*, the First Law reads: "Every body perseveres in its state of resting or of moving uniformly in a right line, unless it is compelled to change that state by forces impress'd thereon."[3] Many students of Newton have speculated on the reason why there is such a Law I in addition to Law II, since it may seem to us that the former is simply a special case of the latter when the impressed force is zero.

There are at least three historical bases for Newton's having stated Laws I and II separately. First, in chronological importance, is the influence of Descartes. Descartes's *Principia philosophiae*, as I have shown elsewhere, was the undoubted source of Definition III and Law I (even to the use of the phrase "quantum in se est"), which appear there as the substance of Descartes's "prima lex naturae" and "altera lex naturae." Descartes's presentation of what was to become Newton's First Law is divided into two parts (two "leges naturae"), the first of which deals with the body's tendency to maintain a *state* of motion or of rest, while the second specifies that inertial motion must be rectilinear.[4] The effect of forces, as in collisions, or in the circular motion of a body whirling in a sling, is dealt with in the succeeding laws. Certainly this procedure must have made an impression, conscious or unconscious, on Newton, who in his own *Principia philosophiae* also embodied the principle of inertia in a separate law from that specifying how forces may alter an inertial motion, just as Descartes had done in his *Principia*.

Second, and perhaps even more important, is the influence of Huygens, whom Newton admired so much that he named the new concept of "centripetal force" in his honor.[5] Part Two of Huygens' *Horologium oscillatorium* (1673) is entitled, "On the falling of bodies and their motion in a cycloid" (*De descensu gravium & motu eorum in cycloide*). Huygens begins with a set of Hypotheses, just as Newton did a decade or so later, in the tract *De motu* (written on the eve of the *Principia*) and in the beginning of Book Three of the *Principia* in 1687, "De mundi systemate." The first two Hypotheses in Huygens' *De descensu gravium* are so close in intent to Newton's first two Axioms or Laws of Motion as to permit no doubt whatsoever that they are the source of Newton's first two laws; and thus they help us to see why Newton too had a separate Lex I and Lex II. (See p. 148 below.)

The third historical basis for separating Law I and Law II is the fact that **Law I** embodies a radical departure from traditional physics to the extent that it declares motion (if uniform and rectilinear) to be a "state" and not a "process"—in the Aristotelian sense. This Law I, equating dynamically the "state" of resting and the "state" of moving uniformly in a right line, is thus a clear announcement at the outset that the *Principia* is constructed on the primary axiom of the new inertial physics of Galileo and Descartes, of Kepler,[6] and of Gassendi. In view of the newness of this inertial physics, a separate statement of Law I, without the complicating factors of the quantitative relation of force to change of motion or of the relative directions of force and change of momentum, was obviously of a heuristic value that by far transcended the narrow logical question of whether under certain circumstances Law I might to some degree be implied by Law II as a special case.

In the modern formulation of Newtonian dynamics, in which the concept of a continuous force $\vec{F}$ is primary and the concept of impulse ($\vec{F} \cdot dt$) is derived from it, Newton's First Law does indeed appear to be a special case of the Second Law. But if impulse be primary, and Law II be stated for impulses and changes in momentum

I. BERNARD COHEN

(rather than *rate of* change in momentum), then Law I would be a special case of Law II only for impulses, but not for continuous forces. It is certainly possible that Newton had this distinction in mind since the explanatory paragraph following Law I refers only to continuous forces as examples, and not once to instantaneous forces. From Newton's illustrations of these two Laws of Motion, it would seem that these two laws—as given in the *Principia*—are not really as closely related to one another as is often supposed by those who do not take account of the fact that Newton's Law II, as stated, is restricted to impulsive forces, whereas Law I is not.

This possible distinction between the first two Laws of Motion is related to the fact that in the *Principia* Newton had to deal with two distinct types of dynamically significant forces: the quasi-instantaneous impulse (as the force of percussion: a blow, an impact), and the continuously acting force. In nature, whether in the world at large or in the specially contrived experiments in the laboratory, a single impulse or a set of discrete impulses produces an obvious change in the state of a body. The Second Law expresses quantitatively just how great this change of momentum must be for a given impulse, and it further specifies that the direction of the change in momentum must be the same as the direction of the impulsive or instantaneous force. As we shall see below, Newton was quite aware that continuous forces produce continuous accelerations, and he even applied in the *Principia* the rule that in these circumstances, there is an acceleration proportional to the force, if the force is constant. But since this rule was not stated explicitly in Law II, it must have appeared to Newton to be implied by the Definitions or to be a consequence (as, in the limit) of the Second Law for impulses, or possibly to be so obvious as hardly to be worth mentioning.

But it is far from obvious as to *when* continuous forces are acting. A continuous force is not *seen to act* in the sense that is usually true of instantaneous impulses. When an impulsive force acts on a body we tend to see both an action (cause) and a change of motion (effect). That is, when a blow is given to a ball by a tennis racquet, or an impact is given by one billiard ball to another, we see the physical act of one body striking another, which we interpret as the giving of an impulse, and we see a second phenomenon, the concomitant change in the state of motion or of rest in the struck body. How different this is from the common action of continuous forces, gravity, or electric and magnetic attraction or repulsion. We certainly don't *see* the sun act on Mars in the sense that we see a tennis racquet strike a ball. Indeed, the very existence of such forces within the Newtonian framework may only be inferred, and inferred specifically from the change in the state of motion (or of rest) in the affected body. In this sense the First Law of Motion contains a test for determining whether a continuous force is acting: this test consists of discovering whether or not the "state" of the body is changing. This is the second part of Law I: ". . . unless it is compelled to change that state [of resting or of moving uniformly in a right line] by forces impressed thereon." (I have reference here to action-at-a-distance only. In the case of a stone being whirled at the end of a spring we may both have the feeling of a force acting and see the effect of the spring being extended.)

Let us turn now to the evidence contained in the paragraph following each of the first two Laws of Motion. In the discussion of Law I, Newton does not refer to a body at rest remaining at rest unless acted on by a force, or even tending to "persevere" in its state of rest. Rather he gives a succession of examples in which a body is in motion and in which the body cannot "persevere" in that state because of the action of an external force. The first example is a projectile. There are two basic ways in which Newton says a projectile may be "compelled" to change its "state of uniform motion in a right line": having its uniform linear motion altered because the projectile is (1) "retarded by the resistance of the air," and (2) "impelled downward by the force of gravity." We may observe incidentally that Newton presents here the identical circumstances of Huygens' *De descensu gravium*: first a pure inertial motion (in Hypoth. I), which is then altered (in Hypoth. II) by air resistance and gravity.

The resistance of the air appears also as a cause for altering inertial motion in the remaining two examples, the rotation of a top and the motions of planets and comets which meet "with less resistance in more free spaces" and so "preserve their motions both progressive and circular for a much longer time." These examples of rotating tops (and the "progressive and circular" motions of planets and comets) to illustrate *linear* inertia is, to say the least, startling. But Newton is not adopting a Galilean position of circular inertia; quite the contrary! Circular motion, or any curvilinear motion, is inertial in Newtonian physics only to the degree that it is a combination of two components, of which one is a continuing tangential inertial motion and the other is a constantly accelerated motion caused by a force which makes the moving body leave its otherwise linear path to follow the curved trajectory.

Let us turn now to the Second Law. The discussion (in Motte's translation) reads:

> If any force generates a motion, a double force will generate double the motion, a triple force triple the motion, whether that force be impress'd altogether and at once, or gradually and successively [*successive et gradatim*]. And this motion (being always directed the same way with the generating force) if the body moved before, is added to or subducted from the former motion, according as they directly conspire with or are directly contrary to each other; or obliquely joyned, when they are oblique, so as to produce a new motion compounded from the determination of both.

The character of the "force" in question is determined by Newton's statement that the quantity of motion generated by any "force" is the same "whether that force be impress'd altogether and at once, or gradually and successively." In our interpretation we must be wary of the adverb *"gradatim,"* which means literally "by degrees" or "step by step." Hence Newton's two modes of action are (i) a single stroke or act and (ii) a sequence of distinct stages, degrees, or steps ("successive

et gradatim"). These two modes of action shall be subjected to further analysis below, in considering some of Newton's projected revisions of the Second Law. In
particular, we shall see the important consequences that ensue from defining the
action on an infinitesimal level. But at this point it is important only to indicate that
Newton would not have us understand "gradatim" to imply necessarily a continuous
action during a finite time-interval (in the sense that today we talk of a "gradual"
slope: meaning an even, moderate inclination). There can be no doubt that Newton
intended the Second Law, as stated, to relate discrete increments of force to the
changes in quantity of motion they produce.

Thus the paragraphs following the two laws do seem to suggest that the "forces"
in Law I are continuous, just as the "forces" in Law II appear to be instantaneous
(i.e., very short-lived) forces. This would accord with the need for being able to specify whether or not a continuous (noncontact) force such as gravity, electrical attraction
(or repulsion) or magnetic attraction (or repulsion) may be acting,[7] to the degree—
as mentioned above—that we cannot see the "cause," as is possible when a blow
is given to one object by another. We have, of course, no way of knowing whether
Newton intended his readers to draw such a conclusion from his examples. Furthermore, the First Law is still valid even if we there interpret "force" as impulse,
and thus give a consistent interpretation to Law I and Law II.[8] In this case the two
laws are one: the first part a qualitative declaration of the new physics, the second
part a quantitative statement of the magnitude (and direction) of the change of
motion produced by an impact. This is true of impulses, but not of continuously
acting forces.

We must be wary, however, lest we make too much of a distinction—on the
Newtonian level—between the action of continuous forces and impulses. As we
shall see below (in the section on "Impulses and Continuous Forces" and in Appendices I and II), such a distinction, while apparently valid on the finite level,
tends to break down on the infinitesimal level. We shall see, below, that Newton, by
and large, considered continuously acting forces as sequences of infinitesimal impulses
(or as limits of sequences of very small impulses) and also was willing to consider
first-order infinitesimal impulses to be composed of (or susceptible of being broken
down into) a set of second-order infinitesimals. Since we shall see that the latter
could act to produce a kind of continuously varying second-order change of motion
within a first-order infinitesimal instant of time, we must be careful lest we bind
Newton's thinking in an intellectual strait-jacket that satisfies our own requirements at the expense of understanding his.

IMPACT, IMPULSE, AND MOMENTUM: NEWTON'S DEBT TO DESCARTES

The paragraph in the *Principia* explaining Law II (printed above) concludes
with a method of adding the new motion to a previously existing motion. The
method, as stated, appears at first to be that of Corol. 1 to the Laws of Motion.[9]
But there is one major difference. In Corol. 1 it is first considered that each of two

forces may act separately to produce a motion in a given body starting at rest; then both forces act simultaneously *on the very same body at rest*. But in discussing Law II, Newton posits a force acting on a body already in motion. The difference may appear conceptually slight, but it proves to be most significant.

In the "Waste Book," and in a tract written much earlier than the *Principia*, "The lawes of motion," published by H. W. Turnbull, A. R. and M. B. Hall, and recently analyzed by John Herivel, Newton discussed this proposition in a form more like the above-mentioned discussion of Law II than Corol. 1. That is, he first allows the body to be put into motion by one of the blows; and then *while the body is in a resulting steady state of motion*, Newton has it receive a second oblique blow. The parallelogram is formed and the proof proceeds from there on as in Corol. 1. This difference between the early presentation in this tract and the later one (in Corol. 1 to the Laws of Motion in the *Principia*) has been called to our attention by Dr. Herivel, who has quite properly emphasized its significance. But I cannot agree with his tentative suggestion that this is in any way directly related to Galileo's derivation of the parabolic path of a projectile.[10] In any event, as Dr. Herivel himself has warned us, there are at least two fundamental differences between Galileo's presentation of projectile motion and Newton's early version of Corol. 1. First, Galileo posits a "force" (gravity) only in the downward direction, there being none in the horizontal. Second, Galileo's downward force is continuous ("constant"), producing an acceleration, whereas the two "forces" of Newton's proposition are impulses, producing changes in momentum almost instantaneously. If I seem to be dwelling overly long on what may appear to be a minor point of scholarship, may I anticipate the sequel: I have found in this early form of Corol. 1 a neglected source of Newton's fundamental concepts of motion.

In seeking for the origins of this early version of Newton's Corol. 1, we must keep in mind that in Newton's day there were two outstanding examples of the change in "quantity of motion" (or in momentum) produced by a force acting instantaneously or quasi-instantaneously. One is the well-known type of impact or percussion that occurs when a freely moving gross body (say a ball) strikes *another* that may be either at rest or in motion. Modern commentators have generally tended to ignore the other instance, which I hope to show is of even greater importance for our understanding of Newton's Second Law of Motion, and which takes us to the source of Newton's Corol. 1. I have in mind Descartes's ingenious explanation of refraction in his *Dioptrique*. Descartes begins his explanation in terms of the motion of a tennis ball, using the analogy in order to show the validity of Snel's Law as a general principle of the mechanics of bodies; but not necessarily arguing therefrom that all optical phenomena arise from the properties and motions of "particles of light." Descartes's example thus takes us from the motion of gross bodies to the possible motions of sub-microscopic particles.

Descartes has just been considering reflection. As in the figure, let us—following Descartes—imagine a tennis player driving a tennis ball along the line AB. In

I. BERNARD COHEN

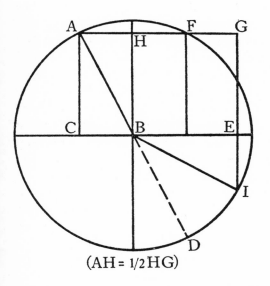

(AH = 1/2 HG)

the case of reflection, the path is altered at the point B so that the tennis ball will bounce up in the direction BF. Descartes then asks us to suppose that at B it encounters not the earth, but a cloth CBE, which the ball may rupture and pass through, losing a part of its velocity, say, one half. Descartes analyzes the motion into vertical and horizontal components; only the vertical component is diminished by the action of the cloth. The result is that the subsequent path will be along the line BI. Next, Descartes considers that CBE represents not a cloth but the surface of water, which acts as the cloth has done, so that the path is again AB + BI. But in order to have an analogue of the refraction of light, the path must be bent *toward the normal* as a ray goes from air into water, *not away from* the normal. Descartes, therefore, must have some action at the interface between the two media to augment the vertical component of the motion rather than to diminish it. Hence, he makes "yet another supposition"; he assumes that at the instant when the ball reaches the point B, it will be struck again by the racquet, "which increases the force of its motion. . . ." I shall not discuss here the significance of this demonstration in either the history of optics or the scientific thought of Descartes, because to do so would necessitate a discussion of the general problem of the corpuscular theory of light and the related question of the relative speed of light in more or less dense media (and of the finite speed of light). This would take us too far afield from our main topic.

The conditions of Descartes's proof are identical to the early form of Corol. 1 in the tract on "The lawes of motion" and in the explanation of Law II in the *Principia*. There can be no doubt that Descartes was Newton's source, since in Newton's optical lectures, the part presumably written in 1670,[11] Newton refers explicitly to Descartes's discussion of the Law of Refraction (or Law of Sines) and actually refers to Descartes's proof. He thus gives testimony of his acquaintance with the whole argument and not merely the results, in the statement: "The Truth whereof the Author [Descartes] had demonstrated not inelegantly, provided he had left no room to doubt of the physical Causes, which he assumed."

Those who first encounter statements that Descartes had a major formative influence on Newton's dynamics are apt to be skeptical, especially when they remember such anti-Cartesian statements as are found in the conclusion of Book Two of the *Principia,* and in the concluding General Scholium, in both of which Newton bitterly attacks the vortical "philosophical romance" of Descartes's *Principia*. But with regard to the Cartesian discussion of refraction, the situation is entirely different. Here we may actually see Newtonian physics in an earlier Cartesian dress. I would submit that it can hardly be a mere coincidence that the conditions of the early form of Newton's Corol. 1 fit so precisely the example given by Descartes. There is nothing like it in the writings of Galileo or of Kepler, nor does anything of this exact sort occur in Wallis' *Mechanica*. How fascinating to see this early version of Corol. 1 as a transformation of a statement of Descartes's, later transformed again in the tract *De motu* (on the eve of the *Principia*) to appear as we find it in the *Principia* itself! Since the Cartesian proof of the Law of Refraction makes use of "forces" that are unambiguously impulses, in the form of blows given to a ball by a tennis racquet, this source of Corol. 1 gives yet another confirmation of the view that the Second Law deals (exclusively) with so-called instantaneous "forces," or impulses.

One other short note on the sources of Newton's Second Law. Newton thought of the Second Law in relation to impact not merely through the influence of Descartes's *Dioptrique* but also because of the problem of impact, of determining just what motions will ensue when one object strikes another in both elastic and nonelastic types of collisions. This topic had occupied the attention of major scientists of the seventeenth century. Important early studies on percussion were made by Galileo, by Baliani, and by Torricelli; and the "Leges Naturae" in Descartes's *Principia* (after the first two dealing with inertia) discussed one by one several varieties of the impact of one body on another. Later in the century the topic was studied with especially rewarding consequences by Huygens and by Wallis and Wren. Wallis' paper in the *Philosophical Transactions* not only introduced Newton to the idea of conservation of momentum, but undoubtedly suggested to Newton—either consciously or unconsciously—the transformation of the Cartesian "Leges Naturae" into "Leges Motus," the Laws of Motion, as Wallis' paper was entitled. Yet another writer on percussion was Mariotte.

In presenting the problem of collision of bodies, in the Scholium following the Laws of Motion in the *Principia*, Newton referred to his predecessors (Huygens, Wallis, Wren, Mariotte) and discussed his own views concerning the imperfect elasticity of even the hardest bodies in nature. No reader could escape the conclusion that the physics of collisions and impacts was central to the dynamical thinking of Isaac Newton. Once again it was Descartes who was of major influence. For Descartes had stressed, in his *Principia*, that the force of a body in motion is measured by the product of its magnitude and its velocity, transformed by Wallis into weight and velocity, and finally transformed by Newton into mass and velocity. On impact, the whole force acts quasi-instantaneously,[12] and if we superimpose Wallis' concept of conservation on Descartes's concept of the force of a body in motion, then the description of the force of impact becomes almost the impulse-momentum form of

I. BERNARD COHEN

CONTINUOUS FORCES AND THEIR ACCELERATIONS: THE CONCEPT OF "IMPRESSED FORCE"

I have said earlier that Newton was perfectly aware that continuous forces produce continuous accelerations, that if such forces are constant they produce constant accelerations, and that such accelerations are in a fixed ratio to the forces for any given mass, where the mass is the measure of the proportionality of forces to accelerations according to the law

$$\vec{F} = k \cdot m\vec{A}$$

We shall see some of the evidence to support this contention in the present section.

But first we must pay a little attention to "impressed force," a concept which occurs in both the first Law (". . . a viribus impressis . . .") and the Second Law (". . . vi motrici impressae . . ."). It is surprising to find Newton using, in his *Principia*, the expression "vis impressa," which we customarily associate with the late medieval writers on dynamics. But "vis impressa" also appears commonly in the seventeenth century, e.g., in the writings of Galileo and Wallis, in a somewhat new sense, and Newton's own use of this concept is highly original. In Definition IV, he says that an "impressed force" is an "action exerted upon a body, in order to change its state," which—as always—means a "state, either of resting, or of uniform motion in a right line." Then, in an explanatory paragraph, Newton makes it clear that this "force consists in the action only" and it "remains no longer in the body once the action is over." Next he says that every new state acquired by a body is subsequently "maintained by *vis inertiae* only."

Now if the "impressed force" *is* the "action," as Newton says so explicitly ("vis impressa est actio . . ."), whereby the state of a body is changed, then the magnitude of this change must be a measure of the "force" through its action. Newton is unambiguous on this point that the "force" or "vis impressa" consists of nothing but that "action"; for he says, in the explanatory sentence, "Consistit haec vis in actione sola. . . ." That an "impressed force" should be the "action" of altering the "quantity of motion," i.e., of altering the momentum, is yet another example of the way in which the Definitions of the *Principia* logically anticipate the Axioms or Laws of Motion.

In this Definition IV, however, Newton does not give any hint as to whether a "vis impressa" need be an instantaneous blow (or a sequence of such discrete blows), or a continuous force acting during a finite time-interval. Under both types of "force" there would be an "action" of changing the body's "state of resting or of moving uniformly in a right line." Actually, Newton had both types of force in mind, since, in the final sentence of the discussion of Def. IV, Newton says specifically that these "impressed forces" may be "of different origins, as from percussion, from pressure, from centripetal force."

By concentrating on the "action" rather than the force, on the change in state or change in momentum, rather than the cause of such change, Newton was able to deal with attractions and centripetal forces as if they had the same physical reality as percussion and pressure. He certainly believed personally in the reality of attractive "forces" acting over vast distances through the celestial spaces, and just as strongly as in the apparently observable "forces" of percussion, but he was surely aware that this would hardly be the case for the majority of his contemporaries. And so Newton couched his Definition in terms that would be unexceptionable, stating merely that by "impressed force" (as contrasted with "inherent force") he meant nothing more than the "action" of producing any observed change of state.

Now it must seem odd that, having defined "impressed force" for both impulsive and continuous forces, Newton then deals in the remaining Definitions V, VI, VII, and VIII only with centripetal, or continuous, forces and does not return to impulsive forces until Law II. By "centripetal force" he means "that by which bodies are drawn or impelled, or any way tend, towards a point as to a centre." As examples, he mentions the magnetic force, and "that force, whatever it is, by which the planets are continually drawn aside from the rectilinear motions, which otherwise they would pursue, and made to revolve in curvilinear orbits. . . ."

Of course, one reason why Newton gives so much space to centripetal force is that the very concept of such a force was a novelty. We have, in fact, seen that Newton not only held it to be his own invention but even explained how he had named it in honor of Christiaan Huygens. For almost all readers, this would have been their first encounter with even the expression "centripetal force," although they might have been familiar with the older concept of "centrifugal force." Furthermore, centripetal force (or any form of continuous force) differs in one marked regard from impulses. An impulse may be measured directly by the momentum it produces, and so the equation

$$\vec{\Phi} = k \cdot \Delta(m\vec{V})$$

is true for all combinations of Φ and m. But in the case of a continuous force, the problem is not so simple. Let us assume a constant continuous "force" F, say the gravitational attraction of the sun. Then, the "action" $\Delta(m\vec{V})$ does not depend only on the "quantity of matter" or the mass m, but also on the distance of the mass m from the center of the sun. But even if we specify that distance, so that the "force" F is now determined and fixed, we still cannot say how much the change in momentum will be, since this will depend on the time during which the "action" occurs. Hence one cannot meaningfully discuss the "action" of a centripetal force: this is unspecified without bringing in other factors.

Newton therefore turns, once he has defined what he means by centripetal force, to three aspects of such forces, the "absolute quantity," (Def. VI), the "accelerative

154   I. BERNARD COHEN

quantity" (Def. VII), and the "motive quantity" (Def. VIII). Each of these is a "measure" of centripetal force. Generally speaking, Newton means the "accelerative quantity" or "accelerative force" when he discusses the properties or effects of a "centripetal force." It is defined as follows: "The accelerative quantity of a centripetal force is the measure of it [i.e., is its measure], proportional to the velocity which it generates in a given time."[14]

To illustrate what he means, Newton first deals with the force or "virtue" ("virtus") of any one and the same magnet (thus, as Whiston noted, keeping the "absolute quantity" constant); this is "greater at less distance and less at greater." Then Newton turns to the "gravitating force" ("vis gravitans")—"greater in valleys, less on tops of exceeding high mountains; and yet less (as shall hereafter be shown), at greater distances from the body of the Earth." Finally, Newton says: "At equal distances, it [the gravitating force] is the same everywhere, because (taking away, or allowing for, the resistance of the air) it equally accelerates all falling bodies whether heavy or light, great or small."

Just as this "accelerative quantity of a centripetal force" (or "accelerative force," as Newton also calls it) is "proportional to the velocity which it generates in a given time," so there is a "motive force" (or "motive quantity of a centripetal force") which is "proportional to the motion [i.e., quantity of motion or momentum] which it generates in a given time." It is to be observed that in each of these two "measures" of a centripetal force, the "accelerative quantity" and the "motive quantity," one must take account of the rate, i.e., use the words "in a given time," which—as we saw above—was not the case for impulses, as in the statement of the Second Law.

The definition of motive force sounds all but like the modern form of the Second Law,

$$\vec{F} = k \cdot m\vec{A} \quad or \quad \vec{F} = k \cdot d(m\vec{V})/dt,$$

that is, force is proportional to the rate of change of momentum. And, indeed, the very choice of words leads us mercilessly from the abstract logic of arbitrary definitions to the physical laws of central forces. According to Newton's physics, whenever there is a change of motion, there must be a force. If the direction of the change of momentum is directed to a point, as in circular motion or the motion of free fall, the motion may be called central, and we assume the existence of a causal agent or a force that is central or centripetal. Let a measure of such a force in a central motion be the change in momentum in a given time, says Newton, or the rate of change in momentum. Call this, he says, the "motive quantity of a centripetal force" or, for short, the "motive force." At once it is suggested to us—by the very name—that there *is* a "force" producing the motion, that this quantity has an independent physical existence, and that in particular, in the case of falling bodies or the motion of the moon encircling the earth, this "motive force" is gravity. And Newton himself, in discussing this Definition, does not talk explicitly about motions generated in given times—as we might have expected from the Definition itself—but discourses at once about weight.

He first says that "weight is greater in a greater body" and "less in a less body." To the uninitiated reader, it is not at all obvious how this property of weight may be related to motion generated in a given time; but it actually is, as is apparent to anyone who has already mastered the Newtonian physics. For Newton is basically only saying again that weight is proportional to quantity of matter, so that if weight is considered as the motive force in Def. VIII, it follows that the velocity generated in any given time is independent of the "body," i.e., its mass or weight.[15] This "centripetency toward the centre" or "weight" is known independently of the motion of descent, for—says Newton—"It is always known by the quantity of an equal and contrary force just sufficient to hinder the descent of the body."

I think that there can be no better index to Newton's revolutionary position in dynamics than his insight into the equivalence of gravitational and inertial mass (to use our contemporary expressions anachronistically) and his recognition of the significance of Galileo's experiments with falling bodies as a demonstration of this fact. That is, he understood the equivalence of mass as the resistance to being accelerated and of mass as the cause of weight or the source of the downward accelerating force of free fall. Indeed, it was Newton who first saw the meaning of Galileo's experiments; precisely because it was Newton who first understood the relation of mass to weight. This required, among other things, a true sense for the Second Law of Motion for continuous forces. This may be seen in the way in which Newton discusses mass and weight in the third paragraph of explanation following Def. VIII (the "motive quantity of a centripetal force").

The "quantity of motion" (or momentum), Newton says, arises from the product of celerity and "quantity of matter" (or mass); hence the "motive force" (measured by the rate of change of momentum) arises from the accelerative force (measured by the rate of change of velocity, or by the acceleration) multiplied by the mass. But at or near the surface of the Earth, the "accelerative gravity or gravitating force" ("gravitas acceleratrix seu vis gravitans") is a constant, the same for all bodies; it follows from the Definition that "the motive gravity or the weight" ("gravitas motrix seu pondus") must be as the mass.[16] In modern numerical language, this is a recognition that the local constant *small g* is not only the experimentally determined 980 cm/sec^2 but is also the constant of proportionality 980 dynes/gram. Now the quantitative value of the acceleration of free fall varies. As Newton says, "if we should ascend to higher regions," we would find "the accelerative gravity [to be] less" and hence the "weight [is] equally diminished," because—as he says explicitly—the weight must always be "as the product of the body [multiplied] by the accelerative gravity." As examples, he mentions "regions, where the accelerative gravity is diminished into one-half," and hence "the weight of a body two or three times less, will be four or six times less." A thought experiment of magnificent proportions!

Newton's insight into mass and weight has thus led him not only to the position that the acceleration of free fall is the proportionality factor between these two quantities. It has also opened up the possibility of equating the "motive force" of free fall with the static (and thus independently observable and measurable) force of weighing. Newton has thus arrived at the unambiguous relation that

$$\vec{W} = m\vec{g}$$

where W is the weight at some one particular place and g is the acceleration at that place. This is not, therefore, a mere "law" for one fixed and specified "weight" of a body, but rather for the acceleration produced by a centripetal weight-force that is expressly said to vary. But no matter how it varies, the mass ("body" or "quantity of matter") remains constant, and under all circumstances the weight-force is proportional to the acceleration produced. Since Newton showed that the falling of bodies on Earth was essentially equivalent to the falling of the Moon, and so on out to the falling of the planets toward the Sun, this Second Law was certainly envisaged as applying to all gravitational forces and thus to all forces of attraction, and by extension to all continuous forces of nature. Surely, there can be no doubt that Newton thus knew and stated explicitly a Second Law of Motion in a form equivalent to

$$\vec{F} = k \cdot (\Delta m\vec{V})/\Delta t = k \cdot m(\Delta\vec{V}/\Delta t)$$

or

$$\vec{F} = k\frac{d(m\vec{V})}{dt} = k \cdot m\frac{d\vec{V}}{dt}$$

although he never wrote such an equation.

In his advance towards this modern form of Law II, Newton used the experimental result that in free fall at any given place, the acceleration is constant for bodies of different weight.[17] He also assumed (though without explicit postulational statement) that the dynamic force pulling a body down to Earth in free fall is identically the same as the static weight, when standing still. He stated unambiguously that although the weight of a body is constant only at any one place, the mass is invariant under all conditions. Since the "vis inertiae" had been said to be proportional to the mass and to measure a body's resistance to acceleration, it followed at once that weight at any one place is proportional to mass, and that at some other place there is a new constant of proportionality, which is the acceleration. But such a result was based on the above-mentioned specific assumptions or postulates; and the identification of weight (considered as an independent quantity) as the postulated motive force could not be done universally, e.g., not for attractions generally. That is, in the case of the motion of the Moon, or of the planets, or of comets, there is no independent "force" as there is for falling bodies on or near the Earth; we cannot stop the motion of the heavenly bodies and, by some kind of balance, determine their "heaviness" or "weight" toward the body at their center of motion.

I would submit that Newton's procedure in thus producing a form of the Second Law out of Def. VIII prior to the formal statement of Law II among the Axioms not only shows again how he anticipated the Axioms or Laws of Motion in the prior Definitions. It equally demonstrates that any form of the Second Law is basically a kind of Definition.

IMPULSES AND CONTINUOUS FORCES

I have shown above that in the introductory section of the *Principia* devoted to "Axiomata sive Leges Motus," the Second Law is stated for impulses and changes in momentum, but that in the preliminary section of "Definitiones," the discussion following Definition VIII presents a form of the Second Law (restricted to gravity) as a proportion between a continuous force and an acceleration (the constant being the mass of the body concerned). It remains to show how Newton conceived the relation between impulses and continuous forces, between the types of "Second Law" applying to the two.[18]

Newton's method of making the transition from impulse to continuous force may be seen in a dramatic fashion in the opening Proposition I of the first Book of the *Principia,* stated in all three editions as follows: "The areas which revolving bodies describe by radii drawn to an immovable centre of force do lie in the same immovable planes, and are proportional to the times in which they are described." The proof proceeds in three steps. First Newton considers a purely inertial motion: uniform and rectilinear. In any equal time-intervals it will carry a body through equal spaces. Hence, with regard to any point S not in the rectilinear path of motion, a line from S to the moving body sweeps out equal areas in equal times. At once, such is the clarity of the Newtonian revelation, an intimate—but hitherto unsuspected—logical connection is disclosed between Kepler's Law of Areas and Descartes's Law of Inertia.

Next, Newton applies the theorem from Descartes's *Dioptrique,* as follows. While a body is pursuing a uniform motion, it is given a blow, or, as Newton puts the matter, "a centripetal force acts at once with a great impulse." By an appeal to Corol. 1 to the Laws of Motion, Newton shows that area is still conserved. But in actual fact it is not Corol. 1 which is used, since the blow is given to a body in motion; this is the condition for that earlier form of this corollary which we saw Newton find in Descartes's *Dioptrique.* Under a regular succession of such blows toward one and the same point, each blow separated from the next by a constant time-interval, area with respect to that point (or center of force) is still conserved. Then Newton proceeds to the limit, whereupon the sequence of impulses becomes a continuous force and the series of line segments becomes a smooth curve. This proof may contain a hint that Newton conceived the Second Law for continuous forces as obtainable in the limit from the Second Law he stated in the *Principia,* just as in the limit a sequence of impulses of increasing frequency becomes a continuous force.[19] But I am not aware of any direct evidence that Newton ever addressed himself specifically to the

I. BERNARD COHEN

dimensional problem: that a continuous force F might be related to the impulse of Law II by being multiplied by the factor of time Δt. We are apt to be misled here because today we take force F to be primary, rather than impulse Φ and we derive the latter from the former by saying that

$$\vec{\Phi} = \vec{F} \cdot \Delta t$$

and that Newton's impulsive force is one that occurs for very small values of Δt. Hence for us, the equation

$$\vec{F} = k \cdot m \frac{\Delta \vec{V}}{\Delta t}$$

leads at once to the limiting form:

$$\vec{F} \cdot dt = k \cdot m(d\vec{V}) = k \cdot d(m\vec{V}).$$

For us, in other words, Newton's "impulse" ($\vec{\Phi}$) is the limit of ($\vec{F} \cdot \Delta t$) for small values of Δt, whereas for Newton, as $\Delta t \rightarrow 0$, $\Phi \rightarrow F$. That F and Φ have different physical dimensions was not a problem for Newton,[20] nor did he ever declare explicitly that these two types of "force" differed by an assumed (or "built-in") factor of time, Δt or dt. Yet, although this topic is not the subject of explicit discussion in the *Principia,* it arises implicitly from the very fact that Newton saw the need of measuring the action of a *continuous force* (a centripetal force) by the rate of its action (Def. VII & VIII), whereas an *instantaneous force* may be measured by the total action without respect to time.

We must proceed with extreme caution, however, in dealing with the distinction between continuous and instantaneous forces—on the level of Newtonian discourse. We tend to make this distinction on the basis of finite forces, whereas much of the *Principia* presents properties of infinitesimal forces, or of finite forces composed of sequences of infinitesimals or as limits of sequences. Indeed, we shall see below (pp. 167–168 and Appendices I and II) that Newton evidently must have conceived an instantaneous force to be a first-order infinitesimal force-impulse that could be broken down into (or was composed of) a sequence of second-order infinitesimal force-impulses (each acting within a second-order infinitesimal time); thus he could even write of a "force" (impulse) acting "uninterruptedly" or "continuously" ("perpetuo").

I would guess that Newton did not ever analyze the logical sequence from impulse to continuous force further than the intuitive conception that a continuous force may be conceived as the limit of a sequence of impulses of infinite frequency. Since Newton had been led by his Definitions to a Second Law for the continuous force of weight, he probably assumed it was *obvious* that the Second Law for impulses implied a Second Law for continuous forces. As stated in the *Principia,* Law II postulated (for impulses) the proportionality of a change in momentum and a "motive force impressed." I have stated earlier the importance of recognizing that by "force impressed" Newton meant the "action" only; so far as I know, no one has pointed out that the Second Law deals with such "action" for the good and proper reason (as Newton quite correctly understood) that in the case of impact or percussion, one cannot quantitatively determine the magnitude of the force or impulse as an independent entity. Hence we see why it was logically necessary for Newton to deal with the action, with the net change in momentum, as dictated by Law II. But for the continuous force, pure "action" does not suffice. For instance, in uniform circular motion through 360°, the net change in momentum is zero, exactly as if the body in question had not moved at all. And yet a force must have been acting since the motion is non-inertial, being non-linear. And in general, the amount of force would depend on the time, thus being more like energy expended than a force which in uniform circular motion ought to be of constant magnitude. And so we see again and again why for continuous forces Newton introduces "time" along with "action," so as to deal with the rate of change in momentum, rather than the change in momentum. (On this point, see Appendix I, below.)

I suggest that in Newton's confusing use of "force" ("vis") for both the continuous force and the instantaneous force, he has given us the key to his signal achievement! For the fact of the matter is, as I read the history of dynamics in the seventeenth century, that it was Newton who for the first time conceived a system of physics embracing simultaneously the action of impulsive forces and centripetal forces. Newton, in a sense, thus combined the Keplerian and the Galilean modes of scientific thought: the action of celestial forces as postulated by Kepler and the physics of percussion as studied by Galileo. Hence the Second Law may serve as a particularly fascinating index to Newton's achievement in the *Principia* because it reveals to us how Newton was able to generalize his physics from the phenomenologically based dynamics of collisions and blows to the debatable realm of central forces, of gravitational attraction, and hence of continuous forces generally.

NEWTON'S REVISIONS OF THE SECOND LAW OF MOTION

Although Newton printed the three Laws of Motion almost without alteration in all the editions of the *Principia*,[21] he was not wholly satisfied with the Second Law and essayed a series of restatements of the law itself and the explanatory paragraph. I have found among Newton's manuscripts no similar attempts to rework either the First Law or the Third Law, although there exists a manuscript fragment containing a discussion of the Third Law in relation to attraction. Newton evidently found less ambiguity or less possibility of misinterpretation in these laws than he did in the Second Law, or perhaps originally he had merely been more felicitous in expressing himself in Laws I and III.

In Newton's own copies of the first and second editions of the *Principia*, there are no manuscript changes in the statement of any of the Laws of Motion; and the only entry relating to these laws directly is a comment on the Second Law which Newton entered into his interleaved copy of the second edition (1713), a comment which appears in a variant form in the third edition (1726) in the Scholium following the

I. BERNARD COHEN

Laws of Motion. The projected revisions of the Second Law occur in loose sheets of manuscript, preserved in the Portsmouth Collection in the University Library, Cambridge. Although the absolutely trivial change in verbiage in the First Law has been discussed again and again, the proposed alterations of the Second Law have not—to my knowledge—hitherto been printed or even mentioned in print. (They occur on fol. 274r, U.L.C. MS Add. 3965.)

Such manuscript texts are particularly valuable in showing us the care with which Newton was apt to revise the *Principia*, rewriting and reworking a part over and over again in an attempt to express himself as accurately and felicitously as possible. Furthermore, successive drafts often enable us to specify Newton's intentions, and thus they lend authority to the interpretations we may propose.

The attempts to reformulate the Second Law may all be dated within five years of the publication of the *Principia*, in the years 1692–93, a period of intense revision of the *Principia* by Newton. I shall present them more or less in chronological order. One sequence, all of which is later cancelled, begins as follows:

Vis omnis [in corpus liberum *add.* & *del.*] impressa motum sibi proportionalem a loco quem corpus alias occuparet in plagam propriam generat.
Every force impressed [on a free body *add.* & *del.*] generates a motion proportional to itself from the place the body would otherwise occupy into its own region [i.e., in its own direction].

On the next line, Newton starts afresh, writing: "Vis omnis impressa motum sibi proportionalem g (Every impressed force g[enerates] a motion proportional to itself"). At once we observe that Newton has introduced three conceptual innovations: (1) he writes of a motion that is generated, rather than a change of motion; (2) he no longer speaks of the new motion as merely being along the right line in which the force acts, but has added a point of origin; and (3) he has recast the sentence to make it read that every force generates a motion, rather than that every change in motion is proportional to (and hence produced by) a force.

But at this point Newton perhaps recognized that his sentence construction differed from that which he had adopted in the *Principia* where the original Lex II (like Lex I & Lex III) is given in the accusative-infinitive construction of "oratio obliqua," whereas the sentences just quoted use the nominative-indicative construction of "oratio recta." In the next version, Newton transfers the intended revision to the form appropriate to "oratio obliqua"; he uses two verbs, one for each part of the law, but both are in the infinitive mood rather than in the indicative, and with the subject consequently in the accusative:

Motum genitum vi motrici impressae proportionalem esse & a loco quem corpus alias occuparet in plagam vis illius fieri.
That a motion generated is proportional to the motive force impressed and occurs from the place which the body would otherwise occupy into the region of [i.e., in the direction of action of] that force.

And now, furthermore, he has reverted to the form of presentation in the *Principia*, at least to the extent of writing about a motion generated being proportional to the "force," rather than a "force" generating a motion; but it is still a motion *generated* and not a *change in motion.*

Newton's next attempt to express Law II is similar to the preceding one in using the indicative mood and in stating that an "impressed force" generates a motion rather than that a motion is generated by an "impressed force":

Vis impressa motum sibi proportionalem a loco quem corpus alias occuparet in plagam propriam generat.

An impressed force generates a motion proportional to itself from the place which a body would otherwise occupy into its own region [i.e., in its own direction].

Finally, the last statement in this sequence returns again to the style of "oratio obliqua," at first starting out "Mutationem motus . . . " as in the *Principia:*

[Mutationem motus *del.*] Motum omnem novum quo status corporis mutatur proportionalem esse vi motrici impressae & fieri a loco quem corpus alias occuparet in plagam qua vis imprimitur.

[That the change in motion *del.*] That every new motion by which the state of a body is changed is proportional to the motive force impressed & is made from the place which that body would otherwise have occupied toward the region [i.e., in the direction] in which the force is impressed.

In these versions, we may see that Newton has removed the ambiguity of the law as printed, by replacing the opening words of the latter, "Mutationem motus," by "Motum genitum." For while "change" ("Mutationem motus") may seem possibly to imply the concept of "rate of change," such expressions as "Motum genitum" or "Motum omnem novum" clearly denote a magnitude, without any possible suggestion of a rate. There is even less ambiguity on this point in the earlier revision, in which it is said: "Every force impressed generates a motion proportional to itself. . . ."[22]

This sequence of alterations may be of interest to the general reader primarily as a characteristic exercise of Isaac Newton in a creative mood, trying again and again to make language an exact expression of his changing thoughts. But the revision attempted on the other side of this same sheet is of a wholly different character and disturbs any simple view of Newton's Second Law as an unambiguous conception of its author, merely relating impulses to the momenta they may produce. Here Newton begins innocently enough with what looks at first glance to be only another version, as follows:

Lex II

Lex II. Motum [in spatio vel immobili vel mobili *del.*] genitum proportionalem esse vi motrici impressae & fieri secundum lineam rectam qua vis illa imprimitur.

I. BERNARD COHEN

Law II. That a motion generated [in a space either immobile or mobile *del.*] is proportional to the motive force impressed and occurs along the right line in which that force is impressed.

With the deletion, this form of Lex II differs from that of the *Principia* only in the improvement in the opening pair of words: "Motum genitum" being used rather than "Mutationem motus."

But it is in fact the deletion that commands our attention. For that expression, "in a space either immobile or mobile," appears as a key to the problem with which Newton was wrestling. In the *Principia,* Law II deals with "mutatio motus" without specifying whether the body on which the force is impressed is at rest or in motion. In the discussion, Newton explains how to proceed if the body is moving initially: the old motion is altered by adding or subtracting the new.[23] But now Newton essays a revision in which he would reduce all conceivable applications of Law II to bodies at rest. A moving body could then be considered to be at rest within its space which moves. It would then be necessary only to assume (or to postulate explicitly) a principle of relativity: that the action of forces (in the sense of the Second Law) is identical in a moving space and in a space at rest. Thus, in the manuscript, the first version of the comment states (in translation):

> [And this motion if the body was resting before the impressed force must be computed in an immobile space according to the determination of the impressed force, but if the body was moving before must be computed in its own mobile space in which the body without the impressed force would be relatively at rest] And the same force will generate the same motion in a uniformly moving space as in an immobile space. Let A, B be two bodies[24]

Evidently Newton was thinking of some situation such as Galileo's famous example of the ship, in which motions occur within the ship at rest just as they do with respect to the ship if the latter is in uniform motion. For instance, apart from the effects of wind or air resistance, a body let fall will always fall straight down with respect to the ship, whether the ship be at rest or in uniform motion; even though if the ship is in uniform motion, the path will simultaneously appear to be a vertical line to an observer on the ship and a parabola to an observer on the shore. In the above extract Newton refers explicitly to a "uniformly moving space," but he did not do so in the sequel. For he replaced the above paragraph by another reading (in translation):

> And this motion has the same determination as [*lit.,* with] the impressed force and happens from that place in which the body, before the force was impressed upon it, was at rest either truly or at least relatively: and therefore if the body was moving before the impressed force, it is either added to its conspiring motion or is subtracted from it if contrary or is added obliquely to it if oblique and is composed with it in accordance with the determination of both.

Newton then proceeds to deal exclusively with the problem of the composition of two oblique motions, that is, the situation in which a force produces a new motion "that is neither parallel to, nor perpendicular to, the original motion to which it is to be added." The text reads (in translation) as follows:

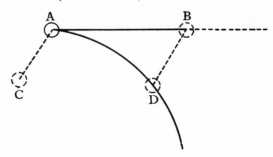

If body A was moving before the impressed force and with the motion which it had in A uniformly continued could have described the distance AB in a given time and meanwhile be urged by the impressed force into a given region: it will have to be thought that the place in which the body is relatively at rest moves together with the body from A to B and that the body through the impressed force is thrown out from this mobile place and departs from it in the direction of that impressed force with a motion which is proportional to the same force. And so if the force is determined, for example, toward the region of the right line AC and in that given time could have impelled the body deprived of all motion from the immobile place A to a new place C, draw BD parallel and equal to AC and the same force in the same time in accordance with this Law will impel the same body from its own mobile place B to a new place D. Therefore the body will move in some line AD with a motion which arises from the motion of its own relative place from A to B and the motion of the body from this place B to another place D, that is from the motion AB which the body shared before the impressed force and the motion BD which the impressed force generates by this Law. From these two motions joined according to their determinations will arise the motion of the body from the line AD. And

Thus Newton has more or less anticipated Corol. 1 to the Laws, giving a proof of the method of composition of two motions. But again it is not exactly the example of Corol. 1 of the *Principia,* in which one considers either that one of two impulses may act separately on a body presumed at rest, or act simultaneously; here once more, the body is initially in uniform motion and then is given an oblique blow, as in the theorem on refraction in Descartes's *Dioptrique.* Observe that while the original motion is said explicitly to have been uniform (". . . uniformiter continuato . . .") the resulting trajectory is curved and not a straight line, thus seeming to imply that the new motion is accelerated and not uniform. This trajectory AD, as drawn by Newton in three separate versions of the figure, is unmistakably a curve; and to a degree that by far exceeds the possibilities of a freehand straight line with a bit

I. BERNARD COHEN

of a curve in it. No! In each case the trajectory is a deliberately drawn and obvious parabola-like curve (or "curved line"), rather than the expected diagonal of a parallelogram. But if the resultant trajectory is such a curve, we would conclude that the "force" must be continuous, producing a constant acceleration, as gravity does, rather than an impulse generating a motion which then continues uniformly.[25]

Nevertheless, and despite the figure, there can be no doubt from the text itself that Newton's "impressed force" is impulsive or instantaneous, and not continuous. For Newton says specifically: "The body through the impressed force is thrown out from this mobile place and departs from it in the direction of that impressed force with a motion which is proportional to the same force." Only for impulses can the "motion" (i.e., "quantity of motion," or momentum) be proportional to the "force." If the "impressed force" were not an impulse, the "motion" generated would not be simply proportional to the "force," but would rather be jointly proportional to the force and the time in which the force acts, as we have seen above. Therefore we would conclude either that Newton was careless in drawing the figure, or that he had—without explicit declaration—taken the step of assuming that the Second Law (stated explicitly for impulses and momenta) implies another Second Law for continuous forces and constant accelerations. We shall see, in a moment, that this is what Newton more or less does in the third and final edition of the *Principia,* stating that the parabolic path of projectiles may be derived from the Second Law in this manner.

The list of possibilities just given is not, however exhaustive. Newton may have had in mind the condition in which a sequence of blows or impulses may be given, rather than just one. Let us suppose that a given impulse Φ may be divided into (or is composed of) a number of parts:

$$\vec{\Phi} = \vec{\Phi}_1 + \vec{\Phi}_2 + \vec{\Phi}_3 + \ldots .$$

Then it follows immediately that one and the same effect will be produced on a moving body (or a body at rest) whether the impulse (Φ) be given "altogether and at once" or (Φ_1, Φ_2, Φ_3, . . .) "by degrees and successively." That is, if each impulse Φ_i produces a change in momentum $\Delta(mV_i)$, then the total change in momentum $\Delta(mV)$ will be the vector sum of the individual changes in momentum,

$$\Delta(m\vec{V}) = \Delta(m\vec{V}_1) + \Delta(m\vec{V}_2) + \Delta(m\vec{V}_3) + \ldots .$$

In both cases, the final velocity will be the same in both magnitude and direction (parallel, but not necessarily coincident). The only difference between the two cases will be that the actual trajectory produced by a single blow (Φ) will be a new straight line, whereas the trajectory resulting from Φ_1, Φ_2, Φ_3, . . . acting successively will be a series of line-segments joined end to end: a portion of a polygon. In the limit, as the time between blows vanishes, the trajectory will become a smooth curve.

It shall be seen below (and especially in Appendices I and II) that such an analysis cannot be made exclusively on the finite level. Since Newton, in his proposed revisions of the Second Law, is dealing with a blow or instantaneous force, the situation is that of an infinitesimal force-impulse acting in an infinitesimal time-unit dt. If we divide up this time-interval into sub-units or parts dt/n, then the limiting condition (as n → ∞) corresponds to an infinitely small quantity (or infinitesimal) but is not, properly speaking, a second-order infinitesimal unit of time. Only by such an analysis on the infinitesimal level can we see how the two modes of action of an impulse—"simul et semel" and "gradatim et successive"—produce the effects illustrated by Newton within the framework of the stated "Lex II."[26]

Newton's discussion helps to clarify one feature of the several revised versions of the Second Law printed earlier in this section: that Newton specified the direction of the new motion as "from the place the body would otherwise occupy" along the direction of the force. Newton must have had in mind a "place" in a possibly mobile space. And indeed this phrase occurs again explicitly in two further versions of the Second Law which appear in the manuscript below the above commentary. They read (in translation from U.L.C. MS Add. 3965, fol. 274r) as follows:

> That motion from a place which a body would otherwise be occupying is proportional to the motive force impressed and is directed toward its region.
> That every new motion by which the state of a body is changed is proportional to the motive force impressed and is made from the place which the body would otherwise be occupying into the region [i.e., in the direction] which the impressed force aims for.

The discussion or commentary which comes next is much the same as the previous one and I shall not, therefore, quote it *in extenso*. But there are two possibly significant differences. The first is that in discussing the motion produced by the "force," Newton's first illustration has the "force" acting along the line of the original motion (initially in the same sense as the motion and then in a contrary sense). The body would have moved from A to a had there been no "force," and from A to B had the "force" been acting on the body at rest. Hence in these two cases, the resultant mo-

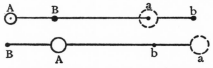

tions from A to b are shown by Newton in the diagrams reproduced here. Newton then deals with the oblique case, in part as follows:

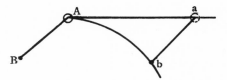

> Whence the translation of the body from a to b will be parallel and equal to the translation of the same body from A to B which the same force in the same

time with the same direction would have been able to generate by acting on that body deprived of all motion.

The situation is equivalent to that of the previous version, i.e., ". . . the force . . . in that given time could have impelled the body deprived of all motion from the immobile place A to a new place C. . . ." Newton now is saying again that a "force" produces a displacement (or "translation") in a given direction *during a given time* on a body at rest. This is not a statement that the "force" has been acting during the given time, for in that case it would be generating a "motion," not a "translation," proportional to the time. In this version Newton has included the opening sentence of the original discussion of Lex II, as printed in the *Principia*, that if "any force generate a motion," a double "force" will generate a double motion, and a triple "force" a triple motion, whether the "force" be "impressed" "at once" or "by degrees and successively." We have seen that this would be true only for impulses and does not have a clear significance for continuous forces, which always generate a motion not proportional to their magnitudes (assuming a constant mass) but proportional to their magnitudes and the time in which they act. We may now interpret Newton's statement in terms of our previous infinitesimal analysis. Whether (1) the infinitesimal blow is given "simul et semel" on a body at rest at A, or (2) an equivalent blow—but broken up into second-order infinitesimal force-impulses—be given on a moving body at A (going from A toward *a*), the net displacements *in any given time* (dt) will be the same: AB and *ab* are equal and opposite sides of a parallelogram. Clearly, however, this result will only hold on the infinitesimal level.

There is one further manuscript revision of the Second Law and comment. It occurs on a burnt sheet of paper. Unlike the previous versions, which are rewritten and worked over, this appears in a fair copy in Newton's hand (*ca.* 1693) with only an occasional crossing-out and revision. This version of the law reads (in translation) as follows:

Lex. II.

Motum omnem novum quo status corporis mutatur vi motrici impressae proportionalem esse, & fieri a loco quem corpus alias occuparet in metam [*replacing* regionem *del., which in turn replaces* plagam] qua vis impressa petit.

That every new motion by which the state of a body is changed is proportional to the impressed motive force, and occurs [is made] from the place which the body would otherwise occupy into the region [i.e., in the direction] which the impressed force aims for.

There follows a comment, which apparently is like the others, including the ultimately curved trajectory.[27]

There is one further piece of documentary evidence to support the foregoing analysis. It occurs in U.L.C. MS Add. 3965, fol. 86r. Here we see that Newton at one time intended to revise the presentation of Corollary 1 to the Laws of Motion. The revision would follow a new version of the paragraph following the enunciation of Lex III. Then, Newton would say that "the meaning and truth of these Laws will become more manifest in the following Corollaries." Corol.1, as stated in the *Principia,* would now become a "Cas.1." A new "Cas.2" would then be added, as follows:

Cas.2. Eodem argumento si corpus dato tempore vi sola M in loco A impressa ferretur uniformi cum motu ab A ad B & vi sola N non simul & semel sed perpetuo impressa ferretur accelerato cum motu in recta AC ab A ad C [,] compleatur parallelogrammum ABDC & corpus vi utraque feretur eodem tempore ab A ad D. Nam reperietur in fine temporis tam in linea CD quam in linea BD et propterea [in utriusque lineae concursu D invenietur]

Case 2. By the same argument if a body in a given time, by a force M alone, impressed in place A, would be borne with a uniform motion from A to B, and by a force N alone, impressed not altogether and at once but continually, would be borne with an accelerated motion along the right line AC from A to C; let the parallelogram ABDC be completed, and the body will in that same time be borne by both forces from A to D. For it will be found at the end of the time both on the line CD and on the line BD and therefore [will be found on the intersection D of both lines].

Case 1, the old Corol. 1, which I have discussed on p. 145 *supra,* dealt with two stages: a single blow M, delivered to a body and producing rectilinear motion, followed by a unitary oblique blow N, producing a new rectilinear motion at some angle to the motion that had been produced by M alone. Now, in Case 2, the "same argument" is used. But here Newton says, the force N is not "impressed" as before, "not altogether and at once" ("non simul & semel"); hence the mode of action must be "gradatim et successive," which is now described as "perpetuo" and which produces accelerated motion ("accelerato cum motu") so as to yield a parabolic path which joins the two vertices of the parallelogram (as in the figure on p. 164), rather than a path along the linear diagonal.[28]

We have no ancillary documents to tell us why, in the early 1690s, Newton was contemplating such an alteration of the statement of the Second Law of Motion,[29] but the nature of the diagram, in all the different versions, would seem to prove that Newton was planning to arrive ultimately at a derivation of a parabolic path, or other curved path, as a consequence of two independent motions: one linear, uniform, and inertial; the other, the result of a continuously acting "force," producing a constant acceleration. This continuous force could be conceived as a sequence of second-order infinitesimal force-impulses equivalent to a first-order infinitesimal continuous force: a micro-example of the physics of visible bodies. For projectiles, the constant acceleration needed to produce the curved path, when combined with an inertial motion, was known to him in the action of the continuous force of gravity.

I. BERNARD COHEN

And we have seen, above, that—even before stating the Second Law in the "Axio-mata sive Leges Motus"—Newton had already exhibited one special case of a Second Law for continuous forces, the action of gravity; presumably this result was obtained merely by the application of intuition to the Definitions. But the critical reader would find it hard to justify the way in which, on either a finite or an infinitesimal level, the Second Law for continuous forces would follow directly from the Lex II of the *Principia*—at least without making explicit further assumptions whose justification would be far from obvious. Possibly this is a major reason why Newton did not expound further, at least in the Leges Motus, the method of "Case 2": action "gradatim et successive."

In his own interleaved copy of the second edition of the *Principia,* Newton wrote out an addition to the comment on Law II, including a hint as to how to get a Sec-ond Law for the continuous force of gravity from the stated Second Law for discrete impulses. But he did not print it at that place in the third edition, but moved it in a slightly altered form to become part of a longer insert into the Scholium concluding the section of "Axiomata sive Leges Motus." This particular addition was evidently intended to explain the statement made in the first two editions (without comment) that by using

the first two Laws and the first two Corollaries, *Galileo* discovered that the descent of bodies varied as the square of the time *(in duplicata ratione temporis)* and that the motion of projectiles was in the curve of a parabola; experience agreeing with both, unless so far as these motions are a little retarded by the resistance of the air.[30]

In the first two editions Newton then passed directly onward to the statement, "On the same Laws and Corollaries depend those things which have been demonstrated concerning the times of the vibration of pendulums . . . ," and then to the application of "the same, together with Law III" whereby Wren, Wallis, and Huygens "did severally determine the rules of the impact and reflection of hard bodies. . . ."

Now, of course, Galileo did not at all use "the first two Laws" to prove that "the descent of bodies varied as the square of the time."[31] But whether he did or not, there can be no question that if gravity does produce a constant and uniform acceler-ation, so that the distances traversed downward in free fall (from rest) are propor-tional to the squares of the times; then the trajectory of a projectile, as Newton says, determined by "the motion arising from its projection . . . compounded with the motion arising from its gravity," will be in the shape of a parabola.[32] Neither New-ton's misinterpretation of Galileo's procedure nor his correct deduction of the para-bolic path is as interesting as his reasoning on how uniform gravity produces a velocity proportional to the time, according to the Second Law of Motion: the miss-ing factor in the versions of the Second Law printed earlier in this section.

Newton's presentation is contained in a single sentence that was arrived at only after many trials. It is certainly a strange circumstance that this sentence, in which Newton has carefully stated the basis for the application of the Second Law to continuous forces, has been so badly translated as to hide Newton's meaning and his very intention from English readers and to cause otherwise well-informed scholars to use this sentence in attributing wrongly to its author a dual use of the word "force" in a single sentence.

The sentence reads, in the Latin and in an English translation, as follows:

Corpore cadente gravitas uniformis, singulis temporis particulis æqualibus æqualiter agendo imprimit vires æquales in corpus illud, & velocitates æquales generat: & tempore toto vim totam imprimit et velocitatem totam generat tempori proportionalem.

When a body is falling, uniform gravity, by acting equally in every equal particle of time, impresses equal forces upon that body and generates equal velocities: and in the whole time impresses a whole force and generates a whole velocity proportional to the time.[33]

The sense appears to be that because gravity is uniform, it acts "equally" in "every equal particle of time," in every instant, in the smallest "atomic" units into which time can be conceivably divided, in units— that is to say—so small that the action of gravity is "instantaneously" impulsive. Now without going into the question as to whether such "instants" or "particles" of time are infinitesimally small or finite though tiny, it follows from the Second Law as stated that in each such "particle of time," gravity—by so "acting equally"—"impresses equal forces upon that body" in the sense of Def. IV and so "generates equal velocities." During a "whole time," made up of the sum of such "particles of time," the "whole velocity" generated will be the sum of velocities generated within the separate "particles of time," and hence "proportional to the [whole] time." In short, if $d\vec{v}$ be the velocity generated in one "particle of time," then in N such "particles of time" the total velocity generated will be $N \cdot d\vec{v}$.

I have referred above to the existence of an earlier version of this idea in the interleaved (and annotated) copy of the second edition of the *Principia* that Newton had in his own library. It reads:

Actio gravitatis uniformis in corpus grave est ut tempus agendi, et vis impressa est ut actio illa et velocitatem generat tempori proportionalem. Et spatium cadendo descriptum est ut velocitas et tempus conjunctim seu in duplicata ratione velocitatis.

The action of uniform gravity on a heavy body is as the time of acting, and the impressed force is as that action and generates a velocity proportional to the time. And the space described by falling is as the velocity and time conjointly or in the duplicate ratio [i.e., as the square] of the velocity.

Yet another version, found among Newton's manuscripts, reads:

I. BERNARD COHEN

Cum vis a gravitate in corpus grave impressa sit ut tempus, corpus illud duplo tempore acquiret dupam [*sic*] vim et duplam velocitatem & describet quadruplam altitudinem cadendo, duplam scilicet ob duplam velocitatem & iterum duplam

Since the force impressed by gravity on a heavy body is as the time, that body in double the time will acquire double the force and double the velocity and will describe four times the height [distance] in falling, double that is because of the double velocity and again double [breaks off].

At about the same time that Newton wrote out the above versions in Latin, he made a similar statement in English, in a document apparently intended for use by Samuel Clarke in replying to Leibniz in the famous correspondence that took place between them. Newton's statement, written by him in English, reads:

> Galileo argued that uniform gravity by acting equally in equal times upon a falling body would produce equal velocities of descent in those times, or that the whole force imprest, the whole time of descent & the whole velocity acquired in falling would be proportional to one another, but the whole descent or space described would arise from the time & velocity together & there be in a compound ratio of them both, or as the square of either of them.[34]

The projected revisions of the Second Law and the basis for using it to derive a curved trajectory for the motion of projectiles have enabled us to see how Newton justified the application of the Second Law in the *Principia* to continuously acting forces of gravity. We have seen Newton state more than once in the *Principia* that such a result was implied by the Second Law, although in point of fact it seemed to follow only from the particular nature of Def. VIII and was not ever proved to be a valid extension of Newton's Second Law save as an intuitive extension of the law from impulses to continuous forces, a step which he never justified by rigorous logic or by experiment. But Newton's intuition served him well, for it enabled him to apply correctly a law which originated in the seventeenth-century problem of impact to the universal problem of the gravitational forces governing the motions of the heavenly bodies. Newton's genius enabled him to transfer the concept of real forces, seen in impact, and in terrestrial weight, to imagined forces such as the forces on moons, tides, planets, and comets, and thereby to construct the first satisfactory dynamics of the world-system. This was the decisive step in constructing the physical system of the *Principia*.

NOTES

[1] The writer would like to express his gratitude to the National Science Foundation for a grant which has supported the research on which this article is based. A longer, and more extensively annotated, version of this paper is scheduled to appear as one of the chapters in the writer's *Newton's principles of philosophy: inquiries into Newton's scientific work and its general environment* (Cambridge: Harvard University Press, 1971).
The present article has been revised, and further material (not included in the original) has

been presented in two Appendices. It differs from the prior version in *The Texas Quarterly* in that some major corrections have been made, notably on the old pp. 148 and 150, corresponding to pp. 164–166 and 167–169 of this book.

² Owing to the limitations of space, it has been necessary to omit a section on Newton's concept of force. This shall be included—as a new section, occurring here—in the complete version mentioned in n. 1 *supra*.

³ Lex I: "Corpus omne perseverare in statu suo quiescendi vel movendi uniformiter in directum, nisi quatenus a viribus impressis cogitur statum illum mutare." This is the First Law as found in the first (1687) and the second (1713) editions; a minor change was made in the third (1726) edition.

The translations of extracts from Newton's *Principia* are (for the most part) given here and throughout this article in the versions of Andrew Motte (1729), unless otherwise specified; but I have occasionally altered these translations, since my purpose is to present an accurate English version and not to record the peculiarities of Motte's style.

⁴ These read as follows:

"First law of nature: that each thing, in so far as it can of and by itself [i.e., by its own force], perseveres always in the same state; and that which is once moved always continues so to move."

"Second law of nature: that all motion is of itself in a straight line; and thus things which move in a circle always tend to recede from the center of the circle that they describe."

On the debt of Newton to Descartes in relation to Def. III and Law I of Newton's *Principia*, see I. B. Cohen: 'Quantum in se est': Newton's concept of inertia in relation to Descartes and Lucretius, *Notes and Records of the Royal Society of London*, 1964, *19*: 131–155; the actual stages of the development of the concept of inertia are traced in detail in Ch. 2 of *Transformations of scientific ideas* (Cambridge, England: at the University Press [1971: in press]), based on the Wiles Lectures given at Queen's University, Belfast, in May 1966. See also A. Koyré: *Newtonian studies* (Cambridge: Harvard University Press, 1965) and John Herivel's book (cited in n. 10, *infra*).

⁵ In a MS containing "Remarks on Leibnitz' 1st Letter to the abbe Conti," Univ. Lib. Cambr. MS Add. 3968, §28, Newton wrote out the following brief statement on the rise of dynamics:

". . . Galileo began to consider the effect of Gravity upon Projectiles. Mr Newton in his Principia Philosophiae improved that consideration into a large science. Mr Leibnitz christened the child by [a] new name as if it had been his own calling it *Dynamica*. Mr Hygens gave the name of vis centrifuga to the force by wᶜʰ revolving bodies recede from the center of their motion [.] Mr Newton in honour of that author retained the name & called the contrary force vis centripeta. . . ." For the context of Newton's remarks see A. Koyré & I. B. Cohen: Newton and the Leibniz-Clarke correspondence, *Archives Internationales d'Histoire des Sciences*, 1962, *15*:62–126, Appendix Three, pp. 122–123.

⁶ In an annotated copy of the second edition of the *Principia* in his own library (and now in the library of Trinity College, Cambridge), Newton wrote out a statement of the difference between his concept of inertia and Kepler's. This interesting contrast occurs in the margin, alongside the statement of Law I, and reads (in translation from the Latin) as follows: "I do not mean the force of inertia of Kepler, by which bodies tend toward rest, but the force of remaining in the same state or resting or of moving." In Latin: "Non intelligo vim inertiae Kepleri qua corpora ad quietem tendunt sed vim manendi in eodem quiescendi vel movendi statu."

⁷ That is, a change in motion (as in the case of a falling body) shows that such a force is acting; but the force may act (as on a body resting on a table) without producing a change in motion. Dr. J. E. McGuire, in commenting on my paper, quite correctly drew attention to this feature of the change in motion being a *sufficient* but not a *necessary* condition for the action of a force.

⁸ The examples in Law III are of both types of force: (1) continuous—a person pressing a stone with a finger, a horse drawing a stone tied to a rope; (2) impulsive (quasi-instantaneous)

I. BERNARD COHEN

—a body impinging upon another. Newton says, "This law takes place also in attractions."

9 The two versions are as follows:

[*Comment on Law II*]	[*Corol. 1 to Laws of Motion*]
"And this motion (being always directed the same way with the generating force), if the body moved before, is added to or subtracted from the former motion, according as they directly conspire with or are directly contrary to each other; or obliquely joined, when they are oblique, so as to produce a new motion compounded from the determination of both."	"A body, acted on by two forces simultaneously, will describe the diagonal of a parallelogram in the same time as it would describe the sides by those forces separately."

10 I know of no evidence whatsoever that Newton had read the *Discorsi* prior to writing the *Principia,* although he did obtain and read a copy of the Latin translation in the 1690s; I have elsewhere assembled a considerable number of indications that he was unfamiliar with the *Discorsi.* Newton did not read Italian, but it may be argued that this is not a decisive factor since he might have picked out the bits of Latin. I may add that probabilities are very great against Newton's having had access to that very rare work, Salusbury's English version of the *Discorsi.* On this topic, see I. B. Cohen: Newton's attribution of the first two laws of motion to Galileo, *Atti del Symposium Internazionale di Storia, Metodologia. Logica e Filosofia della Scienza: "Galileo nella Storia e nella Filosofia della Scienza."* 1967, pp. XXV–XLIV.

See John Herivel: The background to Newton's *Principia* (Oxford: at the Clarendon Press, 1965); the discussion of the parallelogram rule, in relation to Galileo's analysis of the projectile, occurs on p. 39, and the text of "The lawes of motion" on pp. 208 sqq. This tract was first printed by H. W. Turnbull in 1961 in vol. 3 of the Royal Society's edition of Newton's *Correspondence,* pp. 60–64; again on pp. 157 sqq. of A. Rupert Hall and Marie Boas Hall: *Unpublished scientific papers of Isaac Newton* (Cambridge: at the University Press, 1962).

11 The optical lectures were alleged to have been read in four installments, starting in Jan. 1669/70, then in Oct. 1670, in Oct. 1671, in Oct. 1672, according to marginal notes in the deposited version (U.L.C.Dd. 9.67).

12 I have referred in this article again and again to the importance of the form of Newton's Second Law: the "force" (impact) being set equal to the "motion" it produces. In the "Waste Book," among the early "Axiomes" we find a statement of the Law of Inertia much as Descartes had written it ("A quantity will always move on in the same straight line [not changing the determination nor celerity of its motion] unlesse some externall cause divert it"), followed immediately by these two axioms:

"3. There is exactly required so much and noe more force to reduce a body to rest as there was to put it upon motion: *et e contra.*

"4. Soe much force as is required to destroy any quantity of motion in a body, soe much is required to generate it; and soe much as is required to generate it soe much is alsoe required to destroy it."

Thus we may see the young Newton, as he works out his ideas within a kind of Cartesian framework, expressing the main aspects of the Second Law, in a preliminary version in relation to impulse and a form of conservation of motion.

13 I have assumed here that a "force" is measured by its "effect," that is, the "quantity of motion" in a body is a measure of the action of the "force" producing that motion. But, as is well known, in Newton's day there was a considerable controversy as to whether the "force" of a body's motion is to be measured by "mv" or by "mv². " Of course, the "force" might be measured by allowing the moving body to strike a pan of an equal-arm balance, or a dish of soft clay, etc. Colin Maclaurin, who followed Newton closely in all physical questions, and who therefore held that the "force" of a body's motion was (according to Law II) "mv," wrote: "Sir *Isaac Newton,* in his second law of motion, points out to us that the impressed force being considered as the cause, the change of motion produced by it is the effect that measures the

cause; and not the space described by it against the action of an uniform gravity, nor the hollows produced by the body falling into clay. This law of motion is the surest guide we can follow, in determining effects from their causes, or conversely the causes from their effects." *An account of Sir Isaac Newton's philosophical discoveries* (London: printed for the author's children, 1748), p. 137.

[14] Throughout most of Book I, Newton is dealing essentially with point masses, or unit masses; or, expressed differently, the "body" he considers has a constant mass throughout. Hence the mass ("quantity of matter") may be absorbed in the constant, yielding a Second Law of the form $\Phi \propto \Delta V$ (or $\Phi \propto dV$). In Def. VIII, however, Newton introduces a "measure" of centripetal force proportional to dV/dt, which he contrasts with another measure (called the "motive quantity") proportional to $d(mV)/dt$. On the concept of "measure" as used by Newton in the Definitions of the *Principia*, see I. B. Cohen: Isaac Newton's *Principia*, the scriptures, and the divine providence (Appendix I: New light on the form of Definitions I–II & VI–VIII), pp. 523–548 (esp. pp. 537–542) of Sidney Morgenbesser, Patrick Suppes, Morton White (eds.): *Philosophy, science, and method. Essays in honor of Ernest Nagel* (New York: St. Martin's Press, 1969).

[15] The reason is of course that if the same (or an equal) factor appears in weight (providing the motive force) and in the "vis insita" or "vis inertiae" (determining the resistance to a change of state), then the Second Law for continuous forces gives a constant acceleration independent of the mass of the falling body. Def. VIII says that

$$\text{"motive force"} = k_1 \cdot \Delta \, (m\vec{V})/\Delta t$$

but if "motive force" is the weight W, proportional to the mass m of the body

$$W = k_2 m$$

it follows that

$$k_2 m = k_1 m \cdot \Delta V / \Delta t$$

and hence it follows that the acceleration ($\Delta V/\Delta t$) is constant so long as the quantity m on the left-hand side of the equation is identically the same as the quantity m on the right-hand side of the equation. Newton's analysis of Galileo's experiment and his own experiments with pendulums thus lead him to the conclusion that a "gravitational" and an "inertial" mass are "equivalent."

[16] "Hence it is, that near the surface of the earth, where the accelerative gravity, or force productive of gravity, in all bodies is the same, the motive gravity or the weight is as the body; but if we should ascend to higher regions, where the accelerative gravity is less, the weight would be equally diminished, and would always be as the product of the body, by the accelerative gravity. So, in those regions, where the accelerative gravity is diminished into one-half, the weight of a body. . . ."

[17] Newton's famous experiments on mass and weight were made with pendulums of identical length (11 feet) and identical hollow bobs (so as to have the same air resistance). At the center of the bobs, he then placed the same weight of a number of different substances. Any difference in the ratio of mass to weight would have manifested itself by a variation in the period of the pendulum, which did not occur. Newton says (*Principia*, Book III, Prop. VI), "By these experiments, in bodies of the same weight, I could manifestly have discovered a difference of matter less than the thousandth part of the whole, had any such been."

It is interesting to note that in this discussion Newton refers the reader to Section VI of Book II, on pendulums, in particular to Prop. XXIV. Here Newton states the Second Law of Motion for continuous forces, much as we would today: "For the velocity which a given force can generate in a given matter in a given time is directly as the force and the time, and inversely as the matter. The greater the force or the time is, or the less the matter, the greater the velocity generated." Newton does not say that this *is* the Second Law, but rather, that "this is manifest from the second Law of Motion." In other words, the Second Law for continuous forces follows from the Second Law as stated for impulses.

I. BERNARD COHEN

[18] In the present abbreviated version, I have omitted the bulk of the present section.

[19] A careful analysis of all the steps in Newton's proof of Prop. I and of Prop. IV (Bk. I of the *Principia*) and their prior states (as found in the preliminary treatise, *De motu*, the "Waste Book," and the final paragraph of the Scholium to the above-mentioned Prop. IV) shows that Newton was constructing a continuous force out of discrete infinitesimal impulses, and not finite ones. Further, an examination of the infinitesimal basis of many of these dynamical the-orems shows that the question is one of second-order rather than first-order infinitesimals. On this topic see Appendices I and II below. Also D. T. Whiteside's essay-review of Herivel's book (see n. 10 *supra*), in *History of Science*, 1966, 5: 104–117; and Leon Rosenfeld: Newton's views on aether and gravitation, *Archive for the History of the Exact Sciences*, 1969, 6: 29–37. This topic is also explored in Ch. 5, §5 of E. J. Aiton's forthcoming book on *The Vortex theory of the planetary motions* (in press), and in his article: Newton's aether-stream hypothesis and the inverse-square law of gravitation, *Annals of Science*, 1969, 25: 255–260.

[20] This point is well made by R. G. A. Dolby: A note on Dijksterhuis' criticism of Newton's axiomatization of mechanics, *Isis* 1966, 57: 108–115.

[21] The statements of Lex II and Lex III show no variation in the three editions, but Lex I is altered in the third edition (1726). In all three editions, Lex I begins: "Corpus omne perseverare in statu suo quiescendi vel movendi uniformiter in directum, ..." The concluding portion reads as follows in the two forms:

First (1687) & Second (1713) Editions	*Third (1726) Edition*
". . . nisi quatenus a viribus impressis cogitur statum *illum* mutare."	". . . nisi quatenus *illud* a viribus impressis cogitur statum *suum* mutare."

I have italicized the words that differ in the two editions.

I have not found this change anywhere among Newton's MS alterations, and it may possibly have originated with Dr. Henry Pemberton, who edited the third edition of the *Principia* under Newton's direction.

[22] At first encounter, it may seem that Newton's statement about "a free body" was a neces-sary addition and should not have been deleted, after having been added. For clearly a "force" may not generate any motion at all if the body on which it acts is constrained, as might be the case if a blow were to be given to a block of wood nailed to the floor. And even if the blow were of sufficient magnitude to rupture the fastening, some of the "force" would have to be expended in getting the block loose, and the resulting "motion generated" would thus not be proportional to the "force." On reflection, however, this is seen not to be the case at all. What is in question is not "force" in general but a "force impressed" ("Vis omnis impressa"), which is defined specifically as that "force" which alters a body's state of motion or of rest—and, hence, *only* that part of any "force" in general which *does* so alter a body's state.

[23] "And this motion [generated by the force] (being always directed the same way with the generating force), if the body moved before, is added to or subtracted from the former mo-tion, according as they directly conspire with or are directly contrary to each other; or obliquely joined, when they are oblique, so as to produce a new motion compounded from the determina-tion of both."

[24] This comment was cancelled by Newton in two stages, first the portion within square brackets (these are Newton's square brackets), then the remainder. An initial sentence, not cancelled, is identical to the initial sentence in the printed version, which reads (in transla-tion): "If some force generate any motion, a double force will generate a double motion, a triple one a triple, whether it has been impressed at one time and at once or by degrees and successively." The second sentence (of the two) in the printed version has been given in n. 23 *supra*.

[25] But if the motion of the space in the direction $\overrightarrow{AB}$ were accelerated, while the motion $\overrightarrow{AC}$ were uniform, then the curved path would be concave toward AB rather than convex, as New-ton has drawn it. Of course, if by some chance the motion of the space were decelerated, the curve would then have the shape indicated by Newton, that is, be convex toward the line AB.

Needless to say, there is no indication given in the text to justify the assumption that the motion of the space along the direction of the line AB would be either accelerated or decelerated, since Newton says explicitly, ". . . with the motion which it had in A uniformly continued. . . ."

[26] In my discussions of this question with Dr. D. T. Whiteside, he has pointed out that either of two possibilities, "whether—at a finite level—the orbit is built up of a series of infinitesimal discrete force-impulses [Leibniz's favored form] or a series of infinitesimal arcs generated by a continuous force (of second-order infinitesimal discrete force-impulses) [Newton's favored approach], leads to *exactly* the same theory of central forces." The first is, of course, what Newton in 1687 and afterwards calls generation "simul & semel", the latter being "gradatim & successive."

[27] It occurs on fol. 731 *v*, U.L.C. MS Add. 3965.

[28] The revisions made by Newton in successive editions are presented in the forthcoming edition of the *Principia* with variant readings, prepared by the late Alexandre Koyré and I. B. Cohen, assisted by Anne Whitman (Cambridge, Mass.: Harvard University Press; Cambridge, England: at the University Press, 1971). See especially the first volume of that edition, *Introduction to Newton's "Principia,"* by I. B. Cohen, Ch. VII, §2.

[29] At this time, Newton was also considering a different way of beginning Book One, having a wholly new Prop. I (Theorem I), stating that a body revolving uniformly in a circle will be drawn off from its rectilinear motion and brought back continually to the circular path by a force which is directed to the center, and which will be to the force of gravity as the square of the arc described in a given time to the rectangle (product) of the circle and the space which in that same time that body would describe by falling. Following a number of corollaries, some taken from the old Prop. IV, Theorem IV, Newton would add a note that these results were found by Huygens, who showed in his *Horologium oscillatorium* how to compare the force of gravity with centrifugal forces. Descartes, Borelli, and others, Newton said, had discussed these forces, but it was Huygens who first displayed their quantitative measure.

Prop. II, Theorem II, would then state that if bodies moved uniformly along unequal circles, the forces by which they would be drawn off from rectilinear paths and brought back continually to the circles would be as the arcs described in the same times divided by the squares of the radii. The above discussion of Descartes, Borelli, and Huygens now was to appear in Corol. 2 to a new Prop. V.

[30] All revisions entered by Newton in his own copies of the first and second editions of the *Principia* have been included among the variant readings in the new edition (see n. 28).

[31] Newton's complete misrepresentation of Galileo's procedure seems to me strong evidence that he had never read the *Discorsi* before writing the *Principia*. See n. 10, *supra*.

It is interesting to note that Newton's attribution of the Second Law, as well as the First Law, to Galileo appears in his tract on the motion of bodies in uniformly resisting media. "By means of these two laws," he wrote, "Galileo discovered that projectiles under a uniform gravity acting along parallel lines described parabolas in a non-resisting medium."

[32] Newton wants to prove that if "the spaces described [by a freely falling body] in proportional times are as the product of the velocities and the times. . . . And if a body be projected in any direction, the motion arising from its projection is compounded with the motion arising from its gravity. Thus, if the body A by its motion of projection alone could describe in a given time the right line AB, and with its motion of falling alone could describe in the same time the altitude AC; complete the parallelogram ABCD, and the body by that compounded motion will at the end of the time be found in the place D; and the curved line AED, which that body describes, will be a parabola, to which the right line AB will be a tangent at A; and whose ordinate BD will be as the square of the line AB."

I. BERNARD COHEN

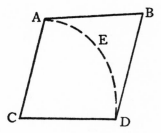

[33] The Motte-Cajori version reads: "When a body is falling, the uniform force of its gravity acting equally, impresses, in equal intervals of time, equal forces upon that body, and therefore generates equal velocities; and in the whole time impresses a whole force, and generates a whole velocity proportional to the time." Since Newton uses the word "vis" only one time less than Motte and Cajori, this passage can hardly illustrate how "Newton uses 'force' in nicely contrasting ways." But see n. 34, *infra*. See, further, I. B. Cohen: Newton's use of "force," or, Cajori versus Newton—a note on translations of the "Principia," *Isis,* 1967, *58:* 226–230.

[34] Univ. Lib. Cambr. MS Add. 3968, §41, fol. 10. This document is printed *in extenso* in A. Koyré & I. B. Cohen: Newton & the Leibniz-Clarke correspondence, *op. cit.,* n. 5, *supra,* p. 118.

In another MS, never published by Newton, he *did* use the word "force" in English in contrasting senses. It is printed *ibid.,* p. 119 (from MS Add. 3968, §41, fol. 44), and reads in part: "The Theory of Projectiles invented by Galilaeo is founded upon the Hypothesis of uniform gravity, & is generally approved by Mathematicians. Now uniform gravity is that which acts with an uniform force & in equal times by acting with equal force upon the body communicates equal forces to it." This statement is a rough draft, not a final version approved for publication.

APPENDIX I

A central problem in any discussion of Newton's Second Law, or of the system of dynamics presented in the *Principia,* is the relation of continuous and impulsive forces. That these two types of forces should be related to Newton's concept of time may be seen at once in the fact that they are defined in terms of the time in which they act: the impulsive force is instantaneous whereas the continuous force produces its effects during a finite interval of time. Because we today make a distinction between the two, we are puzzled by the ease with which Newton passed from one to the other, and even appears to have assumed without any explicit declaration that a Second Law stated for impulses and the change in motion (momentum) they produce could imply a similar law for continuous forces and the rate of change of motion they produce. And, as we have seen in the main body of the present article, Newton (e.g., in the proof of Prop. I, Bk. I, of the *Principia*) considered that a continuous force could be the limit of a series of impulses as the frequency of impulse becomes infinite (or as the time between impulses vanishes), without apparently taking cognizance of the difference in dimensionality of an impulse (proportional to $\Delta(m\vec{V})$) and a continuous force (proportional to $d(m\vec{V})/dt$). In this Appendix, I shall indicate how this procedure is related to Newton's concept of time and I shall then discuss the associated problem of infinitesimal versus finite force-impulses.

In Newton's mathematics, as in his physics, time is almost invariably the primary independent variable on which all other quantities depend. Time—along with space, place, and motion—was not defined in the *Principia;* all four of these quantities were held to be "well known to all." But, in the Scholium following the Definitions, Newton stated that "Absolute, True, and Mathematical Time, of itself, and from its own nature flows equally [*aequabiliter fluit*] without regard to any thing external. . . ." In his *Methods of Series and Fluxions* (1670–71), Newton had previously discussed time as follows:

> We can, however, have no estimate of time except in so far as it is expounded and measured by an equable local motion, and furthermore quantities of the same kind alone, and so also their speeds of increase and decrease, may be compared one with another. For these reasons I shall, in what follows, have no regard to time, formally so considered, but from quantities propounded which are of the same kind shall suppose some one to increase with an equable flow: to this all the others may be referred as though it were time, and so by analogy the name of 'time' may not improperly be conferred upon it. And so whenever in the following you meet with the word 'time' (as I have, for clarity's and distinction's sake, on occasion woven it into my text), by that name should be understood not time formally considered but that other quantity through whose

equable increase or flow time is expounded and measured. [Quoted from D. T. Whiteside's translation, in his edition of *The mathematical papers of Isaac Newton,* Vol. 3 (Cambridge: at the University Press, 1969), p. 73. For the relation between Newton's views of time and Isaac Barrow's, see *ibid.,* p. 17, pp. 71–72 (nn. 82, 84). Newton's concept of time may also be found in his treatise *De quadratura,* Introduction, §§ 1, 2; and see the comment by John Stewart, p. 35 (§6) of his commentary to the translation in Newton's *Two treatises of the Quadrature of curves and Analysis by equations of an infinite number of terms* (London: printed by John Bettenham . . . and sold by John Nourse and John Whiston, 1745).]

Some forty years later, Newton wrote:

> I consider time as flowing or increasing by continual flux & other quantities as increasing continually in time & from ye fluxion of time I give the name of fluxions to the velocitys wth wch all other quantities increase. Also from the moments of time I give the name of moments to the parts of any other quantities generated in moments of time. I expose time by any quantity flowing uniformly & represent its fluxion by an unit, & the fluxions of other quantities I represent by any other fit symbols, & the fluxions of their fluxions by other fit symbols & the fluxions of those fluxions by others, ...[Quoted from *Math. papers.,* Vol. 3, p. 17.]

In this way, Newton held, his "Method is derived immediately from Nature her self," which is not true of other methods, as "indivisibles, Leibnitian differences or infinitely small quantities."

One consequence of a universal or uniform flow of time is that the increment of time is constant under all circumstances. This is equivalent to a quasi-discrete concept of the infinitesimals of a variable time that is not quite continuously flowing. In the *Principia* we find both concepts in use almost interchangeably. The smooth flux appears in Section I, Bk. I, on first and last ratios, whereas the infinitesimally discrete concept seems to occur in actual proofs of the propositions. (On this topic, see the conclusion to Appendix II, below.)

If we consider "dt" as this constant increment of time, we may write a number of equivalent forms of the Second Law of Motion, equivalent—that is to say—in terms of the Newtonian concept of a primitive or fundamental "time" flowing uniformly at a constant rate everywhere, at all times, and under any conditions imaginable. These are:

$$(1)\quad \vec{f} \propto d\vec{V}$$

$$(2a)\quad \vec{f} \propto \frac{d\vec{V}}{dt} = \frac{d^2\vec{s}}{dt^2}, \text{ where } \vec{V} = \frac{d\vec{s}}{dt}$$

$$(2b)\quad \vec{f} \cdot dt \propto d\vec{V}$$

$$(2c)\quad \vec{f} \cdot dt^2 \propto d^2\vec{s}.$$

The only difference between equation (1) and any other in this group is that the constant of proportionality cannot be the same, and it must have a different physical dimensionality. I have used the symbol "f" so as not to impose upon the symbolic representation of Newton's Second "Law" any clear-cut distinction between varieties of "force" (impulse Φ and continuous force F) such as we make today and such as I have made in the body of the article. If the force is itself a variable, then "f" must be the average value during time dt.

It must be kept in mind that in the *Principia* Newton did not usually write equations of motion, but expressed his principles as proportions. Hence the constant of proportionality did not need to appear explicitly, nor had Newton any general regard for physical dimensionality of physical quantities—as in the various forms of "force" (*vis*). This is especially the case since Newton compared forces (as, the different weights an object must have "toward" the Earth at one place and another), rather than computing their numerical values in some given system of units, which would have required a consideration of the physical dimensions of the computed quantities. Thus we may understand how it was possible to hold simultaneously the validity of a Second Law as written symbolically by equation (1) and by equation (2b), whereas to us it would appear at once that the quantity "f" cannot be the same in both equations.

The foregoing discussion derives in good measure from an extended exchange of ideas I have had with Dr. D. T. Whiteside, coupled with a careful re-reading of Newton's mathematical writings as each of the three volumes of the *Mathematical Papers* has appeared. Some of the major aspects of this presentation may be found in Vol. I of J. M. F. Wright's *Commentary on Newton's Principia* (London: printed for T. T. & J. Tegg; and Richard Griffin & Co., Glasgow, 1833), esp. §46 where the significance of "considering dt constant" is introduced, along with the fact that the various forms of the Second Law require "properly adjusting the units of force." The concept of constant increments of time (dt) is found explicitly in many of Newton's writings, e.g., *De quadratura* (*ed. cit.,* Intro., p. 2, §3): "Fluxions are very nearly as the Augments of the Fluents generated in equal but very small Particles of Time...."

Whiteside has published a penetrating analysis of the infinitesimal character of Newton's dynamics (in 1966, in a review article in *History of Science,* ed. by A. C. Crombie & M. A. Hoskin, vol. 5, pp. 104–117, esp. p. 111). In particular, Whiteside has drawn attention to a generally unnoticed aspect of Newton's proof of Prop. I, Bk. I, of the *Principia,* and also of the prior proofs of the Law of Areas, as in *De Motu.* Newton's proof, as we have seen, reduces the continuous curve to the limit of a polygon, and thus—according to Whiteside—replaces the continuously acting central force by the limit of "a series of component, discrete impulses, each acting instantaneously but separated from its predecessor by a measurable if indefinitely small time interval.... [This] model requires its elements to be of a second order of the infinitely small...." Hence, since dt^2 is a constant (a necessary consequence of dt being a constant), Newton's proof of Prop. I, Bk. I, would thus seem to em-

I. BERNARD COHEN

ploy the Second Law in a form expressed by equation ($2c$), or an equivalent form, namely $f \propto d^2 s$. Equation ($2c$) is thus another way of saying that a Newtonian force-impulse may be a second-order infinitesimal.

Similarly, equation ($2b$) is an expression of the Second Law essential to the development of Props. XXXIX-XLI, Bk. I; that is, in the equivalent form, $F \cdot ds \propto V \cdot dV$ (as may be seen in Wright's *Commentary*, Prop. XLI, §302 and §46). Equation ($2b$) states the relation $f \cdot dt \propto dV$, the validity of which is not affected by multiplying both sides by V, so as to get $f \cdot dt \cdot V \propto V \cdot dV$, or $f \cdot dt \cdot \dfrac{ds}{dt} \propto V \cdot dV$, which at once yields $f \cdot ds \propto V \cdot dV$.

Finally, equation ($2a$) corresponds to a form of the Second Law required in the *Principia* for Prop. VI, Bk. I. That is, it yields the "measure" of the force required in this case, where Newton introduces specifically the "least time" in which a body (in "a space void of resistance") "describes any arc just then nascent" as it "revolves in any orbit about an immoveable center." Newton supposes that the versed sine of that arc is drawn so as to bisect the chord and then produced so as to pass through the center of force. Under these circumstances, "the centripetal force in the middle of the arc" will prove to be "as the versed sine directly and the square of the time inversely."

One is led into error by considering that Newton's "force-impulses" are intended to be finite quantities, or even first-order infinitesimals. The first version of my paper contains a fault, deriving from just such an assumption (pp. 164–166, 167–169), corrected in the current state of this presentation. Newton's MS additions to the presentation of the Second Law, which I discuss in the main body of this article, do not lead to error or ambiguity (as, for instance, in not leading to a uniquely definable finite trajectory) so long as we keep in mind that the force-impulses are not acting at a simple first-order infinitesimal level. Thus, in the MS I have quoted (U.L.C., MS Add. 3965.6, fol. 274v), the "vis motrix impressa" is not acting over a finite time-interval, but rather over a first-order infinitesimal time dt, and hence may properly be considered an instance of the Second Law as stated in the *Principia* among the "Axiomata sive Leges Motus," a relation between an impulse (or instantaneous force) and the change in momentum! The parabola-like orbit is thus an infinitesimal orbital segment, produced by a first-order infinitesimal force-impulse which itself proves to be compounded of an infinite number of second-order infinitesimal force-impulses, each of which we may consider to be acting instantaneously in a time-interval which is not the whole interval dt but rather dt/n as $n \rightarrow \infty$, itself infinitesimally small.

FINITE OR INFINITESIMAL IMPULSES, "PARTICLES" OF TIME,
FORCES, AND INCREMENTS OF "QUANTITY OF MOTION"

Whoever reads the *Principia* carefully is aware of the extent to which its principles (Definitions, Laws, Propositions and Lemmata and their respective proofs) are conceived on the level of infinitesimals. This aspect of Newton's dynamics is emphasized for the reader by the prominent display—as Section I of Book I—of Newton's "method of first and last ratios of quantities" which are explicitly presented as the tools needed in order to "demonstrate the propositions that follow."

Almost every proposition of the *Principia* is either developed or proved by taking limits, or depends on anterior propositions that invoke the limiting process. Often the proof is written out in such a way as to permit no ambiguity as to the very instant at which the limit is introduced. It is, indeed, because almost universally Newton's proofs proceed by limits that we may see how absurd it is to make a simple description of the *Principia* as an example of a treatise cast in the mold of classic Greek geometry. Rather, the constant recourse to limits, to "nascent" and "evanescent" quantities, should clarify the level of discourse as "infinitesimal"; and the language of geometry should not mask the true incremental quality of the mathematical thought. Nor should the general absence of a universal algorithm and a familiar symbolism prevent us from recognizing that the *Principia* is written in terms of the calculus (the infinitesimal or differential, if not the integral, calculus) in all but name only. Newton himself was obviously aware of this aspect of his monumental treatise, and he often quoted with pride the conclusion of a statement made in the first textbook of the calculus, the Marquis de l'Hôpital's *Analyse des infiniment petits* (1691): that "M. Newton . . . avoit aussi trouvé quelque chose de semblable au Calcul différentiel, comme il paroît par l'excellent Livre intitulé *Philosophiae naturalis principia Mathematica,* qu'il nous donna en 1687, lequel est presque tout de ce calcul."

Of course, some Propositions (and Lemmata) are unambiguously stated for infinitesimal conditions. Lemma XI, Bk. I, is one of these: "The evanescent [!] subtense of the angle of contact . . . is ultimately [!] in the duplicate ratio of the subtense of the conterminate arc." Or, again, Lemma X, in which Newton discusses the "spaces which a body describes . . . in the very beginning [!] of the motion." We have seen (in the main body of this article) that in proving Prop. I, Newton first deals with a set of discrete impulses, before he introduces a limiting process. In demonstrating Prop. XI, Bk. I ("If a body revolve in an ellipse: it is required to find the law of the centripetal force tending to the focus of the ellipse"), again he develops a set of geometric relations before introducing the limiting condition, that the point Q coincide with the point P.

But Newton does not in every case make it clear as to when he wishes the reader

I. BERNARD COHEN

to understand that the quantities are infinitesimally small rather than finite and merely indefinite. A case in point occurs in Newton's projected revision of the Second Law, in which an error would be made if the conditions were supposed finite: since a single finite blow delivered once to a body moving inertially (and hence uniformly) along a right line cannot produce a parabolic trajectory, but only a new uniformly traced-out rectilinear path. Furthermore, we have seen that Newton does not make plain when the logic of the mathematical argument requires that the infinitesimal quantities must be of the second order rather than simple first-order infinitesimals.

The lack of absolute clarity on such matters may be considered a compliment to the mathematical perspicacity of the reader,[1] but is certainly to be reckoned a major difficulty in understanding the *Principia*. In large measure, confusion arises from the lack of a universal algorithm, developed for the reader in analytical symbols early on and then applied consistently. In rewriting some of Newton's dynamical statements in post-Newtonian mathematical symbolism, I have used both the "Δ" and the Leibnizian "d"; but I would not wish the reader to assume therefrom that there is always a vast and fundamental difference between the two on the Newtonian level. For instance, I have written the impulse-form of the Second Law as

(1) $\Phi \propto \Delta(mV)$

where the "Δ" signifies the discrete incremental quality of a single blow. In this fashion, in the main body of the article, I have intended to convey symbolically the linguistic ambiguity of Newton's original statement. But I believe that on the Newtonian plane the meaning is not seriously altered (if it is indeed altered at all) by writing this Law, as in Appendix I, in the form

(2) $f \propto d(mV)$.

The latter more clearly defines the infinitesimal level of discourse, which is necessary since the impulse f here acts in an instant. The sense is, of course, that $d(mV) = \lim.(\Delta mV)$. This equation (2) thus emphasizes the important insight of the late Alexandre Koyré that the principles of dynamics in the physics of the seventeenth century—whether those of Descartes or those of Newton—tend to be true infinitesimally rather than on the finite level.

Newton tried to hold to the ideals of Greek geometry in the early stages of each task—prior to taking limits. He thus specifically rejected Leibniz's critique, and held that Leibniz had even misrepresented his methods:

> For in this method [*of first & last ratios*] quantities are never considered as infinitely little nor are right lines ever put for arches [*i.e., arcs*] neither are any lines or quantities put by approximation for any other lines or quantities to wch they are not exactly equal, but the whole operation is performed exactly in finite quantities by Euclides Geometry untill you come to an equation & then the equation is reduced by rejecting the terms wch destroy one another & divid-

[1] Or even an indication of inadequacy on Newton's part.

ing the residue by the finite quantity *o* & making this quantity *o* not to become infinitely little but totally to vanish. . . . And this way of working . . . [*is*] as . . . exact & demonstrative as any thing in Geometry. . . .[Quoted from *Mathematical papers,* vol. II, p. 264; see also p. 271.]

Nevertheless, despite the rigorous approach to the theory of limits in Section I of Book I of the *Principia* (in which the doctrine of "first & last ratios" is introduced), it is not always clear at first glance whether quantities are in fact finite or infinitesimal ("nascent" or "evanescent")—and this may become apparent only by a profound analysis of the mathematical circumstances and the consequences of both assumptions. But I have no doubt that there would be no ambiguity for Newton himself, who certainly could see fully—whenever he wished to do so, or was challenged to do so—(and at once) all the mathematical aspects of his presentations. In the absence of any positive evidence, however, we can say no more than that he could and would have made such analyses had he a mind to, but we do not know whether or not he ever did so with regard to all Propositions and Lemmata of the *Principia.* This is the reason why we are forced to make assumptions about Newton's methods, such as has been done in Appendix I. It is as if we were proposing plausible answers that Newton himself might have given to our questions, but without any surety that he was ever asked these questions—by himself as well as by others.

The ambiguity for the reader derives also from Newton's insight: his intuitive leap from a relation between finite quantities to its ultimate limit as one or more of the quantities might either vanish or become infinite. Skipping the intermediary steps, Newton would anticipate the result. Thus in some, but by no means all, instances the infinitesimal end-product creeps into what may appear to be a finite situation. Indeed, this is a general basis for criticism of reckoning with infinitesimals. A mind like Newton's could proceed in this way without making errors, where his contemporaries and we ourselves might stumble.

The modern reader is apt to be confused because Newton does not always make a clear distinction between the "mutatio" (dx) of a fluent quantity (x) and its "celeritas mutationis" $\left(\dfrac{dx}{dt}\right)$. In the famous Lemma II of Book II of the *Principia,* Newton states unambiguously that: "It will be the same thing, if, instead of moments [= "momentaneous increments or decrements" of "quantities I here consider as variable and indetermined, and increasing or decreasing as it were by a perpetual motion or flux"], we use either the Velocities of the increments and decrements (which may also be called the motions, mutations and fluxions of quantities) or any finite quantities proportional to those velocities." This sentence so confused Andrew Motte, who made the English translation of the *Principia,* that he omitted the word "mutations" from the parenthetical expression, which reads "quas etiam motus, mutationes & fluxiones quantitatum nominare licet" in all three editions.

I. BERNARD COHEN

All of these difficulties appear in Newton's concept of time, presented above in Appendix I. We saw there that Newtonian time flows uniformly, so that we may consider "dt" as a constant increment.[2] But is this time itself made up of discrete units or "particles"? Or is it infinitely divisible? Although Newton writes in the *Principia* of "particles" of time, he does not mean finite atoms of time in the sense of finite countable atoms in any sample of matter. This is the sense in which time itself is finitely continuous and only infinitesimally discrete. The "fluxional" basis of the *Principia* thus—paradoxically though it may seem—depends in practice on a discrete kind of infinitesimal of time, in which quantities do not really flow, but rather jerk, jerk, jerk along (to use a metaphor of D. T. Whiteside). But this occurs to our finite eyes on the infinitesimal level only, so that time appears to be flowing smoothly, as postulated by the (equivalent) method of first and last ratios.

In Prop. II, Bk. II, we may see how Newton divides a time-interval into "equal particles," and eventually lets "those equal particles of time be diminished, and their number increased *in infinitum.*" We ourselves would hasten to ask how a continuous flux of time could be made up of discrete units, even infinitesimal ones, but this is basically the embodiment of an anachronous point of view that seeks to impose upon Newtonian science those rigorous tests and strict dichotomies that would deny to the *Principia* those very qualities of ambiguity that are so essential for the functioning of Newton's genius in all its display of power and beauty.

[2] Time for Newton *does* flow uniformly. But perhaps it would be most accurate to say that it is the measure of the flux that can be divided into infinitesimals of equal "length," rather than to insist that Newtonian time itself is *made up of* some sort of "discrete units."

JAMES E. MCGUIRE

Comment*

Professor Cohen's paper is an admirable contribution to our understanding of some of the more vexing problems in the *Principia*. Starting from the widely accepted view that impulse is primitive for Newton[1], his discussion is concerned primarily with Newton's techniques for extending the second law for impulses to cover nonimpulsive forces. And he draws our attention to the fact that the law for continuously acting forces is anticipated in the discussion to Definition VIII to the laws, and that it is presented in a completely generalized form in Proposition XXIV of Book II. Important also is the connection established between Descartes' use of impulses in the proof of his law of refraction, and Newton's use of similar theoretical considerations in the proof of an earlier version of Corollary I to the laws.

I wish to comment on three aspects of Professor Cohen's paper. First, on his treatment of the first two laws of motion in terms of a distinction between two different kinds of force. Next, on his analysis of Newton's use of the concept of action. And lastly, on his views regarding the nature and status of the first law of motion. In connection with this, I shall conclude briefly with my own interpretation of Newton's conception of *vis insita* and *vis inertiae*.

Professor Cohen offers a new basis for a separate law I and law II. His analysis arises from two factors on which he places considerable importance. We only see the effects of continuously acting forces, thus the second part of the first law is needed to determine that the action of such forces is taking place. This is not necessary for the discrete, instantaneous forces with which the second law, as it is formulated, is concerned. As Professor Cohen points out, the forces with which it deals, unlike those of the first law, are observable causal events. He then contends that in Laws I and II, Newton is dealing with two sorts of "impressed motives forces": the one continuous and the other a discrete impulse. And elsewhere, he more strongly contends that the continuous forces with which Law I is concerned are not a single blow, nor even a sequence of discrete blows. Professor Cohen claims that the remarks to the laws and their corollaries support his analysis.

It would seem that he wishes to drop these two laws into very different categorical bins. As he says: "these two laws—as given in the *Principia*—are not really as closely related to one another as is often supposed by those who do not take account of the fact that Newton's Law II, as stated, is restricted to impulsive forces, whereas Law I is not." The first point I should like to make is an obvious, but I hope a clarifying one. It seems clear that Newton did not consider his first law superfluous, precisely because he held that an impressed impulse is the cause of an abrupt change in either velocity or motion. But this is only a sufficient condition for such a change. The second law does not prescribe the necessary conditions. As far as we can tell from its formulation a change of momentum, for instance, could happen in a number of possible ways. This is obviated by the latter part of the first law: it asserts that only an impressed impulse, and no other cause, can alter the state of a body. Thus it clearly lays down the necessary conditions for determining when and how a force is acting. Hence the two laws together constitute the necessary and

JAMES E. MCGUIRE

sufficient conditions for the presence of a force, and for the measurement of its effect. This is so whether a force acts continuously or is an impulse.

The above point makes it plain that these laws, though different, are an integral part of Newton's conception of how forces operate in nature. The interpretation of Professor Cohen tends to blur this, since he strongly stresses that the laws apply to different sorts of forces. Moreover, he suggests that it is not clear, given the formulation of the laws, how these two sorts of impressed forces are to be related. Indeed he implies that one of the major conceptual difficulties in the *Principia* is precisely to work out a relation between the laws governing the two types of forces. I think it is legitimate to ask whether this dichotomy is not too sharp. For if we make a categorical difference between two types of impressed force in terms of a criterion of the complete separateness of the two laws, this would seem to be tantamount to the view that there are two primitive forces in the *Principia*: continuous and instantaneous. Whereas, it seems clear that there is only one external and primitive force—impulse. And, as I shall contend, there is also the internal "property" of *vis insita* which plays an important part in Newton's analysis of interactions between bodies. But more of this in a moment.

As to impulses, Proposition I of Book I amply testifies, as Professor Cohen observes, that when the time intervals between successive impulses become vanishingly small, as it were, these discrete forces give rise in the limit to the *effect* of a continuous force. They are not themselves, however, continuous. And, given impulses, the problem, which is solved to Newton's satisfaction in Proposition I, is that of accounting for continuous effects in nature; it is not that of transforming instantaneous impulses into continuous forces, which is implied if we accept Professor Cohen's strict dichotomy. The latter view has the added difficulty that it is not clear that such a conceptual transformation is meaningful. Thus Newton in Proposition I supposes, rightly or wrongly, that impulses by acting continuously give rise to truly continuous effects, so that it is instantaneous discontinuous motion that becomes apparently continuous, not that discrete impulses become truly continuous forces. If this is so, Newton clearly recognizes a distinction between continuously *acting* forces, and continuous forces. The latter are *not* true forces for the *Principia*. Although he certainly believes in attractive forces, he also takes an agnostic position with respect to their nature. And Newton's thinking is always in terms of impulses.

In any event Newton's problem is not that of *combining* two different types of forces as Professor Cohen suggests, but that of moving from truly instantaneous forces to continuously acting forces, as Professor Cohen *also* states. But we cannot, at the same time, accept both positions. For if Newton had considered these two forces as being primitive and separate, as Professor Cohen seems to hold, it is difficult to see why he would have considered the problem of transforming from one to the other. The more logical move would have been to define two laws of action in relation to the first law: the one for impulse, and the other for continuous forces. Since Newton did not do this, we can only conclude that Professor Cohen does not intend his dichotomy to be a strict one. But then it seems difficult to understand why it should be an argument for the separation of the two laws; however, I agree with him that they are separate, but for reasons other than those which he considers.

Professor Cohen rightly observes that the primacy of impulses in the *Principia* arises from the centrality of collision problems in Newton's dynamical thinking. Indeed, his earliest program in dynamics was probably the hope of extending the scope of the concept of force essential for analyzing collisions, to all forces whatsoever. As we know, this program was not achieved. Nature became for Newton more complex. And he was brought to assert that there are many different types of forces which do not arise from matter and which are in no way reducible to it. It is evident in the *Principia,* however, that Newton holds, for general dynamical purposes, that all forces can be analyzed quantitatively as impulses acting on matter as impressed forces.

This brings me to Professor Cohen's remarks on the key term *actio.* He lays great stress on Definition IV where Newton says that an impressed force "consists in the action only; and remains no longer in the body, when the action is over."[2] This he literally interprets as an identity statement: an impressed force (*vis impressa*) *is* the action. And, moreover, he suggests that Definition IV defines Newton's use of *actio* and *reactio* in the formulation of the third law. It would seem, however, that the use of the term "impress" is a way of characterizing the mode of action of a single impulse or series of impulses, and that thus the action is not in and of itself a type of force. Rather action, as defined, is synonymous with mechanical cause. That is, an impulse causes, by impressing on a body (i.e., by acting), a change of its state. Thus *actio* is neither the impulse in itself nor the change of state in itself. This gives a clear sense to Newton's view that an impressed force consists in action only. Admittedly in the remarks to the third law, and in part of the following scholium to the laws, Newton discusses many examples which the three laws cover in terms of his three types of impressed force: impact, percussion and attraction. And it seems that in these examples "actions" are being used synonymously with forces. But here again, however, I think the above analysis is plausible.

But this exegetical point apart, it is true that Newton uses the term "action" in a very much broader sense than force. Two examples will suffice. In the scholium to the laws, action is used to refer to mechanical "Powers." These do not necessarily have equal action and reaction in the sense of acting in opposite directions. This is the criterion which is clearly stated by the third law. Again, in the scholium where the equal action and reaction of all machines is discussed, Newton states that: "We estimate the action of the agent from the product of its force and velocity."[3] In the context of this discussion, actions are not forces, but *arise from* forces and velocities. And Newton's statement was probably intended to bring work into the ambit of the third law. Newton uses the term "action" in a blanket sense precisely because it allows him to extend his laws to a wide range of cases. Thus, while I do not agree with Professor Cohen that Newton only uses action in one sense as synonymous with impressed force, I do agree, however, that its use helps Newton to make a generalized extension, from impulses to continuously acting forces. As Cohen points out, the reader's attention is focused on the measurement of changes of motion and velocity as a result of something's acting, and not on the causal nature of attraction (p. 154).

Professor Cohen tells us that there are two dynamically significant forces in the *Principia:* those that are active and those that are passive. Referring to a passage in Query 31 of the *Opticks,* where Newton distinguishes passive and active principles, he seems to assimilate that discussion to what Newton tells us in Definition IV of the *Principia* about the distinction between the action of an impressed force, and the *vis inertiae* of a body which solely maintains each new state. It would seem to me that these texts are not equivalent. In the *Opticks* Newton is summarizing the three laws of the *Principia* as they apply to passive matter, and contrasts the "passive" principle *vis inertiae* (which determines the status of all the laws of motion) with active principles discussed in a later part of the same passage. One of the main points that Newton is concerned to make, is that active principles are not one with *vis inertiae* and, *a fortiori,* not so with the laws of motion. Active principles ultimately account for the motion of passive matter in the world, and "conserve" and "recruit" its varieties. By treating these passages as equivalent, Professor Cohen seems to interpret the term *actio* in Definition IV to be a *type* of active principle which characterizes the forces in the *Principia* which produce or alter the quantity of motion in matter. Since these forces act on matter endowed with a *vis inertiae,* and since Professor Cohen construes action to mean active in the sense of Query 31, he is led to categorize two different kinds of forces. This identification also seems to lie behind the suggested view that certain forces are continuous, as distinct from being instantaneous.

In order to justify my remarks, I want to conclude by offering yet another basis for a separate Law I and Law II. There are, it seems to me, two irreducibly different kinds of "explainers" in the *Principia.* External impulses, which are causes for Newton, and an internal *vis insita* in each bit of matter. The first law does not state that inertial motion is natural, either in the sense of being uncaused, or in the sense of representing ideal and nonrealizable motion. I will contend that in the *Principia* inertial motion is real and that for Newton it is something to be explained. This is the purpose of Definition III. It defines and characterizes *vis insita* as an internal, inherent and innate "property" of all bodies. Since in the Definition it is linked but not identical with *vis inertiae,* Newton gives an independent statement of Law I.

Before discussing Definition III to substantiate these contentions, it will first be helpful to deal briefly with some of the relevant presuppositions of Newton's thought. Like many of his contemporaries, he was unquestionably committed to a strict subject-predicate logic which tended to exclude relational propositions as invalid. Thus the essence of a thing must be a true or absolute property of it, which does not depend on the existence of other things. For Newton both extension and *vis insita* fall into this category. Gravity, on the other hand, is a property which determines the spatial relations among bodies. It is in this sense not an essential attribute of matter, and Newton felt the need to explain it. The relational nature of gravity, then, was probably at the heart of his rejection of it as essential to matter.[4]

The nature of Newton's logical commitment can be further illustrated from one of his early writings. In *De Gravitatione,*[5] where he gives a series of criticisms of Descartes' theory of motion, he characterizes relative motion as a mere external designation. But "physical and absolute motion is to be defined from other considerations than translations, such translation being designated as merely external."[6] Newton is here distinguishing in terms of the medieval doctrine of extrinsic and intrinsic designations, relative from absolute motion. Relative motion, being "merely external," gives only a geometrical characterization of a body with respect to others. This tells us nothing about its intrinsic or necessary attributes. Using an argument which in spirit is much like that which Leibniz employed in his *De Ipsa Natura*[7] to show that a "state of motion" cannot exist at an instant, Newton concludes "that Cartesian motion is not motion, for it has no velocity, no definition, and there is no space or distance traversed by it."[8] Their arguments both purport to show that mere extrinsic designations do not tell us what a body actually is. And both thinkers consider matter to have dynamical properties which cannot be determined geometrically. For Newton it is something which truly moves dynamically in absolute space, independently of other things. Similarly, Leibniz considers matter to be truly endowed with a nonextended force, which acts as an internal principle of change.

In the light of this background I want to consider Definition III. It is primarily concerned with the nature of *vis insita.* Although Newton speaks of a *vis,* his doctrine would seem to be that every body is actually endowed with a natural and inherent disposition to maintain itself in a state. That a body either preserves itself in a state of resting, or a state of moving, is so simply *because* it has this internal and absolute property.

There is no question of Definition III and Law I being equivalent. The Definition is concerned with an absolute dispositional property which all bodies have independently of each other. On the other hand, the law defines the observable "state of *inertiae*" of a body, which is itself a manifestation of this hidden property. Thus an independent statement of Law I is needed, for *vis insita* is different from an external impulse. A state of *inertiae* can be treated geometrically in terms of relative motion, and as such is an external designation. But *vis insita* explains absolute motion and rest, and in itself is nongeometrical. And Newton seems to have thought that the *Principia* provided techniques for connecting what he took to be empirical facts such as *inertiae* and absolute entities like *vis insita*.[9]

There seem to me to be *three reasons* which support the validity of this interpretation. Definition III in no way bears the mark of being residually influenced by either pre-inertial or impetus physics. Newton's discussion more probably indicates medieval influences of another sort. The key is the sentence which states of *vis insita*: "*Exercet vere corpus hanc vim solumodo in mutatione status sui per vim aliam in se impressam facta, estque.*"[10] Not only does a body preserve its present state by virtue of its *vis insita*, but it also *acts*, so far as it can, to maintain that state. That is, the disposition to maintain its state is "exercised" when an external force impresses upon it. Thus matter is not entirely passive, though it has a passive disposition to act, nor is it in any sense self-acting. It seems clear that this reflects a medieval distinction between something's having a disposition to act, and its acting under certain conditions. We know that Newton was exposed to medieval thought as an undergraduate, and in particular that this very doctrine is broadly discussed by Magiri whose *Physiologiae Peripateticae* he read.[11]

In Rule III of Book III hardness (solidity), impenetrability and inertia are plainly distinguished. This is not surprising. For Definition III makes it clear that inertia is a very special type of resistance. This can be clarified if we ask what the difference is between a body being solid, and hence being potentially resistant, and the same body also having a power of resisting by means of a *vis insita* proportional to its quantity of matter. Newton has two notions of resistance. A solid body occupies a place. Hence it physically resists penetration, so that another body cannot get into its place unless it gives way. But bodies also have an innate property which acts both as resistance internal to the body, and as impulse from the body, whether they are at rest or in motion. This is quite a different notion from that of resistance by virtue of merely occupying a place.

This brings me to the last reason. Since *vis insita* involves an idea of resistance which is unrelated to occupancy of place, it is not a relativistic notion based on the mutual solidity of bodies. Newton is concerned to stress that "the exercise of this force may be considered as both resistance and impulse."[12] And he plainly rejects a restriction of resistance to bodies at rest, and of impulse to those in motion. This he claims is merely a relativistic distinction, or an external designation. "But motion and rest, as commonly conceived," Newton states, "are only relatively distinguished; nor are those bodies always truly at rest, which commonly are taken to be so."[13] Thus a *vis insita* is not something attributed to matter because of its state relative to something else, but is intrinsic to matter and independent of its states, though of course manifested by them.

Conclusion. The concept of a "state of *inertiae*" is purely geometrical. For Newton it was meaningful to suppose that in the absence of external impediments, a body would be in either an absolute state of resting or of moving. This would be explained by its inherent disposition, or its *vis insita*. Hence he formulated Law I. But in the physical world bodies do interact. Thus the third Law becomes a fundamental statement indicating how bodies endowed with this internal property interact, or how they interact with

JAMES E. MCGUIRE

forces, since Newton also held that it applied to attractive forces. In this context the second law, both for impulses and for continuously acting forces, is a law of action, stating how bodies and forces, acting and reacting, will change in magnitude and in direction.

NOTES

*The following discussion is based on an earlier and somewhat different version of the paper by I. B. Cohen [Ed.].

[1] E. J. Dijksterhuis was the first to point this out in the original Dutch version of the classic study translated into English as *The Mechanization of the World Picture,* Oxford, Clarendon Press, 1961. In another and independent study Brian D. Ellis came to the same conclusion, "Newton's concept of motive force," *J.H.I.,* volume 23, 1962, pp. 273–8. These pioneering studies have not had the effect which they richly deserve.

[2] Sir Isaac Newton, *Mathematical Principles of Natural Philosophy,* edited by F. Cajori, Berkeley, California, 1962, p. 2.

[3] *Ibid.,* p. 28.

[4] I am not, of course, suggesting that gravitational force was merely a spatial property for Newton. But with respect to its spatial characteristics Newton held it to be an extrinsic designation in a very general sense. This can be brought out by considering the consequence of a position which he certainly held: namely that it is meaningful to suppose the existence of a single-body universe in which we would still be able to determine the intrinsic qualities of that body. It is at once clear that for Newton the particular proposition to the effect that a body must be *some* distance from another body does not indicate an intrinsic designation. This is clearly compatible with Newton's theological doctrine that matter depends for its existence and motion on the will of God. *Vide,* J. E. McGuire, "Body and Void and Newton's *De Mundi Systemate,*" *Arch. for Hist. of Exact Sc.,* Vol. 3, No. 3, 1966, pp. 227–228.

[5] A. R. Hall and M. Boas Hall, *Unpublished Papers of Isaac Newton,* Cambridge, 1962, pp. 89–155.

[6] *Ibid.,* p. 128.

[7] C. I. Gerhardt, *Die Philosophischen Schriften von G. W. Leibniz,* Berlin, 1875–90, Vol. IV, p. 513.

[8] Hall and Hall, *Unpublished Papers,* p. 131.

[9] These are discussed for both absolute rotation and translation in the Scholium on space and time.

[10] Isaac Newton, *Philosophiae Naturalis Principia Mathematica,* London, 1686, p. 2.

[11] Ioannis Magiri, *Physiologiae Peripateticae,* Coloniae, 1629, Caput III, pp. 49–57. There is not space in this reply to trace the influence of this scholastic background on Newton in the detail it deserves.

[12] Newton, *Mathematical Principles,* p. 2.

[13] *Ibid.,* p. 2.

C. TRUESDELL

Reactions of Late Baroque Mechanics to Success, Conjecture, Error, and Failure in Newton's *Principia*

NEWTON'S *Principia* IS CITED WITH AWE BY HISTORIANS OF SCIENCE AND even writers of physics texts; its worth is attested by the price a copy of the first edition commands from bibliophiles; but all these mostly join in expressing their awe and their valuation by venerating the book from without, not venturing to profane the shrine by opening its covers to peer inside. It is a very hard book to read. If a page from the middle of it were copied on a typewriter and handed to a professor of the history of science who had just detailed Newton's magnificent discoveries to his class, he might well fail to recognize it as coming from the pen of his hero. It is densely mathematical. On many pages there is not a single word concerning what historians and physicists now call physics. The new professionalized history of science joins social science in excluding, if politely and often tacitly, mathematics from the sciences. Unlike the historians of today, Newton's contemporaries and successors did not revere him as a seer and a prophet. They respected him as a mathematician of gigantic power.

Now a mathematician has a matchless advantage over general scientists, historians, politicians, and exponents of other professions: He can be wrong. *A fortiori,* he can also be right. There are errors in Euclid, and, to within a set certainly of measure zero on the ordinary human scale, what Euclid proved to be true in ancient Greece is true even in the colossal, unprecedented, nucleospatial totally welfared today. In the advance through the physical, social, historical, and other sciences, the demarcation between truth and falsehood grows vaguer, until in some areas truth can be rezoned as falsehood and falsehood enshrined into truth by consensus of "acknowledged experts and authorities" or even popular vote. One professor discussing the doctrines of Karl Marx may label them as grave errors; a second, equally qualified, may present them as problematic, partly true and partly not so; while a third, living in a different part of the world, may proclaim them as the quintessence of human knowledge. In the mathematical sciences as taught by the colleagues of these same three social scientists, there is no disagreement as to what is true and what is not. A mistake made by a mathematician, even a great one, is not a "difference of point of view" or "another interpretation of the data" or a "dictate of a conflicting ideology," it is a mistake. The greatest of all mathematicians, those who have discovered the greatest quantities of mathematical truths, are also those who have published the greatest numbers of lacunary proofs, insufficiently qualified assertions, and flat mistakes. By attempting to make natural philosophy into a part of mathematics, Newton relinquished the diplomatic immunity granted to non-mathematical philosophers,

FIGURE 1. Isaac Newton (1643–1727), after an engraving of 1712 by John Smith, following a painting by Sir Godfrey Kneller

FIGURE 2. James Bernoulli (1655–1705), portrait in 1686 by his older brother Nicholas Bernoulli, in the Alte Aula, Basel

FIGURE 3. John Bernoulli (1667–1748) after an engraving done in 1741–1742 by Johann Jakob Haid and Aug. Vindelic, following a painting by Johann Rudolf Huber. Bernoulli points to a figure explaining his solution of the brachistochron.

FIGURE 4. Daniel Bernoulli (1700–1782), portrait by Johann Niklaus Grooth in 1760, in the Alte Aula, Basel

C. TRUESDELL

FIGURE 5. Leonhard Euler (1707–1783), portrait in 1753 by Emanuel Handmann, in Kunstmuseum, Basel

FIGURE 6. J. Le Rond D'Alembert (1717–1783), after an engraving published as the frontispiece to Volume 2 of the third edition of Diderot's Encyclopédie, 1778

FIGURE 7. J.-L. Lagrange (1736–1813)

FIGURE 8. Christiaan Huygens (1629–1695), after a painting by Kaspar Netscher in 1671, Collection Haags Gemeente-museum—The Hague

C. TRUESDELL

chemists, psychologists, etc., and entered the area where an error is an error even if it is Newton's error; in fact, all the more so because it is Newton's error.

The mistakes made by a great mathematician are of two kinds: first, trivial slips that anyone can correct, and, second, titanic failures reflecting the scale of the struggle which the great mathematician waged. Failures of this latter kind are often as important as successes, for they give rise to major discoveries by other mathematicians. One error of a great mathematician has often done more for science than a hundred impeccable little theorems proved by lesser men. Since Newton was as great a mathematician as ever lived, but still a mathematician, we may approach his work with the level, tactless criticism which mathematics demands.

The *Principia* is a book on the mechanics of the solar system seen within a half-formulated, half-sensed rational mechanics as a whole. In the century following its publication, down even until the work of Laplace, the *Principia* influenced nearly all mechanical researches. Two great challenges offered by the *Principia* may be seen at once and distinguished, for the answers to them are almost disjoint:

1. To determine in greater precision the motion of a system of mass-points subject to universal gravitation.
2. To discover and set forth the general rational mechanics which Newton sought and to apply it to the motion of ordinary bodies on the earth: deformable masses of finite extent.

Most eighteenth-century researches on theoretical mechanics respond to one or the other of these challenges. Historians of physics, from Mach on into our own day, have studied the history of the first so exclusively as to fall into the delusion that Newton himself had solved the second, and that the three laws set at the head of his book really suffice as a basis for mechanics as a whole. No modern specialist in mechanics shares this opinion; even if it were true today, to project it backward to the century from 1687 to 1787 would be most unhistorical, for Newton himself made no such claim, either outright or by implication or tacitly in his own work in the second field, and the great savants of the eighteenth century who struggled their lives long to master the mechanics of rigid and flexible and fluid and elastic bodies would consider it poor pay indeed for their labors to be told by some pedagogue that they were merely "applying Newton's laws."

A total estimate of the reactions to the *Principia* would have to include a summary of eighteenth-century work on the problem of three bodies and on perturbations in the solar system. I am not competent in celestial mechanics and must therefore keep silent about it, even about its history. While today an astronomer does not seem to need to know much about mechanics, it was a different matter in Newton's day, since physics had not yet been cut up into compartments, and students of natural science had not yet reached certainty as to what was unimportant to them. The specialist did not yet exist.

At the time he wrote the *Principia,* Newton showed little interest in any part of mechanics save the motion of heavenly bodies. He treats these first as points moving subject to two forces alone: universal gravitation and their own inertia. So as to justify a model in which such immense bodies as the sun, earth, and moon are represented as mathematical points, he then proved that the force of attraction between two homogeneously layered spheres is directed along the line of centers and is independent of the diameters. Here, as in several earlier places in the book, his program of deduction from the laws breaks down. While he once refers to the third law, which in fact he does not need, the arguments rest on a rule for adding infinitely many forces. No such rule was given explicitly by him, but apparently he thought the vector law for pairs of forces sufficed. This law he had stated as Corollary II to the Laws of Motion, but the proof, resting on Corollary I, is false.[1] If we overlook this use of unstated axioms, common and excusable in works of great originality, we can regard Newton's program as brilliantly successful.

Newton himself was not satisfied. In earthly experience, bodies move in media, and these media resist their motion. The heavenly bodies move in something, too. If we are to complete a unified mechanics based on laws common to the earth and the heavens, we must take account somehow of such resistance as heavenly bodies may encounter. Moreover, the proof that big spheres are dynamically equivalent to concentrated masses then fails. If the resistance on a tennis ball in air is small, it need not be so on a great planet moving at enormous speed in the faraway heavens.

Newton faced this problem in Book II of the *Principia*. This is the part of the *Principia* that historians and philosophers, apparently, tear out of their personal copies. Newton may have hoped to show that resistances according to all simple laws influenced the motion of a "body," ultimately, in much the same way. After finding, on the contrary, that the effects of friction according to various hypothetical laws are different, he was impelled to seek the true nature of the resistance offered to a finite body by a fluid medium. According to his metaphysics, explanation of celestial mechanics was to be sought in earthly mechanics. Obviously, such a metaphysics is not confined, like the mind of a physicist today, to regard inertia and gravitation as the beginning and end of "classical" mechanics. Not having been taught in a physics course to shut out most ordinary facts as being only "unphysical" or "approximate" or "macroscopic," Newton sought the laws of the heavenly medium just where he had sought the laws of inertia, namely, in earthly experience. Since the laws of fluid motion on the earth were unknown, Newton had to find them. This is not so easy. While there is only one kind of inertia, there are many kinds of fluids, and the variety of their behaviors is bewildering. Newton envisaged a fluid alternately as composed of discrete particles "fleeing each other" or as a "continued" medium. His program of rational deduction from the axioms then broke down completely, and in many places he took refuge in merely qualitative remarks, sometimes labelled as "corollaries" although they are no more proved from the propositions than the propositions themselves are proved from the axioms. The arguments are made still more difficult by being not entirely conjectural: Here and there a few lines or even pages of regular mathematical proof of the easier

C. TRUESDELL

tia G J minor effe poteft quam affignata quavis. Eft autem
(ex natura circulorum per puncta *ABG*, *Abg* tranfeuntium)
AB quad. æquale *AG* x *B D* & *Ab quad.* æ-
quale A g x *b d*, adeoq; ratio A B *quad.* ad
A *b quad.* componitur ex rationibus A G ad
A g & B D ad *b d*. Sed quoniam *J* G affu-
mi poteft minor longitudine quavis affignata, fieri poteft ut ratio A G ad *A g* minus
differat a ratione æqualitatis quam pro
differentia quavis affignata, adeoq; ut ratio
A B quad. ad *A b quad.* minus differat a ratione *B D* ad *b d* quam pro differentia
quavis affignata. Eft ergo, per Lemma I,
ratio ultima *A B quad.* ad *A b quad.* æqualis
rationi ultimæ B *D* ad *b d*. *Q. E. D.*

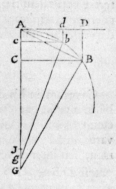

Cas. 2. Inclinetur jam *B D* ad *A D* in angulo quovis dato, &
eadem femper erit ratio ultima *B D* ad *b d* quæ prius, adeoq; eadem ac *A B quad.* ad *A b quad. Q. E. D.*

Cas. 3. Et quamvis angulus *D* non detur, ~~tamen anguli D,d~~
ad æqualitatem femper vergent & propius accedent ad invicem
quam pro differentia quavis affignata, adeoq; ultimo æquales e-
runt, per Lem. I. & propterea lineæ *B* D, *b d*, in eadem ratione
ad invicem ac prius. *Q. E. D.*

Corol. 1. Unde cum tangentes *A D*, *A d*, arcus *A B*, A *b* & e-
orum finus B *C*, *b e* fiant ultimo chordis A B, A *b* æquales; erunt
etiam illorum quadrata ultimo ut fubtenfæ B *D*, *b d*.

Corol. 2. Triangula rectilinea *A D* B, A *db* funt ultimo in tri-
plicata ratione laterum A *D*, A *d*, inq; fefquiplicata laterum *D* B,
d b : Utpote in compofita ratione laterum A *D* & *D* B, A *d* & *d b*
exiftentia. Sic & triangula A B C, A *b c* funt ultimo in triplica-
ta ratione laterum B *C*, *b c*.

Corol. 5. Et quoniam *D B*, *d b* funt ultimo parallela & in duplicata ratione ipfarum *A D*, A *d*; erunt areæ ultimæ curvilineæ

FIGURE 9. A typical purely mathematical passage in the *Principia,* reproduced from a
copy, annotated in Halley's hand, now in the library of the University of Texas

details rise, as they do throughout the writings of Galileo, to lend the appearance of logic to what seems in fact to be guesswork.

The areas treated are as follows:

1. General and obscure assertions about resistances and motions of parts of a fluid.
2. Resistances of spheres and cylinders in a rare static medium.
3. The motion of a continued fluid falling through a hole in a vessel, based on statics.
4. Resistances of cylinders, spheres, and spheroids in a continued fluid, either of infinite extent or confined by a canal.
5. General remarks on the propagation of pressures through a heap of particles.
6. Oscillation of an incompressible fluid in a U-tube.
7. The speed of surface waves and the nature of the fluid motion giving rise to them.
8. The speed of sound in a gas.
9. The resistances of cylinders and spheres spinning in a fluid with internal friction.

In his study of these miscellaneous problems of fluid mechanics, Newton seems to have forgotten what his original purpose was. He nowhere applies to the solar system his conclusions about resistance, perhaps because they are so varied and so hypothetical as to defy any such application. He concludes Book II with a proposition intended to destroy Descartes's vortex theory of the planets, but the proposition itself is unconnected to what went before and is meaningless without definition of the terms used, and the "proof," like that of the earlier and false proposition on the "cataract," rests upon an unsound principle of solidification.

While in celestial mechanics and the simpler motions of "bodies" Newton had centuries and even millenia of sound observation and sound special theory on which to base his "intuition," as the physicists today like to call the application of common sense to previously organized experience, in fluid mechanics he had few guides. Book II is almost entirely original.

In writings on the history of science today, as in all aspects of social intercourse, it becomes increasingly bad taste to call a spade a spade. In the particular application to the history of science, the compulsion to euphemy assumes the form of solemn denial that there is such a thing as wrong in science. All that matters is how the scientists of one epoch thought and felt about nature, their own work, and the work of others. In particular, the beginner is enjoined above all not to take sides, like the positivist historians of the last century, and set past science into categories of true and false according as it does or does not agree with what is taught in school science of our own day.[2] However admirable this philosophy may be in promoting peace and mutual love among historians of science, it disregards one aspect of science that is not altogether negligible, namely, that scientists seek *the* truth, not *a* truth. He who refuses to "take sides" in science in effect negates science itself by

C. TRUESDELL

denying its one and common purpose. He reduces science to just one more social manifestation. In so doing, not only does he by implication belittle the great scientists of the past, but also he sins against history, for in his attempt at historical impartiality he destroys the object, namely science, the history of which he claims to write.

Newton's treatment of the efflux of water from a vessel is a case very much to the point here. In the first edition, he gave an essentially static argument which in fact sets aside his own laws of motion; after learning that his end result contradicted experiment, he replaced the whole passage in the second edition by an argument far less plausible, based on an *ad hoc* fiction of a cataract of melting ice. Thus Newton himself clearly believed then that his first treatment had been at fault, but he did not say how. Instead, he manufactured a maze to lead to a different answer he at that time considered right. In a language where a spade is called a spade, the first treatment of the efflux problem is wrong, while the second is a bluff. Much the same may be said of the calculation of the velocity of sound, for which Newton in the second edition introduced the fiction of the "crassitude of the solid particles of the air" so as to insert what would nowadays be called a "fudge factor" yielding the desired numerical value from a recalcitrant theory.

It was these two flimsy and unmathematical props, the "cataract" and the "solid particles of the air," no better than the vortices of the Cartesians, that drew the strongest criticism upon the *Principia*. However successful was Book I, Book II was a failure as an essay toward a unified, mathematical mechanics.

With its bewildering alternation of mathematical proof, brilliant hypothesis, pure guessing, bluff, and plain error, Book II has long been praised, in whole or in part, and praised justly, as affording the greatest signs of Newton's genius. To the geometers of the day, it offered an immediate challenge: to correct the errors, to replace the guesswork by clear hypotheses, to embed the hypotheses at their just stations in a rational mechanics, to brush away the bluff by mathematical proof, to create new concepts so as to succeed where Newton had failed. It is not an exaggeration to say that rational mechanics, and hence mathematical physics as a whole and the general picture of nature accepted today, grew from this challenge as it was accepted by the Basel school of mathematicians: the three great Bernoullis and Euler, on the basis of whose work Lagrange, Fourier, Poisson, Navier, Cauchy, Green, Stokes, Kelvin, Helmholtz, Kirchhoff, Maxwell, and Gibbs constructed what is now called classical physics. Between 1700 and 1750 the Basel school met occasional competition from Taylor, MacLaurin, Clairaut, and d'Alembert, though of these only the last did work of any breadth.

It is wrong to picture the Basel geometers as disciples of Newton. Rather, they began as doubting opponents, who accepted, grudgingly, only some isolated results. Newton's achievement, great though it was, was far from enough to cause the revolution in scientific thought historians of the last century and ours have been pleased to imagine. In the first place, three major mechanical systems which had

Sunto Sphæræ quotcunq; concentricæ similares *AB, CD, EF*
&c. quarum interiores additæ exterioribus componant materiam
densiorem versus centrum, vel subductæ relinquant tenuiorem;
& hæ, per Theor. XXXV, trahent Sphæras alias quotcunq; con-
centricas similares *GH, IK, LM*, &c. singulæ singulas, viribus
reciproce proportionalibus quadrato distantiæ *SP*. Et compo-
nendo vel dividendo, summa virium illarum omnium, vel ex-
cessus aliquarum supra alias, hoc est, vis qua Sphæra tota ex concentricis quibuscunq; vel concentricarum differentiis composita
AB, trahit totam ex concentricis quibuscunq; vel concentricarum differen-
tiis composi-
tam *GH*, erit
in eadem ra-
tione. Auge-
atur numerus
Sphærarum
concentrica-
rum in infini-

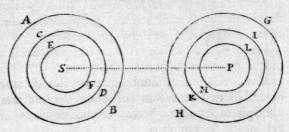

tum sic, ut materiæ densitas una cum vi attractiva, in progressu
a circumferentia ad centrum, secundum Legem quamcunq; cres-
cat vel decrescat: & addita materia non attractiva compleatur u-
bivis densitas deficiens, eo ut Sphæræ acquirant formam quamvis
optatam; & vis qua harum una attrahet alteram erit etiamnum
(per argumentum superius) in eadem illa distantiæ quadratæ ratione inversa. Q. E. D.

Corol. 1. Hinc si ejusmodi Sphæræ complures sibi invicem per
omnia similes se mutuo trahant; attractiones acceleratrices sin-
gularum in singulas erunt in æqualibus quibusvis centrorum dif-
tantiis ut Sphæræ attrahentes.

Corol. 2. Inq; distantiis quibusvis inæqualibus, ut Sphæræ attrahentes applicatæ ad quadrata distantiarum inter centra.

Corol.

FIGURE 10. Newton's proof of the proposition that the resultant attraction of two homogeneously layered spheres is as the inverse square of the distance between their centers,
from the *Principia*

fit $\frac{2d}{e}S$ & latitudo eadem quæ foraminis, poffet eo tempore defluendo egredi de vafe, hoc eft columna $\frac{2d}{e}SF$. Quare motus $\frac{2dd}{ee}SFV$, qui fiet ducendo quantitatem aquæ effluentis in velocitatem fuam, hoc eft motus omnis tempore effluxus illius genitus, æquabitur motui $AF \times V$. Et fi æquales illi motus applicenter ad FV; fiet $\frac{2dd}{ee}S$ æqualis A. Unde eft dd ad ee ut A ad $2S$, & d ad e in dimidiata ratione $\frac{1}{2}A$ ad S. Eft igitur velocitas quacum aqua exit e foramine, ad velocitatem quam aqua cadens, & tempore T cadendo defcribens fpatium S acquireret, ut altitudo aquæ foramini perpendiculariter incumbentis, ad medium proportionale inter altitudinem illam duplicatam & fpatium illud S, quod corpus tempore T cadendo defcriberet.

Igitur fi motus illi furfum vertantur; quoniam aqua velocitate V afcenderet ad altitudinem illam S de qua deciderat; & altitudines (uti notum eft) fint in duplicata ratione velocitatum: aqua effluens afcenderet ad altitudinem $\frac{1}{2}A$. Et propterea quantitas aquæ effluentis, quo tempore corpus cadendo defcribere poffet altitudinem $\frac{1}{2}A$, æqualis erit columnæ aquæ totius AF foramini perpendiculariter imminentis.

Cum autem aqua effluens, motu fuo furfum verfo, perpendiculariter furgeret ad dimidiam altitudinem aquæ foramini incumbentis; confequens eft quod fi egrediatur oblique per canalem in latus vafis, defcribet in fpatiis non refiftentibus Parabolam cujus latus rectum eft altitudo aquæ in vafe fupra canalis orificium, & cujus diameter horizonti perpendicularis ab orificio illo ducitur, atque ordinatim applicatæ parallelæ funt axi canalis.

Hæc omnia de Fluido fubtiliffimo intelligenda funt. Nam fi aqua ex partibus craffioribus conftet, hæc tardius effluet quam pro ratione fuperius affignata, præfertim fi foramen anguftum fit per quod effluit.

T t 2   Denique

FIGURE 11. Newton's argument that the reaction issuing from a vessel is the same as that which would be required to keep the hole stopped up, in the first edition of the *Principia*, 1687

been treated with greater or lesser success by others were left out by Newton. These are:

1. *Rigid bodies*. Newton's famous remark about the inertia of a spinning top did not lead him to attempt any specific theory of rotation, nor did he mention the problem of the pendulous oscillation of a finite body, a correct solution to which, based on special assumptions, had been published by Huygens in 1673.

2. *Flexible bodies*. The problems of the vibrating string and the catenary curve had been widely discussed even before Newton's birth. If most of the work of Beeckman and Huygens remained unpublished, this fact did not keep it from being noised abroad. Mersenne had published his empirical laws of vibration in 1625; Pardies, his beautiful solution of the suspension bridge problem in 1673. Newton must have known much if not all of this, but his writings do not mention anything in this area of study.

3. *Elastic bodies*. While Galileo had discussed the rupture of solid bodies, and while various authors had published attempts on the theory of elasticity, Newton's nearest approach comes in his description of the pressure of a gas composed of particles. Newton must have known not only Hooke's vociferations on elasticity, made excessively public in 1678, but also the magnificent note of 1684 in which Leibniz initiated the mathematical theory of stress and gave the first application of integral calculus to problems concerning contact forces. Moreover, Newton's claim that the pressure varies as the density *only* if the intermolecular force is of one special kind is wholly wrong.

Newton's work in mechanics opened a new stream of thought, which immediately became the most powerful of all. However, it by no means stopped or absorbed the others at once. These others were:

1. *Statics*

   a. *The Parallelogram of Forces and the Law of the Lever*. While by example Newton taught us to use statically conceived forces in kinetic problems, his explanation of forces suggests that they can be detected only when they give rise to motions. If this were true, there would be no science of statics. It may seem a paradox that although it was Newton above all who showed us how to turn knowledge gained from equilibria so as to solve problems of motion, his handling of mechanics was weakest where statics was involved. In 1687, the year of the *Principia*, Varignon published his *Project of a New Mechanics*, in which the principle of the parallelogram of forces, inferred from a rather Aristotelian viewpoint, is applied to the solution of a class of problems untouched by Newton. While the book is pedestrian, it bears witness that the didactic tradition of Stevin, long prior and hence independent, was still very much alive, as in fact it is today. The law of the lever had been known since antiquity. The numerous unsuccessful attempts, including Varignon's, to derive it from the equilibrium of forces are not germane to my subject.

C. TRUESDELL

generari quo tempore Globus duas tertias diametri fuæ partes, velocitate uniformiter continuata defcribat, ut denfitas Medii ad denfitatem Globi, fi modo Globus & particulæ Medii fint fumme elaftica & vi maxima reflectendi polleant: quodque hæc vis fit duplo minor ubi Globus & particulæ Medii funt infinite dura & vi reflectendi prorfus deftituta. In Mediis autem continuis qualia funt Aqua, Oleum calidum, & Argentum vivum, in quibus Globus non incidit immediate in omnes fluidi particulas refiftentiam generantes, fed premit tantum proximas particulas & hæ premunt alias & hæ alias, refiftentia eft adhuc duplo minor. Globus utique in hujufmodi Mediis fluidiffimis refiftentiam patitur quæ eft ad vim qua totus ejus motus vel tolli poffit vel generari quo tempore, motu illo uniformiter continuato, partes octo tertias diametri fuæ defcribat, ut denfitas Medii ad denfitatem Globi. Id quod in fequentibus conabimur oftendere.

PROPOSITIO XXXVI. PROBLEMA VIII.

Aquæ de vafe Cylindrico per foramen in fundo factum effluentis definire motum.

Sit $ACDB$ vas cylindricum, AB ejus orificium fuperius, CD fundum horizonti parallelum, EF foramen circulare in medio fundi, G centrum foraminis, & GH axis cylindri horizonti perpendicularis. Et concipe cylindrum glaciei $APQB$ ejufdem effe latitudinis cum cavitate vafis, & axem eundem habere, & uniformi cum motu perpetuo defcendere, & partes ejus quam primum attingunt fuperficiem AB liquefcere, & in aquam converfas gravitate fua defluere in vas, & cataractam vel columnam aquæ $ABNFEM$ cadendo formare, & per foramen EF tranfire, idemque adæquate implere. Ea vero fit uniformis velocitas glaciei defcendentis ut & aquæ contiguæ in circulo AB, quam aqua cadendo & cafu fuo defcribendo altitudinem IH acquirere poteft; & jaceant IH & HG in directum, & per punctum I ducatur recta KL horizonti parallela lateribus glaciei.

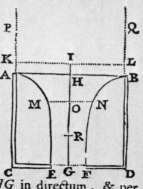

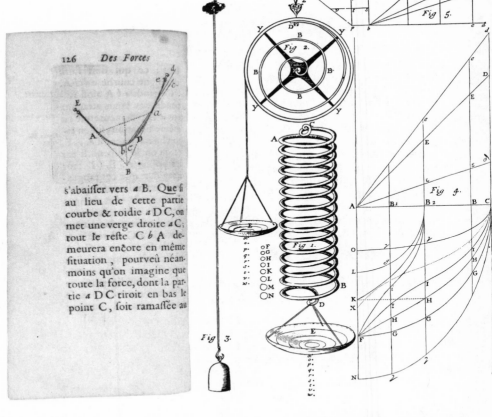

Inside Figure 13 (page reproduction):

126   *Des Forces*

s'abaiſſer vers *a* B. Que ſi
au lieu de cette partie
courbe & roidie *a* D C, on
met une verge droite *a* C;
tout le reſte C *b* A de-
meurera encore en même
ſituation, pourveû néan-
moins qu'on imagine que
toute la force, dont la partie *a* D C tiroit en bas le
point C, ſoit ramaſſée au

FIGURE 13. Pardies' solution of the problem of the suspension bridge (1673)

FIGURE 14. The plate from Hooke's pamphlet, *Lectures De Potentia Restitutiva, or of Spring, Explaining the Power of Springing Bodies,* 1678

206   C. TRUESDELL

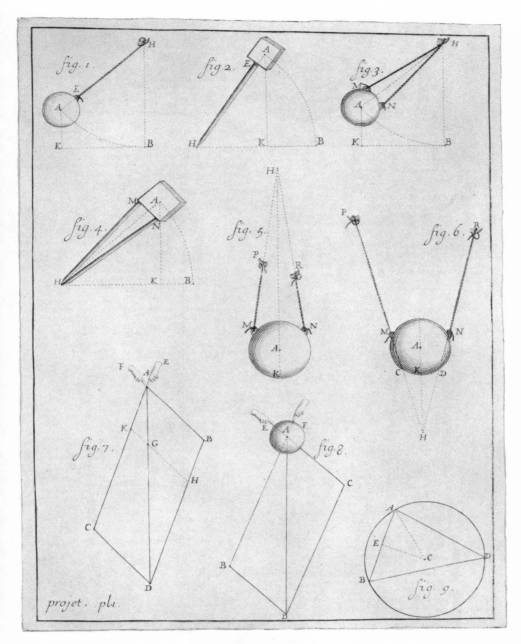

FIGURE 15. Plate 1 from Varignon's *Projet d'une Nouvelle Méchanique*, 1687, one of many illustrating the parallelogram of forces

sur P, repose aussi sur I, & partant comme G O à G P, ainsi seront les pesanteurs qui reposent sur I & H.

Conclusion. Une colomne donc reposant, &c.

COROLLAIRE.

Il est manifeste par ce que devant, que voulant recognoistre la raison de la pesanteur reposant sur I, à celle qui repose sur H, qu'on doit à ceste fin mener les perpendiculaires K L, M N, coupant l'axe és poincts O, P; & que la raison de G O à G P seroit la requise; ainsi donc, lors que la pesanteur de la colomne est notoire, qu'aussi seront les pesanteurs de celles qui reposent sur chacun poinct, tel que H, I.

JUSQUES ICY ONT ESTE déclarées les proprietez des pesanteurs directes; suivent les proprietez & qualitez des obliques, desquelles le fondement general est compris au Theoreme suivant.

THEOREME XI.   PROPOSITION XIX.

Si un triangle, a son plan perpendiculaire à l'horizon, & sa base parallele à iceluy; & sur un chacun des deux autres costez un poids spherique, de pesanteur egale; comme le costé dextre du triangle, au senestre; ainsi la puissance du poids senestre, à celle du poids dextre.

Le donné. Soit A B C un triangle ayant son plan perpendiculaire à l'horizon, & sa base A C parallele à iceluy horizon : & soit sur le costé A B (qui est double à B C) un poids en globe D, & sur B C un autre E, egaux en pesanteur & en grandeur.

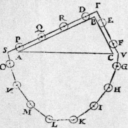

Le requis. Il faut demonstrer que comme le costé A B 2 au costé B C 1, ainsi la puissance ou pouvoir du poids E à celle de D.

Preparation. Soit accommodé à l'entour du triangle un entour de 14 globes, egaux en pesanteur, en grandeur, & equidistans, comme D, E, F, G, H, I, K, L, M, N, O, P, Q, R, enfilez d'une ligne passant par leurs centres, ainsi qu'ils puissent tourner sur leurs susdits centres, & qu'il y puisse avoir 2 globes sur le costé B C, & 4 sur B A, alors comme ligne à ligne, ainsi le nombre des globes au nombre des globes: qu'aussi en S, T, V, soyent trois poincts fermes, dessus lesquels la ligne, ou le filet puisse couler, & que les deux parties au dessus du triangle soyent paralleles aux costez d'iceluy A B, B C; tellement que le tout puisse tourner librement & sans accrochement, sur lesdits costez A B, B C.

DEMONSTRATION.

Si le pouvoir des poids D, R, Q, P, n'estoit egal au pouvoir des deux globes E, F, l'un costé sera plus pesant que l'autre, donc (s'il est possible) que les 4 D, R, Q, P, soyent plus pesans que les deux E, F; mais les 4 O, N, M, L, sont egaux aux 4 G, H, I, K; parquoy le costé des 8 globes D, R, Q, P, O, N, M, L, sera plus pesant selon leur disposition, que non pas les 6, E, F, G, H, I, K, & puis que la partie plus pesante emporte la plus legere, les 8 globes descendront, & les autres 6 monteront : Qu'il soit ainsi donc, & que D vienne, où O est presentement, & ainsi des autres; voire que E, F, G, H, viennent, où sont maintenant P, Q, R, D, aussi I, K, où sont maintenant E, F : Ce neantmoins l'entour des globes aura la mesme disposition qu'auparavant, & par mesme raison les 8 globes auront le dessus en pesanteur, & en tombant feront revenir 8 autres en leurs places, & ainsi ce mouvement n'auroit aucune fin, ce qui est absurde. Et de mesme sera la demonstration de l'autre costé : La partie donc de l'entour D, R, Q, P, O, N, M, L, sera en equilibre avec la partie E, F, G, H, I, K; que si on oste des deux costez, les pesanteurs egales, & qui ont mesme disposition, comme sont les 4 globes O, N, M, L, d'une part, & les 4, G, H, I, K, d'autre part; les 4 restans D, R, Q, P, seront & demeureront en equilibre avec les 2 E, F; parquoy E aura un pouvoir double au pouvoir de D; comme donc le costé B A 2, au costé B C 1, ainsi le pouvoir de E, au pouvoir de D.

Conclusion. Si un triangle donc a son plan, &c.

COROLLAIRE I.

Soit A B C un triangle comme devant, & A B double à B C, & soit D un globe sur A B, double à E, qui est sur B C; en F soit un poinct ferme, par dessus lequel la ligne D F E puisse couler sans empeschement, ainsi que D F, F E soyent paralleles aux costez du triangle A B C, procedantes des centres des globes; il appert que D, E seront encor en equilibre, puis que cy-dessus P, Q, R, D, l'estoyent à E, F; parquoy comme A B à B C, ainsi le globe D au globe E.

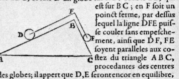

COROLLAIRE II.

Soit maintenant l'un des costez du triangle, comme B C (qui est moitié de l'autre A B) perpendiculaire à A C, comme cy joignant; le globe D, qui est double à E, sera encor en equilibre avec E, car comme le costé A B à B C, ainsi le globe D au globe E.

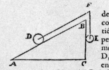

COROLLAIRE III.

Soient derechef les mesmes posées, mais au lieu du poinct ferme F, soit adaptée une poulie comme icy, ainsi que D F demeure parallele à A B, & que E soit un

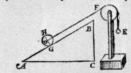

poids de quelle figure que ce puisse estre, egal en pesanteur à celuy de devant; iceluy avec D, seront encor en equilibre, parquoy comme A B à B C, ainsi D à E.

COROL-

FIGURE 16. The argument for the parallelogram of forces in Stevin's *De Beghinselen der Weeghconst,* 1586, as republished in French in 1634

C. TRUESDELL

b. *Virtual Work*. While the principle of virtual work may be of Peripatetic origin, a correct formulation of it had been sketched by Descartes, and it was to remain on the periphery of mechanics until Lagrange made it his principal axiom in 1788.

c. *The Action of Contact Forces*. The concept of interior forces exerted by the parts of a body on each other is difficult to trace, but it was skirted by Galileo and used explicitly in the treatise of Pardies.

2. *Dynamics*

a. *The Principle of Energy*. A particular principle of energy had been laid down as an axiom and used with brilliant success by Huygens. Another was published by Leibniz in 1686, the year the *Principia* was licensed.

b. *The Principle of Inertial Force*. Although it is customary to attribute this principle to Newton or d'Alembert, there is no evidence that Newton had a grasp of it sufficient for application to finite bodies, and certainly it was known and used widely before d'Alembert's treatise of 1743, where, in fact, it can be located only with difficulty.

While the parallelogram of forces, the law of the lever, the principle of virtual work, the action of contact forces, and the principle of energy had extensive earlier histories and were to be absorbed in or united to the Newtonian stream, the principle of inertial force grew independently from the same antecedents as did Newton's mechanics, found its first expression in 1686, and finally incorporated Newton's dynamics and every other. It was James Bernoulli's idea to set aside Huygens' special principle of energy and determine the oscillation of a pendulous body by an appeal to statics. The law of the lever is taken as valid in motion as well as at rest, provided the motion itself be regarded as giving rise to forces per unit mass equal to the accelerations reversed. James Bernoulli does not get this principle quite right, but he is the first to come near it. He proposed and applied it correctly, though only in the context of the pendulum, in his great paper of 1703.

Though it was many years before this great unifying principle was grasped in general form, we see today that to make it useful, a far more developed, explicit statics was necessary. This, too, we owe in the main to James Bernoulli. It is well known that the catenary curve was determined in 1690 by John Bernoulli, Huygens, and Leibniz in a public contest. It is less well known that all three used special devices for arriving at the equations to be solved. Newton, and with him the British school, took no part in this work, nor is it even in the slightest detail influenced by Newton's book, published only three years before. Immediately thereafter, in 1691–1704, James Bernoulli, who had been unable to match his younger brother's brilliance and who had failed to appear among the solvers of the great problem at the appointed time, pondered the general nature of perfectly flexible lines in equilibrium, subject to arbitrary loading. Here the devices of Leibniz and John Bernoulli would not work, and of course the old approach of Huygens was hopelessly elab-

Lemma 2.

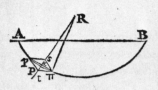

In aliquo articulo vibratio-nis ſuæ induat Nervus tenſus, inter punɛta A & B, formam curvæ cujus-vis A p π B. Tum dico quod ſit incrementum ve-locitatis punɛti alicujus P, ſeu acceleratio oriunda a vi tenſionis Nervi, ut curvatura Nervi in eodem punɛto.

Demonſtr. Finge Nervum conſtare ex particulis rigidis æqualibuꞵ infinite parvis p P & P π, &c. & ad pun-ɛtum P erige perpendicularem P R = radio curvaturæ in P, cui occurrant tangentes p t & π t in t, iis parallelæ π s & p s in s, & chorda p π in c. Tum, per Principia Me-chanicæ, vis abſoluta, quâ urgentur particulæ ambæ p P & P π verſûs R, erit ad vim tenſionis fili, ut s t ad p t ; & hujus vis dimidium, quo urgetur particula una p P, erit ad Nervi tenſionem, ut c t ad t p, hoc eſt, (ob tri-angula ſimilia c t p, t p R) ut t p vel P p ad R t vel P R. Quare, ob tenſionis vim datam, erit vis accelera-trix abſoluta ut $\frac{P\,p}{P\,R}$. Sed eſt acceleratio genita in rati-one compoſitâ ex rationibus vis abſolutæ direɛtè & ma-teriæ movendæ inverſè ; atq; eſt materia movenda ipſa particula P p. Quare eſt acceleratio ut $\frac{1}{P\,R}$, hoc eſt ut Curvatura in P. Eſt enim Curvatura reciprocè ut radius circuli oſculatorii. Q. E. D.

E 2

Prob. 1.

FIGURE 17. Brook Taylor's treatment of the vibrating string in the *Philosophical Trans-actions* No. 337, 1714

$$\alpha\, d\, t^2 : 2\, a = \mathrm{F}\,\beta\, d\, t^2 : p\,\theta^2, \text{ donc } \alpha = \frac{2\, a\, \mathrm{F}\,\beta}{p\,\vartheta^2} = \frac{2\, a\, p\, m\, l\,\beta}{p\,\vartheta^2} =$$

$$\beta\quad \frac{2\, a\, m\, l}{\vartheta^2}.$$

VI. Nous remarquerons d'abord, que l'on peut reprefenter le tems donné θ par une ligne conftante de telle grandeur que l'on voudra : il faudra feulement avoir foin de prendre, pour exprimer les parties variables & indeterminées du tems, des lignes t qui foyent à la ligne qu'on aura prife pour marquer θ, dans le rapport de ces parties variables du tems au tems conftant & donné, pendant lequel un corps pefant parcourt l'efpace a. On pourra donc fuppofer θ telle, que $\vartheta^2 = 2\, a\, m\, l$: & en ce cas on aura $\alpha = \beta$. Donc puisque $d\, p = \alpha\, d\, t + \nu\, d\, s$, il faut que $d\, q$ ou $\nu\, d\, t + \beta\, d\, s$ foit $= \nu\, d\, t + \alpha\, d\, s$.

VII. Pour déterminer par ces conditions les quantités α & ν, On remarquera, que comme $d\, p = \alpha\, d\, t + \nu\, d\, s$, & $d\, q = \nu\, d\, t + \alpha\, d\, s$, on aura $d\, p + d\, q = (\alpha + \nu) . (d\, t + d\, s)$; & $d\, p - d\, q = (\alpha - \nu) . (d\, t - d\, s)$. d'où il s'enfuit

1°, que $\alpha + \nu$ eft egale à une fonction de $t + s$, & que $\alpha - \nu$ eft egal à une fonction de $t - s$.

2°. Que par confequent on aura $p = \dfrac{\Phi\, (t + s) + \Delta\, (t - s)}{2}$ ou fimplement $= \Phi\, (t + s) + \Delta\, (t - s)$; & $q = \Phi\, (t + s) - \Delta\, (t - s)$, d'où l'on tire P M ou $s\, (p\, d\, t + q\, d\, s) = \psi\, (t + s) + \Gamma\, (t - s)$, $\psi\, (t + s)$ & $\Gamma\, (t - s)$ exprimant des fonctions encore inconnuës de $t + s$ & de $t - s$.

l'equation generale de la courbe eft donc

$$y = \psi\, (t + s) + \Gamma\, (t - s).$$

VIII.

FIGURE 18. D'Alembert's paper of the vibrating spring, showing the first appearance of the partial differential equation, in the *Mémoires de l'Académie des Sciences,* Berlin, for 1747

Reactions of Late Baroque Mechanics

orate. In the end, James Bernoulli found four independent proofs of the general differential equations:

   a. By the balance of forces acting on an infinitesimal element.
   b. By the balance of moments acting on an infinitesimal element.
   c. By the principle of virtual work.
   d. By the principle of minimum potential energy.

The first two are the most important, for they point toward the general theory of stress, and they show that when applied to a particular and sufficiently special system, the two independent basic principles of mechanics may fall into equivalence.

To get the equation of motion of the vibrating string, anyone today knows that he needs only apply "Newton's second law" to an infinitesimal element, or, more elegantly, apply to the static equation of the catenary James Bernoulli's principle of reversed accelerations. In his famous paper of 1713, Taylor followed the former path and obtained, if in obscure form, one of the two partial differential equations of finite motion, but he had no idea what to do with it, and he fell into a morass of guesswork to obtain only the fundamental mode. As late as 1727 John Bernoulli, following Huygens in using the discretely loaded string as a model, could do little better. The differential equation was first recognized as the basic and sufficient statement of the mechanical principles for this particular system by d'Alembert in 1746. In the sixty years since the *Principia* enough mathematics had been created that a fully mathematical statement of the problem could be recognized as such and put to use.

After James Bernoulli's exhaustive analysis of the general catenary, he was in a position to attack the far more difficult problem of the elastic beam. Here the equilibrium of forces and the equilibrium of moments are not at all the same thing, and the action of a part of the beam on its neighbor must be represented not only by a contact force but also by a contact couple. In a series of deep and difficult researches in 1691–94, James Bernoulli went far toward understanding these facts, and he obtained the correct differential equations of the elastica. His basic principle was the equilibrium of moments.

While the work of James Bernoulli shows not the slightest influence from Newton's, the English approach found a great champion in Daniel Bernoulli, son of John and nephew of James. It was Daniel Bernoulli who first applied to a deforming mass Newton's idea that the resultant force on a body, whatever its form and nature and internal motion, is the rate of change of its total momentum. In 1727 he calculated in this way the force exerted on a wall by a jet of water playing steadily upon it. We could describe this work as an alteration of one of Newton's problems in such a way as to render just Newton's own approach.

However, when Daniel Bernoulli came to the motion of water in tubes, he could find no key in his uncle's work or in Newton's, and he turned instead to a primitive and unconvincing principle of impulse and energy, reminiscent of Newton's groping toward the law of linear momentum.

C. TRUESDELL

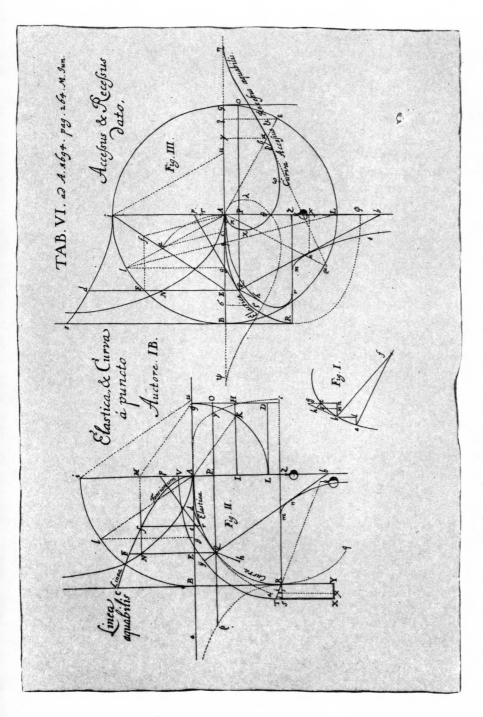

FIGURE 19. James Bernoulli's figure for explaining his treatment of the elastica, from the *Acta Eruditorum* for June, 1694

While Daniel Bernoulli discovered his law of hydraulics in 1730, it was not published until 1738. His old father, John Bernoulli, thereupon attacked the method as being indirect and replaced it by another, "resting solely on dynamical principles, denied by no one." These principles are (1) calculation of the difference of internal pressures on opposite sides of a slice of fluid and (2) the linear momentum principle. This work is simultaneous with D'Alembert's on the vibrating string and shares with it priority in application of the balance of forces to all the parts of a system with infinitely many degrees of freedom. In work done earlier but published later, Euler had obtained the equations of finite motion for a string by passing to the limit from the discretely loaded one. Priority is not important. The evidence, while failing to reveal Newton and his disciples as being in possession of tools sufficient for competent treatment of hydraulic or flexible motion, confirms such progress in the concepts of statics by the 1740s that three savants were able, independently, to apply the principle of linear momentum correctly to two of the simplest models of extended bodies on the earth.

Advance so far had been gained through the study of particular cases and particular systems like the compound pendulum; once this point had been reached, generalization to more spatial dimensions was relatively easy, and of course it was Euler who gave us the theories of flexible membranes and of perfect fluids.

The principle of moment of momentum and its applications lie deeper. Here, I remind you, there is not one word of help in the *Principia* or in the work of Huygens on oscillation; in the early 1700s the difficult and cryptic papers of James Bernoulli on the pendulum and on the elastica were the only reliable guides. In the first draft of the *Mechanica*, written about 1730 but not published[3] until last year, Euler broke off just after beginning to try to determine the motion of a body first forced to rotate about two perpendicular axes and then freed. In the book[4] as finished in 1734, everything concerning rigid bodies has been suppressed. In their correspondence in the 1730's Euler, John Bernoulli, and Daniel Bernoulli all complained that the "ordinary principles" of mechanics were insufficient to determine the motion of a rigid body, and none of them was able to find the new general principle needed, although all three did succeed, by special devices, in obtaining differential equations for physical systems somewhat but not much more general than Huygens' pendulous body. In particular neither they nor anyone else knew how to describe, let alone determine, a rigid motion whose axis is not restricted to lie in one plane. The first non-planar case of rigid motion that had to be faced squarely came up in Euler's researches on the stability of ships. So as to discuss the problem of small vibrations of a floating body, he had no choice but, like Newton before him in the problem of efflux, to abandon the known principles of mechanics and resort to conjecture. His "hypothesis"[5] was a happy one: that every rigid body has three orthogonal axes about any of which it may oscillate freely in infinitesimal motion. We shall come back to his hypothesis in a moment.

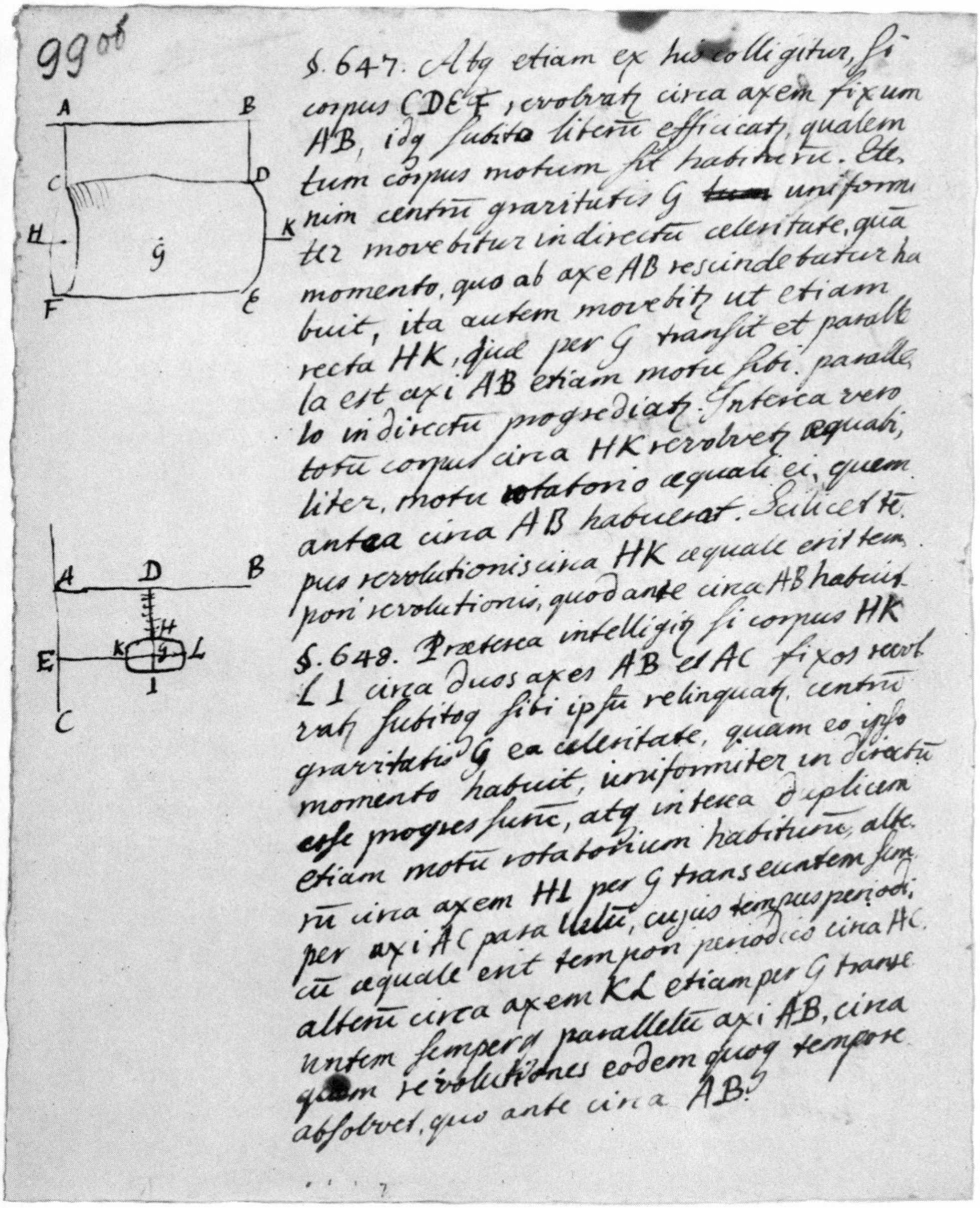

§. 647. Atq etiam ex his colligitur, si corpus CDEF, evolvat circa axem fixum AB, idq subito liberum efficiatq, qualem tum corpus motum fit habiturum. Etenim centru gravitatis G uniformiter movebitur in directu celeritate, qua momento, quo ab axe AB rescindebatur habuit, ita autem movebitq ut etiam recta HK, quae per G transit et parallela est axi AB etiam motu sibi parallelo in directu progrediat. Interea vero totu corpus circa HK revolvetq aequaliter, motu rotatorio aequali ei, quem antea circa AB habuerat. Scilicet tempus revolutionis circa HK aequale erit tempori revolutionis, quod ante circa AB habuit.

§. 648. Praterea intelligis si corpus HK LI circa duos axes AB et AC fixos revolvat, subitoq sibi ipsi relinquat, centro gravitatis G ea celeritate, quam eo ipso momento habuit, uniformiter in directu esse progressurum, atq interea duplicem etiam motu rotatorium habiturum, alterum circa axem HI per G transeuntem, semper axi AC parallelu, cujus tempus periodicu aequale erit tempori periodico circa AC, alterum circa axem KL etiam per G transeuntem semperq parallelu axi AB, circa quam revolutiones eodem quoq tempore absolvet, quo ante circa AB.

FIGURE 20. Conclusion of the manuscript of Euler's *Mechanica seu Scientia Motus*, showing his unsuccessful attempt to treat the motion of a rigid body, written about 1730, first published in 1965 (reproduced here from the Archives of the Academy of Sciences, Leningrad, by courtesy of Dr. G. K. Mikhailov)

ita vt OC fit diftantia centri ofcillationis ab axe. Confideremus autem corpus extra fitum verticalem detrufum, eiusque centrum grauitatis in G, ita vt ipfi angulus GOC fit defcribendus, donec in fitum aequilibrii pertingat. Vis autem, quae corpus ad hunc motum angularem follicitat, eft pondus corporis quo in directione GH deorfum vrgetur. Sit nunc maffa feu pondus corporis $=$ M eiusque momentum inertiae refpectu axis per centrum grauitatis G tranfeuntis et axi ofcillationis paralleli $=$ S erit huius corporis momentum refpectu axis ofcillationis $= S + M . OC^z$. Momentum autem grauitatis ad motum angularem circa O generandum eft M. GO. fin. O; ideoque vis gyratoria erit $= \frac{M . GO . fin . O}{S + M OC^2}$. Contemplemur nunc pendulum fimplex og aequali angulo goc a fitu verticali oc diftans cui in g pondufculum infinite paruum p fit alligatum circa o ofcillans, erit vis gyratoria, qua pondufculum p ad angulum goc abfoluendum animatur $= \frac{fin . O}{oc}$. Si ergo haec vis gyratoria aequalis fuerit priori, pendulum fimplex og et compofitum OG fimul in fitum verticalem peruenient, quia vtrique aequalis angulus eft percurrendus. Faciamus ergo $\frac{M . CO . fin . O}{S + M . OC^2} = \frac{fin . o}{oc}$ prodibit $oc = \frac{S + M . CO^2}{M . CO}$ quae eft longitudo penduli fimplicis ifochroni, feu diftantia centri ofcillationis in pendulo compofito OC ab axe ofcillationis, erit ergo centrum ofcillationis in Z, vt fit $OZ = CO + \frac{S}{M . CO}$; Vnde apparet centrum ofcillationis perpetuo infra centrum grauitatis G cadere, effeque interuallum $CZ = \frac{S}{M . CO}$.

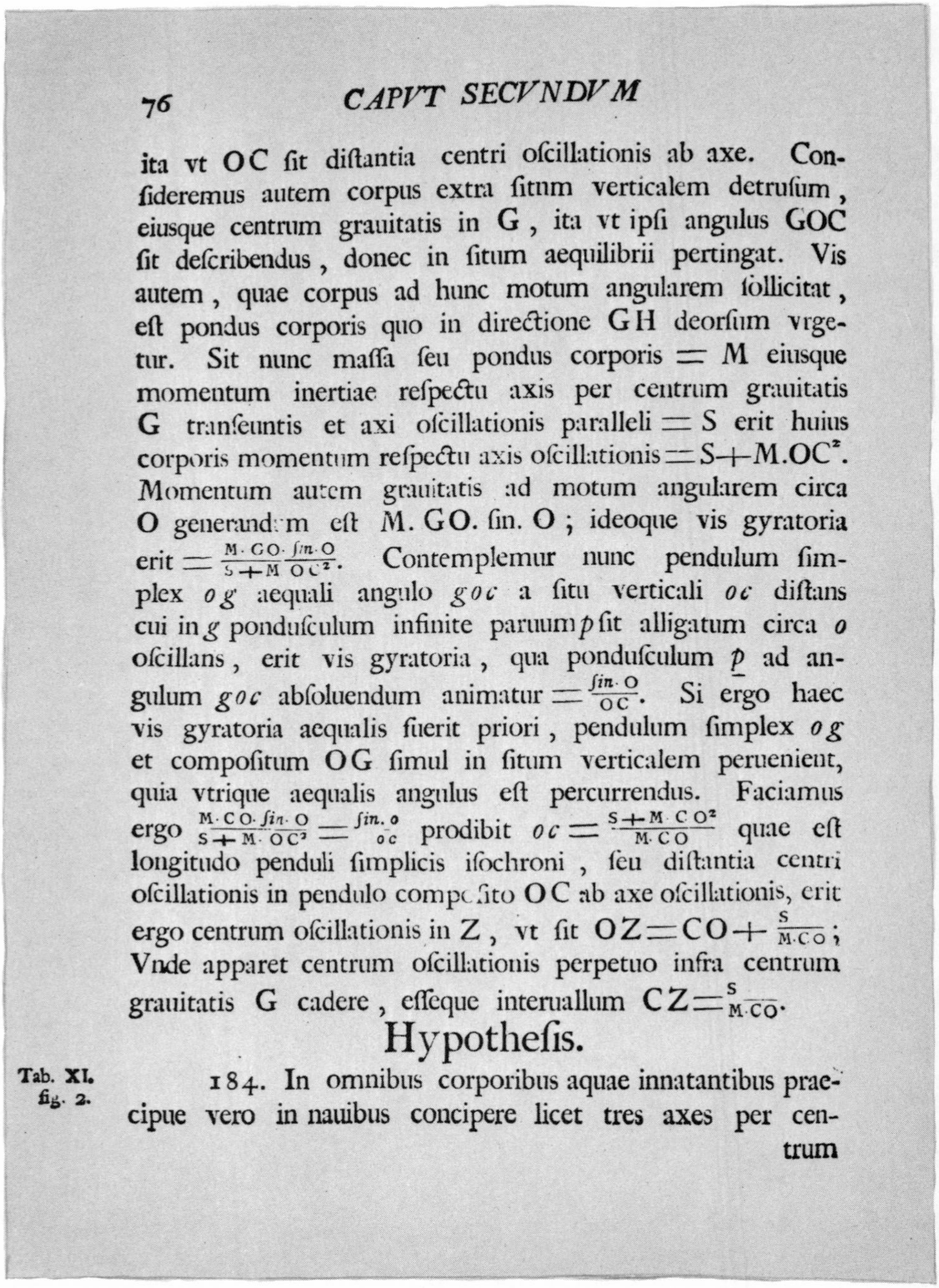

Hypothefis.

Tab. XI.
fig. 2.

   184. In omnibus corporibus aquae innatantibus praecipue vero in nauibus concipere licet tres axes per centrum

FIGURE 21. The first conjecture of the principal axes of inertia, in Euler's *Scientia Navalis,* completed about 1738, published in 1749

trum grauitatis G tranfeuntes inter fe normales, primum verticalem fcilicet CGP, fecundum horizontalem AGB fpinae RS parallelum, in plano diametrali fitum ARSB et tertium EGF pariter horizontalem, fi quidem nauis fuerit in ftatu aequilibrii, et ad priorem AGB normalem. Deinde ponere licet corpus huiusmodi a viribus follicitantibus circa vnumquemque horum axium ita conuerti poffe, vt motus gyratorius circa vnum horum axium non turbetur a motibus gyratoriis circa reliquos.

Scholion 1.

185. Ex fuperioribus fatis intelligitur corpus circa alium axem liberum et immotum gyrari non poffe, nifi circa quem omnes vires centrifugae fe deftruant. Quamobrem fi vires follicitantes corpus circa alium axem rotare conentur, motus orietur maxime irregularis, cum etiam axis inclinetur; quem motum definire difficillimum etiamnum eft. Huic igitur incommodo medela afferetur, fi talis motus irregularis refolui poffet in duos vel tres motus rotatorios circa axes fixos fimul factos; tum enim cognito motu circa quemque axem feorfim, motus totus inde facile colligeretur. Quamuis autem haec refolutio accurate non fuccedat, tamen fi ad praxin refpiciamus, tuto fatis adhiberi poterit, fi tres illi axes inter fe fuerint normales; tum enim motus circa vnum minime a motibus circa reliquos turbabitur. Praeterea vero fi hi axes ita fint comparati vt corpus circa quemli' et feorfim immotum gyrari queat, refolutio ifta eo magis veritati erit confentanea. In nauibus autem, ad quas hanc tractationem praecipue accomodare inftitui, huiusmodi tres axes

K 3   vel

FIGURE 21 (Continued).

Reactions of Late Baroque Mechanics

The development of the general theory of rigid motion was slower than the brilliant successes of Huygens and Euler in these key examples might lead us to expect. The treatment of various special cases by Euler and Daniel Bernoulli gradually built up enough experience with different mechanical ideas to indicate which one was the easiest to apply. No one today will be surprised to learn that the quickest and surest was James Bernoulli's principle of regarding reversed accelerations as forces per unit mass. This principle was adopted also by D'Alembert in 1743, if in a rather obscure form. As always, Euler's treatment was clearest and most direct, and it was he who first made it plain that in certain special systems, namely, those consisting of rigid bars linked together, the principle of moment of momentum must be laid down as an independent basic law.

The statements I have just made are misleading in that they are phrased by hindsight. To us, today, it is clear that the principle of moment of momentum, as a consequence of James Bernoulli's law of reversed accelerations applied to the ancient law of the lever, was used again and again in the mechanical researches of the early eighteenth century, especially those of Euler. Since, however, the principle of moment of momentum had not yet been stated, the geometers of that day did not know they were applying it. Indeed, they were discovering it, discovering it by the commonest method for discovering general laws of theoretical physics, namely, generalization from special cases by discarding the differences and retaining the common features.

Three problems were critical and central for the development of a general mechanics. All three consisted in discovery of differential equations of motion for particular kinds of space-filling bodies:

1. A rigid body
2. A perfect fluid
3. An elastic bar

All three of these problems were solved by Euler. The first stage of his thought culminated in the idea that the principle of linear momentum could be expressed, once and for all, as a set of differential equations. Not until 1747 did Euler see, and he was the first to see, that for *all* discrete systems the equations of motion are of the form

$$m_k \ddot{x}_k = F_k,$$

where the force F_k acting on the kth body is prescribed. While physicists call these "Newton's equations," they occur nowhere in the work of Newton or of any one else prior to 1747. It is true that we, today, can easily read them into Newton's words, but we do so by hindsight.

Once he had this idea, it did not take Euler long to propose as the one and general law of mechanics

$$\ddot{x}dm = dF,$$

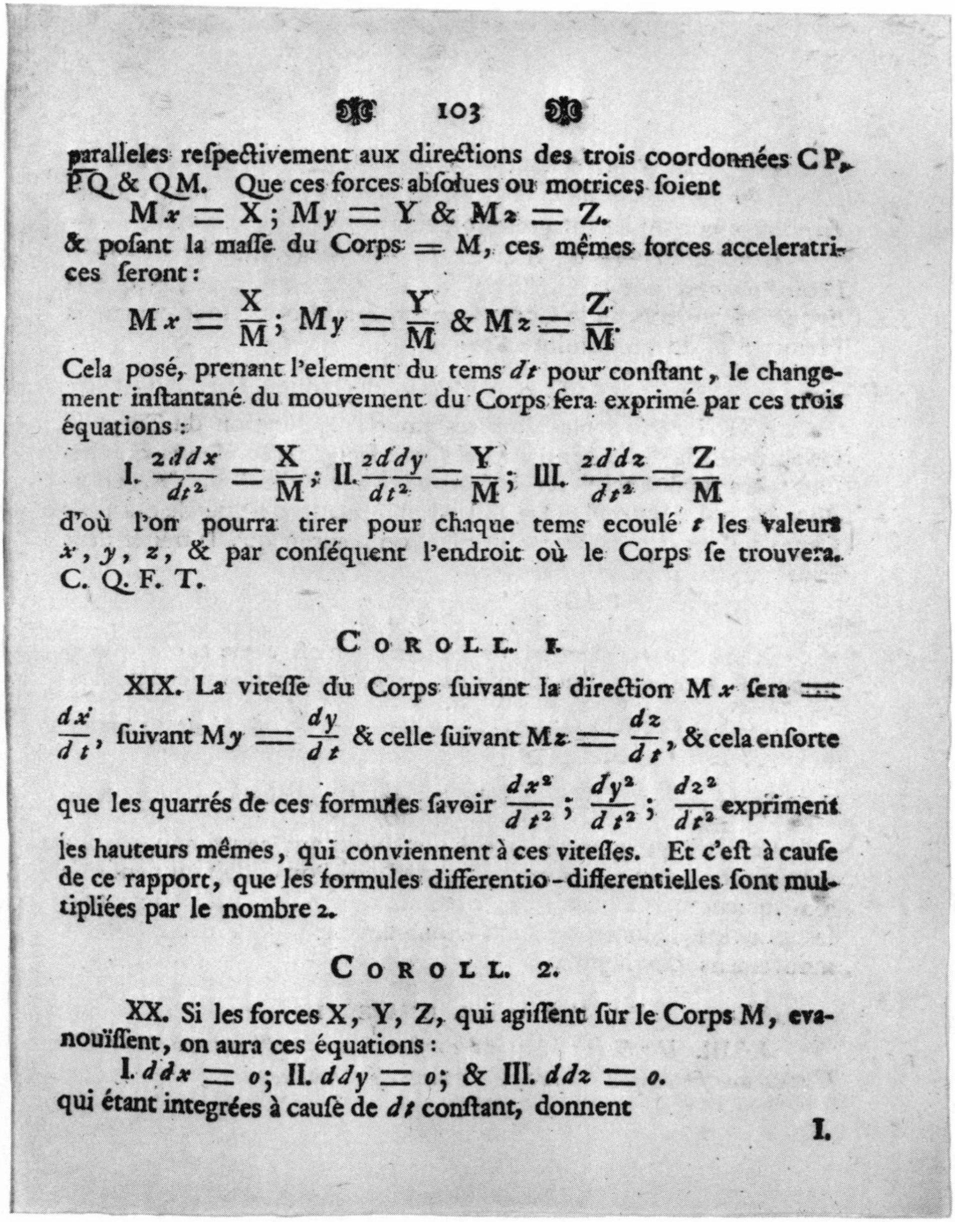

paralleles refpectivement aux directions des trois coordonnées C P, P Q & Q M. Que ces forces abfolues ou motrices foient

$$M x = X; M y = Y \& M z = Z.$$

& pofant la maffe du Corps = M, ces mêmes forces acceleratrices feront :

$$M x = \frac{X}{M}; \quad M y = \frac{Y}{M} \& M z = \frac{Z}{M}.$$

Cela pofé, prenant l'element du tems dt pour conftant, le changement inftantané du mouvement du Corps fera exprimé par ces trois équations :

$$\text{I. } \frac{2ddx}{dt^2} = \frac{X}{M}; \quad \text{II. } \frac{2ddy}{dt^2} = \frac{Y}{M}; \quad \text{III. } \frac{2ddz}{dt^2} = \frac{Z}{M}$$

d'où l'on pourra tirer pour chaque tems ecoulé t les valeurs x, y, z, & par conféquent l'endroit où le Corps fe trouvera. C. Q. F. T.

COROLL. 1.

XIX. La viteffe du Corps fuivant la direction M x fera = $\frac{dx}{dt}$, fuivant M y = $\frac{dy}{dt}$ & celle fuivant M z = $\frac{dz}{dt}$, & cela enforte que les quarrés de ces formules favoir $\frac{dx^2}{dt^2}$; $\frac{dy^2}{dt^2}$; $\frac{dz^2}{dt^2}$ expriment les hauteurs mêmes, qui conviennent à ces viteffes. Et c'eft à caufe de ce rapport, que les formules differentio-differentielles font multipliées par le nombre 2.

COROLL. 2.

XX. Si les forces X, Y, Z, qui agiffent fur le Corps M, evanouïffent, on aura ces équations :

$$\text{I. } ddx = o; \quad \text{II. } ddy = o; \quad \& \text{ III. } ddz = o.$$

qui étant integrées à caufe de dt conftant, donnent

I.

FIGURE 22. The first statement of the "Newtonian equations" for discrete systems, in Euler's memoir on celestial mechanics in the *Mémoires de l'Académie des Sciences,* Berlin, for 1747

cette viteſſe ſoit egale à celle qu'un corps grave acquiert en tombant de la hauteur v, il faut prendre $\dfrac{dx^2}{dt^2} = v$, ou l'elément du tems

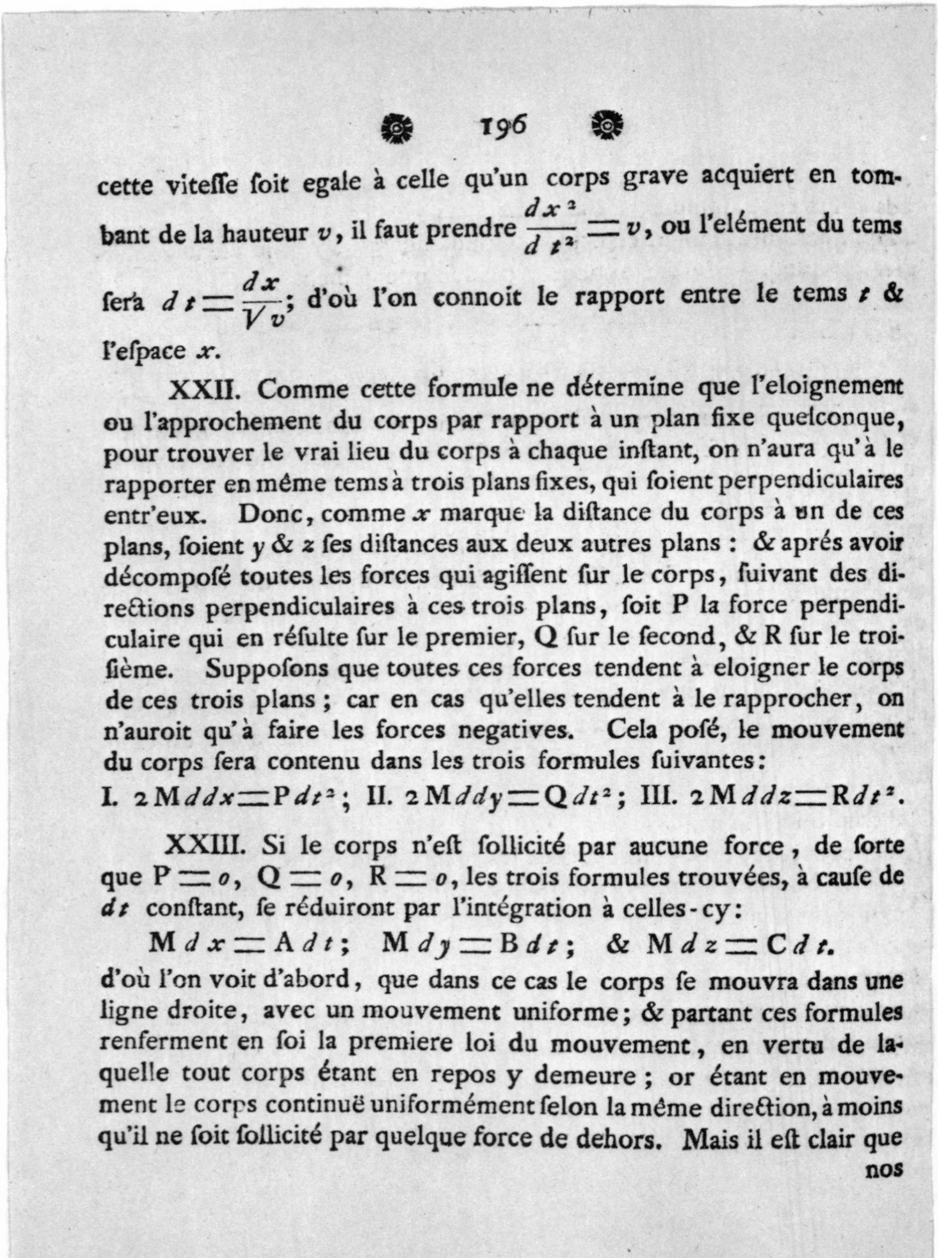

ſera $dt = \dfrac{dx}{\sqrt{v}}$; d'où l'on connoit le rapport entre le tems t & l'eſpace x.

XXII. Comme cette formule ne détermine que l'eloignement ou l'approchement du corps par rapport à un plan fixe quelconque, pour trouver le vrai lieu du corps à chaque inſtant, on n'aura qu'à le rapporter en même tems à trois plans fixes, qui ſoient perpendiculaires entr'eux. Donc, comme x marque la diſtance du corps à un de ces plans, ſoient y & z ſes diſtances aux deux autres plans : & aprés avoir décompoſé toutes les forces qui agiſſent ſur le corps, ſuivant des directions perpendiculaires à ces trois plans, ſoit P la force perpendiculaire qui en réſulte ſur le premier, Q ſur le ſecond, & R ſur le troiſième. Suppoſons que toutes ces forces tendent à eloigner le corps de ces trois plans ; car en cas qu'elles tendent à le rapprocher, on n'auroit qu'à faire les forces negatives. Cela poſé, le mouvement du corps ſera contenu dans les trois formules ſuivantes:

I. $2M\,ddx = P\,dt^2$; II. $2M\,ddy = Q\,dt^2$; III. $2M\,ddz = R\,dt^2$.

XXIII. Si le corps n'eſt ſollicité par aucune force, de ſorte que $P = o$, $Q = o$, $R = o$, les trois formules trouvées, à cauſe de dt conſtant, ſe réduiront par l'intégration à celles-cy:

$M\,dx = A\,dt$; $M\,dy = B\,dt$; & $M\,dz = C\,dt$.

d'où l'on voit d'abord, que dans ce cas le corps ſe mouvra dans une ligne droite, avec un mouvement uniforme; & partant ces formules renferment en ſoi la première loi du mouvement, en vertu de laquelle tout corps étant en repos y demeure ; or étant en mouvement le corps continuë uniformément ſelon la même direction, à moins qu'il ne ſoit ſollicité par quelque force de dehors. Mais il eſt clair que

nos

FIGURE 23. Euler's "New Principle of Mechanics" i.e. the general principle of linear momentum, in the *Mémoires de l'Académie des Sciences,* Berlin, for 1750

or, in the modern notations of Stieltjes integrals,

$$\int_P \ddot{x}\,dm = F(P),$$

where $F(P)$ is the resultant force acting upon the arbitrary part P of the body.

If we ask, how can this idea have been missed, we can answer only by profitless and unconfirmable guessing about how people thought and felt in days long past. However, there can be no doubt of the fact, and we ought not to be so childish as to follow Mach and the standard historical writers on physics in their implication that everyone knew the Newtonian equations, whether or not these had yet been written down.[6] The key example is the problem of general motion of a rigid body, which, as I mentioned, Euler in the 1730's was the first person to face squarely, and which he could at first solve only by resort to hypothesis, a hypothesis he cautiously limited to small motion. However, the moment he had his "New Principle of Mechanics," as he called it in 1750, he confirmed its usefulness by applying it to the motion of a rigid body so as to obtain the general differential equations which, unlike most of his discoveries, are named after him today. Shortly thereafter he was able to prove as a theorem his "hypothesis" of fifteen years earlier that in any body there is an orthogonal triad of free rotation and to liberate it from any restriction to small motion.

We all know that the equations of motion of a rigid body express the balance of moment of momentum, not of linear momentum, so we might conjecture that Euler, like a modern physicist, must have made some hypothesis about mutual forces such as to maintain rigidity. Here hindsight misleads, for in the Age of Reason no real, producing geometer (and here I wittingly exclude Boscovich) ever introduced hypothetical forces beyond gravity in the interior of a body unless compelled to. Euler proposed instead an exclusion principle: Since a body does not spontaneously assume any motion in virtue of whatever internal forces there may be within it, these do not contribute to any of its motions as a whole. We know today that this principle is false in general, but for rigid bodies, it leads to the correct equations. We may say with hindsight that to discover the general equations of rigid motion Euler used a special device to *avoid* the principle of moment of momentum, just as Huygens had used a different special device to avoid it when he determined the center of oscillation. It should be unnecessary to remark, though unfortunately it is not, that the general motion of a rigid body affords a mechanical problem far too subtle for any savant of the seventeenth century, no matter how great.

The problem of the elastica is of a still higher order of conceptual difficulty. In one of his earliest researches, Euler in 1728 had succeeded in unifying the catenary and the elastica in a single theory as far as equilibrium was concerned. Obviously, the basic principle had to be the balance of moments. These two systems are of such a kind that balance of forces, while of course it holds, need not be considered. To get equations of motion is a different matter. While the nature of the contact force could be left aside in the problem of equilibrium, for the problem of motion it could not.

Here Euler had a second earlier success to guide or misguide him, namely, his hydrodynamics. After having simplified and generalized the hydraulic theories of Daniel and John Bernoulli in 1750–51, Euler was in a position to extend the ideas to three-dimensional fluid bodies. D'Alembert in a devious and obscure essay submitted for a prize in 1749 had woven a number of correct equations for rotationally symmetric or plane flow into a tissue of philosophy, conjecture, doubt, sophomorisms, and error. Just at this time Euler was attacking the same and more general problems. As always, his approach was brilliantly simple and easy. He introduced the concept of fluid pressure, the action of the fluid on one side of an imagined boundary on that on the other. By assuming this contact force to be perpendicular to the surface, no matter what the state of motion of the fluid, and by applying his differential form of the principle of linear momentum, Euler derived the basic equations of hydrodynamics in a few pages. The Bernoullian tradition had taught him how to calculate the resultant force on a one-dimensional element, and his own calculus of partial derivatives enabled him to extend the idea to three dimensions.

The simple modes of infinitesimal vibration for straight elastic bars had been found by Daniel Bernoulli and Euler in their youthful days, even before there were equations of motion. The partial differential equation of small motion was obtained straightaway by Euler the moment he had the general principle of linear momentum. Finite motion offers a problem of a different order of difficulty.

After having studied this problem on and off for fifty years, Euler found the key to it, as simple as it is powerful. This key is to regard the moment of momentum as *an independent basic law of mechanics*, and to decline to specify the contact force and contact couple, either in magnitude or in direction. In this way Euler in 1771 was able to write down the general equations of mechanics for a plane deformable line. After doing this, he found it easy to state the general principle of moment of momentum:

$$\int_P p \times \ddot{x}dm = L(P),$$

where p is the position vector and L is the total torque, including couples if need be, applied to the part P of the body. In his final memoir of 1775, he laid down the two principles as fundamental and independent: On every part of every body, the total force equals the rate of change of total momentum, and the total torque equals the rate of change of total moment of momentum, where these torques that are moments of forces are taken with respect to the origin of p, that origin being a fixed point. These are *Euler's laws of motion*. The nature of the forces acting, and in particular the nature of contact forces, varies from one kind of body to another. This same distinction had been made by James Bernoulli in 1705, but he had not attained correct general principles. Again with hindsight, we may say that at the beginning of the eighteenth century the mathematics of three-dimensional space had not been developed sufficiently to make possible clear and precise physical thought about space-filling bodies in general. With Euler's memoir of 1775, the whole program of rational mechanics becomes clear. There are the two general laws, *common to all bodies* but insufficient to specify their motions. The *differences* between bodies are represented by *constitutive equations,* which specify the nature of their response to their surroundings. The constitutive equations studied in the eighteenth century are those defining the discrete system, the rigid body, the perfectly flexible line, the perfectly flexible sheet, the elastica, and the perfect fluid, with a few others which are less important. All these fit easily into the general scheme laid down by Euler in 1775. In fact, this scheme remained general enough for all of mechanics for at least 100 years.

Something must be said about Lagrange's *Méchanique Analitique*, published in 1788. In it, the basic axiom of statics is the principle of virtual work, stated explicitly and in some generality. Dynamics follows by the Bernoulli-Euler principle of reversed accelerations. While today this generalized axiom is often attributed to D'Alembert, Lagrange himself claims, and justly so, that it replaces the much more complicated principle D'Alembert had proposed as a general basis for mechanics.

Almost as much nonsense has been written about the *Méchanique Analitique* as about the *Principia* and the *Two New Sciences.* Although Lagrange's book is far easier to read with understanding than is Newton's or Galileo's, still it does not seem to be easy enough for most historians of science to penetrate. There are few errors, few novelties, and many routine manipulations in it. While it contains interesting historical parentheses, the presentation of mechanics is strictly algebraic, with no explanation of concepts, no illustrations either by diagrams or by developed examples, and no attempt to justify any limit process by rigorous mathematics. It does not enter at all a number of the fields opened by Newton, and it leaves unmentioned most of the deeper and harder problems of mechanics solved by the Basel geometers in the century preceding it. In particular, it does not include the general principle of moment of momentum. It could not do so, because the principle of virtual work does not yield the principle of moment of momentum until the nature of the contact forces is made somewhat explicit. Cauchy had still to be born and to create the general concept of stress, by which all theories of space-filling bodies are united.

Other great problems set before the world as challenges in the *Principia* remained unsolved, some even untouched, a century after it was published. The theory of infinitesimal surface waves waited for Laplace, Kelland, and Airy, who derived it from Euler's equations of fluid dynamics. Newton's ideas on fluid friction were to be taken up by Navier and Stokes; while the latter was to see the error of Newton's solution for the spinning cylinder and correct it, the problem of the spinning sphere remains unsolved today. The flow of fluid from an orifice, after a special result found ingeniously by Borda in 1766, was to be studied successfully on the basis of Euler's hydrodynamics by Kirchhoff and Helmholtz, but only in the plane, and the three-dimensional theory is scarcely touched today. While D'Alembert and Euler had derived wave equations for flexible solids and gases, the first satisfactory explanation of the observed velocity of sound was found in the early years of the nineteenth century, and a theory inclusive enough to allow loud sounds to reinforce while weak sounds die out was first discovered only last year by Coleman & Gurtin.

tems les efpaces parcourus par le corps m fuivant les lignes p, q, r, &c. Donc $mP \times \delta p$, $mQ \times \delta q$, $mR \times \delta r$, &c, feront les *momens* des forces mP, mQ, mR, &c, agiffantes fuivant ces mêmes lignes, p, q, r, &c.

Or la formule générale de l'équilibre confifte en ce que la fomme des *momens* de toutes les forces du fyftême doit être nulle (Part. I, Sect. 2, art. 2); donc on aura la formule cherchée en égalant à zéro la fomme de toutes les quantités

$$m \left(\frac{d^2 x}{dt^2} \delta x + \frac{d^2 y}{dt^2} \delta y + \frac{d^2 z}{dt^2} \delta z \right)$$
$$+ m \left(P \delta p + Q \delta q + R \delta r + \&c \right),$$

relatives à chacun des corps du fyftême propofé.

7. Donc fi on dénote cette fomme par le figne intégral S, qui doit embraffer tous les corps du fyftême, on aura

$$S \left(\frac{d^2 x}{dt^2} \delta x + \frac{d^2 y}{dt^2} \delta y + \frac{d^2 z}{dt^2} \delta z + P \delta p + Q \delta q + R \delta r + \&c. \right) m$$

pour la formule générale du mouvement d'un fyftême quelconque de corps, regardés comme des points, & animés par des forces accélératrices quelconques P, Q, R, &c.

Pour faire ufage de cette formule, on fuivra les mêmes regles que pour la formule de l'équilibre; ainfi il faudra appliquer ici tout ce qui a été dit dans la feconde Section de la premiere Partie, depuis l'article 3 jufqu'à la fin, en obfervant que les différentielles marquées par la note ou caractériftique δ dans la formule précédente répondent aux différentielles marquées par la caractériftique ordinaire d dans la formule de l'équilibre, & fe déterminent par les mêmes regles & les mêmes opérations.

B b 2

FIGURE 24. The general principle of virtual work as stated by Lagrange in the *Méchanique Analytique,* 1788

In being asked to speak about reactions to the *Principia*, I am grateful for an assignment licensing an approach simpler than that most of the other speakers have chosen. Here, unpublished documents are almost irrelevant, since only historians of today, not scientists of Newton's time or any other, have had a chance to react to them. So as to survey the reactions to Newton's published work, I must first correct common misconceptions as to what Newton's achievement and program in physics really were. One such misconception, put forward in the eighteenth century by a few interpreters not to be numbered among creative scientists and then adopted by almost all physicists and historians from the nineteenth century on, is that Newton insisted all of natural philosophy should be founded on calculations of central forces.

Whatever may have been the speculations Newton chose not to publish, the works he did release do not justify imputation to him of so narrow a view of nature. In the first place, it would have to rest largely on one sentence in the preface to the *Principia* and on the comments at the end of the "Queries" in the *Opticks*. The exaggerated weight often laid upon these few pages may reflect the fact that while a mathematician may need a day to get through a page of the *Principia*, then he has it beyond quibble, but anybody can read the "Queries" in ten minutes and go on arguing about them forever. The "Queries" are not science; they show Newton from a side he withheld usually and would have been better advised to have withheld without exception; at best, they are prophecies of science. Their interest lies not in themselves but in the mere fact that it was Newton who wrote them. Second, even if we must tarry over these fleshless speculations, we cannot justly read into them atomism in the narrow sense later given to the word. Newton's fancied atoms were "solid, massy, hard, impenetrable, moveable." Of these five adjectives, three are not punctual. The repulsion experienced by two solid, hard, impenetrable grains, however small, when they strike each other, is not an action at a distance but a contact force. Contact forces, if crudely handled by Newton, are nevertheless nowhere excluded by him. His treatments of water waves, efflux, and resistance of a continued fluid rest on concepts, vague though they be, of contact forces, not between corpuscles but in an infinitely divisible medium. Newton's particles are "even so very hard, as never to wear or break in pieces." Breaking cannot be denied unless there are pieces into which to break. The "particles" are "particulae," little parts, not mass points; they fill a small region, which contains infinitely many points. I do not deny that Newton here and there proclaimed an atomistic view of nature, but I see equally that in his own *practice* he was far from adhering without exception to the 39 Articles the nineteenth-century headline writers and the text compilers of today strap him to with the hagiography of a Parson Weems. Even in the explicit statement of the third law of motion in the *Principia*, where only forces between pairs of "bodies" are mentioned, Newton does not demand that they be central. In chanting that electromagnetism destroyed Newton's views, the physicists force upon him a program that may have been once theirs but was not his.

Writings on the history of science all too often proclaim and develop an antithesis between "Newtonian" and "anti-Newtonian" science in the nineteenth century, using the supremacy of central interatomic forces as the shibboleth. I do not deny that central forces had their passionate partisans and opponents, but among these enthusiasts I do not find any mathematical theorists but those of the second rate, or, oftener, mere journalists of science. The great mathematicians who gave us "classical" physics do not fall into either category. Cauchy and Poisson created theories of solids alternatively as assemblies of point centers and as plena, and they proved that the two models were equivalent, more or less. Maxwell created both the kinetic theory of gases and the electromagnetic theory of the aether; he showed, incidentally, that in his kinetic theory no result inconsistent with the conception of a gas as a continuum could ever be derived by correct mathematics. These men tower above the idle speculators who claimed all and proved nothing for their atoms or subtle fluids. Cauchy, Poisson, and Maxwell were neither "Newtonian" nor "anti-Newtonian" in the historians' sense. Like Euler before them, they bore Newton's mantle. While Euler is regarded often, and with some justice, as an upholder of Cartesian metaphysics, in his *practice* of mechanics he was the truest of all Newton's ultimate disciples, for he took over, ennobled by abstraction, and fixed by explicit and exact application, all of Newton's fruitful ideas and merged them with James Bernoulli's to form what we know now as "classical mechanics." Indeed, what physicists today call "Newtonian mechanics" has little direct relation to Newton's own work but is rather a combination of Euler's mechanics with Lagrange's.

The heritage of science cannot be equated to its history. We do injustice to a great scientist if we merely chronicle his views and actions, or even if we cast the arithmetic sum of all his scientific work. If we excise judgment, we insult the goddess we claim to worship. While he who writes the history of Charles II need not himself be an expert tennis player and keep a costly international stall of mistresses, he who approaches Newton without having himself experienced the neurosis of scientific thought, the perverted solitary ecstasy of creation, and the aristocratic duelli of polemics at the summit,[7] is not likely to get nearer than did poor puerile Brewster and Rigaud to the real science of Newton. Even if the difference is merely that a historian can less painfully imagine himself in the slippers of a Charles crowned by a garland of doxies than in the "absolute space, . . . always like and immobile" of a Newton with only fluxions of that equable fluent, "absolute, true, and mathematical time" as his companions, the difference is essential. Charles is dead beyond recall. A scientist does not so die. Newton is alive today, just as are the Hadamard and the Birkhoff some of us met in the flesh, the Hilbert all of us know through his disciples. Newton is alive, not in the barren speculations of the "Queries" but in the solid, permanent, mathematical pages of the *Principia,* in the program he there laid down for us and illustrated by brilliant examples, and in the great new concept he there taught us to use.

First, the program. Often quoted but invariably misread is Newton's own statement: "Utinam caetera Naturae phaenomena ex principiis Mechanicis eodem argumentandi genere derivare liceret." It is right to translate "ex principiis Mechanicis" as *from mechanical principles,* but only in the vague, inclusive sense the word *mechanics* had in the seventeenth century, already explained by Mr. Hill. Many, on the contrary, read this passage as if Newton had meant *from mechanical principles* in the sense of the nineteenth-century physicists' mechanics, namely, "from my own three laws of motion." As one of its definitions of *mechanic,* with a quotation from Congreve in 1697, the Oxford Dictionary gives "working like a machine, having a machine-like action"; another, supported by a quotation from 1663, "acting or performed without exercise of thought or volition"; and "practical as opposed to speculative," with the following quotation from a mathematical book of 1570: "A speculative Mechanicien . . . differereth nothyng from a Mechanicall Mathematicien." The physicists' and historians' use of *mechanical* as distinguished from *optical, electromagnetic,* etc., is too recent even to be mentioned in the dictionary, which comes near it only in the antithesis to *chemical,* quoting an example a full century after Newton's time. Newton himself, while he regarded force as a "mechanical" idea, mentioned "electric" and "magnetic" forces. The electromagnetic vacuum of Maxwell, Hertz, and Lorentz is just as consonant with Newton's "ex principiis Mechanicis eodem argumentandi genere" as were the ponderable aethers of Newton's own early and late speculations.[7]

The aspect of Newton's program least regarded in historical studies is that on which he himself laid greatest weight, namely, that it is *mathematical,* not only mathematical but *rigorously* mathematical. The word *mathematical* appears in the title and frequently in the text, always with a capital letter. In the preface Newton, after reminding us of the old distinction between rational and practical mechanics, continues: "Since, however, artificers are wont to operate with small accuracy, *mechanics* has come to be distinguished thus from *geometry,* that whatever is accurate is classed as *geometry,* whatever is less accurate, as *mechanics.* Notwithstanding, the errors are of the artificers, not of the art. He who operates less accurately is the less perfect mechanic, and if any one could operate with greatest accuracy, he would be the most perfect mechanic of all." Going on to explain the nature of geometry, Newton concludes, *"Geometry,* therefore, is founded in mechanical practice and is nothing else than that part of *universal mechanics* which sets forth and proves the art of measuring accurately. . . . *Rational mechanics* will be the science of the motions that result from any forces whatever, and of the forces that are required for any motions whatever, accurately set forth and proved." Those who read Newton's "ex principiis mechanicis eodem argumentandi genere" as referring only to the one following sentence regarding forces among the particles disregard not only the page before it, from which I have just given extracts, but also the ten lines above it, where in describing his book Newton speaks of "our mathematical principles of philosophy," "propositions mathematically proved," and "mathematical propositions"—three references to mathematical proof. "The same kind of reasoning" means, in plain English, *proved by rigorous mathematics from mathematical axioms.* Newton's preface, if read straight through, makes his program plain: to construct a *mathematical* natural philosophy, in which geometry is only the simplest part but a perfect specimen of method.

Against this program there were, indeed, hostile reactions, especially among the poets and musicians of the early romantic movement, as Mr. Haskell mentioned; they are fully expressed in the autobiography of Berlioz. On the course of physics itself, they had little effect. Most of the evidence for positive contributions by nonmathematical theorists of physics rests on misconceptions about the nature of mathematics. Faraday's disclaimer is often parroted unhistorically, without a reminder that for him, who, like a modern mathematician, dealt directly with precise and abstract concepts and operations, the word *mathematics* referred only to the ritual algebra of pedagogues in the barrenest period of British mathematics, when the blind use of x, y, z and a, b, c connected by plus and minus signs was allowed to usurp the word that before then did signify and now again does signify the precise theory of relations and sets.

Since the literature of the history and philosophy of science, despite the good intentions and efforts of the best students in those fields, remains jejune in its credulity as to the nature and function of mathematics, I append here some remarks of Maxwell in the preface to the first edition of his *Treatise*: "As I proceeded with the study of Faraday, I perceived that his method of conceiving the phenomena was also a mathematical one, though not exhibited in the conventional form of mathematical symbols. . . . Faraday's methods resembled those in which we begin with the whole and arrive at the parts by analysis. . . . I also found that several of the most fertile methods of research discovered by the mathematicians could be expressed much better in terms of ideas derived from Faraday than in their original form," A modern student of natural philosophy might summarize the difference thus: Faraday preferred global statements of physical laws, but since the mathematical tools necessary for exploiting them locally (Green's transformation, etc.) did not yet exist, Faraday's mathematics seemed to be distinct from that already symbolized and commonly taught; Maxwell, two generations later, easily constructed methods for interconverting local and global statements; the full power of the global viewpoint began to be appreciated in Hilbert's time; the modern creative theorist prefers global principles whenever he can find them. Thus the *real* history of science, the science that is alive and growing, upholds Maxwell's judgment that Faraday as a theorist was certainly a mathematician, and a great one. (Not every great mathematician is a master of *all* aspects of the mathematics cultivated in his day. Some look more to the future than to the past.) Those historians who adduce Faraday as an example of a nonmathematical theorist and hence a rebel to Newton's program not only fail to understand what mathematics is but also do Faraday himself a great injustice. They judge him in terms of the mathematics of his own day, while he himself, like other great theorists, could plead a much better case before the higher tribunal of the mathematicians of

C. TRUESDELL

our day. Faraday may serve indeed as a proof, if one were needed, that the mathematical high priests of any one period are rarely the best mathematicians in it.[9]

While some programs remain programs only, even if they are projected by so great a man as Newton, and thus may be trodden as paving stones upon the road of good intentions, others stand erect as summaries of practice. As well as many of the former kind, Newton left us one of the latter. In the middle of the *Principia,* as a tailpiece to some of its most brilliant successes, Newton wrote, "Eodem sensu generali usurpo vocem impulsus, non species virium & qualitates physicas, sed quantitates & proportiones Mathematicas in hoc Tractatu expendens: ut in Definitionibus explicui. In Mathesi investigandae sunt virium quantitates & rationes illae, quae ex conditionibus quibuscunque positis consequentur: deinde ubi in Physicam descenditur, conferandae sunt hae rationes cum Phaenomenis ut innotescat quaenam virium conditiones singulis corporum attractivorum generibus competant. Et tum demum de virium speciebus, causis, & rationibus physicis tutius disputare licebit." "In the same general sense I take over the word "impulse," pondering in this treatise not kinds of forces and physical qualities, but quantities and mathematical proportions, as I explained in the definitions. In mathematics are to be investigated the quantities of forces and such rules as may follow from whatever conditions be laid down. Whenever we descend therefrom into physics, these rules are to be compared with the phenomena so as to disclose what conditions of forces answer to the several kinds of attractive bodies." Newton closes with a characteristic sneer: "And then, finally, argument about the kinds, causes, and physical rules of forces will be safer." He implies that such argument will get us nowhere, but it does not matter, since the real work, the mathematics, is done, so the rest is what you will. Whatever his theology and philosophy, this is Newton's grand lesson for us: Disregard the "causes"—whatever that strange word may mean—and cleave to relations among the phenomena. Indeed, "cause" is only a verbal crutch for beginners who do not grasp the concept of function in mathematics. In laying out this program, Newton was not alone. In the course of a concrete, specific research on elasticity, Leibniz wrote, "his paucis consideratis, tota haec materia redacta sit ad puram Geometriam, quod in physicis & mechanicis unice desideratum." "These few things having been considered, the whole matter is reduced to pure geometry, which is the one aim of physics and mechanics."

Those who regard the eighteenth century as a period when Newtonian science stood still make the error of equating "Newtonian" to "British." Those who find it a barren period in physics fail to learn a lesson from Newton and Leibniz. While first physics relieves philosophy of some of its burdens, at the second stage mathematics reduces the physics of a given class of phenomena to a bare minimum and thereby frees physicists to turn their speculations elsewhere. In brief, the aim is to clear out such physics as is unnecessary, which is most of it. No man before or after ever brought so great a range of physics under the control of specific, explicit, final mathematical theory as Euler did. He was so successful that most of his discoveries are not even credited to him, being taught today to all and dismissed by the physicists today as obvious or mathematical and hence, presumably, God-given to physicists at birth. Euler's work lies entirely within the scientific programs of Newton and Leibniz, and his specific principles of mechanics unite theirs in their common features, discard them in differences, and merge them into new, embracing concepts.

Our second great legacy from Newton, the specific one, is the concept of force given *a priori*. To the insight that place and time and body and motion and mass are not enough, that decent correlation of the phenomena demands another primitive element, Newton won through alone and imperfectly. As Mr. Cohen has remarked, Newton's "vires" in the statements of his laws are granules[10] of impulse, not forces as we conceive them today. As further remarked by Mr. Cohen, if in somewhat different words, Newton's own laws, if taken strictly, are insufficient even for what he himself claimed to prove from them, let alone to serve as basis for "classical mechanics." It took half of the eighteenth century to render Leibniz' calculus the lingua franca of physical science and hence clear the way for Euler to teach us to walk upright without the crutches of tiny impulses and other shadowy, imprecise granules. The concept of force resisted longer. Clear and sufficient mathematical axioms for systems of forces, at the level of Hilbert's axioms for points and lines and Carathéodory's axioms for distributions of mass, were first proposed by Noll, no earlier than 1960, and are still under revision by him and others.

In surveying reactions to the *Principia*, I did not idly adduce work done only recently. I hope it is not out of place to mention to distinguished philosophers and historians of science that classical mechanics, the mechanics loosely called "Newtonian," is not the corpse it is often pictured as being. Mr. Stein has given me courage by alluding to the higher levels of concept and precision possible for classical space-time. Refinement and extension of the concept of force is one of the central areas of research in the rational mechanics of deformable bodies today. We stand here upon the shoulders of more giants than one. It is from Newton's *Principia* that our forebears learned how to use the concept of force given *a priori*. The structure which that concept binds together we owe to many great mathematicians; among the founders, Newton is joined by Huygens, Leibniz, and James Bernoulli, and the great architect is Euler.

NOTES

[1] In modern terms, with granules of impulse replaced by forces, the proof of Corollary I is roughly as follows. Given two forces f_1 and f_2, let them produce motions $x_1(t)$ and $x_2(t)$ in a body of mass m. Then by Law II,

$$f_1 = m\ddot{x}_1, \qquad f_2 = m\ddot{x}_2 .$$

Addition yields

$$f_1 + f_2 = m(\ddot{x}_1 + \ddot{x}_2) .$$

From kinematics, accelerations add vectorially, say $\ddot{x}_1 + \ddot{x}_2 = \ddot{x}_3$, but by Law II

$$f_3 = m\ddot{x}_3 .$$

Hence $f_1 + f_2 = f_3$. That is, forces add vectorially. This argument applies only to *resultant* forces on bodies. In statics, these resultant forces are all 0, and every step in the proof reduces to $0 = 0$. The vectorial composition of the parts of a force with resultant 0 is essential in statics, and in particular in the theory of attraction. It cannot be derived from any laws which relate forces only to the motions they produce.

C. TRUESDELL

² Lest this remark seem unfounded, I append a quotation from Mr. Cohen's eulogy of the late A. Koyré, published in *Isis,* Volume 57, p. 161 (1966). Asserting that Koyré was "more than any other responsible for the *new* history of science," Mr. Cohen explains, "He rejected the kind of history in which a modern scholar remarks that this was correct and that was wrong judging each statement, not in the context of the time in which it was composed, but rather grading it from the viewpoint of our own presently accepted theories and collections of facts. Such historians, according to Koyré, were not engaged in conceptual analysis; they were not attempting to understand what the men of science of the past were thinking and even accomplishing with the mathematical, theoretical, and experimental tools then available. Professor Koyré was interested—first and foremost—to find out the degree to which men of science in the past may have been 'right' in the terms of their own times, not ours."

It is amusing to carry the new historians' impartiality in science a little further. If science, which presumably remains even for them the theory and demonstration of the phenomena of nature, is time-conditioned, social, and institutional, like politics and moral philosophy, are such also the phenomena themselves? If purely mechanical perpetual motion and purely chemical transmutation of elements are impossible today, as we are now taught in school, were they perhaps possible in the times of Leonardo and Newton?

³ Euler, *Mechanica seu Scientia Motus,* pp. 93–224 in *Manuscripta Euleriana* II, ed. G. K. Mikhailov, Moscow and Leningrad, Izdat. Nauka, 1965. See Section III and especially the last paragraph, §648.

⁴ Euler, *Mechanica sive motus scientia analytice exposita,* Petropoli, 1736, 2 vols. = *Opera omnia* II, *1 & 2.*

⁵ Euler, *Scientia Navalis* . . . I (completed 1738), Petropoli, 1749 = *Opera omnia* II, *18* (1968). See §184.

⁶ It is enlightening to read what Euler himself wrote in 1747 when he took up, by no means for the first time, the general problem of the planetary system. "To solve these problems, I shall use a method a little different from that which others who have written on this subject have used. First, they tried to determine the true velocity of the body, from which they sought the motion at each instant; and from this velocity compared with the space traversed they determined the place where the body should appear at each instant. So as to avoid this rather tedious operation, and since in astronomy the true velocity of the heavenly bodies is never wished, I have found means of reaching straightaway an equation connecting the time elapsed with the apparent place of the planet . . . . Finally, according to my method, I am not obliged to take account of the curvature of the line that the body describes, and by this means I avoid much laborious research, above all when the motion of the body does not take place even approximately in the same plane. This great advantage is included in the following *Lemma* . . . .

Lemma

"XVIII. If a body *M* is acted upon by the arbitrary forces, to determine the instantaneous change that these forces produce in the motion of the body."

The outcome, as the reader may see for himself in Fig. 22, is the "Newtonian equations", there numbered I, II, III. Euler apparently considers the *principle* these equations express to be so well known that it requires no reference and no proof. He merely affirms the equations.

What then are the "method a little different" and the "great advantage"? As Euler writes, these lie in the *general conception,* which is new in that it requires no geometric restrictions or devices. To apply in three dimensions the intrinsic conception of Newton, Euler had had to construct a differential geometry of skew curves, and a large part of his *Mechanica* is taken up by cumbrous manipulations concerning what we should now call curvature and torsion. The "method a little different" sweeps all this away.

Clearly, Euler did not regard his own innovation here a great one; he attributes to it only mathematical convenience. Just as clearly, it was this small innovation that showed him within three years the way to what he unhesitatingly called a *new principle* of mechanics: The linear momentum principle for each element of volume in an arbitrary space-filling body.

⁷ Cf. the remarks of Mr. Manuel, which, set against Mr. Hill's, may serve to remind us that

in the age of Charles II and Newton, blessed by Apollo and Venus, the "normal" of iatro-psychological philosophy did not exist, either in word or in concept.

[8] Newton continues in this passage, "For many things move me to suspect somewhat that they all may depend upon certain forces by which the particles of bodies through causes not yet known are driven toward one another and cohere according to regular figures, or are driven away and withdraw from one another. . . ." The phrase "secundum figuras regulares" is usually translated "*in* regular figures," as if Newton had suggested geometric arrays of atoms, while in fact it is not so specific and could refer, as the phrase "geometrical figures" often did at that time, merely to use of specific mathematical functions. The classical *figura* means not only "form, shape, figure" but also "quality, kind, species, nature, manner," and in the writing of Galileo and others "geometrical figures" are said to describe or specify a situation where a modern author would use the term *function*. Thus, I think, Newton's own attempts to describe flows of a "continued" fluid in Book II involve coherence of "the particles of bodies . . . according to regular figures," although they make no use of atoms or central forces. Indeed, Newton himself tells us as much in the Preface, where he lists among the "natural powers" he will treat "the resistance of fluids and forces of that sort, whether attractive or repulsive . . ." and he mentions not only Book I but also Book II as pertaining to his general program. The forces of coherence and resistance in space-filling bodies do satisfy Newton's principle of "action and reaction," although in general they are not central forces.

[9] There may be some hope that scientists will refuse to let pass by default the misconceptions about the histories of their own fields that the new professionalized history of science is busy to create by its refusal to recognize that science is still alive. The general periodical *Endeavour* in its issue for September, 1967, printed an unsigned commemorative editorial which in one page gives a sounder character of Faraday than an entire recent biography, *e.g.* "It is a remarkable fact that although Faraday knew little beyond simple arithmetic, and affected to see little need of mathematics, he clearly had a kind of mathematical intuition that guided him with scarcely a fault through the new fields he opened up."

[10] Those who appeal triumphantly to these granules as evidence that Newton conceived all of nature as corpuscular may set themselves the task of explaining why Newton did not similarly chop up into gobbets his absolute space and equable time.

REFERENCES

Most, though not all, of the works mentioned in this lecture are analyzed and referenced in my three introductions to volumes in L. Euleri *Opera Omnia*:

1. Rational fluid mechanics, 1687–1765, *L. Euleri Opera Omnia* (2) 12, IX–CXXV (1954).
2. I. The first three sections of Euler's treatise on fluid mechanics (1766); II. The theory of aerial sound, 1637–1788; III. Rational fluid mechanics, 1765–1788. *L. Euleri Opera Omnia* (2) *13*, VII–CXVIII (1956).
3. The Rational Mechanics of Flexible or Elastic Bodies, 1638–1788, *L. Euleri Opera Omnia* (2) *11₂*, 435 pp. (1960).

For the center of oscillation, among other things, see

4. E. Jouguet, *Lectures de Mécanique*, Paris, Gauthier-Villars, 2 vols., 1908–1909.
5. R. Dugas, *La Mécanique au XVIIᵉ Siecle*, Neuchatel, Griffon, 1954.

For the principle of moment of momentum:

6. C. Truesdell, Whence the law of moment of momentum? *Mélanges Alexandre Koyré 1*, pp. 588–612 (1964). Reprinted, with corrections, as Chapter V of C. Truesdell, *Essays in the History of Mechanics*, New York, Springer, 1968.

For the concept of stress:

7. C. Truesdell, The Creation and Unfolding of the Concept of Stress, Chapter IV of Truesdell, *Essays in the History of Mechanics*.

While it is customary to refer to Mach's book, for all matters treated in this lecture the account given there is totally unreliable.

C. TRUESDELL

ARTHUR E. WOODRUFF

Comment

I fear that Dr. Truesdell has been somewhat carried away from his original theme in response partly to my comments on the oral version of his paper. Dr. Truesdell wields a mighty ax which sometimes misses its proper target, but he cannot be accused of skirting the issues. I will seek to share the latter virtue by summarizing the comments I made at Austin and adding some further ones.

Just as we have learned that mechanics did not begin with Galileo, Dr. Truesdell has shown us with great clarity that it did not end with Newton. There is no disputing the flaws in the *Principia* and the accomplishments of the Bernoullis and Euler; as he has said, these are facts. My own wish was to supplement his paper with a few remarks on another aspect of the influence of the *Principia*—that is, the action-at-a-distance physics of the early nineteenth century. However seriously Newton may have really meant the words quoted by Dr. Truesdell and so many others at this conference, they seemed to express a program of comprehending the other phenomena of nature by means of central forces mathematically expressed as actions at a distance. Ampère was explicitly pursuing the method by which Newton "derived" the law of gravitation when he found his law of force between current elements.

> I have consulted experience alone to establish the laws of these phenomena, and I have deduced from them the only formula which can represent the forces to which they are due; I have made no research into the cause which one could assign to these forces, being fully convinced that any research of this sort should be preceded by the purely experimental knowledge of the laws, and by the determination, uniquely deduced from these laws, of the value of the elementary forces, the direction of which is necessarily that of the line determined by the material points between which they exert themselves.[1]

Wilhelm Weber followed the same line in developing his more inclusive force law. There is no question that the claim of proceeding "without hypothesis" was, if the word "hypothesis" be used in its modern sense, a delusion. The global approach of Faraday and Maxwell was more fruitful. Finally, Ampère and Weber were wrong. But their contemporaries, including Maxwell, agreed that these laws correctly represented the then known facts of electricity. A proper understanding of history includes a knowledge of both these truths. Surely Dr. Truesdell would not join those who extol Newton's *Opticks* in the light of much later evidence for the wave-particle duality. Furthermore, some of the conceptual structure of the "wrong" electrodynamic theories was incorporated by Lorentz into our classical electromagnetism.

With much of Dr. Truesdell's further animadversions I have a great deal of sympathy. Picture-thinking is not mature science. Dr. Truesdell's taste leans toward the most mature and well-codified science in contradistinction to the earlier, ill-formulated fumblings in which many of us are undoubtedly more interested. "Often the report of one trained surveyor outlasts the braying of a thousand heroes."[2] But the identification of science with its mathematical structure is mostly a modern phenomenon, Leibniz to the contrary notwithstanding; witness Newton's evident seriousness about the aether, or other causes for gravitation, or the nineteenth-century preoccupation with mechanical models. These impress us with their general barrenness. But the idea of an undulatory aether was at one time not fruitless, and the idea of the atom is still alive. A model may serve as a scaffold for a mathematical theory, and in the process become itself stripped of its initial substantiality, its impress surviving in the abstractions of the theory. On the other hand, if not so embodied, the model may become a curiosity, an object on a junk-pile. Perhaps Rutherford's atom is an example of the former, and Boscovich's of the latter situation. Boscovich has been forgotten by the scientists, although now he has been enjoying a vogue among the historians. It would be easy to dismiss this as symptomatic of the superficiality of the last-named profession, if it were not that so many of the nine-teenth-century scientists did at least pay Boscovich lip service. The development of concepts is as important to science as their subsequent inclusion in a mathematical theory. Unfortunately, it is also a good deal more obscure.

NOTES

[1] *Théorie Mathèmatique des Phènoménes Electro-dynamiques Uniquement Déduite de l'Expérience* (Paris, 1827), p. 2.

[2] C. Truesdell, *Six Lectures on Modern Natural Philosophy* (New York, 1966), p. 90.

ARTHUR E. WOODRUFF

E. L. SCHÜCKING

Newtonian Cosmology*

INTRODUCTION

N EWTONIAN COSMOLOGY IS THE APPLICATION OF NEWTON'S THEORY OF
gravitation to the universe as a whole. This theory was put forward by Milne
and McCrea in 1935. Its naming after Newton may not be very well justified
because Newton was—modulo my ignorance in Newtonology—not successful in such
a world-wide application of his theory. The only evidence known to me that he had
thought about this possibility is his letter to Richard Bentley of December 10, 1692

> ... if the matter was evenly disposed, throughout an infinite space [he wrote]
> ... some of it would convene into one mass and some into another, so as to
> make an infinite number of great masses, scattered at great distances from one
> to another throughout all that infinite space. And thus might the sun and fixed
> stars be formed. ...

It may be interesting, however, to discuss the question why such a simple and
beautiful theory as Newtonian Cosmology was not already formulated centuries ago.
I shall describe Newtonian Cosmology briefly in its crudest form and then discuss in
turn conceptual difficulties of this theory which may have been responsible for the
strange delay in its formulation.

A. NEWTONIAN COSMOLOGY

The universe is taken as a three-dimensional Euclidean space homogeneously
filled with matter of density $\rho = \rho(t)$ called the substratum. Consider two arbitrary
points A and B of the substratum with distance $R = R(t)$. We compute then the
acceleration of B with respect to A as if it were caused by the mass contained in a
sphere with center A and radius $R(t)$.

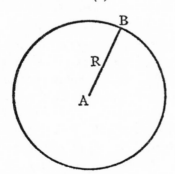

$$\ddot{R} = -\frac{GM}{R^2}, \qquad (1)$$

$$M = \frac{4\pi}{3}\rho R^3 = \text{const.}$$

* Supported by Grant AF-AFOSR 454–65.

The infinite amount of matter outside this sphere is neglected. The motion is assumed to be purely radial $\vec{x} = R(t)\, \vec{x_0}$, $\vec{x_0} =$ const. and thus by eliminating $\vec{x_0}$ we have

$$\dot{\vec{x}} = \vec{v} = \dot{R}(t)\vec{x_0} = \frac{\dot{R}}{R}\vec{x}.$$

The sphere is thus frozen into the substratum. Equation (1) is the equation of the Kepler-problem for purely radial motion, i.e., vanishing angular momentum. It must have been well known to Newton because this is the differential equation which describes in the absence of a resisting medium the motion of a falling apple. A first integral of (1) is obtained by multiplication with $\dot{R}$. We get

$$\tfrac{1}{2}\dot{R}^2 = \frac{GM}{R} + h, \quad h = \text{const.}$$

We call this energy integral the Friedman equation. For $h < 0$ (elliptic case) we obtain the cycloid solution

$$R = \frac{GM}{-2h}(1 - \cos\tau); \quad \pm\sqrt{-2h}\,(t - t_0) = \frac{GM}{-2h}(\tau - \sin\tau),$$

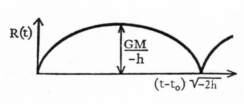

which describes the locus at the rim of a wheel with radius $\dfrac{GM}{-2h}$ rolling on the time-axis. By putting $h = -c^2$ and taking $\tau = \dfrac{\pi}{2}$ one obtains the Newtonian analogue of the presently most fashionable model of a spherical or elliptical universe in Einstein's theory of gravitation with R as its radius of curvature. So much for Newtonian Cosmology.

B. THE NOTION OF THE UNIVERSE

(a.) The idea that the cosmos is a time-dependent dynamical system appears in many primitive creation and destruction myths, as given by the Bible for example. Though a commonplace in the mind of man, to accord it serious consideration as a scientific notion based on sound principles was a revolutionary thought of extreme boldness. The protagonist, as far as I know, was Alexander Friedman, a Russian meteorologist and aviation champion of dubious morals. How shocking and surprising this Friedmanian idea was is illustrated by the following incident.

When Friedman published his paper in 1922 in the *Zeitschrift für Physik*, Einstein saw it and checked Friedman's calculations. He found an error and published an anti-Friedman paper in the *Zeitschrift* in which he expressed his satisfaction that

General Relativity was vindicated by showing that a non-static universe did not exist. This actually, he maintained, was the true significance of Friedman's calculation. Soon afterwards Einstein learned, however, that not Friedman but he, himself, had committed the mathematical felony of dividing by zero and he wrote a short, sour note in the *Zeitschrift für Physik* confessing his guilt without expressing any satisfaction about the existence of the totally new solutions of his field equations.

Friedman's idea that the universe was not static and eternal like a crystal but ephemeral like the fireworks of a gigantic explosion is one of the most far reaching and fascinating concepts ever conceived by a scientist. Since the historians of science have not quite kept up with "The Roaring Twenties" you might search in vain for his biography in non-Soviet encyclopedias. Newtonian Cosmology in the pre-Friedmanian area was plainly incapable of explaining the static universe of Democritus and Bruno where all change and evolution were no more than the ripples of waves on an eternal ocean. Friedman's equation $\ddot{R} = -GM/R^2$ had no solution R = const.

(implying $\ddot{R} = 0$) for $M > 0$, $R > 0$. This theory appeared automatically wrong when held against the static background of conventional thinking about the cosmos.

I shall introduce here a side remark on Sir Isaac's cosmology as sketched in the Bentley letter. He was perhaps considering as the initial phase the state of highest dilution of matter in the cycloid universe for maximum R introducing a perturbation that led to condensation, i.e., breakup into protostar clouds. But apparently he did not see that the system as a whole had to collapse. Perhaps he never worked it out.

(b.) *Spatial Extension.* The universe of modern science is approximately homogeneous. That means the density of the averaged mass-distribution is spatially constant. This cosmos is a world without center. Democritus may have had this idea already, Cusanus got hold of it in his mystical deliberations, and Bruno became the Jesus Christ of this new *Weltanschauung.*

Bruno's concept of an infinite centerless universe, populated by an infinite number of suns separated by the immensely vast, dark, empty, and silent interstellar spaces marks a turning point in man's thinking about the universe. The so-called Copernican revolution, though important for finding the laws of nature, was a mere trifling correction to our picture of the universe, an irrelevant amendment to local topography. One wonders whether historians who take Copernicus so seriously are not still mistaking one little planetary system for the universe.

Such an attitude, prevalent in Newton's day and after, makes it difficult to try an ansatz $\rho = \rho(t)$ for the universe, since this is a very poor approximation for the solar system. As Newton's fourth letter to Dick Bentley shows, he got fed up with initial homogeneity pretty soon because he could not explain the angular momentum of the planets in this way.

Kant's revival of Bruno's idea did not break the spell because soon a serious objection to this concept was raised. E. Halley and then Olbers pointed out that an even density of luminous matter leads to an infinite surface brightness of the sky (Olbers' paradox). We know that the darkness of the night sky simply expresses the fact that the universe expands because the redshift dims the light of the distant sources.

It was only after the advent of Hubble's observations that the homogeneous model of Newtonian Cosmology became the simplest and most natural ansatz for this theory.

C. THE INERTIAL SYSTEM

Newton's *Principia* has one important flaw that is not usually mentioned at all in modern physics textbooks. It concerns the definition of an inertial system and though it can be circumvented in the discussion of finite systems, it shows up unavoidably in any theory of a homogeneous universe.

The serious flaw in Newton's principles is that an operational definition of an inertial system can be given only in the absence of matter. By a *Gedanken* experiment Newton was able to define a nonrotating reference system but he was unable to fix the system operationally with respect to purely translational accelerations. When treating the mechanics of the solar system he simply assumed that the center of mass of the planetary system rests with respect to the absolute space. Such an assumption does not cause trouble in systems with a total finite mass for which a center of mass can be defined. But for a universe with an infinite total mass this trick no longer works. In a homogeneous non-empty universe immediately the question crops up: where is the inertial system? And Newton's reference to absolute space is no help whatsoever in determining the translational degree of freedom of an inertial system.

Let us look at the situation in the homogeneous universe described earlier where the acceleration of point B with respect to point A was computed. We had silently assumed that A had an inertial system fixed in the origin when we did our calculation, but A was not distinguished in any way. We could do the same calculation with a sphere through A centered on B and would get the same relative acceleration between A and B. But this time B would own the inertial system. If we allow such systems as fixed in A and B to be inertial systems we are immediately at variance with Newton's *Principia* because according to his principles inertial systems may not have relative accelerations. This seems to indicate clearly that Newtonian theory is simply not applicable to systems with infinite mass. After Milne and McCrea had proposed Newtonian cosmology Kurth raised this objection to their treatment and came to the same conclusion. But it might well be that other people had looked into that matter earlier, and had discarded a Newtonian Cosmology on the grounds that the introduction of an inertial system would spoil the dynamical homogeneity: A has it but not B.

D. THE RANGE OF GRAVITATION

There was another point in the foregoing derivation that must undoubtedly have aroused suspicion: the assumption that one could simply neglect the gravitational

E. L. SCHÜCKING

field contributed by all the matter outside the sphere about A. This assumption must appear to be quite arbitrary when one computes the gravitational potential from the formula

$$\phi\left(\vec{x}\right) = \int \frac{d^3\vec{x}' \, \rho(\vec{x}',t)}{\left|\vec{x} - \vec{x}'\right|}$$

since this integral is plainly divergent. This difficulty was already troubling astronomers in the nineteenth century. Seeliger and Neumann proposed to vary the $\frac{1}{r^2}$-force or the $\frac{1}{r}$-potential to a $\frac{1}{r^2}e^{-\lambda r}$-force or a $\frac{1}{r}e^{-\lambda r}$-potential, respectively. The last expression is the so-called static Yukawa potential and corresponds to a finite rest mass for the particle field connected with gravitation. Both proposals would lead to a finite expression for the gravitational potential of homogeneous mass distributions. Since there was no empirical justification for this arbitrary alteration of a fundamental law, these proposals were not well received. Herr Geheimrat Professor Dr. Hugo von Seeliger, the czar of late nineteenth-century astronomy in Germany, could not prevent a virtually unknown "observator" at the Berlin Observatory from daring to question his views in this matter in the *Astronomische Nachrichten!* Even German demigods were not safe in questioning Newton's law. The potential difficulty also stressed by Einstein in his 1916 popular book on relativity led to the generally accepted conclusion that Newtonian theory is not applicable to infinite systems.

E. A SELF-CONSISTENT NEWTONIAN THEORY

The difficulties mentioned above make it understandable that Newtonian Cosmology was formulated so belatedly and seemed to offer so little appeal after its invention. Its main asset, however, was that it gave exactly the same equations for the time development of the universe as the Friedman theory and allowed for a much simpler derivation.

From the point of view of Einstein's theory of gravitation it was not difficult to see how the conceptual structure of the theory had to be mended. Instead of inertial systems one had to introduce local inertial systems and the gravitational potential had to be transformed in a transition from one such system to another. Besides this, new relaxed boundary conditions were necessary for the determination of the potential. With these conceptual changes the theory was also capable of dealing with infinite mass distributions.

It is, however, well known that Newton's theory is only a very good approximation for the description of gravity and not compatible with the local validity of special relativity. Newton's theory as compared to Einstein's plays a role in physics like the Bohr theory compared to quantum mechanics—a useful and simple approximation that sometimes allows us to derive correct results in a much simpler way.

JÜRGEN EHLERS

Comment

Since I am in agreement with Professor Schücking about the contents of Newtonian Cosmology, rather than criticize his paper I should like to take up again a few items which have been mentioned briefly in his lecture and which, in my opinion, deserve elaboration, in particular since these matters are closely related to several discussions which we heard during this symposium.

The questions I wish to discuss are these: How are inertial frames of reference defined in Newtonian Mechanics, and what is the relation between any two such frames?

The defining property of an inertial frame F is that every free particle, i.e., every particle not subject to forces, moves with constant velocity in a straight line relative to F. To obtain such a frame, we could choose a free particle O as the origin of a (spatial) rectangular Cartesian coordinate system (x, y, z), and construct the axes such that other free particles move in straight lines also. The last prescription (or Newton's famous bucket-experiment or Foucault's pendulum experiment) serves to define "nonrotating" coordinate axes.

Before we can accept this definition of an inertial frame we have to ask: How do we identify in reality a free particle?

To exclude electromagnetic forces we should take electrically neutral particles (with vanishing electric and magnetic moments); to exclude friction we should have the particles moving in a vacuum. Assuming that this can be done, we still have to ask: How can we remove the gravitational force acting on our particle?

As far as we know, we cannot shield particles from the gravitational attraction of other bodies. Moreover, all types of test particles—whatever their chemical constitution, or shape, or size—move in the same orbit in a given gravitational field, if they are released from the same initial position with the same initial velocity. This fact has been tested already by Newton, and it has been confirmed by Dicke, Roll, and Krotkov at Princeton in 1963 with staggering accuracy (10^{-11}). Hence, we cannot eliminate the gravitational force, if we experiment in a given region of space-time.

A way out of this difficulty which would, in principle, work if the masses of the universe were confined to a bounded region of space would be to remove test particles from all the gravitating bodies, and set up an inertial frame of reference by observing these asymptotically free particles.

However—and here cosmology enters the discussion—observations indicate that the observable part of the universe, which at present has a radius of about 10^{10} light years, is more or less uniformly filled with clusters of galaxies, and there seems to be no sign of a dimming out of matter at large distances which would suggest an "island-universe." Moreover, most scientists would find it necessary or at least very desirable that the identification of an inertial frame, so fundamental for dynamics, should be based on criteria which require only local laws and local observations.

For these reasons, the above characterization of inertial frames is rejected—not, admittedly, for iron-clad logical or empirical reasons, but because of that somewhat vague mixture of "empirical evidence" and "programmatic principles" which leads scientists to change their fundamental assumptions whenever they become convinced that a new set of assumptions will provide a truer model of reality—whatever that may mean.

In our case, the new proposal, which has been made (after preliminary work by E. A. Milne and W. H. McCrea, 1934) by O. Heckmann and E. Schücking in 1955, consists of rejecting as fictitious the concepts of "free particle" and "inertial frame" in their original sense, and replacing them by "freely falling particle" and "nonrotating frame": In a nonrotating frame, a freely falling particle, i.e., a particle subject only to gravitational forces, moves in accordance with the law

$$\ddot{\vec{x}} = \vec{g}\,(\vec{x},t),$$

where $\vec{g}$ is a vector field called the gravitational field relative to the frame considered. It follows that if F is such a nonrotating frame, then every frame F^1 the axes of which have constant angles with those of F is again such a frame, whether F^1 has a (translational) acceleration with respect to F or not. So, in the new dynamics, even the acceleration of a particle has no absolute meaning; it can be arbitrarily changed by changing the frame of reference.

It has been shown that Newtonian mechanics can be reformulated without difficulty such that these "nonrotating frames" take the place of the previous inertial frames (the "body alpha" of C. Neumann) or the still earlier absolute space of Newton.

The modified theory of dynamics removes a discrepancy between "local" mechanics and cosmology which existed in the earlier version of the former: In conventional mechanics, only frames in uniform relative motion are considered as dynamically equivalent, whereas in cosmology a basic assumption, the cosmological principle, states that all frames of reference attached to "typical" galaxies are dynamically equivalent, in spite of the fact that the latter are accelerated relative to each other.

A second merit of the modified theory is that it narrows the gap between Einstein's general theory of relativity and "Newtonian" mechanics: Accelerated frames are considered as equivalent for the same reason as in Einstein's theory, and the "guiding field" which is responsible for the motion of freely falling particles is considered as determined by the distribution of masses (and, possibly, symmetry or boundary conditions); it cannot be split without arbitrariness into an inertial field (the body alpha) and a gravitational field.

These considerations show that Newtonian mechanics is still an evolving part of physics which helps us to understand new branches of empirical science as well as it aids us in clarifying, by means of comparison and analogy, the meaning of more recent and more abstract theories.

REFERENCES

O. Heckmann and E. Schücking, Z. *Astrophysik 38*, 95–109 (1955); 40, 81–92 (1956), and earlier papers cited therein.

A. Trautman, contribution to *Perspectives in Geometry and Relativity*, B. Hoffmann (ed.), pp. 413–425, Indiana University Press, 1966.

H. Weyl, *Philosophy of Mathematics and Natural Science*, Atheneum, New York, 1963; especially Part II, chapter I, section 16.

PHILOSOPHICAL ANALYSIS OF NEWTON'S SCIENTIFIC ACHIEVEMENTS

ROBERT PALTER

Newton and the Inductive Method

To the Memory of Robert Hamilton Boyer, December 1, 1932–August 1, 1966

THE HYPOTHETICO-DEDUCTIVE METHOD DOMINATES METHODOLOGICAL TALK about science today. Two quotations, both very recent, will illustrate this. In the words of a scientist, "The method actually used by science is a combination of induction, inspiration, and deduction; it is called the *hypothetico-deductive* method . . .";[1] in the words of a philosopher, "the hypothetico-deductive method [is] the coping stone of our present-day science."[2] As for what constitutes the hypothetico-deductive method, there is pretty general agreement that it involves (1) the *formulation* of a hypothesis, (2) the *deduction* of consequences of this hypothesis, and (3) the *testing* of these consequences by observation and experiment.[3] This three-step pattern of formulation-deduction-testing goes back at least to Christiaan Huygens who states it quite explicitly in the preface to his *Treatise on Light* (1690).[4] It should not go unnoticed, however, that Huygens introduces at the very beginning of his treatise what is in effect a severe restriction on the application of the method, when he insists that any truly *explanatory* hypothesis in physics must be formulated in terms of "mechanical motions." Scientists and philosophers today are fond of reiterating that we have outgrown this commitment to a narrowly conceived "mechanical philosophy," but surely even our vaunted permissiveness in the choice of scientific hypotheses has *some* limits, dictated by pragmatic historical considerations (what kind of hypotheses have worked well in the past?), if not by *a priori* ontological considerations (what are the ultimate categories of physical reality?). But I hasten to say that my point here is only to suggest the existence of important complexities lurking behind the familiar three-step pattern, and not at all to impugn the usefulness of that pattern as a methodological construct.

If analysis of the hypothetico-deductive method has brought to the fore what might be called the *logical* role of hypotheses in scientific explanation and testing, analysis of experimental procedure has disclosed what might be called the *heuristic* role of hypotheses in suggesting and interpreting experiments. I would emphasize that the distinction I have in mind is that between two *roles* played by hypotheses in scientific investigations rather than between two *kinds* of hypotheses. It may be, of course, that certain kinds of hypotheses are more suitable for playing one of these two roles rather than the other. Thus, an extremely vague hypothesis or a hypothesis based on analogy may be untestable at a certain time and yet serve to call attention to a particular realm of phenomena and even to suggest specific observations and experiments to be made on these phenomena. A precisely formulated hypothesis on the other hand—perhaps a mathematically formulated hypothesis—will often be testable by the very experiments it suggests, though it *may* also suggest experiments that do not bear at all on its own validity.

Recent discussions of what I have called the heuristic role of hypotheses often seem to echo older views. Thus, we find Duhem arguing that in physics—if not in more primitive sciences such as physiology—"it is impossible to leave outside the laboratory door the theory that we wish to test, for without theory it is impossible to regulate a single instrument or to interpret a single reading."[5] The first part of this assertion seems unexceptionable: one's experimental design is inevitably influenced by the theory one intends to test. (Whether there can be significant experiments which are not designed as tests of theories at all is a question to which we will come presently—indeed it constitutes one of my basic themes.) Furthermore, the regulation and interpretation of one's instruments may very well involve a complex set of theories. What is not clear, however, is that the latter set of theories will necessarily include the theory being tested; and indeed in another place Duhem seems to say that the physicist interprets an experiment in terms of "the theories he regards as established,"[6] which presumably do *not* include the theory being tested.

(In failing to distinguish hypotheses and theories—not to mention laws—I have simply been following many of the recent expositors of the hypothetico-deductive method. Such failure may beg important methodological questions. My concern here, however, is less with critical evaluation of the hypothetico-deductive method than with Newton's conception of the inductive method. For my purposes it will also be possible to forego any elaborate inquiry into Newton's use of the term "hypothesis.")

One other role of hypothesis (or theory) in science which has been much emphasized of late is the *semantical* one, that is to say, the way in which the meanings of scientific terms reflect the character of the hypotheses one accepts. Once again, this view has been anticipated by Duhem, who writes, "According to whether we adopt one theory or another, the very words which figure in a physical law change their meaning. . . ." On the other hand, it should be noted that Duhem exempts the entire class of what he calls "commonsense laws" from this sweeping semantical thesis, so that "the law 'We see the flash of lightning before we hear thunder' has for the physicist who knows thoroughly the laws of disruptive electrical discharge the same clarity and certainty as it had for the Roman plebeian who saw in a stroke of lightning the anger of Capitoline Jupiter."[7] Some contemporary philosophers have been far less cautious, with consequences that are more paradoxical than enlightening.[8]

Summing up, then, we may say that recent methodological discussions of science have attributed three distinct roles to hypotheses (or theories):

(1) Hypotheses function *logically* in explanation and testing.

(2) Hypotheses function *heuristically* in suggesting and interpreting experiments.

(3) Hypotheses function *semantically* in helping to specify the meanings of certain terms.

While there is every reason to suspect that these three roles of hypotheses have significant interrelations, any uncritical conflation of the three will very likely lead to confusions and paradoxes.[9] What I wish particularly to stress here, however, is the effect which this fixation on hypotheses or theories has had on the study of the nontheoretical or purely *inductive* side of scientific investigation.

The problem of induction—construed as the search for some rationally comprehensible connection between past events and future contingencies, or more generally between evidence and hypothesis—is widely discussed in philosophy today. But induction as a method—not simply some vague generalized appeal to empirical data but a deliberate process of deriving or eliciting generalizations from observations and experiments—is out of favor among philosophers of science. The pejorative term "inductivism" has been introduced to refer to a method which, we are told, is doomed to futility no matter how inspired its practitioners because it is in principle impossible to apply. My own claim in this paper is that Newton both characterized an inductive method[10] and used it in some of his most important scientific work, and furthermore that this method is fundamental to empirical science. Newton's formulation of his inductive method occurs in each of his two major published books on natural philosophy: in Book III of the *Principia* as "Rules of Reasoning in Philosophy" and in Query 31 of the *Opticks* as "the Method of Analysis." There is, I believe, no essential difference in the two formulations, but I quote the latter passage since my central concern will be with certain aspects of Newton's optical studies.

"As in Mathematicks, so in Natural Philosophy, the Investigation of difficult Things by the Method of Analysis, ought ever to precede the Method of Composition. This Analysis consists in making Experiments and Observations, and in drawing general Conclusions from them by Induction, and admitting of no Objections against the Conclusions, but such as are taken from Experiments, or other certain Truths. For Hypotheses are not to be regarded in experimental Philosophy. And although the arguing from Experiments and Observations by Induction be no Demonstration of general Conclusions; yet it is the best way of arguing which the Nature of Things admits of, and may be looked upon as so much the stronger, by how much the Induction is more general. And if no Exception occur from Phænomena, the Conclusion may be pronounced generally. But if at any time afterwards any Exception shall occur from Experiments, it may then begin to be pronounced with such Exceptions as occur."[11] I do not claim that this Newtonian inductive method is the *only* method of science, nor do I claim that it should be preferred to all other scientific methods. Indeed, I hold that Huygens' hypothetico-deductive method is complementary to Newton's inductive method, and that Newton and Huygens

ROBERT PALTER

use *both* methods, sometimes in a single investigation. For example, the very structure of Newton's first publication (the letter of 1671-2 on light and colors) consists of successive applications of the hypothetico-deductive method (to refute various unacceptable explanations of Newton's elongated solar spectrum), and the inductive method (to establish the correct explanation); while the over-all hypothetico-deductive structure of Huygens' *Treatise on Light* has room for certain subordinate but highly important inductive investigations (such as Huygens' measurement of the crystallographic angles of Iceland spar). The uniquely important fact about the Newtonian inductive method is that it is, at bottom, responsible for the objectivity and the cumulative character of science. These features of science it would be paradoxical and intellectually irresponsible to deny, and I must confess uncertainty as to whether any recent critics of inductivism seriously *intend* to deny them whatever the apparent tendency of their arguments.

I turn now for an illustration of Newton's inductive method to his investigation of optical interference phenomena and in particular of the "rings" which bear his name. Newton himself was not, of course, the first to observe these colored rings, and indeed his interest in the rings had very likely been awakened by a reading of Hooke's *Micrographia* not long after its publication (which was at the very beginning of 1665). Hooke had described the regular "consecution" (or succession) of colors, comparing it to the rainbow though, as he pointed out, the order of the colors was different in the two cases. Hooke also recognized the dependence of the rings on the thickness of the transparent medium in which they appeared; below a certain thickness and above a certain thickness the rings disappeared, but Hooke did not succeed in actually measuring these limits. On the basis of these considerations it is not unreasonable to say that Newton was motivated in his investigation of the rings by Hooke's hypothesis of an underlying periodicity in the regular succession of colors. Using my earlier distinction, however, I should want to add that this hypothesis was functioning heuristically rather than logically in Newton's investigation: though much too vague to use as a premise for deducing quantitative consequences, Hooke's hypothesis was apparently capable of initiating Newton's successful search for that method of measuring the thickness of the medium which had eluded Hooke himself. Not the hypothetico-deductive method then, but the method of analysis—the inductive method—was used by Newton "to discover and prove the original Differences of the Rays of Light in respect of Refrangibility, Reflexibility, and Colour, and their alternative Fits of easy Reflexion and easy Transmission. . . ."[12] "Discover and prove": like his fellow inductivist J. S. Mill, Newton holds that the inductive method is capable both of *discovering* and of *proving* "general conclusions." "Proof" here does not refer to a species of strict logical or deductive reasoning; the latter is usually called "demonstration" by Newton, who restricts its use to mathematics including, of course, the mathematical principles of natural philosophy or rational mechanics.[13] Viewed only as a procedure of *proof* (in this qualified sense), Newton's inductive method will be acceptable to some in the form of a program whose goal would be a system of rules (sometimes called an inductive logic) for assigning "degrees of proof," or probabilities, to hypotheses on various possible sets of evidential data. But such a system of rules, if achievable at all, would almost certainly bear little resemblance to the actual processes of scientific discovery, Newton's or anyone else's. It should be added that proponents of inductive logic join most other philosophers of science today in rejecting the very possibility of a "logic of discovery." On the other hand, the key to understanding Newton's inductive method lies, I believe, in a recognition of just this interdependence of proof and discovery: the initial evidence for the conclusion is just that it was discovered by means of a properly designed experiment—what Newton calls a "crucial experiment." This does not of course preclude *further* testing (or "proving")[14] of the conclusion by additional experiments, that is, by means of the hypothetico-deductive method. But the "general conclusions" to which Newton refers are not first *discovered* by guesswork or plausible hypothesizing and only then *confirmed* by amassing empirical evidence.[15]

It follows that a close analysis of Newton's experiments is essential for an understanding of his inductive method. Immediately we appear to be confronted with a methodological problem of our own. Which of Newton's various accounts of a given experiment shall we study: the published or the unpublished version, the original, rudimentary or the later, elaborated version? In fact, I believe our results with respect to the nature of Newton's inductive method will be relatively independent of which versions we study, though of course in practice one will want to examine all available versions. But I'm afraid that the above methodological point may be seized on by some philosophers in order to insinuate the thesis that every experiment is essentially conditioned by the theoretical commitments of the experimenter so that, for example, if Newton changed his views on the optical aether over a period of time, then any optical experiments performed by him during this period would similarly change in significance—he would not be performing or even discussing the "same" experiment if his optical theory had altered. I reject this dogma, just as surely as Newton would have rejected it. Newton was well aware of the necessity for restraining the influence of one's theories on one's observations; thus, in some early notes on Hooke's *Micrographia* (probably written within several years of its publication) Newton accuses Hooke at one point of "fram[ing] his observation to his erroneous Hypothesis."[16] The opposite dogma is equally misguided, namely, the notion that there is some pristine Ur-Experiment which, if we could only reconstruct it from Newton's writings, would give us the pure uninterpreted data on which Newton, whatever his practice, ought to have relied. There is no such experiment and there are no such data. But this does not mean that there can be no reproducible experiments or reproducible experimental results—some ideal of reproducibility independent of the experimenter's particular conceptual and

ROBERT PALTER

physical apparatus indeed constitutes the guiding principle of any competent experimenter. Let me, however, turn to particulars.

Book II of Newton's *Opticks* (first edition: 1704) deals mainly with interference phenomena produced by reflecting light from the surfaces of thin transparent media. The first two parts of Book II and much of Part III (everything through Prop. VIII) are transcribed practically verbatim from the "Discourse of Observations" which was read at several meetings of the Royal Society in 1675–76; the remainder of Part III and all of Part IV are new. Further, the fundamental observations and measurements on the colored rings between two contiguous lenses with which Part I opens may be traced back to two early Newton manuscripts, one written about 1666 and the other a few years later.[17] Not only do the later experimental techniques often resemble the earlier, but sometimes we find that the same piece of apparatus has been used repeatedly over a period of years (e.g., a certain biconvex lens whose radius of curvature is taken as 100 feet in one of the manuscripts reappears in the "Discourse of Observations" and the *Opticks* with a corrected radius of 102 feet together with Newton's recognition of a slight difference in curvature of the two faces). As far as Newton's theoretical commitments go, two things must be kept in mind. First, Newton seems never to have wavered in his belief that light consists of corpuscles, nor in his fundamental argument against the pulse theory of light, namely, that light could not travel in straight lines if, like sound, it consisted of pulses in a medium.[18] However, it must be added that Newton did have to modify his early belief that his optical researches on color would provide detailed support for the corpuscle theory of light.[19] Thus, the corpuscles which figure so prominently in Newton's early optical writings are deliberately excluded from the original text of the *Opticks*[20] and reappear only in the Queries. Second, Newton's attitude toward an optical aether seems to have undergone significant shifts during the years from 1666 (the probable date of his earliest systematic essay on colors) to 1717 (the date of the second English edition of the *Opticks*). Part of the evidence for this is the fact that in his earliest optical writings Newton does not hesitate to include even within the confines of a single "proposition" experimental results on the one hand and speculative talk about an aether medium on the other;[21] while in the *Opticks* the aether has no place at all until Queries 17–23 are added to the second English edition. The reasons behind this shift in Newton's ideas on aether, while not entirely clear, are certainly complex. Mr. Westfall has suggested as one decisive reason that by the time that Newton was composing the *Opticks* he no longer believed in the possibility of an aether medium pervading all space.[22] This requires us to assume that Newton later reversed himself once again on the subject of the aether when he accorded it a central explanatory role in the Queries of the *Opticks*. While I find nothing inherently implausible about this account, I should like to suggest another account (not necessarily incompatible with the former) based on a possible evolution in Newton's methodological ideas. Why not assume that Newton gradually came to the view that proper method in natural philosophy required a strict separation of inductively established generalizations and of speculative hypotheses? After all, we have already noted that Newton did *not* ever alter his views about the nature of light; the exclusion of light corpuscles from the *Opticks* can perhaps be explained then by a methodological prohibition against mixing propositions derived from optical phenomena and speculative hypotheses—no matter how probable—concerning the ultimate nature of light.

In his study of the colored rings Newton used essentially a single experimental technique for producing the rings: he pressed together two glasses, generally either prisms or lenses, and when this pair of glass surfaces with an air layer between them was observed by means of reflected or transmitted light, the colored rings made their appearance. Newton focuses his attention on certain properties of the colored rings; these include their number, color, relative intensity, breadth, and size, as well as the thickness of the transparent medium corresponding to a given ring. Since it is not the color as such that interests Newton, but rather the orderly recurrence of rings of the same color, we see that all six of these properties are in the broad sense "mathematical" (though only three of the properties—number, size, and thickness of medium—are actually counted or measured by Newton).[23] The entire series of experiments on the rings may be summarized by saying that in each experiment Newton studies either a correlation between two of these properties or else the effect on one or more of them of varying some one factor in the experimental arrangement. The factors varied include the angle of the incident light (or, what amounts to the same thing, the angle at which the rings are viewed); the direction in which the rings are viewed (i.e., either by reflected or by transmitted light); the color of the incident light; and the nature of the thin layer of transparent medium (air, water, glass, or mica). The experimental results are described in twenty-four "Observations." What we get under this rubric are not "raw data" but rather in each case a reasonably careful account of the experimental arrangement and a generalization based on—or as Newton says "collected" from—the experimental data.

I will not pause to summarize these observations but turn instead to Newton's attempt to derive from his observations on the colors of "thin transparent plates" a series of generalizations concerning the broad topic of the interaction of light and bodies. That these generalizations are formulated as numbered "Propositions" is an indication of the importance and the degree of cogency which Newton attached to them. Beginning with some seven propositions on the colors of natural bodies, Part III of Book II of the *Opticks* goes on to attempt a mechanical explanation of reflection and refraction in terms of hypothetical forces, and then after a proposition asserting the finite velocity of light (to which, up to this point in the *Opticks*, Newton had deliberately avoided committing himself), concludes with the famous sequence of propositions on fits of easy transmission and easy reflection. What I wish to draw attention to is the argument Newton uses to introduce the "fits." The first and fundamental proposition (XII) on the fits may be paraphrased as follows: Every ray of light, while passing through a refracting medium, oscillates between two periodically varying states consisting in a disposition to be either easily transmitted or easily reflected when it reaches the surface of the next refracting medium. The recurrences of the disposition to be easily transmitted are called *fits of easy transmission*; the recurrences of the disposition to be easily reflected are called *fits of easy reflection*; and the space traversed between recurrences of fits of the same type is called the *interval of the fits*.

The key experimental result on which Newton bases this proposition is the mathematical rule expressing a simple periodic relation between thickness of the air layer between two contiguous lenses and the corresponding recurrence of alternating colored and dark rings. The succession of integers representing relative thicknesses of air layer starts with zero (where the lenses are in contact and the air layer therefore vanishes) and continues indefinitely to higher and higher values (since there appears to be no natural upper limit to the diameter of the rings and hence to the thickness of the corresponding air layer). Thus, by an obvious application of Newton's principle that "Nature . . . is wont to be simple, and always consonant to itself,"[24]—which Newton himself doesn't in this context even bother to mention—one obtains the desired generalization (Proposition XII).

Has Newton succeeded in merely generalizing the measured periodicity of the colored rings in thin transparent plates or has he, more or less covertly, introduced a speculative element into his account of fits? I believe there can be little doubt that such an element is present in Newton's account, but it is worth seeing exactly where and how it enters. That light-rays possess *some* spatial and temporal periodicity is a proposition which is still perfectly acceptable today (and *a fortiori* it should have been perfectly acceptable to all post-Newtonian opticians). The critical questions to be answered concerning Newton's particular formulation of this periodicity are two: first, what are these *rays* which are said to possess the fits; second, what are the two opposite *states* whose recurrence constitutes the fits?

The notion of a light-ray was introduced by the Greeks and has persisted throughout the entire later history of optics; furthermore, throughout that history light-rays were consistently represented in the geometrical guise of straight lines; and finally, light-rays have close observational counterparts in visible *light beams* (as when light is reflected from tiny particles of dust). Nevertheless there is a fundamental ambiguity in the notion, stemming from the various possible answers to the question of just what it is that moves when one speaks of the propagation of light. Newton makes a determined effort to undercut this ambiguity by defining light-rays in what might be called a "quasi-operational" mode. This definition, with which the *Opticks* opens, goes as follows: "By the Rays of Light I understand its least Parts, and those as well

Successive in the same Lines, as Contemporary in several Lines." And Newton's comment on the definition is this:

> For it is manifest that Light consists of Parts, both Successive and Contemporary; because in the same place you may stop that which comes one moment, and let pass that which comes presently after; and in the same time you may stop it in any one place, and let it pass in any other.[25]

I call the definition quasi-operational because, though formulated in terms of actually performable operations ("stopping" light or "letting it pass"), these operations may become inapplicable before the conceptual limit referred to in the definiens—"the least Light or part of Light"—can be reached. In view of the existence of diffraction effects the operations in question do in fact become inapplicable when one attempts to reduce the size of a light beam too much (relative to the wave length of the light) by interposing opaque barriers in its path. Newton, of course, knew of and indeed studied certain diffraction effects, but it is doubtful if he recognized their serious implications for his notion of light-rays; the natural interpretation of diffraction phenomena for Newton was to assume that in passing through small apertures or near opaque barriers, the corpuscles of light were simply bent out of their straight-line paths by short-range forces. Leaving aside diffraction effects and the special circumstances in which they can be detected, however, we may say that Newton's notion of light-rays is indifferent with respect to various alternative assumptions about the nature of light. (Is light corpuscular or undulatory? Are the ultimate parts of light finite or infinitesimal in size? Is there a space-pervading medium associated with light or not?)

Turning now to the question of what constitutes a state of easy reflection, we note first of all that *reflexibility* of rays is defined by Newton as a "Disposition to be . . . turned back into the same Medium from any other Medium upon whose Surface they fall."[26] This seems straightforward enough: surely the corresponding nondispositional term "reflexion," and its correlative "transmission," are about as close to pure observational terms as one is likely to get in the science of optics, their meanings being easily specifiable with the help, if need be, of familiar objects and their properties such as mirrors and transparent substances. Furthermore, the notions of reflection and transmission of light have been employed consistently throughout the entire history of optics beginning with the Greeks. It would seem that, like the notion of a light-ray, these two notions are indifferent with respect to considerations concerning the nature of light and how it interacts with bodies; or at least that the meanings of the two notions are invariant with respect to a broadly inclusive set of optical theories.

If Newton had been content in his treatment of fits with the mere assertion of their existence while light is passing through a refracting medium, he could perhaps have forestalled certain later objections to the fits, though at the cost of impoverishing both the content and the heuristic power of his account. Instead, he both generalized the notion of fits by asserting their presence in light at all times and in all situations, and also attempted to specify somewhat more closely the connection between the fits and surfaces of refracting media. Neither of these extensions of his fundamental propositions on fits need be explained, I would emphasize, by anything like a secret addiction for speculative explanatory processes on Newton's part; both elaborations of the fits are in general accord with Newton's professed inductive method. This is obvious in the case of the generalization of the fits themselves where Newton suggests that "probably [light] is put into such fits at its first emission from luminous Bodies, and continues in them during all its progress."[27]

Turning to the interaction between fits and refractive media, we encounter in the *Opticks* (Book II, Part III, Prop. XII) the following succinct argument. (1) The alternate reflection and transmission (or refraction) of light-rays as they pass through thin plates of a refracting medium depend on *both* surfaces of the plate because they depend on the distance between the plates. This conclusion is confirmed by the fact (noted in Observation 21) that if *either* surface of a thin mica plate be moistened, the colors are weakened. (2) The actual reflection and refraction occur at the *second* surface, for if they occurred at the first surface prior to the arrival of the rays at the second surface, they would not depend on the second at all, contrary to our first conclusion. (3) The reflection and refraction must be influenced by some "action or disposition" propagated from the first surface to the second because otherwise they would not depend on the first surface at all, contrary to our first conclusion. (4) Finally, then, it is only natural to ascribe to this action or disposition the periodic character earlier ascribed to the fits. The net result of this argument is thus to leave open the possibility of splitting off the periodic character previously conceived in terms of a varying *state of the rays themselves* and attributing it instead to a new action or disposition whose existence is postulated *over and above the existence of the rays*. Newton is careful not to assert the truth or even the probability of this multiplication of optical entities but his sole mechanical illustration of the fits takes full advantage of it by referring both to light-rays and to a medium capable of propagating vibrations induced by the action of the light-rays.

I should like now to point out what I take to be the single false step in the argument we have been considering. The second step of the argument presupposes without explicitly saying so that the alternate reflection and refraction of the light-rays incident on a thin plate must take place either at the first or at the second surface, but *not at both surfaces*. Then, by excluding the first surface, Newton can conclude that the optical processes in question must take place at the second. But why couldn't there be reflection and refraction of light-rays at *both* surfaces? I see nothing in the deliberately abstract[28] formulations of Newton's argument to preclude this possibility. And indeed, Newton knew of just such a "two-surface" explanation of the colored rings in the form of Hooke's pulse-theory of light. Hooke's idea was that when a light-ray falls on the refracting medium, "part" of it is reflected and another "part" is refracted into the medium, whereupon the latter is reflected at the other surface and, after a second refraction at the initial surface, rejoins the directly reflected ray. The resulting combined pulse then somehow—and this is the weakest side of Hooke's theory—yields a light-ray of a particular spectral color.[29] Psychologically, it is perhaps not too difficult to see why Newton failed to recognize the possibility of reflection and refraction (or transmission) occurring at both surfaces of the refracting medium: he had in the first place little use for Hooke's nonquantitative account of the colored rings; but, more important, it would require some pretty ingenious speculations to explain how, on any corpuscular theory of light, the rays could be reflected and refracted at both surfaces. Most difficult to understand would be how light *transmitted* at both surfaces could yield darkness, or absence of light, since this might appear to violate expected conservation laws for light corpuscles. Still, such a hypothesis could conceivably be devised,[30] and in any case Newton's own methodology demands that as clear a line as possible be maintained between inductive reasoning and speculative hypothesis.

Let me now attempt to summarize the salient features of this discussion on the development of Newton's scientific and methodological views. It must be admitted, first of all, that in some mysterious way Newton possessed from the very outset of his scientific career an extraordinary flair for devising "crucial experiments"—by which I mean, following Newton, experiments whose results may be plausibly extrapolated into a general, usually mathematical, formula in accordance with such simple methodological rules as: "to the same natural effects we must, as far as possible, assign the same causes."[31] Newton's particular beliefs about the nature of light at no time exerted a significant influence on his choice of a particular sequence of experiments or on the technical details of any one of these experiments. That Newton experimented so painstakingly on optical periodicity can be attributed to his trust in his inductive method; Huygens, intellectually dominated by a different method (the hypothetico-deductive method), after making a few casual measurements on the colored rings, quietly dropped the subject.[32] On the other hand, Newton's varying *interpretations* of his experimental results reflected the vicissitudes of his aether concept, the gradual clarification of his methodological views, and his firm belief in a corpuscle theory of light. It seems to me that only some such account as this does justice to all that is presently known about the concrete details and the historical development of Newton's optical studies. And I take it for granted that any adequate general account of scientific inquiry ought to be capable of doing justice to Newton's optical studies—surely one of the greatest triumphs of experimental method in the early history of modern physics.

NOTES

This work was supported in part by the National Science Foundation (Grant GS-1209).
[1] Marshall Walker, *The Nature of Scientific Thought* (1963), p. 25. Note that here induc-

ROBERT PALTER

tion is taken to be *part* of the hypothetico-deductive method. Other writers *identify* the hypothetico-deductive method with induction.

". . . there are but three steps in the process of induction:—

(1) Framing some hypothesis as to the character of the general law.

(2) Deducing consequences from that law.

(3) Observing whether the consequences agree with the particular facts under consideration" (W. S. Jevons, *The Principles of Science,* 2nd ed., pp. 265–6).

And, more confusedly, F. Dessauer ascribes to Galileo the discovery of the "inductive method" which "begins with the deductive establishment of a working hypothesis" ("Galileo and Newton: The Turning Point in Western Thought," *Spirit and Nature,* ed. J. Campbell, p. 296). William Kneale warns against just this identification:

"Some logicians have been so impressed by the importance of hypotheses in what we commonly call the inductive sciences that they have confused together the notions of induction and hypothetical method, supposing all induction to be an application of the hypothetical method and every use of hypotheses an instance of induction" (*Probability and Induction,* p. 104).

[2] Paul J. Olscamp, tr., Descartes, *Discourse on Method, Optics, Geometry, and Meteorology* (1965), p. xxxiv. Olscamp sees Descartes as one of the originators of the hypothetico-deductive method.

[3] For a recent account which includes these three steps see C. B. Joynt and N. Rescher, "The Problem of Uniqueness in History," *History and Theory,* I, 2 (1961), 150–62; reprinted in G. H. Nadel, ed., *Studies in the Philosophy of History* (1965), pp. 3–15. Joynt and Rescher add a fourth step—examination of the data—which precedes the other three. The thesis of their essay is that the hypothetico-deductive method is applicable to historical investigations.

[4] R. B. Braithwaite is wrong when he writes, "it took a long time for scientists to realize that the hypothetico-deductive inductive method of science was epistemologically different from the prima facie similar deductive method of mathematics; and that, in properly imitating the deductive form of Euclid's system, they were not *ipso facto* taking over his deductive method of proof" (*Scientific Explanation,* p. 353). Huygens was perfectly clear about the distinction in question when he described his optical results as consisting of "demonstrations of those kinds which do not produce as great a certitude as those of Geometry, and which even differ much therefrom, since whereas the Geometers prove their Propositions by fixed and incontestable Principles, here the Principles are verified by the conclusions to be drawn from them; the nature of these things not allowing of this being done otherwise" (Preface, *Treatise on Light,* tr. S. P. Thompson, p. vi). And Newton was equally clear (see below, n. 13).

[5] Pierre Duhem, *The Aim and Structure of Physical Theory,* tr. P. P. Wiener (1962), p. 182. Duhem's French here is not entirely unambiguous: ". . . il ne peut plus être question de laisser à la porte du laboratoire la théorie qu'on veut éprouver, car, sans elle, il n'est pas possible de régler un seul instrument, d'interpréter une seule lecture." Does the word "elle" refer to the theory under test or, as in Wiener's translation, to theory in general (which, of course, might include the theory under test)?

[6] *Ibid.,* p. 159.

[7] *Ibid.,* p. 167.

[8] See D. Shapere, "Meaning and Scientific Change," *Mind and Cosmos,* ed. R. Colodny; P. Achinstein, "On the Meaning of Scientific Terms," *J. of Philosophy,* 61 (1964), 497–509, with P. Feyerabend's rejoinder, "On the 'Meaning' of Scientific Terms," *ibid.,* 62 (1965), 266–74; A. Fine, "Consistency, Derivability, and Scientific Change," *ibid.,* 64 (1967), 231–40; and I. Scheffler, *Science and Subjectivity* (1967).

[9] For example, it is only by distinguishing the three roles of theoretical (as opposed to observational) assertions that one is able to see the sense in which W. Craig's theorem on the replacement of auxiliary expressions does *not* make theoretical assertions dispensable in science. Though all of the deductive connections (but not necessarily all of the inductive, or probabilistic, connections) among the observational terms of a theory may be expressed by a certain set of purely observational assertions, this set is generally infinite and hence can hardly

serve the usual heuristic purposes of a theory (economical summary of many diverse results, suggestion of analogous theories in other domains, etc.). Again, there is a vast semantical difference between the original theory and the "equivalent" set of purely observational assertions in that only the former enables us to talk about theoretical entities. For the first of these points see C. Hempel, "The Theoretician's Dilemma," in *Minnesota Studies in the Philosophy of Science*, II, ed. H. Feigl *et al* (reprinted in Hempel's *Aspects of Scientific Explanation* [1965]), and C. Hempel, "Implications of Carnap's Work for the Philosophy of Science," in P. A. Schilpp, ed., *The Philosophy of Rudolf Carnap* (1963). For the second point see H. Putnam, "Craig's Theorem," *J. of Philosophy, 62*, 10 (May 13, 1965), 251–60.

[10] Given the immense prestige of the hypothetico-deductive method today, it is scarcely surprising that some students of Newton's work should attribute the formulation of the method to him. See, for example, "Isaac Newton and the Hypothetico-Deductive Method" by R. M. Blake in *Theories of Scientific Method: The Renaissance through the Nineteenth Century*, ed. E. H. Madden (1960), Chap. VI. Blake argues—incorrectly, I believe—that Newton's "true" method is precisely the hypothetico-deductive method of Huygens, but that Newton felt compelled by the exigencies of polemical debate to cast his "hypothetical" results in a misleadingly rigid geometrical mode. See nn. 4 and 13.

[11] Isaac Newton, *Opticks*, 4th ed. (reprinted 1931), p. 404.

[12] *Ibid.*, Query 31, p. 405.

[13] Compare Newton's letter to Oldenburg of June 11, 1672, H. W. Turnbull, ed., *Correspondence of Isaac Newton*, I, p. 187: "I should take notice of a casuall expression wch intimates a greater certainty in these things than I ever promised. viz: The certainty of *Mathematicall Demonstrations*. I said indeed that the *Science of Colours was Mathematicall & as certain as any other part of Optiques*; but who knows not that Optiques & many other Mathematicall Sciences depend as well on Physicall Principles as on Mathematicall Demonstrations: And the absolute certainty of a Science cannot exceed the certainty of its Principles."

[14] In Newton's time "to prove" could mean either "to establish by argument" or "to test."

[15] And surely J. M. Keynes is wrong when he says that Newton's "experiments were always, I suspect, a means, not of discovery, but always of verifying what he knew already" ("Newton, the Man," *Essays in Biography*, p. 313). Keynes wishes to have us see Newton as "the last of the magicians," but are we really to suppose that Newton's "magical" powers extended to the prediction of the quantitative results of all his optical experiments on interference and diffraction phenomena?

[16] A. R. Hall and M. B. Hall, *Unpublished Scientific Papers of Isaac Newton* (1962), p. 412. The observation in question concerns an apparent lengthening of the horizontal diameter of the sun and an apparent shortening of the perpendicular diameter, which Hooke attempts to explain by his theory of atmospheric refraction. Incidentally, Newton was also well aware of the heuristic role of hypotheses in experimental investigation: "For hypotheses should be subservient only in explaining the properties of things, but not assumed in determining them; unless so far as they may furnish experiments" (I. B. Cohen, ed., *Isaac Newton's Papers and Letters on Natural Philosophy* [1958], p. 106).

[17] The first has been published in part by A. R. Hall ("Further Optical Experiments of Isaac Newton," *Annals of Science, II*, 1 [1955], 27–43), and the second in its entirety by R. S. Westfall ("Isaac Newton's Coloured Circles twixt Two Contiguous Glasses," *Archive for History of Exact Sciences, 2*, 3 [1965], 181–96).

[18] In what must be one of his earliest writings on light, his notes on Hooke's *Micrographia*, Newton already raises this objection against Hooke's pulse theory of light (Hall and Hall, *op. cit.*, p. 403). But Hooke misunderstood. Thus he enters in his diary for January 1, 1675/6 the claim that "Mr. Newton had taken my hypothesis of the puls or wave" (*Diary of Robert Hooke 1672–1680*, ed. H. Robinson and W. Adams, p. 206). This is undoubtedly a reference to Newton's "Hypothesis of Light" (read Dec. 9 and 16, 1675, before the Royal Society), which includes the description of a mechanism designed to account for the colors of thin plates, namely, the hypothesis of "vibrations" or "waves" in an aethereal medium (I. B. Cohen, ed., *op. cit.*, pp. 185, 193; H. W. Turnbull, ed., *op. cit.*, I, pp. 370, 377–8).

ROBERT PALTER

[19] Westfall says of the paper which probably constitutes Newton's first systematic investigation of colored rings that "a good half of his initial interest in the rings lay in his expectation that they would confirm the corpuscular nature of light" (*loc. cit.*, p. 187).

[20] This policy of exclusion sometimes reaches absurd lengths. Thus, in one of Newton's attempts to demonstrate the sine law of refraction from theoretical considerations concerning the interaction between light-rays and refracting media, he refuses to specify what these rays of light might be, referring instead to "any Motion or moving thing whatsoever" (*Opticks*, p. 79) which can be acted on by a force perpendicular to the refracting surface. But what besides corpuscles could be acted on by a force? In another version of this same demonstration in the *Principia* (Book I, Section XIV) Newton does not hesitate to refer to the "moving things" as "very small bodies," although, ever cautious, he speaks of "the analogy . . . between the propagation of the rays of light and the motion of bodies . . . not at all considering the nature of the rays of light, or inquiring whether they are bodies or not; but only determining the curves of bodies which are extremely like the curves of the rays" (*Principia*, ed. F. Cajori, pp. 230–1).

[21] See, e.g., R. S. Westfall, *loc. cit.*, p. 191 (Propositions 2 and 4).

[22] See R. S. Westfall, "Uneasily Fitful Reflections on Fits of Easy Transmission," in this volume. In his hypothetical account of fits following Proposition XII, *Opticks*, Book II, Part III, Newton refers to vibrations produced by light-rays in "the refracting or reflecting Medium or Substance." The term "aether" is eschewed; whereas in an earlier version of this same hypothetical explanation, to be found in his "Hypothesis of Light" of 1675 (H. W. Turnbull, ed., *op. cit.*, I, pp. 377–8; I. Cohen, ed., *op. cit.*, p. 193), Newton refers quite explicitly to "aethereal vibrations."

[23] And, of course, for Newton color and degree of refrangibility are instances of ordered sets exhibiting a "natural" one-one correlation. In identifying the colors of light-rays, however, Newton uses only the ordinal scale of degrees of refrangibility.

[24] *Principia*, Book III, Rules of Reasoning in Philosophy, Rule II, p. 398.

[25] *Opticks*, pp. 1–2.

[26] *Opticks*, Definition III, p. 3.

[27] *Opticks*, p. 282.

[28] Compare Newton's letter to Oldenburg of June 11, 1672, *Correspondence* I, p. 174: "I chose to . . . speake of light in generall terms, considering it abstractedly as something or other propagated every way in streight lines from luminous bodies. . . ."

[29] Robert Hooke, *Micrographia* (reprinted 1961), pp. 65–6.

[30] Newton speculates (*Opticks*, p. 280) that the action or disposition propagated from one surface of the refracting medium to the other may consist in a "circulating or vibrating motion" either of some hypothetical medium or of the rays themselves. Newton's hypothesis is of the former type, while subsequent physicists such as Boscovich formulated a hypothesis of the latter type involving corpuscles with magnetic-like polarities (something like the hypothesis which Newton himself proposed to account for double refraction). See *Roger Joseph Boscovich*, ed. L. L. Whyte (1961), pp. 193–4, and V. Ronchi, *Histoire de la lumière* (1956), pp. 221–5.

David Brewster, in his *A Treatise on Optics*, gives an account of Newton's fits which is historically inaccurate in that it completely ignores Newton's medium. Instead, Brewster attributes "sides" or "poles" to the light corpuscles themselves and imagines each corpuscle to be rotating about an axis perpendicular to its direction of motion. According to Brewster, "A less scientific idea may be found of this hypothesis, by supposing a body with a sharp and a blunt end passing through space, and successively presenting its sharp and blunt ends to the line of its motion" (new ed. [1853], p. 155).

[31] *Principia*, Book III, Rules of Reasoning in Philosophy, Rule III, p. 398.

[32] I owe this reference to Huygens' study of the colored rings to R. S. Westfall's paper, "Uneasily Fitful Reflections on Fits of Easy Transmission," in this volume. Westfall suggests that Huygens later forgot his recognition of the periodicity of light when it could not be fitted into his theory concerning the nature of light.

HOWARD STEIN

Newtonian Space-Time*

M Y REMARKS TODAY AND TOMORROW WILL BE BASED UPON A RATHER
lengthy paper, written with several simultaneous objectives:
(1) To cast light upon the issues involved in a celebrated passage of intellectual history, and incidentally to clarify some of the purely historical circumstances;

(2) By elucidating those issues, to help furnish insight on related questions of
current interest;

(3) To promote an attitude toward philosophical questions that was a prevalent
one in the seventeenth century, that seems to me sound and admirable, and
that seems not to be prevalent today.

The subject is Newton's doctrine of space and time; but I want to begin by outlining, in the language of present-day mathematics, not what Newton says about
this, but what is in actual fact presupposed by the science of dynamics that we associate with his name.

The structure of space-time according to Newtonian dynamics—two formulations:

A. (1) The "world" W, the set of "events" (whatever physical interpretation the
word "event" is to have), is totally ordered by the (asymmetric and transi-
tive) temporal relation "earlier than": that is, the relation "neither is
earlier," called "simultaneity," is an equivalence. The quotient of W by
the relation of simultaneity is *time*; in other words, if by an "instant" we
mean an equivalence-class of events under simultaneity, then time is the
set T of all instants.[1]—There is furthermore intrinsic in W a structure that
determines for T a particular notion of *ratio of intervals*; and this ratio
satisfies a simple set of conditions, which taken together characterize T as
a *one-dimensional real affine space* (or Euclidean line), whose affine structure is compatible with the ordering it inherits from W.

(2) There is intrinsically determined *for each instant* a notion of *ratio of distances* (among events belonging to that instant); and this ratio satisfies a
rather intricate set of conditions, which can be summed up by the statement that *any class of simultaneous events is a subset of a three-dimensional
Euclidean space* (the ratio of distances among events agreeing with the
ratio derived from the Euclidean structure). If we assume further that at
no instant do all events lie in a plane, then the entire three-dimensional
Euclidean space of each instant is effectively defined by the structure postu-

lated. The union of all these instantaneous spaces may be thought of as the *locus of all possible events*; it is called "space-time."

(3) The instantaneous three-dimensional spaces, which so far as (2) goes are entirely separate, form part of a larger connected structure: space-time is, intrinsically, *a four-dimensional real affine space*—that is, it possesses a a notion of "straight line," having the same properties in respect of intersection (and so also parallelism) as in a Euclidean space of four dimensions. (The straight lines of space-time are to be thought of as representing all possible *uniform rectilinear motions.*[2]) Moreover, the natural projection of space-time upon T (assigning to every possible event its "epoch" or "date") is an affine mapping; and the Euclidean structures of the instantaneous spaces are compatible with their affine structures as the fibers of this mapping.

The technicalities of this account need not too much concern those to whom they are unfamiliar; but it is important to remark that the structure required by (3), which I shall refer to as the "kinematical connection" of space-time, and which is essential in order to have a framework for the analysis of *motion*, cannot be derived as a consequence of (1) and (2): this structure is constrained by (1) and (2), but is far from being determined by them.—I have expressed the structure of Newtonian space-time as a set of conditions upon the world of events. Before giving a second version of this structure, it may be helpful to summarize the first still more succinctly in terms of space-time alone:

Space-time is a four-dimensional real affine manifold, given together with: a one-dimensional real affine manifold ("time"); an affine projection of the former manifold onto the latter; and, on each fiber of this projection, a Euclidean metric compatible with the affine structure.

B. If S is a three-dimensional Euclidean space and T a one-dimensional affine space, the *Cartesian product* S✕T—that is, the set of ordered pairs (*s,t*) whose first member, *s*, belongs to S, and whose second member, *t*, belongs to T—has, in a natural way, all the structure just postulated for space-time. But S✕T has in addition a particular *spatial projection*, whose fibers define a preferred family of parallel straight lines or (briefly) a *time-axis*. Conversely, if in space-time we pick any direction transverse to the instantaneous spaces, we get a well-defined projection onto the space of any instant, having fibers parallel to that chosen direction; and this defines a representation of space-time as a product S✕T. The fact that space-time has no preferred time-axis is called (in the present context) the "principle of Galilean relativity"; and the structure of space-time can be characterized as the structure obtained from S✕T by applying the principle of Galilean relativity. In S✕T we have something that can be called "enduring space": the spatial projection can be viewed as a mapping that assigns to every possible event its place, just as the temporal projection assigns to every possible event its date; in other words, for each point of space, the fiber of the spatial projection over this point—which is a line parallel to the time-axis—can be regarded as "the point, persisting through time." Applying Galilean relativity obliterates this structure: removing the time-axis, it leaves the projection on T but not that on S.

Now let us turn to Newton's famous scholium, in the *Principia,* on time, space, place, and motion.

Newton says that although kinematical notions are so familiar that he doesn't need to define them, their ordinary application gives rise to certain preconceptions or "prejudices" that he is concerned to remove. To this end he proposes to distinguish these notions into "absolute and relative, true and apparent, mathematical and common"; and he clearly intends the "absolute, true, and mathematical" notions to furnish the kinematical substratum of his dynamics. "Absolute, true, and mathematical time," which "of itself and from its own nature flows equably without regard to anything external," is just the structure T: the one-dimensional affine space, upon which space-time has a natural affine projection that preserves its chronological ordering. And "absolute space," similarly, is the structure S, but *identified with the set of lines parallel to the time-axis in* S×T—or in other words, *with a given mapping of the world of events upon it*: for Newton says that absolute space "in its own nature, without regard to anything external, remains always similar and immovable"—clearly implying that it has an identity through time.—On the other hand, *phenomena*, to which dynamics must be applied, and *measurements*, which afford the means of application, always involve the "relative" and "apparent" notions: "relative, apparent, and common time, is some sensible and external (whether accurate or unequable) measure of duration by means of motion, . . . such as an hour, a day, a month, a year"; and "relative space is some movable dimension or measure of the absolute spaces; which our senses determine by its position to bodies . . . ."

These distinctions are responsible for Newton's having had a rather bad press amongst philosophers since the late nineteenth century. The chief problem is how *phenomena*, which by definition bear directly upon the "apparent" notions, can give us any information about the so-called "true" ones; in other words, how Newton's "absolute, true, and mathematical" notions can have any empirical content. Newton indeed discusses this question in the scholium—most notably in the celebrated account of the phenomena in a spinning water-bucket—but his elucidation has usually been dismissed as inadequate.

The scholium ends with a striking remark:

But how to collect the true motions from their causes, effects, and apparent differences, and conversely from the motions whether true or apparent to collect their causes and effects, shall be explained more fully in the sequel. For to this end have I composed the following treatise.

260   HOWARD STEIN

—Now, what does he mean by that? The intimation that the entire *Principia* was composed to explain how to determine absolute motion has been rejected by some with shocked and fervent rhetoric. But it seems to me that one does well, in a case like this, to read the book and see whether it does what the author says he intends it to do.

The central argument of the *Principia* is to be found in the first part of Book III, on the System of the World—that is, as we should say, on the solar system. The dominant question of natural philosophy in the seventeenth century was the question of the structure of this system, and in particular the question whether it is the earth or the sun that occupies its true fixed center. Newton succeeded in giving a very solid and decisive answer to the general question; and to the particular question, whether the earth or the sun is at the center, he gave an answer that was quite surprising: Neither. The argument upon which this answer was based is a most beautiful one, and repays careful study. Although Newton's exposition is in most respects extremely lucid, it conceals certain subtleties, and the reasoning is less straightforward than it has generally been taken to be. Let me summarize the salient points.

The premises of the argument, in Newton's formulation, are statements about astronomical phenomena, summing up the best data on the motions of the planets and their satellites essentially in the form of what we know as Kepler's laws (taken as characterizing the *relative* motions). Alongside these premises are the general principles of force and motion: the Laws of Motion that stand as "Axioms" at the beginning of the *Principia*, and a formidable battery of theorems derived from them in the preceding Books, especially Book I. (It is, by the way, these theorems that Newton specifically refers to as the "mathematical principles of philosophy.") And the argument is conducted in accordance with yet another class of premises or principles, which Newton in later editions calls "Rules of Philosophizing," although in the first edition they are simply listed as "Hypotheses" together with the astronomical premises. The presence of this third class of principles shows that Newton does not present his argument as simply a mathematical deduction from astronomical premises and principles of mechanics. It is also not a deduction from these together with the Rules of Philosophizing—the latter function as guiding principles rather than as premises or precise rules of inference. But in saying that the argument *conceals* subtleties I have in mind more than this: the reasoning has this extraordinary character, that *its conclusions* (so far from being logical consequences) *stand in formal contradiction to its premises*. For according to the theory of universal gravitation, which is of course the product of this argument, Kepler's laws (which were its premises) cannot give an exact representation of the motions of the planets.

From a quite abstract point of view, one could describe this situation by saying that Newton found a simple general postulate which accounts for the premised phenomena in close approximation—and that he then chose to regard the general postulate as exact, in preference to the empirical laws of the phenomena. But this description does not do justice to Newton's argument. The astronomical phenomena that Newton starts from can be represented, according to his analysis, by supposing the major astronomical bodies to be surrounded by central acceleration-fields whose intensities vary inversely with the square of the distance from the center; this yields Kepler's laws exactly. Newton's demonstration of this fact led his greatest contemporaries, Huygens and Leibniz, to accept the inverse square law in astronomy; indeed Huygens, who had previously doubted that Kepler's laws were more than an empirical approximation to the planetary motions, was actually convinced by Newton's theory that Kepler's laws hold exactly! Huygens and Leibniz both, however, *rejected* the theory of universal gravitation, as theoretically objectionable and empirically unproved. Since Huygens and Leibniz were men of formidable intellect—and Huygens in particular a skillful and profound investigator of nature; and since on the other hand Newton's fantastic conclusion that *all bodies attract one another*—and how really extraordinary a conclusion this was, and even (compared with our ordinary experience of bodies) still is, only the dulling effects of what we call "education" can have succeeded in obscuring[3]—has proved to be entirely correct; there is *prima facie* reason to consider that there may be something both sound and deep in the method that led Newton along this path where his great contemporaries could not follow.

A detailed analysis of this matter would take me too far from my central topic, but I shall try to sketch the main outlines. Newton's argument can be described as having three principal stages. The first, and logically simplest, made the greatest impression at the time. It is the purely mathematical demonstration (given in Book I) that Kepler's laws for a system of bodies moving about a fixed body are *equivalent* to the statement that the accelerations of the moving bodies can be derived from a single inverse-square acceleration-field. (This result is essentially contained in Propositions I-III, Proposition IV Corollary 6, Proposition XI, and Proposition XV, of Book I. Its straightforward application to the astronomical case is given in Propositions I-III of Book III—although Newton's concise discussion of these Propositions touches upon some subtler points, which I pass over.) The second stage is also very clearly expounded, and is concentrated in Propositions IV-VI of Book III. Its conclusion, obtained through appeal to the Rules of Philosophizing, is that the accelerations of the heavenly bodies are due to the same *vis naturæ* or *potentia naturalis* that manifests itself in our daily experience as the *weight* of bodies; in other words, that the inverse-square acceleration-fields of the major bodies are *gravitational* fields that affect all bodies near them. The crucial step in this stage of the argument is the famous comparison of the moon's acceleration with that of falling bodies on the earth: Newton shows that the former is to the latter as the square of the earth's radius is to the square of the radius of the moon's orbit—so that if the moon were brought down to the earth, and its acceleration continued to increase according to the inverse square law, that acceleration would reach just the magnitude of the acceleration of falling bodies, and would therefore simply *be* what we should call the acceleration due to the moon's "weight." A full discussion would demand that more be said here, about the extrapolation involved in imagining the

HOWARD STEIN

moon brought down to the earth, and about the character of the link so established between the terrestrial phenomenon of weight and the astronomical motions, not only of the moon but of all the other bodies. However, the broad argument is clear, and all competent readers of the *Principia* found it convincing; up to this point, Huygens and Leibniz in particular gave full agreement.

The third stage of Newton's argument is in point of fact a little hard to locate in his text. Its conclusion is the law of universal gravitation; and this is essentially stated in Proposition VII of Book III and its Corollaries. But the proofs of these statements are very short, and consist largely in appeal to what has already been shown; one feels uneasily that something may have been smuggled in. Careful analysis finds two crucial points. The first is the question, how far the extrapolation involved in what I have called the second stage is to be carried, and how exact it is to be assumed to be. The question arises for the following reason:—One of the assertions of Newton's theory that Huygens dissents from is what the latter calls "the mutual attraction of the whole bodies." By this he means—in distinction from the mutual attraction of the small particles of bodies, which he rejects *a fortiori*—the attraction between the major bodies of the solar system. But since the second stage of the argument has concluded that *all* the major bodies are surrounded by inverse-square acceleration-fields, that is gravitational fields, which affect *all* the bodies about them, it would seem to *follow* that these bodies affect one another; that, for instance, the sun gravitates towards each planet, Jupiter and Saturn towards one another, and so forth. Huygens does not say how he is able to escape this conclusion; but there is really just one way he can, namely by refusing to extend the inverse square law arbitrarily far—i.e., by supposing the validity of that law restricted to some finite region, beyond which the gravitational field decays more rapidly and even goes to zero. There is reason to believe that this was Huygens's conscious supposition, made not just from skepticism of the reach of empirical generalization (for to *doubt the exactness* of such a generalization is very much less than to *believe an equally definite contrary statement*: here, for example, the statement that the acceleration of Saturn towards Jupiter is not what Newton thinks, but zero), but made on the basis of Huygens's own theory of the mechanical cause of gravity, which could hardly be reconciled with Newton's unrestricted linear superposition of gravitational fields.[4] For Newton, on the other hand, it is a fundamental principle of method to press empirical generalizations as far and as exactly as possible, subject to empirical correction; and to do so without regard for theoretical considerations of a speculative kind.[5]

We may thus say that the beginning of the third stage of Newton's argument consists in a sort of rigorous construction that he places upon the conclusion of the second stage. But the most critical point is Newton's application of the Third Law of Motion to any gravitating body and the body towards which it gravitates. Newton does not insist that what he calls the "centripetal force" on the gravitating body is truly an attraction, exercised by the central body; yet he argues as if the Third

Law required the force on the gravitating body to be coupled with an equal and opposite force on the central body. Huygens, who assumes the force of gravitation to be exerted by an ether, objects explicitly and with justice to this step, which roughly amounts to the assumption that even if an ether does enter the interaction, momentum is conserved separately amongst the *visible* bodies.[6] The step is critical, because it is by this argument that Newton concludes *all* gravitation to be mutual; concludes, therefore, that every particle of matter, having weight proportional (at a given place) to its mass, is also a center of gravitational force, with a strength proportional to its mass.[7]

So much, then, for our outline of the argument that led to the law of universal gravitation. Before connecting this with the questions that chiefly concern us, I should like to make two comments of a historical nature on the theoretical controversy that Newton's work aroused. The first remark is, that when Newton responds to criticism of the *Principia*, he appears to rest his case for universal gravitation, not upon the *argument leading to* the theory, but upon the *extremely detailed agreement of its consequences with observed phenomena.* Thus he writes to Leibniz on 16 October 1693:

> What that very great man Huygens has remarked on my work is acute. . . .
> But . . . since all the phenomena of the heavens and of the sea follow accurately,
> so far as I am aware, from gravity alone acting in accordance with the laws
> described by me, and nature is most simple; I myself have judged that all other
> causes are to be rejected. . . .

Among the points concerned in this detailed agreement were: the beginnings, at Newton's hands, of a satisfactory representation of the motion of the moon; the first explanation of the precession of the equinoxes; and the theory of the tides. (Newton's explanations of the precession and of the tides were explicitly rejected by Huygens.)—And the second remark is, that one particular point of detailed agreement—one indeed that would most probably have convinced Huygens at least of the mutuality of the astronomical forces (if not of the universality of gravitation)—was not established at the time Huygens read the *Principia*. I refer to the mutual perturbation of the orbits of Saturn and Jupiter near the conjunction of those planets. I have not found an account of the circumstances in any of the histories of mechanics or of astronomy that I have examined; but the second volume of Newton's collected correspondence contains a letter written to Flamsteed, the Astronomer Royal, in December 1684, inquiring about a possible deviation of Saturn's motion at its conjunction with Jupiter; and contains Flamsteed's reply, somewhat indecisive, but negative. The first edition of the *Principia* (published in 1687) discusses this perturbation without any claim that it is observable. But the second edition (published in 1713) describes the mutual perturbation as observable, and Saturn's deviation in particular as having "perplexed" astronomers. And in fact one finds, in

HOWARD STEIN

a notation by David Gregory dated 4 May 1694 (reproduced in Volume III of Newton's correspondence), the following:

> At Saturn's and Jupiter's most recent conjunction [their] Actions upon one another were manifest; indeed before the conjunction Jupiter was accelerated and Saturn retarded, after the conjunction Jupiter retarded and Saturn accelerated. Whence Corrections of the Orbits of Saturn and Jupiter by Halley and Flamsteed, which were afterwards perceived to be worthless . . . .

(The point of the last remark is that the deviations of the two planets from the courses predicted for them were not due to errors in the determination of their orbits, and could not be used to compute more accurate orbits, since what was observed was in fact a perturbation. Evidently neither Flamsteed, to whom Newton had addressed his inquiry several years before, nor Halley, Newton's good friend, had thought at first of the effect predicted by Newton.)

In any case, Newton's analysis begins from phenomenological and therefore relative motions, and leads to a comprehensive account of the forces of interaction in the solar system. But now if this *dynamical* account is accepted, it has implications beyond the phenomenological premises that led to it—indeed, as I have just explained, it even implies *phenomenological corrections* to those premises; and these implications of the dynamical theory concern in part what Newton calls the "true" or "absolute" motions. Newton's own exposition is characteristically clear and succinct. Following Proposition X of Book III we find (in the second and third editions):

HYPOTHESIS 1. *That the center of the system of the world is at rest.*

This is acknowledged by all, while some contend that the earth, others that the sun, is at rest in the center of the system. Let us see what from hence may follow

I ask you to note that Newton makes no attempt here to argue the *truth* of this "Hypothesis"; he merely proposes to examine the consequences, in the light of his theory, of a common presupposition of the whole cosmological controversy. Then:

PROPOSITION XI. *That the common center of gravity of the earth, the sun, and all the planets, is at rest.*

The proof is trivial: the center of gravity of an isolated system (which the solar system can be taken to be) is either at rest, or in uniform rectilinear motion; but if the center of gravity were in uniform rectilinear motion with non-zero velocity, there could obviously be no fixed point in the system at all (since the configuration of the system is at least roughly stable); therefore to uphold the Hypothesis we must suppose the center of gravity to be at rest.—But from this we have the conclusion:

PROPOSITION XII. *That the sun is agitated by a perpetual motion, but never recedes far from the common center of gravity of all the planets.*

.   .   .   .

Corollary. Hence the common center of gravity of the earth, the sun, and all the planets, is to be esteemed the center of the world. For since the earth, the sun, and all the planets, mutually gravitate one towards another, and are therefore . . . in perpetual agitation, . . . it is plain that their mobile centers cannot be taken for the quiescent center of the world. If that body were to be placed in the center towards which all bodies gravitate most (as is the common opinion), that privilege ought to be allowed to the sun. But since the sun moves, that resting point is to be chosen from which the center of the sun departs least—and from which it would depart still less if only the sun were denser and larger and so were less moved.

If we compare the entire argument whose structure I have now described, with Newton's statement of his intention at the end of the scholium on time and space, I think we can only conclude that the performance corresponds very well with the promise: from motions, either true or apparent—and here more particularly from *apparent* motions—to arrive at the knowledge of their causes and effects; and from the causes, effects, and apparent differences, to collect the true motions.—The intricacy of the theoretical and empirical connections is worth emphasizing. Perhaps it has seemed puzzling that Newton speaks of arriving at the knowledge of the causes *and effects* of the motions. But in fact it is just as *an effect of the earth's true rotation* that Newton predicts its oblate shape—for which geographical evidence was still lacking; and it is only on the basis of this shape, known from the theory but not yet confirmed by direct measurement, that Newton is able—bringing to bear the full power of his theory of gravitation—to account for the precession of the equinoxes.

What can be said of the explicitly "hypothetical" element in Newton's elucidation of the true motions: the hypothesis that the center of the world is at rest? We know the answer: there is no way, on the basis of observations and of the principles of Newtonian dynamics, to establish the truth of this hypothesis; for Newtonian dynamics satisfies the principle of Galilean relativity, according to which one cannot distinguish a state of rest from any other state of uniform irrotational straight-line motion. We know this answer; and Newton did too, and formulated it quite clearly in the fifth Corollary to the Laws of Motion. In the light of this fact, and of the very carefully hypothetical form of Newton's statement about the center of the world, it appears to me that Newton's philosophical analysis of the kinematical presuppositions of his dynamics emerges as acute and *almost* unexceptionable. The qualification lies in this, that although he is clear that dynamics does not provide any way to distinguish motion from rest, Newton does not seem to have conceived the philosophical possibility that *that distinction cannot be made at all*; that is to say, that the spatio-temporal framework of events does not intrinsically possess the structure of the Cartesian product $S \times T$, but a weaker structure. One easily understands why Newton should not have conceived this possibility; even Poincaré, at the end

HOWARD STEIN

of the nineteenth century, could express the view that if rotation is real then motion must be real, and if acceleration is real then velocity must be real. But the more abstract point of view that mathematics has now made available allows us to see, today, that these considerations are specious, and that the true structure of the space-time of Newtonian dynamics, with its Galilean invariance, is the one I have already described, in which there is an absolute time but no absolute space—that is to say, a natural mapping upon T but none upon S. The point that is really crucial for kinematics is that within this structure *there is no absolute or intrinsic notion of velocity, but there is an absolute or intrinsic notion of velocity-difference*—and *therefore* of rotation and of acceleration.

If as I have said it is not surprising that Newton failed to conceive the possibility of such a structure for the space-time of the real world, I regard it as one of the astonishing facts of intellectual history that a contemporary of Newton's did conceive exactly this possibility, and maintain it as the truth. I mean Huygens, who expresses himself to this effect in a number of late manuscript fragments on the question of absolute and relative motion. These fragments have been repeatedly discussed, but they have not in my view been estimated at their true worth; partly because of a certain confusion in Huygens's philosophical conception, which somewhat obscures his exposition; but more, I think, because the true conceptual situation has not been well understood. No one else before Einstein matched Huygens's appreciation of the fundamental importance of the so-called "special principle of relativity." And when Einstein put the matter in its true light, it was in the context of electrodynamics rather than mechanics, therefore of Lorentz-invariance rather than Galilean invariance—a context which required a quite drastic revision of mechanics itself; and fairly soon the far deeper issues of general relativity emerged. As a consequence, rather little attention has been paid to the intrinsic relativity theory of Newtonian dynamics.

In conclusion today, I want to explain briefly what I have just said about velocity and velocity-difference in Newtonian space-time:—The instantaneous state of motion of a particle is represented, in the structure defined at the beginning of this lecture, by a tangent-vector to space-time, "normalized" by the requirement that its time-component be unity: namely, the vector with unit time-component that is tangent to the particle's space-time trajectory at the instant in question. If one asks for the *velocity* of the particle, one wants the "space-component" of this vector; and this is not a well-defined notion, unless a projection of space-time onto space is given—that is, the projection onto time being present from the start, unless space-time is endowed with the structure $S \times T$. On the other hand, if we consider two different states of motion (whether at the same time or at different times), the difference of their representative vectors will be a well-defined space-time vector *with time-component zero*. Such a vector, at any space-time point, is tangent to the instantaneous space in which that point lies; that is, it can be regarded in a natural way as a spatial vector. This is the velocity-difference vector, from which the absolute acceleration-vector of a trajectory can be derived. And the existence of this velocity-difference vector where no well-defined velocity vectors exist allows us to make perfect sense of Huygens's statement that when a body is in rotation its parts, although maintaining constant geometrical relations amongst themselves, are mutually in relative motion (by which he means that they have non-zero velocity-differences); and yet that one cannot say, or meaningfully ask, how much "real" motion any one of them has—this being, he says, "nothing but a chimera, and founded on a false idea."

In tomorrow's talk, I shall comment upon the philosophical background of Newton's views of space and time, and on some of the philosophical controversy to which those views have given rise, from his time to our own.

II

It is not only in respect of the role played by Newton's kinematical conceptions in his positive work that I believe commentators to have erred: I think too that they have misconstrued Newton's chief reasons for making an issue of the distinctions he proposes, and for using the language he does to express them. We are accustomed to seeing Newton's doctrine of space contrasted with that of Leibniz, who held the essence of space to be *relational*: that is, he held that space is constituted essentially by the *spatial relations of bodies,* and he wanted to explicate those relations in terms of something more fundamental. The relationship between Newton's doctrine and Leibniz's is in fact of very great interest. But to understand Newton's scholium on time, space, place, and motion properly, it is necessary to realize that in it he was concerned to differentiate his theory not from Leibniz's but Descartes's. Establishing this difference was important to Newton for two reasons: Descartes's physics and cosmology constituted the most influential view in the scientific world at the time; and Descartes's mechanics was based upon a very confused semi-relativistic concept of motion, on which it would have been hopeless to build a coherent theory. In other words, the "prejudices" that Newton says his scholium was intended to remove were, in large part, those of the scientific community, and his aim was to establish a new technical terminology as the foundation for a coherent theory.—In part, however, the "prejudices" were of a theological character; and so we find at the climax of the scholium the following passage:

> . . . [I]f the meaning of words is to be determined by their use, then by the names time, space, place, and motion, their measures [i.e., the relative quantities] are properly to be understood; and the expression will be unusual, and purely mathematical, if the measured quantities themselves are meant. Upon which account, they do strain the sacred writings, who there interpret those words for the measured quantities. Nor do those less defile the purity of mathematical and philosophical truths, who confound real quantities themselves with their relations and vulgar measures.

HOWARD STEIN

The last two sentences are a characteristic example of Newton's condensed rhetoric. Not only do they state Newton's view of the proper way to read the Bible and the proper way to pursue philosophy, they also contain a twofold gibe at Descartes; for Descartes in his *philosophy* used a concept of motion as relative that allowed him to claim *theological orthodoxy* by maintaining that in the proper or philosophical sense the earth is to be regarded as at rest. And we also have here, incidentally, an example of the crudeness with which Newton's words have often been read: for the clause accurately translated by Andrew Motte as "they do strain the sacred writings," Florian Cajori, in his revision of Motte's version, changes to "those violate the accuracy of language, which ought to be kept precise"—thereby violating the accuracy of language, and ruining the sense of the passage.[8]

The evidence that Descartes was Newton's main philosophical target in the scholium is presented in detail in the paper I have mentioned. It is based upon a careful study of the text of the scholium, and a comparison with the second Part of Descartes's *Principia Philosophiæ*. The conclusion that I drew from this comparison I later found strikingly confirmed by an essay of Newton's, unpublished till 1962, treating substantially the same questions as the scholium, in a far more expansive style, in the explicit guise of a refutation of Descartes. I don't think it would be useful to pursue this matter today, because the details seem to me—like Descartes's physics itself—of fairly narrow historical rather than philosophical interest. My reason for emphasizing the point at all is that I believe it relevant for the philosophical assessment of Newton's discussion to understand that he was addressing himself to the clarification of an undeniably confused conceptual scheme.

But there is a passage in that recently published essay that has no counterpart in the scholium, and seems to me of considerable interest. It is a little prolix; I shall quote it with some excisions:

> Lastly, that the absurdity of this position [of Descartes's] may be made most clear, I say that it follows thence that a moving body has no determinate velocity and no definite line in which it moves. And all the more, that the velocity of a body moving without resistance cannot be said to be uniform, nor the line to be straight in which its motion is accomplished. . . .
>
> But that this may be clear, it is first of all to be shown that when some motion is finished, it is impossible according to Descartes to assign a place where the body was at the start of the motion. . . . For example, if the place of the Planet Jupiter a year ago be sought; by what criterion, I ask, can the Cartesian Philosopher describe it? Not by the positions of the particles of the fluid matter [that is, the ether], for the positions of these particles have changed greatly since a year ago. Nor can he describe it by the positions of the Sun and fixed stars; for the unequal influx of subtle matter through the poles of the vortices . . . , the Vortices' undulation . . inflation . . . and absorption, [all of which are processes described by Descartes in Part III of his *Principia,*] and other truer causes, such

as the rotation of the sun and stars about their own centers, the generation of spots, and the passage of comets through the heavens, change both the magnitudes and the positions of the stars so much, that perhaps they do not suffice to designate the place sought for but with an error of several miles—much less can the place be accurately described and determined by their help, as a Geometer would require. Truly there are no bodies in the world whose relative positions remain unchanged with the passage of time . . . . And so there is no basis from which we can now designate a place that was in time past, or say that such a place is any more to be found in nature. . . . And so as of the place of Jupiter a year ago, it is manifest according to Descartes's doctrine that, of the place of any moving body, not God himself (a new state of things holding) could describe it accurately and in a Geometrical sense; since on account of the changed positions of bodies it does not exist in nature any more.

Now since after any motion is completed the place in which it began . . . cannot be assigned nor any longer exists: that space traversed can have no length; and . . . it follows that the moving body can have no velocity; which is what I first wished to show. Further, what was said of the starting-point . . . should be understood similarly of all the intermediate places; and therefore, as the space has neither a starting-point nor intermediate parts, it follows that there was no space passed over, and thus no direction of motion, as I wished secondly to show. . . . So it is necessary that the determination of places, and therefore of local motion, be referred to some immobile being, such as is extension alone, or space so far as it is seen as truly distinct from bodies. And this the Cartesian Philosopher may more readily admit if he observes that Descartes himself had an idea of this extension distinct from bodies. . . . And that the gyrations of the vortices, from which he deduced the force of the ether in receding from their centers, and therefore the whole of his mechanical Philosophy, are tacitly referred to that generic extension.

I believe that if Huygens and Leibniz, who commented adversely upon the scholium in favor of a relativistic view of motion but never exchanged views on the subject with Newton, had been confronted with the argument of this passage, a clarification would have been forced that could have promoted appreciably the philosophical discussion of space-time—and of scientific concept-formation in general. When I say "promoted appreciably," I mean in fact to a point that has not become commonplace even today. Contrary-to-fact conditionals in history are of dubious worth, and the basis of my suggestion will perhaps appear somewhat subjective: in studying the writings of these three men—Newton, Huygens, and Leibniz—I have found striking, not only their intellectual power, but even more the extraordinarily high plane of discussion in which they engaged, from which the subsequent generations of scientific-philosophical controversy seem to me a serious falling-off. To put it as simply as I can, these were—with all due allowance for personal anfractuosities

HOWARD STEIN

—serious men, concerned with real problems of understanding the world even more than with pet ideas or the scoring of points in debate. And this seems, in point of fact, rare.

What Newton points out in the passage I have quoted is the need for what I called, in yesterday's lecture, a "kinematical connection," to allow one to discuss trajectories, velocities, and so forth. The point of central philosophical interest is that such a "connection" is indeed required for the formulation of the principles of mechanics, and that *it cannot*—as Newton quite clearly indicates—*be defined in terms simply of the spatial relations of bodies.* (For Newtonian space-time as I have presented it, this is just the remark that the mapping upon time and the Euclidean metric on each instantaneous slice of space-time do not determine a unique four-dimensional affine structure.) And this point affects the program of Leibniz quite as much as the fanciful cosmology of Descartes. Alongside the instantaneous geometry assumed (at the time) by everyone, and *whether or not* the spatial relations of that geometry can be explicated in terms of more fundamental properties and relations of bodies as Leibniz wished, it is necessary for mechanics to assume that further structure that has appeared in our discussion as the four-dimensional affine structure of space-time: this is the "immobile being" that Newton says is required. Huygens came closer than Newton did to understanding the mathematical structure of this being; but Newton perceived clearly its independent nature, in the conceptual framework of the mechanics which they shared, and Huygens did not. As for Leibniz, careful examination shows that his attempt to carry out within mechanics his program for the philosophical foundation of the theory of space and time miscarried disastrously—just because he never faced the issue posed by Newton in the passage above. For like Descartes, Leibniz postulated the primacy in nature of uniform rectilinear motion—even while maintaining a relativistic view of motion and (more radically) a relational theory of space; Leibniz indeed held uniform rectilinear motion to be "the natural motion" in so fundamental a sense that, according to him, any deviation from such motion in any other circumstance than the collision of bodies would constitute a miracle.

It is often claimed that the general theory of relativity has demonstrated the correctness of Leibniz's view. This is a drastic oversimplification. It is no more true in the general theory than in Newtonian dynamics that the geometry of space-time is determined by *relations among bodies.* If the general theory does in a sense conform better to Leibniz's views than classical mechanics does, this is not because it relegates "space" to the ideal status ascribed to it by Leibniz, but rather because the space—or rather the space-time structure—that Newton requires to be real, appears in the general theory with attributes that might allow Leibniz to accept it as real. The general theory does not deny the *existence* of something that corresponds to Newton's "immobile being"; but it denies the rigid *immobility* of this "being," and represents it as interacting with the other constituents of physical reality.

It is perhaps a natural tendency for commentators on intellectual history to emphasize oppositions. It is an unfortunate consequence of this tendency that issues
which, in their own time, were vital and charged with the potentiality of honest interaction, come to appear as rigid and ritualistic as the duello. In the correspondence
of Huygens and Leibniz, for example, on the question of absolute or relative motion,
one finds the following things:—The correspondence is initiated by a critical remark of Huygens about a paragraph in Leibniz's notes on Descartes's *Principia*:
Huygens interprets Leibniz as *objecting* to the view that motion is merely relative;
and says that for his own part he holds just such a view, "undeterred by the reasoning and experiments of Newton in his Principles of Philosophy, which I know to
be in error—and I am eager to see whether he will not retract this in the new edition
of the book. . . . Descartes did not sufficiently understand the matter."—Leibniz
in reply affirms his allegiance to a similar view, and says: "Mr. Newton acknowledges the equivalence of hypotheses"—i.e., the principle of relativity—"in the case
of rectilinear motions, but in regard to Circular, he believes that the efforts the circulating bodies make to recede from the center or axis of rotation reveals their absolute motion. But I have reasons that make me believe nothing breaks the general
law of Equivalence. It seems to me, however, that you yourself, Sir, were once of
Mr. Newton's opinion in regard to circular motion."—And Huygens answers: "As
for absolute and relative motion, I am amazed at your memory—namely your recalling that at one time I was of Mr. Newton's opinion in regard to circular motion.
Which is so, and it is only 2 or 3 years since that I discovered what is truer."—Leibniz's closing response is: "When I said to you one day in Paris that it is hard to know
the true subject of Motion, you answered that this was possible by means of circular motion, which gave me pause; and I remembered it when I read almost the
same thing in the book of Mons. Newton. . . ."—Now, a feature of this correspondence that I find very striking is the circumstance that, in spite of the strength
and the importance of their differences with Newton,—which are certainly not to
be depreciated,—these two philosophical antagonists are very far from finding Newton's doctrine bizarre; so much so that one of them acknowledges having held the same
view as Newton, independently, for a major part of his scientific career, and the other
says that when he learned this view from the first it "gave him pause." To me, this
circumstance appears quite irreconcilable with, for instance, the following statement
of Reichenbach's, in reference to this very correspondence:

> [Leibniz and Huygens] feel themselves repelled by the spiritualistic way of
> thinking, derived from Henry More, of this physicist who, whenever he left the
> domain of his narrower specialty, became a mystic and a dogmatist.

And Reichenbach continues:

> They both know that the crude reification of space that Newton shares with the
> epistemologically unschooled mind in its naive craving for realism cannot pos-
> sibly be right. . . . Huygens even expresses the conjecture that Newton will

HOWARD STEIN

correct his views on the problem of motion in the new edition of the *Principia,* so sure does he feel in his rejection of the Newtonian absolutism.

There is no doubt that Huygens felt sure of his ground; but is not his expectation rather a testimony of his admiration for Newton's genius than of his contempt for Newton's "dogmatic mysticism"? And is not the basis of his expectation the fact that he sees Newton on the same road that he himself had traveled?—And note the tendency, from Newton's adjective "absolute," which he applies in its logical sense to concepts that are not "relative" to something,[9] to derive the epithet "absolutist" for Newton himself.[10] What this seems to me to show is just how dulling it is to view a struggle with real problems through the smoky air and accumulated dust of later sterile controversies.

One particular source of misjudgment about the philosophical issues of the seventeenth century, I think, is a confusion about the very word "philosophy." For instance, Newton's criticism of Descartes is that Descartes's several formulations of the fundamental meaning of the word "motion" are inconsistent, and that none of them can satisfy what for Newton is the crucial test of a *philosophical* conception of motion: namely that it make possible an adequate expression of the principles of dynamics. Descartes's own dynamics is in effect, according to Newton,—and in verifiable fact: the *Principia* of Descartes is a confused, but by no means an obscure book,—based on quite different ideas of place and motion than his "official" ones. We have seen Newton refer these ideas to what Descartes calls "generic" extension, and we have seen him appeal to the followers of Descartes to recognize the identity of this Cartesian generic extension with the space of Newton's own doctrine. His appeal concludes with the statement I quoted a few minutes ago: "And . . . the gyrations of the vortices, from which he deduced . . . the whole of his mechanical Philosophy, are tacitly referred to that generic extension."—Now E. A. Burtt says:

> When we come to Newton's remarks on space and time . . . he takes personal leave of his empiricism, and a position partly adopted from others, partly felt to be demanded by his mathematical method, and partly resting on a theological basis, is presented, and that in the main body of his chief work. Newton himself asserts that "in philosophical disquisitions," which apparently means here when offering ultimate characterizations of space, time, and motion, "we ought to abstract from our senses, and consider things themselves, distinct from what are only sensible measures of them." This is surely a peculiar observation from a philosopher of sensible experience.

I hope it is enough to place this quotation alongside the previous discussion, to make plain its sad inadequacy. But what seems to me almost unbelievably obtuse is Burtt's interpretation of what Newton really meant by "philosophical disquisitions." Apparently he forgets the very title of that "disquisition," Newton's "chief work," of which the scholium with its characterizations of space and so forth is so small a part; namely, *Mathematical Principles of Natural Philosophy.* Burtt's work deserves respect, as a pioneering study of the philosophy of seventeenth-century science. Nevertheless, taking the words of a man like Newton to mean "apparently" what one thinks they might be likely to mean,—without paying very careful attention to the evidence that indicates what they did in fact mean,—and on such a basis finding in his utterances all sorts of inconsistency, inadequacy, and unintelligibility, ought to be regarded as shocking; in fact it is shockingly common. Burtt's summary judgment is that: "In scientific discovery and formulation Newton was a marvellous genius; as a philosopher he was uncritical, sketchy, inconsistent, even second-rate." I do not think this judgment is of any value.

The words that Burtt quotes are neither peculiar nor obscure, unless they are read, anachronistically, with connotations they acquired in later metaphysical discussion. For example, Newton doesn't mean by "things themselves" what Kant means by "Dinge an sich": he means what Kant would call "Gegenstände der Erfahrung," objects of experience; and the statement that "we ought to abstract from our senses, and consider things themselves, distinct from what are only sensible measures of them," has nothing to do with a departure from empiricism in any sense in which "empiricism" applies to Newton at all. "Geometry," Newton tells us, "is founded in mechanical practice," and is indeed a part of mechanics; but geometry is also founded upon the use of terms in a precisely controlled way—a way that, while learned from experience, does certainly "abstract from our senses." Newton would never have agreed with Hume that a finite volume contains a finite number of points (because there is a minimal quantum of what can be perceived).

The general situation, with respect to the question of the empirical content of the kinematical notions that Newton calls "absolute, true, and mathematical," appears to me to be this:—These notions are part of Newton's *theoretical apparatus.* We have come to know that the critique of the empirical content of theoretical notions is indeed of great importance in science; but that it cannot be managed by simple translation of theoretical terms into some kind of "observation language." In this respect Newton's use of the "absolute" kinematical notions should be regarded as of the same class with his use of such theoretical notions as "force" or "attraction" or "gravitation." His philosophical investigation of the system of the world led Newton to conclude that things themselves all mutually attract one another, although this attraction amongst the objects around us is quite inaccessible to our ordinary sensible measures. The same investigation led to the conclusion that the sun bobs about and the earth turns. Is the conclusion that all things attract of a different kind from the conclusion that the earth turns? Improved technique did of course allow the former conclusion to be tested, and a hundred years after the *Principia* Cavendish measured gravitational forces in the laboratory. But in the scholium Newton discusses this precise question about the second conclusion: how "absolute" motion can be determined empirically; and one might suggest that Foucault's pendulum experiment, for instance, was as striking a confirmation of Newton's theory of rotation as Cavendish's torsion-balance experiment was of his theory of gravitation. Of course, both were confirmations of theories for which strong confirmation did already exist: for gravitation, the planetary perturbations and the precession of the equinoxes; for rotation, the earth's equatorial bulge—and, one perhaps ought to add (although it was not to my knowledge adduced at the time), the direction of propagation of the weather, which is a sensible phenomenon of impeccable qualifications.

Are the experiments of Cavendish and of Foucault genuinely parallel cases? Against this it may be urged that the evidence of Cavendish is rather direct: the experiment detects, by the observed displacement of the bar of the balance—which puts the wire into torsion—the existence of a torque upon the wire when the test masses are brought close together. On the other hand, the Foucault experiment only shows a kind of geographical fact (like the motion of the weather): the plane of oscillation of the pendulum rotates, at a rate that depends upon terrestrial latitude; the experiment does not and cannot show that this precession of the plane of oscillation is due to the earth's state of motion. The difference is real; but it is important to understand in what it consists, and in what it does not consist. In the scholium, Newton suggests how one might go about testing whether an observed force is due to rotational motion: namely, by applying a torque to vary the rotational state, and observing how the force responds—in particular, whether variation in one sense increases the force and variation in the other sense diminishes it. In the present case, the torque would have to be applied to the earth, so as to change its state of rotation; the experiment is therefore, unfortunately, technologically unfeasible. On the other hand, the limitation *is* purely technological; and as a matter of fact, a partial substitute for Newton's test will soon be quite feasible, namely a Foucault experiment on the surface of the moon, to verify that the precession there differs from that on the earth to the extent demanded by the difference in rotational velocities (and, of course, the difference in gravities). So we see that an extension of Foucault's experiment would allow us to verify that the force there observed depends upon the state of rotation of the system, just as the experiment of Cavendish shows the force observed in that experiment to depend upon the distance between the two bodies and upon their masses.

Nevertheless a question remains. Suppose the extended Foucault experiment indeed shows that the force varies with the earth's state of rotation. How does this establish that the particular state corresponding to null force is, as Newton asserts, the state of null "absolute" rotation?

Now, this is obviously in large part a question about words and meanings. If one denies—on whatever grounds—that "absolute" space and motion can be well-defined notions at all, then one obviously cannot accept *any* experimental result as confirming that the earth possesses a certain quantity of "absolute" rotation. But it is surely nonsense to deny the *definability* of "absolute" motion, since prior to definition—or to some stipulation of conditions to be satisfied—the mere constitution of a word confers no logical attributes whatever upon it. One can with reason deny only the intelligibility of some proposed definition, or the realizability of some proposed set of conditions.

I make these rather pedantic and trivial remarks, because that part of the philosophical controversy—and especially in recent times—that has tended to fasten upon the adjective "absolute" as a deprecable one, is fairly infected with disregard of these simple considerations. Let me give two elementary examples; a little later I shall discuss a third and more substantial one.

The first example is from H. G. Alexander's introduction to his edition of the Leibniz-Clarke correspondence. After recounting the phenomena and the theoretical considerations on which Newton bases his discussion of absolute space and time, and concluding that "only a frame of reference with respect to which the earth is rotating . . . is an inertial frame," Alexander says:

> One would like to believe that this is all Newton meant when he introduced the concepts of absolute space and time. Such an interpretation is supported by his equating the distinction between absolute and relative space and time, with the distinction between "mathematical and common" space and time. This recalls the distinction made in his preface . . . between geometry and mechanics. There geometry is said to be concerned with ideal straight lines and circles even though "artificers do not work with perfect accuracy." Similarly one might interpret the scholium as saying that space and time are ideal entities which it is helpful to consider in theory, although they may not exist in reality.
>
> Unfortunately it is easy to cite other passages in which Newton treats absolute space and time as real even though perhaps unknowable. . . . [T]hese show that Newton thought he was doing more than just identifying the set of frames of reference with respect to which the laws of dynamics would take the simplest form.

The second example is from a paper by Stephen Toulmin:

> . . . [O]ne need no more assert that Newton was committed by his theory of dynamics to the objective existence of a cosmic substratum called "absolute space" than one need say that a geometer . . . is committed to the quasi-material existence of an invisible network of geometrical entities interpenetrating the world . . . . What matters for Newton's dynamics is that his theory—which includes, of course, the distinction between inertial frames and others—should have a physical application. . . .
>
> I question, therefore, whether the *objective existence* of absolute space was or need have been the central issue for Newton. Its "reality" or applicability, as a concept, is a different matter. . . . It is in this respect—in taking Newton to be concerned not with the objective existence of a hypothetical entity called Absolute Space so much as with the applicability to the world of nature of two

kinds of spatial and temporal concepts, which he labels "absolute" and "relative"—that I chiefly contest the received interpretation of the scholium on space, time, and motion.

In both of these passages one observes what I should characterize as a loose and uncontrolled manipulation of verbal distinctions. What exactly do these authors *mean* by "ideal entities which it is helpful to consider in theory," or by a notion or theory that "has a physical application",—as opposed to entities that "exist in reality," or to "the objective existence of a cosmic substratum"? If the distinction between inertial frames of reference and those which are not inertial is a distinction that has a real application to the world; that is, if the structure I described yesterday is in some sense really exhibited by the world of events; and if this structure can legitimately be regarded as an explication of Newton's "absolute space and time"; then the question whether, in addition to characterizing the world in just the indicated sense, this structure of space-time also "really exists," surely *seems* to be supererogatory. It is quite true that the discussion of these questions became involved with issues of logical and metaphysical terminology, and of theology: Is space a substance, an attribute, or something other than these? Is space "ideal" or "real"? Is God in space, or is space an idea of God, or neither? And so on. And a careful study of the philosophy of a man who discusses such questions ought to take account of his discussion of them. But when two philosophers disagree about whether, for instance, space is real or ideal, their disagreement—this is a point one would hope had become commonplace in the era of linguistic analysis—is at least as likely to be based upon different usages of the terms "real" and "ideal" as upon different views about space. Unless one undertakes a critical study of this usage, as neither Alexander nor Toulmin does, comment upon such issues ought to be eschewed; to speak of a "cosmic substratum" or of "the objective existence of a hypothetical entity called Absolute Space," as if such terms had a clear meaning and moreover a clearly objectionable one, is just sophomoric.

It is important to be very clear about one point: the notion of the structure of space-time cannot, in so far as it is truly applicable to the physical world, be regarded as a mere conceptual tool to be used from time to time as convenience dictates. For there is only one physical world; and if it has the postulated structure, that structure is—by hypothesis—there, once for all. If it is not there once for all— and that is what the evidence today indicates overwhelmingly, of the structure of Newtonian space-time—then it is not there at all; although of course it may still be (as the evidence also indicates, overwhelmingly) that a structure is there that approximates, in some sense, to the postulated one. On this point—the "reality" of space and time as an objective framework of the phenomenal universe (although as regards their mode of being he regards them as "ideal" things)—Leibniz can be quite as forceful as Newton:

. . . [S]pace and time taken together constitute the order of possibilities of the one entire universe, so that these orders—space and time, that is—relate not only to what actually is but also to anything that could be put in its place, just as numbers are indifferent to the things which can be enumerated.

Newton, on the other hand, is by no means so far as one might be led to suppose from Leibniz's view that the essence of space and time is in some sense relational. Leibniz's phrase, that space is "an order of situations," which occurs in his correspondence with Clarke, and which Clarke finds absurd, actually appears verbatim in Newton's scholium. And the following remarkable passage occurs in the essay of Newton's from which I have quoted before:

. . . [J]ust as the parts of duration have their individuality from their order, so that (for instance) if yesterday could change places with today and become the later of the two it would lose its individuality and be no longer yesterday but today: So the parts of space have their individuality from their positions, so that if any two could exchange their positions, they would thereby exchange their individualities, and each would be converted numerically into the other. By their mutual order and positions alone are the parts of duration and space understood to be just what they are in fact; nor have they any other principle of individuation besides that order and those positions, which therefore they cannot change.

We clearly do not have here a "crude reification of space"—or an "epistemologically unschooled mind in its naive craving for realism." The idea formulated by Leibniz as the principle of the identity of indiscernibles is obviously a familiar one to Newton; and he bases upon it a view of the standing towards one another of the parts of space that is strikingly similar to Leibniz's. Not identical, however: the relations that constitute space and give its parts their individuality are according to Newton *internal* relations; that is to say, he is content to postulate the entire structure of space, without attempting to derive it from or ground it in the relations of non-spatial entities.

But I want to come back to the Foucault experiment—or for that matter the water-bucket experiment—and to the question whether such phenomena do provide an adequate criterion for applying the notion of "absolute" rotation.

One must beware—as I hope I have already implied—of the tyranny of words. How we use them is certainly not indifferent, and to assume that it is conduces to loose thinking—as in the case of Descartes, who slides the words "motion," "motion in the common sense," and "motion in the proper sense," about, to a degree that vitiates his dynamics. But how we use them is also not imposed upon us by some fixed standard, and much unclarifying dispute over theoretical doctrines has been occasioned by one party's assumption that some word used by the other party *must* have a certain meaning, which is not the meaning the second party intends. Words face in two directions, towards men and towards things; they are instruments of communication and of thought, and must be used in a way that respects both the recep-

HOWARD STEIN

tivity of the audience and the structure of the things they refer to. When from a consideration of the nature of things we are led to propose a change or refinement in the use of words, the way to make the change is never uniquely determined by the subject. To judge such a proposal fairly one must attempt to divorce prejudice, to examine what the *proposed* meanings are and whether they have been (or can be) made clear, and to examine propositions formulated in the new terms in order to see whether they are true and instructive statements about the things they refer to. Otherwise criticism risks the shallowness of those who maintain that a poem must rhyme.

The proper question about Newton's doctrine, therefore, is not whether space, time, and motion really are as he takes them to be, but whether his definitions make sense and whether the things he says are correct statements about the things he means. The water-bucket experiment and Foucault's pendulum make *something* visible. In Newton's terms this something is called "absolute rotation." It is when this is correctly understood that Foucault's experiment can be seen as fully analogous to Cavendish's. The latter is not designed to show—nor can it be shown, for the proposition makes no sense—that the force detected in it should be called "gravitation"; and it is not designed to determine the cause of that force. What it shows is that a force occurs just as predicted by Newton's theory, in which that force is called "gravitation" and is said to be associated universally with the masses and distances of bodies. Just so Foucault's experiment exhibits the occurrence of a force predicted by Newton's theory, in which that force is said to be associated universally with what in the theory is called the "absolute rotational velocity" of a body.

Reichenbach makes a very interesting mistake about this (and this is the third example I promised earlier). He asks us to imagine, reflecting upon a famous comment of Mach's, that the universe is in a sense given twice: that there are two world-systems, each with its "earth" and its "star-sphere," vastly far apart but still accessible to observation; and that each earth is at rest with respect to the other star-sphere but rotates with respect to its own. According to Mach, he says, if centrifugal forces appear on the one earth they ought to appear on the other as well. Suppose that it proves otherwise, and more particularly that centrifugal forces are observed on the earth E_1, whose fixed-star heaven is F_1, but not on the earth E_2, whose star-sphere is F_2. Reichenbach says that according to Newton these observations would "establish absolute space," and would compel us to recognize that E_1 and F_2 are in rotation while F_1 and E_2 are at rest. But Reichenbach objects that the opposite interpretation—E_1 and F_2 at rest, F_1 and E_2 in rotation—can still be maintained. With this interpretation, he says, we introduce the general principle: if the fixed-star shell F rotates relative to absolute space, it produces a gravitational field on its earth E; so E_1 but not E_2 is subject to this gravitational attraction, which is the same as what on Newton's interpretation is called "centrifugal force." Both interpretations distinguish between states of motion which are indistinguishable from the point of view of purely relative kinematics,—since the systems (E_1, F_1) and (E_2, F_2) are indistinguishable from this point of view, and yet by hypothesis show different phenomena,—but they make the distinction differently. And Reichenbach concludes that if the observations agree, as supposed, with Newton's prediction against Mach's, then *"there exists absolute space, but its state of motion cannot be determined."*

There are actually two mistakes in this. The first is that Reichenbach's alternative interpretation is just not tenable in the form he proposes. We have only to suppose a third system (E_3, F_3), in which the earth and the stars are at rest with respect to one another and to F_1 and E_2. According to Newton, E_3 and F_3 are then at rest, and there should be no centrifugal force. But according to Reichenbach's alternative, since F_3 (like F_1) rotates, there should be a gravitational attraction upon E_3. If we assume that the facts support Newton, Reichenbach's alternative would have to be modified in a rather complicated way. The general situation, so far as this point is concerned, is the following:—*However* one formulates the principles of Newtonian dynamics, these principles do in fact allow one to single out a *unique* class of "inertial" or "Galilean" reference systems, and thereby a *unique* rotational state, which is the state that Newton calls *absolute rotational rest*. If one chooses to formulate the dynamics in terms of some other choice of a state of rotational rest, the formulation is possible although a little involved; but what is of greatest systematic interest is the fact that one could *deduce* the arbitrary character of the choice, and one could still single out that unique rotational state (whether or not it be called "absolute rest") that Newton points to. This first mistake, then, concerns the form and substance of the detailed theory. The second is the mistake in critical procedure that I have just been arguing against. To make the point most sharply, I ask you to suppose that the structure of Newtonian dynamics were a little different from what it is, namely that in some way it singled out *two different* unique states of rotation. (By "different unique states" I mean not just that the pair of states is distinguished from all other states, but also that each of the two states is uniquely characterized as distinct from the other.) Suppose that Newton had chosen, for whatever reasons,—esthetic, theological, economic, psychiatric,—to call one of these two states, explicitly identified, "the state of absolute rotational rest." Then Reichenbach's statement, "There exists absolute space, but its state of motion cannot be determined," could be sharpened to mean that we can actually determine two definite states, but cannot tell which of them is the state of rest. And this would be wrong. For Newton would (we assume) have told us what *he means* by rest—how *he intends* to use the word—and this meaning on our supposition does single out a definite state. The only way to interpret Reichenbach's assertion as correct would be by taking it to mean that there is also another way in which the term "absolute rest" might have been used, in this suppositious theory. But this, while in the case contemplated an interesting remark—and one that might induce us to modify the terminology—could not be construed as saying that any part of the Newtonian formulation is wrong. If, on the other hand, the Newtonian theory singled out a pair of states, but afforded no intrinsic way to distinguish between them, then the statement that "there exists absolute space" would be of dubious content, but

HOWARD STEIN

the statement that "its state of motion—if it exists—cannot be determined" would be true, not just in the sense that *there is nothing that forces us to use a word in one way rather than another,* but in the sense that *there is no way to state unambiguously in terms of the theory how the word is to be used.*—The actual case of Newtonian dynamics corresponds to neither of these alternatives, when we consider only the concept of rotation: there is singled out within the theory one and only one unique rotational state, and while we are free to call this the state of absolute rotational rest or to refrain from using that term, if we do choose to use it at all, and to base our use upon the theory, there is really no other way. It is when we consider translation as well as rotation that we are led, as Huygens was, to deny not just the *determinability* but the *existence* of absolute space; for what Newtonian dynamics singles out is a *class* of states of motion, within which it allows no intrinsic distinctions to be made; but this class has the peculiarity that all its members have *the same rotational character.*

I should, then, summarize Newton's general position roughly as follows:—In philosophical disquisitions, one ought to rely neither upon immediate appearances, nor upon the common usage of words that play a crucial role; for common usage is not always adequate to the formulation of requisite principles. Now the science of dynamics has to deal with the phenomena of motion, and requires precise notions in order to build mathematical demonstrations. And the principles of dynamics, already discovered by earlier investigators and applied successfully to many phenomena, distinctly require a view of motion and therefore of place and space that cannot be explicated in terms simply of the geometrical relations among bodies. Therefore the only philosophical procedure is to adopt that conception of space and motion on which alone dynamics can be based—which implies, in particular, that (as in Newton's investigation of the solar system) considerations of *force* as well as of change of relative position must be brought to bear in order to determine the true state of motion or rest of bodies.

Viewed so, Newton's analysis of the notions of space and time is, but for the one shortcoming I have mentioned, a classic case of the analysis of the empirical content of a set of theoretical notions.

I should like to add a comment on the connection of Newton's views of space and time with his theology. Burtt emphasized this connection, and pointed out the affinity of Newton's theological ideas with those of Henry More (an affinity already noted by Leibniz). The observation is certainly both valid and interesting. But the corollary that one often finds asserted (for instance by Burtt in the passage I have quoted before), that Newton's doctrine of space, time, and motion, is based in part on his theology, is a *non sequitur*—and for the attempt to understand and evaluate that doctrine, a red herring. There is no serious reason to suppose that Newton, who rejected the doctrine of the Trinity on the basis of a critical analysis of texts, would have adopted a notion of space as the foundation of his mechanics because that notion formed part of the theology of Henry More. Newton's intellectual interests were far ranging; he desired, as Keynes has so vividly told us, to read the riddle of the Universe; but he was not an enthusiast: his attempts upon that riddle were passionate and possibly obsessive, but they were also very careful, accurate, and critical. It is surely more plausible that More's theology was (in part) acceptable to Newton because its conceptions agreed with those required by mechanics (as the conceptions of the philosophy and theology of Descartes did not). That is what Newton himself tells us, in effect; the celebrated passage on God in the General Scholium to Book III of the *Principia* concludes: "And thus much concerning God; to discourse of whom from the appearances of things, does certainly belong to Natural Philosophy." In the scholium on space and time, on the other hand, he tells us that we ought not to base our philosophical conceptions upon the authority of sacred texts, since these speak the language of ordinary discourse, not of philosophy.

NOTES

* Two lectures, based upon a longer paper written for the Newton conference at the University of Texas (November 10–12, 1966). A shorter talk based upon that paper was delivered at the conference; the present version was presented at The Rockefeller University, February 2 and 3, 1967.

It is a pleasure to acknowledge a great debt of gratitude to Abner Shimony, for advice, criticism, and unstinting encouragement while this paper was being conceived and written.

Some of the work leading to the paper was done during the author's tenure of a National Science Foundation Senior Postdoctoral Fellowship.

1 This represents a fundamental point of difference from the space-time of special relativity, in which there is an asymmetric order-relation "earlier than" for which the ordering is *not* total: the relation "neither is earlier" is not an equivalence, and therefore the definition of time as a quotient-set of W fails.

2 Straight lines that lie in an instantaneous space can be so regarded only in an extended sense, as representing "infinitely fast motions."

3 Huygens, for instance, wrote: "I am astonished that Mr. Newton has taken the trouble to construct, upon such an improbable and audacious hypothesis, so many Theorems and as it were a complete theory of the actions of the heavenly bodies. I mean his hypothesis that all the little particles of diverse bodies attract one another, in reciprocal squared ratio of the distances." That this remark, despite Huygens's own rejection of "the improbable and audacious hypothesis," is not ironical but expresses honest admiration, is clear from the sequel: "He may have been led to his theory . . . by the book . . . by Borelli . . .; but he was unable to penetrate the true foundations as did Newton—who had the advantage of knowing the measure of centrifugal force by the Theorems I have given."

4 It is somewhat ironic that just after stating his dissent from "the mutual attraction of the whole bodies," in his *Discours de la Cause de la Pesanteur*, Huygens expresses his acceptance and his admiration of Newton's theory that the astronomical force is gravitation, and remarks —somewhat wistfully, one feels—that while he had himself long supposed the underlying cause of weight to act near the sun as well as near the earth: "I had not at all extended the action of weight to such great distances, as from the Sun to the Planets, nor from the Earth to the Moon; because the Vortices of M. Des Cartes, which formerly had seemed very probable to me and which I had still in mind, stood in the way." Thus he shows regret at having failed to explore the possibility Newton did explore so successfully, for the sake of a theory he

formerly inclined towards but now rejects; and does so just when he has dissented, under the influence of his new theory, from the further conclusions that Newton was led to.

⁵ This is precisely the content of the fourth Rule of Philosophizing (added in the second edition of the *Principia*): "In experimental philosophy, propositions collected by induction from phenomena ought to be held for true, either accurately or very nearly, notwithstanding contrary hypotheses, until other phenomena occur, by which they are rendered more accurate or subject to exceptions.—This is to be done that the argument of induction be not destroyed by hypotheses." An equally forceful statement of this rule occurs in the *Opticks*: ". . . Analysis consists in making Experiments and Observations, and in drawing general Conclusions from them by Induction, and admitting of no Objections against the Conclusions, but such as are taken from Experiments, or other certain Truths. For Hypotheses are not to be regarded in experimental Philosophy. And although the arguing from Experiments and Observations by Induction be no Demonstration of general Conclusions; yet it is the best way of arguing which the Nature of Things admits of, and may be looked upon as so much the stronger, by how much the Induction is more general. And if no Exception occur from Phaenomena, the Conclusion may be pronounced generally. But if at any time afterwards any Exception shall occur from Experiments, it may then begin to be pronounced with such Exceptions as occur."

⁶ It seems that this irrelevance of the ether in the net gravitational interaction, on Newton's theory, contributed (alongside the argument he ordinarily adduces of the extreme rarity of the interplanetary medium) to Newton's doubt whether an ether causes gravity.—On the subject of this doubt, concerning which a number of comments were made at the Texas Newton conference, I have one small remark to add. Consider the following statement made by Fatio de Duillier, in a letter of 30 March 1694:

> Mr. Newton is still undecided between these two opinions. The 1ˢᵗ, that the cause of Weight is inherent in matter by an immediate Law of the Creator of the Universe: & the other, that Weight is produced by the Mechanical cause that I have discovered. . . .

While Fatio is not a reliable witness to the degree of favor shown by others towards his own hypothesis, the tolerance towards an ether theory of gravitation that he attributes to Newton is consistent with other statements of Newon's public attitude at the time. What I chiefly wish to suggest, however, is that although Newton clearly was then leaning away from an ether theory of gravitation, none of the statements of this leaning indicates a rejection of ethers altogether in physics. One should distinguish skepticism about the ether as a cause of gravitation from skepticism about the existence of hidden elastic fluid media affecting *some* physical interactions. I am not convinced that Newton ever showed serious doubt on the latter point. (Note the statement in Corollary 2 to Proposition VI, Book III—in all editions of the *Principia*—that the particles of an ether too must have weight. This obviously places in an awkward position any theory of weight as the *effect* of an ether; but on the question of the existence of an ether of some kind, it is at least neutral.)

⁷ The lines of the astronomical argument are somewhat obscured by the fact that it is the Third Law, rather than the induction already made, that Newton invokes in Corollary 1 of Proposition V to establish the mutuality of the astronomical forces. This use of the more vulnerable of the two available arguments may have contributed to Huygens's dissent on the point.

⁸ I am indebted to Professor I. B. Cohen for the remark that Cajori's transgression was not executed single-handed. In revising Motte's translation, Cajori made use of that of Robert Thorp. The latter rendered the clause "vim inferunt sacris literis, qui voces hasce de quantitatibus mensuratis ibi interpretantur" (third edition; first identical, save that there is no comma and "Sacris" appears for "sacris") as "those violate the accuracy of language, which ought to be kept sacred, who interpret these words for the measured quantities"; Cajori merely changed "sacred" to "precise."—This is an edifying history of the corruption of a text; its moral is *Caveat lector!* It is really hard to understand how Cajori, confronting Newton's Latin text and the versions of Motte and Thorp, made his choice.

⁹ For instance, what Newton calls "absolute quantity" of the earth's gravity is a property of the earth itself, which we call the earth's "gravitational mass"; in contrast with the "ac-

celerative quantity" of the earth's gravity, which varies from place to place and is a property of a point in a given position relative to the earth—the intensity of the earth's gravitational field at that point; and in contrast with the "motive quantity" of the earth's gravity, which depends both upon the place and the body acted on—the weight, or attraction exerted upon the body by the earth.

[10] Reichenbach refers to Newton as "the great dogmatist of absolutism"; Mach (whose treatment of Newton is quite sympathetic) mentions "his metaphysical liking for the absolute"; and Hermann Weyl—who usually writes pure gold—calls him "Newton, the absolutist."

HOWARD STEIN

DUDLEY SHAPERE

The Philosophical Significance of Newton's Science

I
N A FAMOUS PASSAGE IN THE PREFACE TO THE FIRST EDITION OF HIS *Principia,*
Newton declared that:

I offer this work as the mathematical principles of philosophy, for the whole
burden of philosophy seems to consist in this—from the phenomena of motions
to investigate the forces of nature, and then from these forces to demonstrate
the other phenomena. . . . I wish we could derive the rest of the phenomena of
Nature [besides those dealt with in this work] by the same kind of reasoning
from mechanical principles, for I am induced by many reasons to suspect that
they may all depend upon certain forces by which the particles of bodies, by
some causes hitherto unknown, are either mutually impelled towards one another, and cohere in regular figures, or are repelled and recede from one another.[1]

Newton's statement is characteristically cautious: the "burden of philosophy" is not
described categorically; it only "*seems* to be . . . ." Again, he only *suspects,* on the
basis of "many reasons," that his view is correct—phenomena "*may* all depend
upon certain forces," etc. And finally, at the end of the paragraph from which the
quoted passage is taken, he notes the possibility that there may be "some truer method
of philosophy." In spite of these qualifications, however, and in spite of some more
specific uneasiness which, as we shall see later, Newton himself (to say nothing of
his contemporaries) felt about the adequacy of this statement as a description of
the whole, ultimate burden of philosophy—despite all this, the passage is important
for understanding the logic behind the greater part of Newton's own scientific (or
"philosophical") reasoning, as well as the problems and approaches of a whole tradition of succeeding thinkers. For in many ways, this passage defines those problems
and approaches—that tradition. Besides prefacing a monumental example of "philosophy," reaching specific conclusions, in terms of the motions and forces of particles, about a vast body of "phenomena of Nature," and thus providing "many reasons" for suspecting that the approach may prove successful in other domains, this
statement of "the whole burden of philosophy" lays down a program for further
work. It establishes at once an ideal or goal of scientific investigation—a picture of
what a completed science would look like—and a set of categories in terms of which
the attempt to reach that goal should be made. It provides, that is, a statement of the
terms in which proper possible ultimate explanations are to be formulated. The phenomena of nature—all of them—are to be approached and explained in terms of
"forces" directed radially toward or away from "particles" which (to add a gloss to

the passage) are at rest or in motion in an infinite space. And a completed science would be one which explained all the phenomena of nature in terms of the interactions, through such forces, of such particles moving in space. And, finally, the principles of explanation of nature are to be expressed in the language of mathematics, the symbols of which are to be interpreted as standing for the forces, particles, and motions which exist in nature.

More detailed examination of the body of Newton's writings brings out further features of this picture of the aims, language, and subject-matter of science. At the end of the *Opticks*, Newton suggests, after having presented a number of reasons, that

> All these things being consider'd, it seems probable to me, that God in the Beginning form'd Matter in solid, massy, hard, impenetrable, moveable Particles, of such Sizes and Figures, and with such other Properties, and in such Proportion to Space, as most conduced to the End for which he form'd them; and that these primitive Particles being Solids, are incomparably harder than any porous Bodies compounded of them; even so very hard, as never to wear or break in pieces; no ordinary Power being able to divide what God himself made one in the first Creation. While the Particles continue entire, they may compose Bodies of one and the same Nature and Texture in all Ages: But should they wear away, or break in pieces, the Nature of Things depending on them, would be changed. . . . And therefore, that Nature may be lasting, the Changes of corporeal Things are to be placed only in the various Separations and new Associations and Motions of these permanent Particles.[2]

Stripped of their theological trappings, these remarks stand out both as a sketch of the "particles" of Nature and as a sketch of units to be appealed to in proper ultimate explanations. For to say that "God in the Beginning form'd Matter" in such a manner is, in part, one way of saying that no further explanation need be sought for the particles and their properties: they are explanatory, not in need of explanation. The assertion of their indestructibility has the same logical force. And, finally, the location of all "Changes of corporeal Things . . . only in the various Separations and new Associations and Motions of these permanent Particles" tells us what it is that needs to be explained: changes, under which heading must be included qualitative changes, e.g., of color, sound, etc., which are to be explained in terms of the motions (and forces) of particles. (It should also be added that *differences* of such qualities, e.g., of colors, as well as *changes* thereof, are to be explained thusly.) Further, as we shall see, the "changes" which are to be explained also include, for Newton, certain types of motions of the particles themselves, while other such types do not (at least in the same sense) require such explanation.[3]

The "other Properties" with which the particles are endowed are forces; one, a *vis inertiae*, which Newton equates (Definition III, *Principia*) with the *vis insita*:

> The *vis insita*, or innate force of matter, is a power of resisting, by which every Body, as much as in it lies, continues in its present state, whether it be of rest,

286   DUDLEY SHAPERE

or of moving uniformly forwards in a right line . . . this *vis insita* may, by a most significant name, be called inertia *(vis inertiae)* or force of inactivity.

This "innate force of matter," as has often been noted,[4] is akin to the "impetus" of the fourteenth-century Parisian school of Buridan, Oresme, and others; but the differences between the two concepts must not be passed over lightly. In the first place, Newton's *vis insita* opposes change of state of rest as well as of motion; impetus was definitely only a moving force, fully in the Aristotelian tradition of *omne quod movetur ab alio movetur* (everything that moves must be moved by something). A body at rest had no impetus. Secondly, Newton's force is "innate" and invariable; for most of the impetus theorists, on the other hand, impetus was something which could be added to or taken away from a body.[5] Thirdly, the *vis insita* or *vis inertiae* acts to keep a moving body moving in a specific way: rectilinearly, and at a uniform velocity; but there was rarely, among the fourteenth-century impetus theorists, a clear statement of precisely how impetus would affect the velocity of the body, and much confusion existed as to the kind of curve in which the body would move under the influence of impetus.[6] And finally, impetus was a force which *kept* the body (particle) going in motion, which drove it as a mover, in the old Aristotelian sense, the only difference being that impetus was an internal mover. Newton's *vis inertiae,* on the other hand, does not act to *keep* the body moving, but manifests itself *only* when its response is called up to resist some external agency which is trying to alter the state of motion or rest of the body.[7]

In addition to the *vis inertiae,* there are other sorts of forces also:

> It seems to me farther, that these Particles have not only a *Vis inertiae,* accompanied with such passive Laws of Motion as naturally result from that Force, but also that they are moved by certain active Principles, such as is that of Gravity, and that which causes Fermentation, and the Cohesion of Bodies.[8]

These "active forces" also originate in particles, but it is they that act to change the state of motion or rest of other particles. They are thus, in the language of *Principia,* "impressed forces" (or, perhaps better, the causes of impressed forces).

> Definition IV. An impressed force is an action exerted upon a body, in order to change its state, either of rest, or of uniform motion in a right line.
>
> This force consists in the action only, and remains no longer in the body when the action is over. For a body maintains every new state it acquires, by its inertia only. But impressed forces are of different origins, as from percussion, from pressure, from centripetal force.

Indeed, Newton maintained an open mind as to the kinds of such "active forces" there might be:

> . . . it's well known, that Bodies act one upon the other by the Attractions of Gravity, Magnetism, and Electricity; and these Instances shew the Tenor and Course of Nature, and make it not improbable but that there may be more at-

tractive Powers than these. For Nature is very consonant and conformable to her self.[9]

There are some crucial differences between the concepts of *vis inertiae* and *vis impressa*. The *vis inertiae* of a body, as was remarked above, does not (as the concept of impetus did) explain the continuance of a body in its state of rest or uniform rectilinear motion, in the sense of being an internal pushing agent causing that body to be or continue in that state. Let us examine this point further; for one might suppose that, even though Newton's own definition is (or should be) perfectly clear on this point, it would at least have been consistent for the concept of inertia to be interpreted as referring to an internal force causing a body to continue at rest or with uniform velocity. That this is not even a *possible* interpretation—that to treat *vis inertiae* as a cause *in the same sense* as impressed force (the only difference being that the former is internal, the latter external) would lead to contradiction—is shown by the following considerations. First, if it were such a force, then, as Jammer points out,[10] the third law of motion would be violated: for what would be the equal and opposite reaction? And if there were, in this exceptional sort of case, no equal and opposite reaction, then the unresisted force constantly acting on the body (from within) should, on other sound Newtonian principles, produce a constant acceleration instead of a constant velocity. Furthermore, inertia is a constant, unvarying property of a body, while the uniform rectilinear velocity which the body possesses can take on any of an infinite number of values. But it is a logical property of the notion of "cause" (or "causal explanation"), or at least of the most usual usage of that expression, that a variation in an effect requires a corresponding variation in the cause.[11] Thus it is no accident that inertia—the inertial mass—enters into calculations in Newtonian physics not as a "force" causing or explaining the rest or uniform rectilinear motion of a body; rather, it enters into other sorts of calculations entirely: fundamentally,[12] into calculations of the *impressed* forces acting *on* the body (or, when the forces are known, into calculations of the body's response thereto); or, when inertia acts as "impulse," when "the body, by not easily giving way to the impressed forces of another, endeavors to change the state of that other" (Definition III), it enters into calculation of the *impressed* forces which the body exerts on *other* bodies. Inertia, like other characteristics of bodies (particles), manifests itself in interactions with other bodies—in its effects on and responses to other bodies—not as an internal driving *vis* maintaining the body in its "inertial" state.

The differences between *vis inertiae* and *vis impressa* may be characterized in either of two alternative ways. On the one hand, we may rest content with Newton's use of the term *"vis"* in connection with inertia, and, concomitantly, we may describe the role of the *vis inertiae* as being that of a cause (or as providing a causal explanation) of a body's maintaining an inertial state. But if we do so speak, we must remember that the terms *"vis"* and "cause" are being used in a sense very different from that in which they are used in connection with impressed forces. It is clearly the latter

288   DUDLEY SHAPERE

that, in Newton's physics, play the role of "causes" *in the sense that* they are (or, more precisely, originate in) independent agencies in terms of which variable effects are to be explained. And in this sense, the *vis inertiae* is not an internal pushing-agent counterpart of the *vis impressa*—a distinct agent causing a certain kind and degree of effect; it is essential to particles, definitory (or at least forming part of the definition) of them.

There are undoubtedly historical precedents for Newton's use of the word *"vis"* in connection with inertia, and for our describing the role of inertia as that of a "cause" of a body's maintaining its state of rest or uniform rectilinear motion: Aristotle himself, after all, spoke of "nature" as "a source or *cause* (aitia) of being moved and of being at rest . . ." etc.[13] But on the other hand, it must also be recalled that it was against just such sorts of "explanations," among others, that sixteenth- and seventeenth-century philosophical revolutionaries were objecting when they protested all appeals to internal, invisible, "occult" causes as not being *truly* explanatory.

For this reason, as well as because of the potential confusion resulting from the use of the same term for two very different ideas, it is therefore tempting to make the distinction between *vis inertiae* and *vis impressa* explicit by saying that the fact that a body is at rest, or is in uniform rectilinear motion, is not to be explained (causally) in terms of the *vis inertiae*—or, for that matter, for Newton, in terms of any other sort of "force." (That is, in this sense of the word "cause," and in the sense in which a "force" is a "cause" of the behavior of particles, *vis inertiae* is not a force.) Being in an inertial state is, indeed, on this use of the term "cause," not to be explained causally in terms of *anything*: bodies (particles) simply *do* continue in a state of rest or uniform rectilinear motion unless compelled to change that state by external (impressed) forces. Inertial motion (or rest) is thus *uncaused*; and it is further tempting to put this point positively by saying that the inertial state is "natural" to bodies, what requires causal explanation being any deviation from such a state.

Characterization of the inertial state as "natural" is not uncommon. One of the most recent descriptions in this vein is that given by Margula Perl, who also quotes a very early similar description:

> The first [law of motion, the] "Law of Inertia," is probably the least problematic, and Maclaurin's comment that "From this law it appears why we inquire not in philosophy concerning the cause of the continuation of the rest of bodies, or of their uniform motion in a right line" is still probably the best comment on the law.[14]

In spite of the frequency of this way of characterizing the inertial state, and of contrasting it with accelerated motion, however, calling the inertial state of a body "natural" has its dangers too. As with all such technical terms, one must be wary here of being misled. For example, the notion of "natural" applied as above to inertial motion (or rest) is not in every way the same as the notion of "natural" in Aristotle. For bodies in Newton's science to respond to impressed forces by accelerating in specific ways can in one sense be characterized as being just as "natural" as for them to continue in uniform rectilinear motion in the absence of such forces. Thus the word "natural" applied to the inertial state must not be taken as the opposite of "unnatural"—a contrast that is easy to make in connection with Aristotle's usage. But if we understand the term "natural" as meaning simply "not in need of explanation in terms of external agencies," we shall see shortly that Newton's science may be viewed in an illuminating way in terms of this distinction: in a way which, in taking account of the differences between *vis inertiae* and *vis impressa* in Newton's science, does not do violence to the actual intent of those concepts, and in a way which, further, brings out important features of his science as compared and contrasted with other scientific traditions.[15]

The preceding discussion enables us to see, behind the Newtonian views outlined above, a deep background framework of ideas concerning the nature of explanation and related notions. For there is, lying behind Newton's approach, a family of concepts or terms which, in at least some important uses, are strongly interlocked with one another—so much so that the applicability of one such concept or term may (in those uses or senses) be said to "imply" something about the applicability of the others. Whether such relationships should be referred to as "logical," or, with Wittgenstein, as "grammatical" (suggesting that they are relationships between linguistic terms or usages), or simply as "conceptual," and whether (and in precisely what way) anything would be gained by referring to them as "non-empirical," are real and important issues. But I will not consider these issues at present, but will simply use the terms "logical," "conceptual," "grammatical," and "non-empirical" indiscriminately.[16] In any case, the family of thus interrelated terms (concepts) relevant to the present discussion includes "explanation," "change," and "cause."[17] And the relevant relationship between these concepts is expressed adequately enough for present purposes in the philosophical dictum, "Every change (or every event) must have a cause (or, requires a causal explanation)."

In many uses—the uses which are of primary relevance to the discussion of Newton's science—these terms are also linked "logically" to another class of terms which includes the terms "entity" and "behavior (of entities)," in such a way that implications hold between the concepts of "change," "cause," and "explanation" on the one hand, and "entity" and "behavior (of entities)" on the other. Thus it is a logical truth—not an "empirical" one, in any clear sense of that difficult term—that, in the senses relevant here, "The cause of any change must lie in the behavior of an entity." Further, a very important point, for our purposes, is that the "entity" whose "behavior" causes a "change" must—and this "must" is, again, a sign that the point is a logical (conceptual, grammatical) one, not an "empirical" one—lie "outside of," or be "external to" or "independent of" the change (changing event, changing entity) itself.[18]

DUDLEY SHAPERE

But all this network of interconnected concepts is not sufficient for the purpose of application: for that, it must be made specific. For, though the interrelationships outlined do hold for those uses of these terms which are relevant here, they leave open a number of questions. What, precisely, is to count as an "entity"—something capable of behaving, of causing (and, it may be added, of being affected)? What is to count as the behavior of an entity? As a change? As something happening "outside of" or "independent of" an event or change? And how, specifically, is the behavior of an entity linked to the causing (the causal explanation) of some change or event?

The principle of inertia as contrasted with the Aristotelian view of motion provides a well-known example of how such specification can, and needs to be, made, and of how it can be made differently by different thinkers (and, indeed, of how the specifications can be *characteristic* of the theories and their differences from one another). For the Aristotelian tradition, rest—at least of an element in its natural place—was "natural" (in our sense, even if in others also) to a body: it did not constitute a change requiring a causal explanation in the sense outlined above (the "nature" of the body was the "cause" of that behavior[19]). Motion, on the other hand—or at least violent motion[20]—did count as such a change, and required an external cause constantly applied in contact with the moving body. Upon removal of the cause, the body would (if in its natural place) come to rest immediately or (if not in its natural place) immediately assume its natural motion toward its natural place of rest.

The concept of inertia constituted a shift as to what it is about motion that needs to be explained in terms of an external cause, and what does not. Certain sorts of motions—uniform rectilinear ones—are now put into the same category as rest had been in for the Aristotelian tradition. For whereas uniform rectilinear motion (at least when "violent") required, in Aristotelian physics, a constantly applied external cause, it no longer does so in Newtonian physics. To put the point in terms of the preceding discussion, inertial motion no longer counts as the *kind* of "change" that requires a causal explanation: accelerations are such "changes." Care must be exercised here: for though it is true that, in one sense, even inertial motion can be called a "change"—it is change of position—nevertheless the mere fact that a body changes position is not, for Newton, sufficient ground for asking for a causal explanation— an explanation in terms of an external agency responsible for the behavior. What *counts* as the kind of "change" requiring a "cause" has, in Newtonian science, shifted from its Aristotelian meaning; in the sense of the term "change" in which "every change requires a cause," not all kinds of motion are "changes."[21]

The whole of Newton's conception of the subject-matter of science can, in fact, be profitably viewed as a set of such specifications of the general network of concepts involving "change," "explanation," "cause," "externality," "entity," and "behavior." The kind of "change" that requires explanation in terms of a "cause" is, as we have seen, acceleration—and, it must be added, all "qualities," such as colors and sounds and their differences and changes. What does not require such explanation is the state of uniform rectilinear motion, of which rest is a special case. This is in opposition to the Aristotelian specification, according to which rest and motion (at least when violent) are not on a par, uniform rectilinear motion (at least when violent) being included in the class of changes requiring explanation in terms of a cause.

Further, the notion of "mass" is a specification, in Newton's physics, of what counts as an entity (or at least as an ultimately real or fundamental entity, all other so-called entities being associations of mass-particles, and all their properties and behavior being ultimately explainable in terms of the motions of masses and the forces centered therein). The notion of mass-centered, centrally-directed forces is a determinate expression of what counts as a cause, along with the motions of bodies which alter the strength of those forces with respect to other bodies within their range. The motions of particles, and their impression of forces on other bodies (including the variation of those impressed forces with the changes of relative position of the particles concerned) specifies what counts as the "behavior" of entities. And, finally, the notion that a cause must be "external" to its effect is reflected, and specified, in the fundamental explanatory role played in Newtonian physics by impressed forces.

These specifications are summarized in part, though implicitly, in the laws of motion, particularly in the first two. For we can look on those laws as making, in effect, the distinction made above between "natural" and "deviant" behavior—between behavior that does not require explanation in terms of a cause (an "external" cause) and behavior that does. The laws distinguish, that is, between "behavior" that is "uniform," and which therefore (logically) does not require a causal explanation, and "behavior" that is not "uniform"—behavior that counts as "change" in the sense in which it is a "logical" truth that "every change requires a cause (causal explanation)." The first law of motion ("Every body perseveres in its state of rest, or of uniform motion in a right line, unless it is compelled to change that state by forces impressed thereon") has, among other jobs, the function of telling us that it is only deviations from uniform straight-line motion (or rest) that need to be accounted for in terms of a cause (in the form of an external agency)—ordinarily, at least[22]— and that such deviations are to be accounted for (causally) in terms of "impressed forces." The second law ("The alteration of motion is ever proportional to the motive force impressed; and is made in the direction of the right line in which that force is impressed") spells out in more detail the precise characteristics (the direction and amount) of the forces required to produce a given amount of deviation. And elsewhere in Newton's writings we learn that such forces acting on any particle must ultimately originate in other centers of mass.[23]

In this paper, we have distinguished between two levels in Newton's view of the subject-matter which science is to investigate: first, a general conceptual framework consisting of "logically" related concepts like "change," "cause," and "entity"; and second, a set of specifications of that background framework in terms of such notions as "accelerated motion," "force," and "mass." What seems peculiarly Newtonian is the way the general framework has been specified; for Aristotelian science

DUDLEY SHAPERE

specified some of the same (or, more precisely, a closely related) background frame-work differently.[24] A number of questions arise concerning these different specifica-tions. What warrant is there, ultimately, for selecting one set of specifications of a general background framework rather than another? Are there really "many reasons" which support the Newtonian specification of what counts, e.g., as a "change" re-quiring a "cause," and which cannot be taken account of in terms of the Aristotelian specification? Or is the difference merely a matter of "handling the same bundle of data as before, but placing them in a new system of relations with one another by giving them a different framework, all of which virtually means putting on a different kind of thinking-cap"[25]? Is it a matter of adopting a different "paradigm"[26] with which to approach nature, in the sense that a radically new set of problems to meet, definitions of facts, and standards of acceptability, replaces an old one with which it is not only incompatible but even "incommensurable," and such that no good reasons can *really* be given for its acceptability?

These are important questions, to be sure; but there are also questions that need to be asked about the background framework itself. Is there—*can* there be—only one such framework, which lies (or even which *must* lie) behind all science, past, present, and future? Need there always be one, or is the reliance on such backgrounds some-thing that science outgrows with maturity? (Or, alternatively, does the development of science make it more and more impossible for philosophers to abstract from con-crete scientific theories any such "background framework"?) And if there is more than one background, are there any good reasons for employing, in science, one rather than another, or for abandoning one in favor of another? Is the background framework (whatever may be said about its set of specifications) described ade-quately as a set of "*a priori* assumptions," as "metaphysical presuppositions," or at least as containing a strong element thereof? Again, we may ask whether the back-ground framework is described adequately as a set of "metascientific concepts," the special concern of philosophers, who are supposed to deal (according to some views) not with the actual content of science, but rather with the analysis of those terms which are used in talking *about* science ("metascientific" ones, including such terms as "explanation," "cause," "entity").

Not all of these questions can be answered here, of course; but some light can be thrown on the issues concerned by contrasting the view presented here with certain traditional philosophical doctrines. For, after all, such concepts as "cause," "change," and "entity," which form part of the background of Newton's science as interpreted here, have traditionally been discussed or employed in writings referred to as "meta-physical." The latter word covers so many different ideas as to be almost useless; but there are a few reasonably clear allegations which have been made as to the role of such concepts with regard to science. And none of these roles is played by the background framework as conceived here. Thus, if that framework is characterized as "metaphysical," it is not metaphysical in the most usual or clear senses of classical philosophy. It does not consist of a set of propositions from which the substantive propositions of science can (allegedly) be deduced; nor does it consist of a set of propositions which (allegedly) must be added as premises to some or any scientific propositions in order to deduce further consequences; nor does it consist of a set of "presuppositions" guaranteeing that scientific method will work as a tool of discovery or of induction. On the contrary, the background framework as conceived here consists of a set of concepts (and propositions relating those concepts) which are made specific and applicable by a particular scientific theory.[27]

Nor, again, is there any implication, in the view presented in this paper, that the background framework of Newtonian science consists of a set of concepts which cannot be avoided—which must be employed in *any* attempt, past, present, or future, to characterize the scientific endeavor. Indeed, I have suggested elsewhere, "There is in the range of scientific theories a spectrum of departures from such everyday-life concepts as 'entity' and 'behavior' that makes those terms inadequate to a lesser or greater degree for talking about those theories."[28] Unless we stretch the meanings of the words beyond utility, the concepts of (for example) "entity" and "behavior of entities," which are so naturally applied in discussion of Newtonian physics, become harder to apply to theories which talk, e.g., about electromagnetic fields and variations in field intensities. Thus the framework in terms of which Newtonian science has been discussed here does not consist of a set of necessary, *a priori* propositions (and concepts) in terms of which *any* scientific system must be specified. Nor, correlatively, does it consist of a set of "metascientific" concepts, *at least* in the sense of a set of category-terms for characterizing any scientific theory.

The interpretations given in this paper must not be considered as being concerned with *all* aspects of Newton's work, but only with that facet, illustrated by the passages referred to earlier, which was most influential on the subsequent history of thought: which provided a conception of the aims, methods, and subject-matter of science, and the clarification and extension of which set the problems for a whole tradition of succeeding philosophers and scientists. There are, however, other sides of Newton. Two of these stand out most prominently, though not as facets completely independent of that outlined here, but rather as attempts to answer criticisms, levelled chiefly by continental thinkers, against views connected with those discussed here. On the one side, we find him attempting to answer such objections by giving an account of gravitation in terms of an "Aethereal Medium."[29] And on the other side, we see him answering the same objections by maintaining that, in speaking of attraction, he is not attempting to give an explanation at all, but only a description. The present interpretation is not meant to apply to those views, but rather to provide an account of a central body of Newtonian doctrine in terms of which his adoption of those other views can be understood.

NOTES

[1] I. Newton, *Philosophiae Naturalis Principia Mathematica,* Berkeley, University of California Press, 1946, pp. xvii–xviii.

DUDLEY SHAPERE

2 Newton, *Opticks,* New York, Dover, 1952, p. 400. Another list of properties of particles, somewhat, though not fundamentally, different from the account in the *Opticks,* occurs in *Principia:* "The extension, hardness, impenetrability, mobility, and inertia of the whole, result from the extension, hardness, impenetrability, mobility, and inertia of the parts; and hence we conclude the least particles of all bodies to be also all extended, and hard and impenetrable, and movable, and endowed with their proper inertia. And this is the foundation of all philosophy." (*Principia,* p. 399) The basis of this inference from "macroscopic" to "microscopic" characteristics is Rule III of the Rules of Reasoning in Philosophy: "The qualities of bodies, which admit neither intensification nor remission of degrees, and which are found to belong to all bodies within reach of our experiments, are to be esteemed the universal qualities of all bodies whatsoever." (p. 398) In the light of contemporary quantum theory, such a principle of inference appears naïve and erroneous.

Note the absence of gravity from Newton's lists of the properties of particles. For though gravity, like inertia, is universally found in the bodies we experience, and admits of "neither intensification nor remission of degrees," Newton refuses to draw the conclusion that it is *essential* to matter, a primary property of particles, like inertia: "we must . . . universally allow that all bodies whatsoever are endowed with a principle of mutual gravitation. . . . Not that I affirm gravity to be essential to bodies: by their *vis insita* I mean nothing but their inertia." (*Principia,* pp. 399–400) Action at a distance proved embarrassing enough to Newton to lead him here to make an exception in the application of Rule III, and to distinguish, in this case, between what is essential and what is merely universal in matter.

3 The concept of explanation has traditionally exerted more or less definite types of intuitive appeals, directing analyses of that concept, and, correlatively, of nature and of science, along certain general paths. Such tendencies of analysis have, however, usually been left tacit, and, furthermore, are not necessarily consistent with one another. Among the historically and philosophically more important of these tendencies (together with some sketch of the kind of tacit line of argument accompanying them) are the following. "What require explanation are *changes;* and therefore what does not require explanation, *i.e.,* the fundamental explanatory factors themselves, must be absolutely unchanging. For if they changed (or even, perhaps, if they could change), then those changes (or the possibility thereof) would have to be subject to explanation, and so those factors would not be fundamental explanatory factors at all. And thus if explanation—or at least ultimate explanation—is to be possible at all, there must be explanatory factors which are not subject to change." What require explanation are *differences;* therefore what does not require explanation, the fundamental explanatory factors themselves, must be factors which are 'alike.' " (The remainder of the accompanying argument in this and the succeeding cases is similar to that in the first example.) "What requires explanation is *diversity;* hence what is used to explain must be a 'unity'." "What requires explanation is *complexity;* therefore what is appealed to for the sake of explaining must be 'simple.' " The rationale behind various interpretations of the aims and subject-matter of scientific investigation—e.g., those interpretations associated with atomistic "theories"—have thus not always been purely empirical, but have often rested on such *a priori* considerations as these. There have been a multitude of other such "tendencies," some associated with conflicts between continuum and discrete theories of matter, others connected with controversies as to the respective roles of the concepts of space ("geometry") and matter in scientific explanation, and still others with the tension between traditional "metaphysical" and "empiricist" approaches to explanation. These forces in the development of science have received little or no attention from philosophers of science: yet a thorough analysis of them, and of their precise logical role in the scientific endeavor, seems very much needed.

4 For example, by Dijksterhuis: "Newton still shares Aristotle's view that every motion requires a *motor,* in the modified form of it given by the Paris Terminists, who assumed that this motor resides in the body. The *Vis Inertiae* apparently is identical with the *Impetus* of this school and the *Vis Impressa* of Galileo." (E. J. Dijksterhuis, *The Mechanization of the World Picture,* Oxford, Clarendon, 1961, p. 466.) Dijksterhuis does not discuss any differences between Newton's conception and these earlier ones, but apparently simply equates them.

[5] With regard to this point (as in many other respects), the closest parallel to Newton's view among the impetus theorists, at least until the sixteenth century, was the view of John Buridan. Buridan did look upon impetus as something which was not *self*-expending (as his chief predecessor, Franciscus of Marchia, and his chief immediate successor, Nicole Oresme, maintained); in the absence of counterforces, the impetus will be conserved, according to Buridan, and in this sense is "permanent." It will, however, be destroyed by contrary agencies, if any are present—as Newton's inertia cannot be. For Newton, the measure of inertia is the (inertial) mass of the body, and this is invariant: a body at rest still has it. For Buridan, however, presumably when the impetus is used up in combating external resisting or otherwise corruptive influences, the body comes to rest *and is left with no further impetus*. Buridan's view that the impetus of the celestial spheres, at least, is incorruptible is, of course, no argument against this interpretation; for those impetuses are incorruptible as a matter of *fact* rather than of *logic*. (". . . these impetuses which [God] impressed in the celestial bodies were not decreased or corrupted afterwards because there was no inclination of the celestial bodies for other movements. Nor was there resistance which would be corruptive or repressive of that impetus." (M. Clagett, *The Science of Mechanics in the Middle Ages,* Madison, University of Wisconsin Press, 1959, p. 525)) For such impetuses *would* be corrupted if as a matter of fact there *were* any contrary agencies present. In other words, Buridan's celestial impetus is something imposed by God, inessential to the heavenly bodies. Newton's inertia *cannot* be corrupted; it is constitutive, indeed definitive (at least partially) of particles. A body may be brought to rest (for example) by contrary forces; but it still has the same amount of inertia.

[6] As Clagett (*op. cit.*, p. 520) notes, the successors of Buridan (at least until the sixteenth century) were generally confused as to whether impetus tends to produce uniform motion or accelerated motion; further, "One serious defect of this medieval theory is that there was no sure distinction between rectilinear and circular impetus. It was equally possible to impose rectilinear or circular impetus. We must await the sixteenth century for a clarification of the directional aspects of impetus." (Clagett, *op. cit.*, p. 525) Buridan did, in a "quasi-quantitative" way, according to Clagett, hold that impetus is proportional to the velocity of the projectile (as well as to the quantity of matter—but note that this makes the concept analogous not to inertia, but rather to momentum). (Clagett, pp. 522–23) The impetus theory, in its various manifestations (especially with Buridan) was certainly an important step on the way to the Newtonian conception of inertia, and shows many vital similarities to the Newtonian idea, as I have tried to point out elsewhere (D. Shapere, "Meaning and Scientific Change," in R. Colodny (ed.), *Mind and Cosmos,* Pittsburgh, University of Pittsburgh Press, 1966, pp. 41–85; see especially pp. 71–81). But the differences noted here must not be ignored. It is also true that, with the sixteenth century, particularly with Benedetti, the impetus theory tended more and more clearly toward the Newtonian conception. Even there, however, many of the differences noted here remained.

[7] We must not be deceived here by Newton's remark that inertia "is resistance so far as the body, for maintaining its present state, opposes the force impressed; it is impulse so far as the body, by not easily giving way to the impressed force of another, endeavors to change the state of that other." (Def. III) For this passage does not imply that inertia, like impetus, is the cause of the motion of the body itself.

[8] Newton, *Opticks,* p. 401.

[9] *Ibid.*, p. 376. In this connection, the Halls have noted that Newton "was not even sure whether there was one basic force, or a pair of repulsive and attractive forces, or as many forces as there were classes of phenomena—gravitational, magnetic, electrical, optical, chemical, and physiological—involving such forces." (A. R. Hall and M. B. Hall (eds.), *Unpublished Scientific Papers of Isaac Newton,* Cambridge, Cambridge University Press, 1962, p. 203.)

Newton also considered forces to be *effects* of (accelerated) motions as well as causes thereof; this aspect of his work will not, however, be considered in this paper.

[10] M. Jammer, *Concepts of Mass,* Cambridge, Harvard University Press, 1961, p. 71.

[11] Mill's "Method of Concomitant Variation," when filtered of its many errors and misleading features, reduces essentially to this logical point.

The aspect of the notion of "cause" which will be central in the following discussion is that of "cause of a change"; such notions as "cause of existence" and "cause of difference" will not be discussed, despite the fact that the latter notion, in particular, is important in Newton's science. For in his theory of light, differences of color in a spectrum are explained (causally) by differences in the component rays of white light and their different degrees of refrangibility.

[12] I.e., except when the notion of (inertial) mass (which turns out in calculational practice to be the heart of the notion of "quantity of matter") enters into the *definition* of a quantity, as it does in the definition of "quantity of motion" (Def. II).

Jammer (*Concepts of Mass*, p. 72) argues that "for Newton, in contrast to 'Newtonian mechanics,' 'inertial mass' is a reducible property of physical bodies, depending on their 'quantity of matter.'" It is not easy to see what Jammer means by "reducible" in this connection; as he himself points out, "It is, of course, always rather difficult to state exactly whether two concepts are involved or only one, once a general proportionality between the concepts has been established." (This remark is not entirely correct, for inertial and gravitational mass are, despite their necessary proportionality, clearly distinct in Newtonian physics due to their independent mode of introduction.) Apparently the reasoning behind Jammer's view is that *quantitas materiae* has other properties than inertial mass; he cites gravitational mass. (". . . it is fairly obvious that 'quantity of matter' is still a notion for itself. A careful examination of the text of Book III of the *Principia*, for instance, shows clearly that it is *quantitas materiae* in the original sense of the word which determines the magnitude of gravitational attraction.") Jammer's appeal to gravitation, however, is unfortunate; for, as was pointed out above, gravitational mass is not an essential characteristic of matter, while inertia is. ("Not that I affirm gravity to be essential to bodies: by their *vis insita* I mean nothing but their inertia.") On the other hand, it is true that, for Newton, there are characteristics besides inertia which *are* essential to matter—e.g., solidity, hardness, impenetrability. And in this sense, inertia (inertial mass) constitutes only *part* of the notion (definition, essence) of matter; and—still in this sense—inertia can be said, somewhat confusingly, to be "reducible" to *quantitas materiae*. Jammer's view, when properly interpreted, is thus defensible, although it is rather more innocuous than it might at first seem: for inertial mass is certainly not to be *understood in terms of quantitas materiae*; nor is it caused by the latter, and so is not "reducible" to the latter in either of these interesting senses.

[13] Aristotle, *Physics*, Bk. II, 192b 22.

[14] M. Perl, "Newton's Justification of the Laws of Motion," *Journal of the History of Ideas*, Vol. XXVII (1966), p. 585.

[15] I do not, of course, wish to suggest that this distinction between "natural" and "deviant," as employed here in connection with Newton, is an essential feature of explanation, or of scientific explanation in particular. Specifically, I do not mean to imply that there must be, within any scientific theory, a distinction between two classes of events, one of which includes events always requiring causal explanation, and the other of which includes events not doing so.

[16] Indeed, one must suspect that the distinction between "empirical" and "non-empirical," at least, is highly misleading when applied to the sorts of relationships being discussed here: for many of the same sorts of considerations that count for or against what are usually referred to as "empirical" propositions in science have also counted for or against ideas and interconnections in this "nonempirical" framework of ideas.

[17] Not *all* types or facets of the uses of these terms exhibit the connections here noted, however; thus the term "explanation" has wider uses than those in which it is linked to the notions of "cause" and "change." For example, in such statements as, "Explain how to play chess," "Explain the theory of relativity to me," and "Einstein's theory explains the advance of the perihelion of Mercury," the sense of "explanation" is not that of what has been referred to here as "causal explanation." Again, it is not true that all "explanations" which are appropriately called "causal" are explanations of what may appropriately be called "changes": some causal explanations (e.g., explanations of difference of color in optics) are explanations of differences rather than of changes. (See Footnote 3, above.) And not all "changes" require "causes" either—as the present argument attempts to show, changes of position

do not, for Newton, always require causes. There are similar exceptions in the cases of the other terms discussed here. Nevertheless, there do exist uses (senses) of these expressions in which the "logical" connections asserted do hold.

[18] One sort of objection (there were others also) made in the seventeenth century against "occult causes" rested essentially on this point: that the supposed "causes" were really not explanatory at all, but rather were identical with the object or event to be explained. The requirement that the cause be "distinct from," "external to," or "independent of" the effect thus involves not merely an objection against appealing to causes which cannot be discovered or observed; it involves a "logical" point as to what can *count* as an explanation—as to what can properly be called "an explanation."

[19] See Aristotle's definition of "nature," quoted above.

[20] The Aristotelian and Newtonian conceptions of the relation between force and motion are often distinguished by saying that, for the former, force is the cause of motion, whereas for the latter, force is the cause of change of motion. This way of stating the difference, however, is misleading. For example, apart from reading the notion of force into Aristotelian physics, where it does not unambiguously belong, the view that, for that tradition, all motion requires a "force" applies primarily to violent motion. For while natural motion requires a mover, that mover is, for most of the tradition, the "nature" of the thing moved, and not an external (or, if internal, at least independent) agency.

[21] This is presumably the point behind referring to uniform rectilinear motions (and rest) as *states*: "*Status* of motion: by using this expression Newton implies or asserts that motion is not, as had been believed for about two thousand years—since Aristotle—a process of change, in contradistinction to *rest*, which is truly a *status*, but is also a *state*, that is, something that no more implies change than does rest. . . . Nothing changes without a cause . . . as Newton expressly states. Thus, so long as motion was a process, it could not continue without a mover. It is only motion as *state* that does not need a cause or mover. Now, not all motion is such a *state*, but only that which proceeds uniformly and in a right line . . ." (A. Koyré, *Newtonian Studies*, Cambridge, Harvard University Press, 1965, pp. 66–67).

Later on page 67, Koyré makes an erroneous claim, which he and others have also made elsewhere, that "the law of inertia implies an infinite world." There is no logical reason, based on the law of inertia, why a body should not have its uniform rectilinear motion interfered with by impact against the "walls" of a finite universe.

[22] It is, of course, possible to ask, within Newtonian physics, why a certain particular body continues to move in a straight line with uniform velocity. But though the answer to such a question is to be given in terms of the balance of forces originating in other masses, nevertheless a body would continue in its state of uniform rectilinear motion even if there were no other masses in the universe. Uniform rectilinear motion does not *require* explanatory appeal to the existence of other masses—as accelerated motion always does.

Reformulations of classical mechanics have been constructed which would make illegitimate (or even "meaningless") any talk of the motion of a body in a universe devoid of other bodies. Such a reformulation has the effect of restoring a complete symmetry between the kinds of questions that can be raised concerning uniform rectilinear and accelerated motion. This symmetry is purchased, however, only at the expense of creating another asymmetry—namely, between universes in which there is only one object (particle) and universes in which there is more than one object (particle). (Often the illegitimacy is not limited to universes of only one object, but is extended to those of as many as four or five, on the ground that a "reference-frame" is necessary in order to be able to speak meaningfully of the motion of a particle.)

[23] In this connection, a particularly revealing remark occurs in the context of an argument, in *The System of the World,* to the effect that the stars cannot really go around the earth. If that view were correct, he says, then those stars which do not lie on the celestial equator would describe, in their daily rotations around the earth, circles whose centers would be, not the center of mass of the earth, but rather points on the earth's axis or on extensions of that axis into empty space. But, he declares in refutation of such a possibility, "That forces should be directed to no body on which they physically depend, but to innumerable imaginary points in

the axis of the earth, is an hypothesis too incongruous." (Newton, *The System of the World*, included in the California edition of *Principia*, p. 553.) "An hypothesis too incongruous": there must be a center of mass at the focus of the curve (or, if not, then the force centered there must be the resultant of forces which *are* centered in masses). Only an entity can cause an effect in another entity; and this, too, is a "logical" point.

²⁴ In what sense can the general background framework be said to be (or to have been) "presupposed"? In the case of Newton, it is certainly not suggested that he explicitly formulated such a "background framework," whether in advance of "specifying" it, or at any other period of his career. Nor, however—at the opposite extreme—would it be reasonable to contend that the set of background concepts outlined above constitutes merely a "reconstruction" of his scientific work, and one which, moreover, would have been fundamentally foreign to him and irrelevant to his own thought. There is abundant evidence throughout his writings that he thought of masses as entities acting on one another, causing them to behave in the ways they do (except for that "inertial" behavior which was "natural," requiring no such causal explanation). It is thus plausible to consider the present interpretation as lying between radical description and extreme reconstruction: although the background framework outlined here is not purely descriptive of Newton's most conscious, articulated thought, nevertheless it is an interpretation which has a solid grounding in his writings.

²⁵ H. Butterfield, *The Origins of Modern Science*, New York, Macmillan, 1958, p. 1. The word "framework" in this passage, of course, does not correspond closely to the meaning of "background framework" in our usage.

²⁶ T. S. Kuhn, *The Structure of Scientific Revolutions,* Chicago, University of Chicago Press, 1962. For a discussion of Kuhn's views, see my "The Structure of Scientific Revolutions," *Philosophical Review,* LXXIII (1964), 383–394. The present essay may be looked upon, partly, as showing (with reference to a particular historical case) what elements of Kuhn's view (and that of Paul Feyerabend) are correct, while at the same time avoiding crucial objections against their views. In this connection, the present paper should be read as a continuation of the review of Kuhn and of my article, "Meaning and Scientific Change," referred to above in Note 6. The latter paper ends with a discussion of similarities and continuities between late medieval and Newtonian mechanics, as the present paper begins with a discussion of differences between those theories.

²⁷ The "specification" that has been spoken of in this paper cannot be looked upon as consisting simply of the statement of a premise (e.g., "Deviations from uniform rectilinear motion or rest are changes") which, when conjoined with a "background premise" (e.g., "Every change requires a cause") implies the scientific law (e.g., "Deviations from uniform rectilinear motion require a cause"—though here further specification is necessary to convert "cause" into "force"). For such a way of interpreting the relationship evades the crucial connections between the *terms* involved.

It is almost ironic that the "background concepts" *might* be looked upon as a set of purely "theoretical concepts," defined "implicitly" by their relations to one another, and given an "empirical interpretation" in terms of a set of "correspondence rules" (their specifications). Surely the positivistic tradition would have blanched at the possibility of thus letting "metaphysics" in through the "back door" of science! (This possible "positivistic" way of looking at our "background framework" was suggested to me by Peter Achinstein.)

²⁸ D. Shapere, "The Causal Efficacy of Space," *Philosophy of Science,* XXXI (1964), p. 115.
²⁹ E.g., in Book Three of the *Opticks*.

NEWTON'S INFLUENCE

FRANCIS HASKELL

The Apotheosis of Newton in Art

"HAD THIS GREAT AND GOOD MAN," WROTE JOHN CONDUITT IN A SHORT NOTE just after Sir Isaac Newton's death in 1727, "lived in an age when those superiour Genii inventors were Deified or in a country where mortals are canonised he would have had a better claim to these honours than those they have hitherto been ascribed to; his virtues proved him a Saint and his discoveries might well pass for miracles."[1] Conduitt need not have been so jealous for his uncle's fame. As the century advanced Newton virtually was canonized—not only in England which, with King Charles I, had made such a limited and hitherto unpromising selection of saints, but also in countries which had a superfluity of the more conventional sort.

Well before Newton's death a poet could write of a vision:[2]

'Tis Newton's soul that daily travels here
In search of knowledge for Mankind below,

and the sentiment was echoed on the Continent. Indeed part of the enthusiasm aroused by Newton in England is unquestionably due to the fact that he was the first Englishman ever to attract really serious intellectual attention abroad. Fontenelle, Voltaire, Conti, Algarotti and a host of others spread his reputation throughout the world. Voltaire was not exaggerating when he wrote: "We are now all the disciples of Newton."[3] Such was the enthusiasm that he aroused in Algarotti, author in 1737 of *Newtonianismo per le Dame* soon translated into English as *Sir Isaac Newton's philosophy explain'd for the use of the ladies,* that on the tomb that Frederick the Great had erected for his Italian friend in Pisa were merely inscribed the words: "Algarotto/Ovidii Aemulo/Newtoni Discipulo."

The enthusiasm is easy enough to explain. It has been convincingly argued[4] that the hostility of the Enlightenment to the Catholic Church did not involve a corresponding weakening of religious sentiment. For many people Newton merely replaced a more distant and shadowy creator as an object of adoration—a sentiment naïvely and clumsily expressed the year after his death and echoed throughout the century:[5]

Nature, compelled, his piercing Mind obeys,
And gladly shows him all her secret ways;
'Gainst Mathematics she has no Defence,
And yields t'experimental Consequence

The experiments into light and those into gravitation were of equal importance in arousing such fanatical adoration, for Newton's main achievement, in the eyes of the eighteenth century, was something much greater than either: it lay in showing that in whatever field man chose to explore, he could by his own efforts discover a rational purpose behind creation.

> Nature and Nature's Laws lay hid in night:
> God said, Let Newton be—And all was light.

The literary and philosophical consequences that followed from this assumption have been extensively discussed. I want to talk today about a side to the worship of Newton that has attracted little attention—its effect on the visual arts. And in doing so I have been enormously helped by being able to draw upon a mass of unpublished manuscripts of great interest, shown to me by the librarian of my college, Mr. A.N.L. Munby.

During his lifetime a very large number of portraits were painted of Newton—by Lely, Sir Godfrey Kneller, Vanderbank, Thornhill, William Gandy, and others. The period of his life was probably the dimmest in the whole history of English art, and it seems to me that few if any of these rise much above the mediocre. Certainly none of them presents any particular interest for the present study.

The first great opportunity for a memorial came with the erection of Newton's tomb in Westminster Abbey. This was commissioned from William Kent and the Flemish sculptor Michael Rysbrack by John Conduitt, and it was completed in 1731, four years after Newton's death.[6] (Figure 1) A number of preliminary sketches exist,

FIGURE I

and to these already known I would like to add an unpublished drawing among the Conduitt papers in Cambridge. (Figure 2) This seems to be clumsy enough in concep-

FIGURE 2

tion and weak enough in execution for us to infer that it is by Conduitt himself, and intended as a guide to the artists he had commissioned. We will shortly see that he was very keen on giving practical instructions of this kind. It is interesting because it includes an alternative version of Pope's famous verses, "All Nature and its laws lay hid in Night," and all the essential features of the tomb as it was eventually executed —the reclining figure of Newton, the pyramid, and the globe. Pope's lines were in fact published only in 1735, but we know from a letter that has survived that he and Conduitt were in correspondence about Sir Isaac Newton in November 1727,[7] and it

FRANCIS HASKELL

seems clear that the famous lines were actually written for the tomb, but were then rejected for obvious reasons.

The symbolism is explained in a note in *The Gentleman's Magazine* of April 22, 1731:[8] "Behind the Sarcophagus is a Pyramid; from the middle of it a Globe arises in Mezzo Relievo, on which several of the Constellations are drawn, in order to shew the path of the Comet in 1681, whose period he has with the greatest Sagacity determin'd. And also the Position of the solstitical Colure mention'd by Hipparchus, by which (in his Chronology) he has fixed the time of the Argonautic Expedition— On the Globe sits the Figure of Astronomy weeping, with a Sceptre in her Hand, (as Queen of the Sciences) and a Star over the Head of the Pyramid."

We know that John Conduitt himself was responsible for choosing this highly complex scheme, for among his papers in Cambridge is a note by him outlining his ideas for the bas-reliefs on the sarcophagus itself:[9] "In the Mainground—A boy weighing in a stillyard as in (a) the sun against all the other planets—On one side— a boy looking up to the sky thro' a prism, another looking thro' a reflecting Telescope. On the other side an aloes in a flower pott, to denote Vegetation and a limbeck to denote Chymistry, and a boy near pouring coin out of a horn; if the coins are so large as to be distinguished they may be the coins of K.Wm. Q.Anne. & K.G. those being the reigns in wch he was Master of the Mint." Conduitt, as we will see, was nothing if not thorough. The reliefs, as finally modified, are described in *The Gentleman's Magazine*: "On a Pedestal is placed a Sarcophagus (or Stone Coffin) upon the front of which are Boys in Basso-relievo with instruments in their hands, denoting his several discoveries, viz. one with a Prism on which principally his admirable Book of Light and Colours is founded; another with a reflecting Telescope, whose great Advantages are so well known; another Boy is weighting the Sun and Planets with a Stilliard, the Sun being near the Centre on one side, and the Planets on the other, alluding to a celebrated Proposition in his Principia; another is busy about a Furnace, and two others (near him) are loaded with money as newly coined, intimating his Office in the Mint."

Conduitt's admiration for Newton can also be seen in the bust which he commissioned from Roubiliac and which occupied the most prominent position in his drawing room, represented for us in Hogarth's well known painting of children performing "The Conquest of Mexico."

The tomb in Westminster Abbey aroused a good deal of interest which was reflected in, of all places, Venice. The Abate Conti, a great admirer and one-time friend of Newton, and Francesco Algarotti were both Venetians. For all that, Venice was hardly a center of Newtonian studies, and to avoid the censorship Algarotti had later to publish his book in Milan. Even so it was severely criticized in the Venetian press as potentially subversive.[10] Despite this, reflections of the tomb as it actually was and possible designs for an alternative turn up in a number of drawings and gouaches by Sebastiano and Marco Ricci in about 1730.[11]

We can be pretty certain where the inspiration for these projects came from, for when several years later a Venetian poet Arrighi–Landini came to write a long philosophical poem on Newton's tomb he describes the attempts he made to find out the inscription on it.[12] "It was," he writes, "very kindly given to me by Signor Giuseppe Smith, Consul of the English Nation in Venice, a man as remarkable for his rare talents, his goodness, and sweetness of temperament as for the love which he feels for the fine arts." Joseph Smith had been a prosperous businessman and art collector in Venice since early in the eighteenth century and we know from a number of sources that he was in close touch with Newton's London friends, in particular Dr. Richard Mead, and was a keen admirer of the great scientist. The significance of this connection will become apparent later.

Burial in Westminster Abbey was no doubt a great honor, but it was one that Newton shared with many other men. To appreciate the real nature of the cult that was growing up around him we shall have to look elsewhere. In Stowe, his great country house, Lord Cobham commissioned from Kent and Rysbrack in about 1730 a curious Temple of British Worthies, which included a very strange collection of canonized Whig heroes: Sir Thomas Gresham, "who by the honourable profession of a merchant having enriched himself and his country, for carrying on the commerce of the world, built the Royal Exchange"; Inigo Jones; John Milton; William Shakespeare; John Locke; Sir Isaac Newton; Sir Francis Bacon; King Alfred, "the founder of the English constitution"; Edward, Prince of Wales, "the terror of Europe, the delight of England"; Queen Elizabeth; King William III; Sir Walter Raleigh; Sir Francis Drake; and John Hampden. Beneath the bust of Newton are the magnificently arrogant words: "Sir Isaac Newton, whom the God of Nature made to comprehend his works; and from simple principles, to discover the laws never known before, and to explain the appearance, never understood, of this stupendous universe."

The two traditions which I have just examined—Venetian art and the deification of Newton as one of the great men of England—had, however, already joined forces a few years earlier in what is undoubtedly by far the most interesting project of all those designed to commemorate the great national hero.

Its protagonist is a strange figure, who has been much discussed in recent years— Owen McSwiney. He was an Irish operatic impresario and theatrical manager, at various times in charge of Drury Lane and the Haymarket. He had at one time known Dryden, and when later Dr. Johnson was writing his *Lives of the Poets* he went to McSwiney for information, but was told only that at Wills's coffee house Dryden used to have one special seat in the winter and another in the summer.[13] But as a rule McSwiney was more imaginative and enterprising than this story would suggest, and some time in the mid-1720s he conceived the idea of commissioning some of the leading Italian artists to paint allegories, designed by himself, to commemorate many of the principal British heroes who had emerged from the Glorious Revolution of 1688. Italian sources vividly describe the mystification of the artists as they were called upon in teams of three to execute pictures whose meanings they totally failed

FRANCIS HASKELL

to understand.[14] "It was," wrote Zanotti, "like serving under a captain who kept his orders secret and moved his troops on long journeys without explaining what their purpose was."

These difficulties are easy enough to appreciate. The whole idea of raising monuments and tributes of this or any other kind was a new one. I think that it is true to say that until this period allegorical tributes to individuals had been confined entirely to rulers and to victorious commanders, although, of course, it would be easy enough to find many examples both in antiquity and during the Renaissance of men of letters being honored by simple monuments. Even this, however, was unusual enough by the eighteenth century for it to be commented on as a specifically English habit. "It is worthy of notice," wrote a French author of the Enlightenment in 1767,[15] "that the practice of honoring men of talent with statues is still vigorously maintained by the English, who follow the Greeks and Romans in their esteem for talent as well as in their love of liberty," and he singles out busts of Newton, Locke, Wollaston, and Clarke which had been placed by Queen Caroline in Richmond Park. In fact the practice only became possible in the climate of optimism, patriotism, and sentimentality that prevailed in England after the Whig Revolution.

But, far more than ethical considerations, what really worried the Italian artists and can still baffle us today was the actual content of the symbolism chosen by McSwiney. "In each Piece," he wrote,[16] "is plac'd a principal Urn, wherein is supposed to be deposited the Remains of the deceased Hero. The Ornaments are furnish'd partly from the Supporters and Arms of the respective families; and the Ceremonies supposed to be performed at the several Sepulchres, as well as the Statues and Basso Rilievo's allude to the Virtues, to the Imployments, or to the Learning and Science of the Departed."

In fact there is a good deal of evidence to show that McSwiney's pictures were not understood fully by his contemporaries, nor as highly thought of as he felt to be their due.

Among the first pictures painted was one in honor of Sir Isaac Newton. The artists chosen—for McSwiney insisted that "the Figures, the Landskips, the Buildings and other Ornaments are painted by different Hands; yet the Harmony of the Whole is so well preserved that each picture seems to be the work of one great Master"— were Giovanni Battista Pittoni, then aged forty and at the height of his powers, and the brothers Giuseppe and Domenico Valeriani, essentially theatrical painters of no great interest. All were Venetians. After some years McSwiney's pictures were issued as engravings, and they can best be studied in this way, as the original Newton picture is inaccessible in a private collection in Rome.

It is preceded by an elaborate title-page (Figure 3) which contains many allusions in playful form to Newton's achievements, cunningly arranged into a rococo frieze. At the top there is what appears to be a reference to the transit of the planet Venus across the sun, and a wholly inaccurate version of his experiments with light. Elsewhere are globes, mathematical instruments arranged in the patterns made

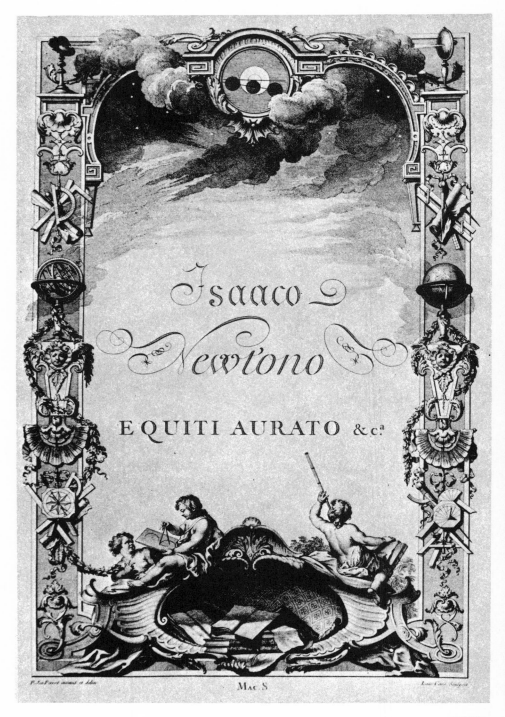

Isaaco Newtono

EQUITI AURATO &c.ª

Mac S

FIGURE 3

FRANCIS HASKELL

familiar by later Renaissance artists with trophies of armor, and at the bottom a shell containing books and putti playing with dividers and a telescope. We then see the bust of Sir Isaac Newton (Figure 4) crowned with a laurel wreath and inserted into

FIGURE 4

a pyramid, which is surrounded by the figures of the zodiac, of which Gemini, Taurus, Scorpio, Leo, and Aries stand out in high relief; while below (Figure 5) is a book,

FIGURE 5

The Apotheosis of Newton in Art

a telescope, a pair of compasses, and an armillary sphere, designed on the Copernican system to illustrate the earth revolving round the sun. This was an instrument used for teaching, and is in no way especially associated with Sir Isaac Newton. Both these drawings are by François Boucher, and present a strange episode in the career of an artist more known for his celebration of the nonintellectual triumphs of the human race.

There then follows the picture itself, for which a number of drawings exist.[17] (Figure 6) At the base Minerva and the Sciences are led weeping to the urn contain-

FIGURE 6

FRANCIS HASKELL

ing Sir Isaac's remains. From a pyramid above the urn is a wholly fanciful allusion to Newton's experiment on the splitting of light. On a raised dais in front of it are allegorical figures of Mathematics and what I take to be Truth; while various figures, clearly representing philosophers, ancient and modern, predecessors of Newton, are studying globes, books, and mathematical equations. Parts of the composition are obviously derived from Raphael's "School of Athens," though it takes place in architectural setting reminiscent of a stage design by Bibbiena. I am, of course, fully aware of the moral cowardice in saying that the characters are merely "ancient and modern philosophers" and in proceeding no further with their identification. My excuse is that, in fact, the figures are not sufficiently characterized for further investigation to be very fruitful, and that, as we will see in a moment, it was just this aspect of the picture that was to cause so much trouble. For at some stage in the proceedings, when this picture had already been commissioned, and probably nearly completed, John Conduitt, Newton's friend, nephew, and successor at the Mint, apparently unaware of the picture's existence, wrote the following letter, dated 4 June 1729, to McSwiney:[18]

I fear you will be much surprised at my very long delay in answering your favour of September last which is owing to my waiting for the advice and opinion of Sir Isaac Newton's friends in relation to the monumental picture to his memory, and I assure you it is but very lately that I could fix upon any design & I hope that resolved upon will please you as much as it does everyone here; it is as follows:

It is proposed to have the monument not in any church because it is impossible to express all his discoveries in so little a place but in the open air & by the seaside as some of those are which you have already done—& by an arm of the sea on the left hand a stately monument of the finest architecture with the proper symbols and attributes belonging to him wch I furnished you with so amply already wch I leave entirely to you—I would have the rest of the picture in some measure resemble the school of Athens—viz—

In one place a groupe of Philosophers looking on a scroll, with Mathematicall figures on the ground at the head of these I would have Pythagoras, Plato and Galileo looking with admiration & Descartes with a dejected countenance, as being concerned for the destruction of his system of Philosophy—I would have Aristotle who it is said threw himself into the Euripus because he could not solve the nature of his tide looking upon the sea rolling to the shore & pointing with admiration to a scroll with a problem of Sir Isaac's upon it showing the course of the tides—I would have him near these other philosophers because he belongs to them, & if it could be expressed he should in some measure triumph over Descartes, who had overturned the Aristotelian system upon the destruction of his by Sir I:N. The next groupe should be of Astronomers & at the head of these I would place Hipparchus, Ptolemy, Copernicus, Tyco Brahe, Kepler and Ulny Brighi. Kepler should be holding up in his hand a celestial globe which the others should be looking upon with admiration—You will find such a groupe in the picture of the school of Athens by Raphael which without doubt you have copies or prints of at Venice. The next groupe and which should be the least conspicuous should be a groupe of Geometers with Euclid, Archimedes and Apollonius at the head of them looking with admiration upon a scroll upon the ground with geometrical problems upon it. On the right hand of the picture should be the arch of a rainbow in the sky & some persons looking upon it with knowledge at the sky not at the rainbow & others through a reflecting telescope. At some distance behind the whole, there may be a beautiful landskip & lontananza.

You will perceive it is not designed to have any genii or poetical fantastical beings in these groups so they are all left to be made use of as you should think proper about the Monument, but it will be absolutely necessary to have the Philosophers, Astronomers and Geometers I have placed at the head of the 3 groupes to be very particularly described, for without that the whole beauty of the design will be lost—You can be at no difficulty to get the face and habits of Pythagoras, Plato, Aristotle, Euclid and Archimedes, Ptolemy & Hipparchus & Apollonius, because there are a number of books with prints of them from old statues or intaglios in almost every library—Tyco Brahe was Knight of the Elephant & is always painted with a flat nose having it is said been unfortunate in his amours but in the life of him & Copernicus writt by Gassendi you will see their pictures very well done & in Helvetius's Prodromius Astronomiae which is a book in all libraries you will find that of Galileo and Ulri Brighi an Arabian prince with short hair and mustachios hanging down, and Kepler who was Astronomer to an Emperor of Germany. As for Descartes who must be very particularly marked out you will find his picture before his own works and in Perrault's Hommes Illustres. As to the mathematical problems & the particular figures of a comet & upon the celestial globe I will have them done here afterwards & only desire you will have the scrolls & the shape of the globe painted.

This you will perceive will be a picture in character & only applicable to Sr I Newton which is what will give it its value with me, & I am persuaded you will forgive me if I tell you that it has been thought your other pictures, though finely painted, are defective in that respect & I have already seen two of them which turned to a quite different design from what they were intended. I mean those for the late Duke of Devonshire & Sir Cloudesly Shovel, the first of which is turned into a Brutus & the other into a Roman Admiral by my Lord Bingley in whose possession they are now. The sketch you intended for Sir Isaac Newton may I hope very easily be (& if not I shall willingly pay charges of the little alterations that can be wanting) applicable to any other great man, but I can not think of having it on any account as a monumental picture to him, nor indeed can I ever be satisfied or pleased with any but one after the design I have now sent you. If you will be so good as to superintend the execution of this I shall be much obliged to you, but it has been so thoroughly considered here by the best judges & is so much to my own fancy that though the ornaments and execution must be left to the painters I would not have any material alterations made in the main design. I must likewise declare that the picture be much broader than it is high, because I have no room in which I could possibly put one of the same height with those sent to the Duke of Richmond. I would have the height of those be the breadth of this, and the breadth of those be the height of this.....

It is clear that Conduitt, although he had not yet seen the picture, was wanting something far more precise than McSwiney had ordered. He was carefully dividing Newton's work into three constituent parts of Philosophy, Astronomy, and Geometry. The triumph of Newton over Descartes, "the French dreamer" as James Thompson called him, was, of course, a commonplace. We know, in fact, that Conduitt was not satisfied with Fontenelle's eulogy, because he suspected the Frenchman of reluctance to admit his compatriot's discomfiture. About this time (as Saxl has pointed out[19]) the same idea received a curious visual expression when a print by Picart of 1707 (Figure 7) representing "Truth sought by Philosophers" was adapted

FIGURE 7

The Apotheosis of Newton in Art

by an English engraver, who made one crucial alteration. (Figure 8) The texts are

FIGURE 8

virtually identical: "Philosophy represented by a stately Woman accompany'd and followed by many Philosophers, conducts 'em to the knowledge of Truth," but whereas in the original French text and illustration it is Descartes who is being led, in the English plagiary it is Sir Isaac Newton.

The illustrations mentioned by Conduitt are indeed easily available, and in fact most of the books referred to could be found in the library of McSwiney's friend and host at the time, Joseph Smith: but was the picture ordered by Conduitt ever in fact painted? Here we face an unsolved problem, and we can only attempt a guess by producing another picture and another letter.

The picture I have never seen in the original, and I have only been able to lay hands on a bad photograph. (Figure 9) The first thing to notice is that it is "much broader than it is high" as Conduitt had requested and as had been arranged by McSwiney (as you will see). On the other hand, we can see at a glance that the figures do not correspond with those that Conduitt had asked for. In fact, with some signif-

314   FRANCIS HASKELL

FIGURE 9

icant exceptions, the painting is virtually a copy of the other one. Let us look at the exceptions: Instead of the urn we now have a reasonably accurate representation of Newton's tomb in Westminster Abbey—and this may well have been the result of Conduitt's intervention. The famous experiment with the prism has now gone altogether. The architecture is far simpler; we do get some glimpse of the open air as Conduitt had demanded, though it is difficult to feel much more influence of the "School of Athens." On the wall of the platform are bas-reliefs which must unquestionably refer in allegorical form to Newton's achievements, though they are indecipherable in the present photograph. Finally some new figures have been added—a philosopher with a scroll in a niche (could this be "Aristotle . . . looking upon the sea rolling to the shore and pointing with admiration to a scroll"?), a representation of Fame crowning Merit in the apse, and two further figures with some broken statuary in the bottom right hand corner possibly representing Descartes or any of the other thinkers Newton was held to have dislodged. Otherwise the paintings are virtually identical.

Having considered both versions of the picture, we may now turn to McSwiney's reply to Conduitt. It was sent from Milan on 27 September 1730:[20]

> I have been out of Venice these three months, and on my arrival here, I found a
> letter from you, sent me by my friend Mr. Smith. In it I see a copy of directions

about the monumental piece to the memory of Sir Isaac Newton. I was formerly favoured with the same notices more than once, and sent you my opinion about them in a letter which I writ to you from Rome in the month of December last and which I put into the French post myself, though I find by what you write that it must have miscarried. I keep no copies of my letters, therefore shall give my present opinion about the piece, as you would have it, and as I intended it.

In all the pieces I have done, there is (in each of them) a Sepulchre wherein I suppose my Hero lies—the Sepulchres are adorned with statues, urns, basso-rilieves etc., allusive to the virtues, arms of the Family etc. of each of 'em. The sepulchres I suppose placed in a solitary situation, and that there is an anniversary ceremony performed on a certain day at 'em—I introduce figures (under each of 'em) properly employed as I think to explain the meaning of the Visitants, and their intentions etc.

'Tis impossible to tell (in such a narrow compass) more than one Man's story, without running into what would be very trivial, and the pieces would resemble the cuts in the *Gerusalemme Liberata*. In the Monument to the memory of the Duke of Malborough I make a soldier, attended with guards etc. as visiting the monument of a great general. I mean nothing more in it but the visit—now if I was to represent his battles, Sieges and abilities as an able counsellor, I have no way to do it but by Medaglions, medals, basso-rilievos, statues etc.

To show you that I have not been negligent in serving you, I have ordered a piece to be done of the same size with those of the Duke of Richmond's—but turned long ways—the perspective and the landscape have been done these six months, but how to dispose of the figures is the great difficulty and I'm afraid impossible, at least to my own satisfaction, and if it can't be done to my satisfaction I'll promise you shall never have it. I wish the gentlemen who assisted you with the plan of the landscape, and the disposition of the several groups of figures would make a small sketch of the picture which will explain the meaning much better than I can understand it by writing.

I would be glad to know what size he intends the figures to be (in a cloth of what length and breadth) and how he would have the resemblances kept of the several philosophers, astronomers etc., and the different meanings expressed of the different groups of figures etc.

In short better heads than mine in Rome and Bologna are puzzled how to contrive it—Sir Isaac Newton's monument is one of the collection which Sir William Morice has, and as soon as I send it to him, be so good as to cast an eye on it and let me have your opinion of it. If it or something like it will please you I will have it well executed by the same or some other able painter; if not I'll try whether anything can be done in the manner you desire; if neither pleases you, then the fifty pounds which I received shall be repaid you by the same hand; this is all I think necessary to be said on this score.

FRANCIS HASKELL

There the correspondence comes to an end. From it, it seems to me that we can infer that McSwiney had the second picture begun with the best intentions in the world of carrying out Conduitt's plan, but that as the difficulties increased, he fell back into his old ways, and had the original picture copied. There is, incidentally, one further point worth noticing about this painting. It is supposed to be signed PITTONI ROMA. If this is authentic (which seems to me more than doubtful) it is the only record that we have that Pittoni ever visited Rome.

These pictures form by far the most elaborate attempts made in the eighteenth century to celebrate Newton in art. They are, of course, by no means the only ones. In Trinity College, Cambridge, is a stained glass window, described by Newton's Victorian biographer as follows:[21] (Figure 10)

FIGURE 10

The Apotheosis of Newton in Art

The subject represents the presentation of Sir Isaac Newton to his majesty King George III [*sic*], who is seated under a canopy with a laurel chaplet in his hand, and attended by the British Minerva, apparently advising him to reward merit in the person of the great philosopher. Below the throne, the Lord Chancellor Bacon is, by an anachronism legitimate in art, proposing to register the record about to be conferred upon Sir Isaac. The original drawing of this picture was executed by Cipriani and cost one hundred guineas.

On the ceiling of the library in Home House, No. 20 Portman Square (now the Courtauld Institute), Newton is featured in a medallion along with Drake, Bacon, Milton, Addison, and other Whig heroes; and there are countless more such memorials, without mentioning innumerable medals and book illustrations in which he appears throughout the century.[22]

The only other large painting I know of is a very late and deplorable work by George Romney. It is of interest only in showing how towards the end of the eighteenth century (and, of course, the trend was accentuated in Victorian times) the heroic gives way to the anecdotal and the genre. Newton is there seen experimenting with his prism while his two nieces look on with suitable expressions of astonishment.

But I want to turn from this pedestrian work and end instead with the strangest of all the projects designed to honor Newton—the plan for a cenotaph made by the visionary French architect and draughtsman Etienne Louis Boullée in 1784.[23] Boullée prefaces his scheme with a rhapsodical invocation—"Esprit Sublime: Génie vaste, et profond! Etre Divin! Newton! Daigne agréer l'hommage de mes faibles talents!"— which sets the tone for his gigantic sphere resting on a cypress covered socle, at the base of which inside stands a small simple tomb, from which because of the spherical walls of the mausoleum the visitor would find it impossible to move. The apex was to be pierced with holes so that by day it would let in light which would appear to issue from the stars and planets. At night, on the other hand, the interior effect was to be one of brilliant sunlight achieved by a form of artificial illumination which was, in fact, not practicable in Boullée's lifetime. Although this fantastic project had considerable influence it goes without saying that—like most of Boullée's ideas—it was never constructed.

In fact by the end of the eighteenth century and with the rise of the Romantic movement Newton's sanctity was being seriously challenged. Blake indeed was first to cast him as the devil, the very incarnation of materialism, who believed that the great mysteries of the world could be solved by a pair of dividers and mathematical calculation. And yet even for Blake he had a certain magnificence, as Satan had had for Milton, and in one of his finer water colors[24] he paid tribute to him as a devil who at least served humanity by letting himself be known.

In 1817, in the studio of the artist Benjamin Robert Haydon, there took place the final reckoning of the Newton legend. The occasion was the "Immortal Dinner," so vividly described by the painter:[25]

Wordsworth was in fine cue, and we had a glorious set-to on Homer, Shakespeare, Milton and Virgil. Lamb got exceedingly merry and exquisitely witty: and his fun in the midst of Wordsworth's solemn intonations of oratory was like the sarcasm and wit of the fool in the intervals of Lear's passion. He made a speech and voted me absent, and made them drink my health. "Now," said

FIGURE 11

The Apotheosis of Newton in Art

Lamb "you old lake poet, you rascally poet, why do you call Voltaire dull?" We all defended Wordsworth, and affirmed there was a state of mind when Voltaire would be dull. "Well," said Lamb, "here's Voltaire—the Messiah of the French nation, and a very proper one too."

He then, in a strain of humour beyond description, abused me for putting Newton's head into my picture; "a fellow," said he, "who believed nothing unless it was as clear as the three sides of a triangle." And then he and Keats agreed he had destroyed all the poetry of the rainbow by reducing it to the prismatic colours. It was impossible to resist him and we all drank "Newton's health and confusion to mathematics." It was delightful to see the good humour of Wordsworth in giving in to all our frolics without affection and laughing as heartily as the best of us.

Wordsworth may have laughed, but he remained silent; for he had seen Roubiliac's magnificent statue of Newton in Trinity Chapel with its superbly apt quotation from Lucretius—"qui genus humanum ingenio superavit"[26] (Figure 11)—and contemplating this finest of all visual homages to the great scientist he had matched it with an equally eloquent tribute of his own.[27]

> The antechapel where the statue stood
> Of Newton with his prism and silent face,
> The marble index of a mind for ever
> Voyaging through strange seas of thought alone.

NOTES

[1] King's College, Cambridge—Newton MSS 212 (14).

[2] John Hughes (1677–1720)—quoted by H. N. Fairchild: *Religious trends in English poetry*, I, p. 251.

[3] In 1778—in *Lettre à l'Academie francaise*, as preface to *Irène*.

[4] C. L. Becker: *The Heavenly City of the Eighteenth Century Philosophers*.

[5] Desaguliers: *The Newtonian System of the World*, 1728, in Fairchild: *op. cit.*, I, p. 357. See also Marjorie H. Nicolson: *Newton demands the Muse*.

[6] M. I. Webb: *Mychael Rysbrack sculptor*, 1954, p. 82.

[7] The correspondence of Alexander Pope, edited by George Sherburn, 1956, II, p. 457 ff.

[8] M. I. Webb: *op. cit.*, p. 84.

[9] King's College, Cambridge—Newton MSS.

[10] *Novelle della Repubblica delle Lettere*, 1738.

[11] See, for instance, Blunt & Croft-Murray: *Venetian Drawings of the XVII and XVIII centuries in the collection of Her Majesty the Queen at Windsor Castle*, London 1957, p. 60—and there are many other examples.

[12] Orazio Arrighi-Landini; *Il Tempio della Filosofia, Venezia* 1755, p. 30.

[13] Whitley: *Artists and their friends in England*, 1700–1799, I p. 9.

[14] For the most recent account of McSwiney's activities, with detailed references to the sources and subsequent research see F. Haskell: *Patrons and Painters* (London & New York, 1963), pp. 287–292.

[15] [Abbé de Guasco]: De l'usage des statues chez les anciens, p. 267.

[16] *To the Ladies & Gentlemen of Taste*, undated: copy in British Museum, 816 m.23 (134).

[17] For the most interesting study of all the related drawings see I. Fenyö "Disegni veneziani

FRANCIS HASKELL

nel museo di Belle Arti di Budapest" in *Acta Historiae Artium Academiae Scientiarum Hungaricae,* tomus VI, fasc. 1–2, 1959.

[18] King's College, Cambridge—Newton MSS.

[19] F. Saxl: *Veritas Figlia Temporis* in Essays presented to Ernst Cassirer, 1936.

[20] Kings College, Cambridge—Newton MSS.

Professor Gombrich kindley drew my attention to the following quotation from Francesco Milizia: *Dell'Arte di Vedere nelle Belle Arti del Disegno* (Venice, 1823), p. 104, which is of considerable interest as it suggests that he may have had access to a version of one of these pictures: "E qual effetto della scuola d'Atene? Se un pittor filosofo volesse rappresentare la filosofia d'Inghilterra, non si contenterrebbe soltanto effigiarvi Bacone, Bayle [sic], Locke, Newton, Priestly, Francklin ec., ma caratterizzerebbe ciascuno di questi valentuomini con quelle cose per le quali ciascuno si è reso insigne. Il ritratto di Newton e poca cosa. Ma un Newton solo può fare un gran quadro co' suoi principii matematici, coll'attrazione, colle flussioni, coll'ottica, colla cronologia, e fin anche con quell'apocalissi, con cui egli volle chiedere scusa al mondo d'averlo illuminato."

[21] Sir David Brewster: *Memoirs of the Life, Writings and Discoveries of Sir Isaac Newton,* II, p. 396.

[22] Two allegories by Januarius Zick in the Landesgalerie, Hanover, are often said to refer to Newton's discoveries, but I can find no evidence to suggest that this is their true subject.

[23] See Boulée's Treatise on Architecture—edited by Helen Rosenau, 1953, p. 83 ff. Starobinski (*The Invention of Liberty,* 1964, p. 207) publishes a very similar Newton cenotaph designed by Pierre-Jules Delépine.

[24] A. F. Blunt: "Blake's ancient of days" in *Journal of the Warburg & Courtauld Institutes,* II, 1, p. 61.

[25] Benjamin Robert Haydon: *Autobiography and Memoirs,* edt. by Alexander P. D. Penrose, 1927, p. 231.

[26] Katherine A. Esdaile: *The Life and Works of Louis Francois Roubiliac,* p. 102.

[27] *The Prelude,* III, 60.

WILLIAM COLEMAN

Mechanical Philosophy and Hypothetical Physiology

To SPEAK OF NEWTONIANISM IN BIOLOGY PRESUPPOSES THE EXISTENCE, presumably in the late seventeenth and early eighteenth centuries, of peculiarly Newtonian modes of biological reasoning. There is, for example, the experimental Newtonian philosophy practiced by Stephen Hales, wherein data accumulated by unparalleled industry and controlled imagination are recorded with apposite numerical precision. No less notable was the more rigorously experimento-mathematical approach of physiologists such as George Cheyne and James Keill. Their calculations, particularly of the strength of the heart muscle and the force of the blood in its vessels, appeared to many the quintessence of Newton mathematical certainty.

I shall not examine here either strictly experimental or mathematical Newtonianism in physiology. Instead, my emphasis falls upon the continuity of the system called the Mechanical Philosophy and, more importantly, upon a characteristic manner of pursuing natural philosophy, and physiology, described as Hypothetical Physics. On exhibition will be the English physician, Richard Mead, the most popular if not the most sound of Newton's physiological advocates.[1]

Newton's barb that he framed (or feigned) no hypotheses was cast against a powerful school of physical reasoning. At issue was the nature of hypothesis and the range of its usefulness in physics. The very term suggested to Newton vain and unsupported speculation; "hypothesis" to others, however, meant the true business of physics and the extreme limit of possible and plausible physical explanation. Newton's foes, these hypothetical physicists, were essentially intellectual democrats. Natural philosophers might legitimately entertain the most diverse opinions— "hypotheses"—if only they did not violate two simple rules of reason and common sense. The hypothesis must not conflict with experience nor could it be manifestly absurd. Experience, however, was usually limited, and ingenious philosophers appeared ever capable of avoiding self-contradiction. The Creator, moreover, worked in many ways and the philosophers realized that they could never be certain that they had captured God's one special way. A range of alternative interpretations was therefore permitted and, indeed, demanded. The hypotheses proffered need guard only self-consistency and some connection with phenomena to remain plausible and useful.

These views were shared and disseminated by Gassendi and Descartes and, with certain limitations, Hobbes.[2] A broader rationale for the hypothetical physics was given by Robert Boyle, although Boyle himself is not at all times representative of this mode of thought.[3] The "good hypothesis" Boyle judged was intelligible and neither "manifestly false" nor self-contradictory. It furthermore explained phenomena or, better, explained the principal phenomenon and remained consistent at least with secondary phenomena. The "excellent hypothesis" had to satisfy additional and more stringent criteria. It required "auxiliary proofs" from other phenomena and was necessarily the most simple possible explanation. It was, ideally, a unique explanation and should "enable the skillful naturalist to foretell future phenomena."

No single hypothesis, however, would fully meet such terms and the hypothetical physicists as well as Boyle appreciated this fact. In practice and even in theoretical utterance the fundamental criterion of uniqueness was violated. Having praised Bacon for urging that erroneous hypothesis conduces more to the discovery of truth than the confusion consequent upon a science without any generalization whatsoever, Boyle continued: "I would have such kind of [hypothetical] superstructures looked upon as only temporary ones, which though they may be preferred before any others, as being the least 'imperfect,' or, if you please, the best in their kind that we yet have, yet are they not entirely to be acquiesced in, as absolutely perfect, or uncapable of improving alterations."[4] Elsewhere Boyle compares those who contemplate physical matters to men who cast different keys to read a document written in cypher. Only a trial can indicate which key is correct. Moreover, the trial gives not a proof of correctness but only suggests which key is most suitable to the problem. The "fitness" of an hypothesis to "solve the phenomena," Boyle concluded, is the essence of the whole enquiry, and uniqueness may or may not enter into consideration.[5] Given the diversity of the physical systems propounded during Boyle's generation we can see that uniqueness, whatever might be an author's pretensions, did not determine the truth of any given hypothesis.

This was unfortunate, for the possibility of a unique and valid hypothesis would have permitted that certainty in interpretation which ever escaped the physicist. Newton states most poignantly that the "mere possibility of hypotheses" will bring us no closer to physical certainty. "For it is always possible," he continued, "to contrive hypotheses, one after another, which are found rich in new tribulations."[6] Newton, of course, could and did contrive hypotheses as well as the next philosopher. He pretended, however, and sometimes with reason, that his hypotheses were not sheer unfounded speculation but were deduced from phenomena carefully established by experiment. And beyond this no reader failed to recall that it was the great Newton alone who had found certainty as well as precision in the mathematical principles of natural philosophy.

Quite apart from the form, it was this element of certainty, and thus uniqueness, which made Newton's mathematical way so injurious to the accepted procedures of hypothetical physics. To those persuaded by the method in the *Principia,* and near the turn of the century they abound in physiology as well as in physics, a long era of what was deemed vain and foolish conjecture appeared at end. In physiology, perhaps, such conjecture had been illogical and without adequate support, but by no means was it at end. In Richard Mead, whose every gesture was to preserve vital and holy the example of his "Chief Philosopher," Newton, we find a superb illustration of the methods of the hypothetical physicist and physiologist.

The eye of the hypothetical philosopher was biased. It pretended impartiality in assessing the criteria of alternative physical explanations but always one hypothesis was discerned to be *primus inter pares*.[7] This was the mechanical or corpuscular philosophy which attributed to matter—its shape, motion, and relative position—the generation of all visible and indeed unseen physical phenomena.[8] From matter and motion could be deduced or illustrated, for example, the movements of heavenly bodies, the nature of light and the formation of colors, and the processes of chemical change. Furthermore, the mechanical hypothesis was promptly introduced into physiological explanation. It gained here much the same ascendancy over rival hypotheses as it had assumed in the physical sciences but remained ever subject, here as there, to the challenge of other hypotheses under the terms of the hypothetical method's loose criteria.

Mechanical and corpuscular interpretations of physiological function emerge clearly from the thought of Galileo, Descartes, and others and flow directly into distinctive schools of medico-physiological thought.[9] Newtonian mathematics was but a later, primarily English, appendage to mechanical physiology. None spoke more eloquently on this latter subject than Mead's mentor, the Scots physician Archibald Pitcairne. Pitcairne, a mathematical student of David Gregory and trained in medicine in Edinburgh and France, seems fiercely opposed to the hypothetical physics.[10] The search for "Physical Causes" has been and remains "entirely useless and unnecessary to Physicians," said Pitcairne, who continued: "It is not allowable to advance anything into a principle either in the Theory or Practice of Physick, which the Mathematicians . . . call in question. . . ."[11] Observing Pitcairne's own physiological system one discovers that his mathematics are so applied as to be but one additional, albeit seemingly unmechanical, hypothesis added to the scientific warehouse. Pitcairne depended greatly upon Bellini's contention that aberrations in the circulation of the blood accounted for virtually all pathological states. Most importantly, secretion, to Bellini and Pitcairne the essential physiological phenomenon, was due to the dynamics of the circulating fluid. Due to differential rates of flow consequent upon the varying diameters of different vessels, secretions—material particles—of lesser or greater magnitude would be produced and then distributed in appropriate vessels. Such a claim, Pitcairne believed, obviated the need for pores with a special figure, the favorite of the more mechanically inclined, and denied any appeal to the action of ferments, a gesture Pitcairne saw no better than a reversion to the qualities and faculties so dear to philosophically orthodox physicians.[12]

Pitcairne's mathematics, never given in detail, were intended to describe the behavior of material particles and the fluid which conveyed them in terms little different from those used by other mechanical philosophers. Pitcairne claimed,[13] and Mead easily believed, that here was a great improvement on customary physiological explanation. The new mathematics of Newton contributed just that sense of security the physiologist had wanted. It was false security, of course, and worse yet, it in no way eliminated the desire or the necessity to fall back upon inherently imprecise

WILLIAM COLEMAN

corpuscular principles and the band of secondary hypotheses which these always generated.

Gratuitously sharing the splendor of the new mathematical wonders but holding firmly to old, and casting new, hypotheses on physical causes was the dubious Newtonian, Richard Mead. Mead was a conspicuous figure in London science after the turn of the century.[14] His medical practice, including among the regular patients the royal family, Alexander Pope, and Isaac Newton, was exceedingly successful, and the remarkable breadth of his reading, in both classical and modern authors, put him, as it did his intimate friend and fellow Newtonian Richard Bentley, among the most erudite men of the generation.

Two theoretical essays record Mead's general physiological views and exemplify both the obscurity and contradictions of assumed Newtonian influences in biology. They do so not merely because Mead patently adopts Newtonian conceptions and terminology, but because in them is found much of the essential irrelevance of Newton's innovations to the thought of an influential and supposedly genuine Newtonian.

Mead first attempted (*Mechanical account of poisons,* 1702) to explain the action of poisons, particularly that of the viper, on the living body. It was to be, he claimed, a "mechanical account" and was based upon a most singular juxtaposition of the ideas of Bellini, Pitcairne, and Newton. Boyle in 1663 had discussed the effect of the viper's bite. He concluded that the rage of the animal was the active agent and not the venom. He reported, however, experiments by John Wilkins and Christopher Wren which proved that opium, at least, when injected into dog's veins, induced death. Boyle thereupon called for further experiments on the effect of poisons but he executed none himself.[15] Between 1663 and 1702 such experiments were performed and these Mead reported and amplified with great satisfaction, for they showed clearly that it was the venom and nothing else which contributed to the viper's deadly bite.[16] Mead added to these demonstrations a masterful anatomical description of the viper's jaws, teeth, and secretory glands. Published as an appendix, this splendid contribution constitutes the only portion of Mead's volume of enduring value.

But these were mere phenomena; Mead demanded explanation. He hoped, he said, to "discover the footsteps of Mechanism" where before only occult principles were esteemed. This required some undertanding of the general regimen of the body or, following the customary seventeenth-century expression, a knowledge of "Humane Oeconomy." Happily, it was widely known that the "body of man was . . . a hydraulic machine contrived with the most exquisite art, in which there are numberless tubes properly adjusted and disposed for the conveyance of fluids of different kinds." "Upon the whole," Mead added, "health consists of regular motions of the fluids, together with a proper state of the solids, and diseases are their aberrations."[17] Poisons, too, worked their aberration and their effect took hold in the principal body fluid, the blood.

Mead asks us to observe a drop of viper venom under the microscope. As it dries it loses its homogeneous appearance and breaks up into countless minute salt crystals of "incredible Tenuity and Sharpness." These are the poison's lethal agents. Injected into the blood they rapidly irritate surrounding membranes and this, as Bellini taught, induced a massive secretion of body fluids into the area, hence, inflamation. Moreover, the deadly "Spicula" mixed intimately with the mass of the blood where the effect was to "so disjoin and disunite the Parts of it, that its Mixture must be quite altered" and the blood was thus rendered unfit for the maintenance of life.[18]

To this point Mead's theory is mechanical in the usual sense; that is, matter and motion, plus the configuration of matter, account for the phenomena. But Mead's subtlety went beyond this and found a place in toxicology for Newton's "Great Principle of Action in the Universe," attraction. Poisons, according to this simplistic interpretation, are foreign bodies which disrupt the harmonious balance of forces in the blood. These forces are naturally geometrical, that is, they are an additional instance of the ubiquity of (gravitational) attraction. Just how this disturbance takes place we are not informed. Poisons, moreover, present sharp protuberances and without fail these pierce the many "small Globules" floating in the blood. Characteristic of such globules was the fact that they contained an expansive "elastick Fluid" which rapidly dispersed in the blood when the globule was ruptured. The elastic fluid then served as a "nimble vehicle to the acute Salts." Here was the true explanation of the systemic effect of poisons whose small quantity could scarcely induce such general consequences. The elastic fluid transported widely the damaging crystals and, what was more, restored to them in some unstated manner "their decreasing Force."[19]

Among Mead's foremost concerns was the identification of the cause or causes of periodic diseases, above all, recurrent fevers. To this end he published in 1704 a brief essay on medical theory whose central postulate is of a singular nature.[20] His argument, Mead claimed, was wholly Newtonian; in reality it more closely followed astrological tradition, albeit in partial mathematical dress.

Newon's theory of the tides and their extension to the atmosphere underlay Mead's speculation. The sun and moon exerted marked and regular alterations in the level of the sea and, more importantly, in the density of the atmosphere. The health of the human body, Bellini and Pitcairne had taught, was contingent upon the free flow of body fluids and therefore upon the absence of congestion in the vessels. A heavy, close atmosphere was dangerous because it interfered with fluid motion in the circulatory vessels and disrupted the all-important function of the lungs in stirring the blood and preserving its correct state of mixture.

In support of his hypothesis Mead offered rude calculations of the magnitude of the atmospheric tides. One compared the combined effect upon the sea of sun and moon with that of the earth's centrifugal force. Using data given by Newton (*Principia,* III, Propositions 36–37), Mead developed a series of proportions which instructed him that the combined force of sun and moon was to the centrifugal force as 1:8123.   Now, the earth's centrifugal force was sufficient to raise water some 85,000 feet; sun and moon together would therefore be able to raise water perhaps ten to eleven feet.[21] In an unspecified manner this demonstration of celestial control was

WILLIAM COLEMAN

assumed to work upon the atmosphere as well as the sea. For those unversed in mathematics Mead brought forward Edmond Halley's "True theory of the tides." As guarantee for his reasoning Mead informed his readers, that *"all Natural Effects of the same kind have the same causes."*[22] These are Newton's words and were scarcely to be questioned.

The barometer seemed to provide clear evidence that tides in the atmosphere, if they existed at all, were either trivial, completely irregular, or virtually undetectable. Against this criticism Mead offered elaborate argumentation and very little evidence.[23] The critics were not answered, but their attack was both redirected and ignored. It was the principle which mattered, the principle that atmospheric tides could exist (and therefore must exist) and that they could be described in ostensibly quantitative manner. The hypothesis and its curious mathematical decoration were not to bend before contradictory phenomena or patent medical irrelevance.[24]

Whatever be made of the substance of Mead's speculations they tell us much about Newtonianism in biology. Mead sees no incongruity between full liberty in casting hypotheses on a most *ad hoc* basis and claiming that his hypotheses enjoy the protection of mathematical vigor. His remarkable statement to this effect betrays the logical infelicities of prominent elements in a so-called Newtonianism. Referring to the poison theory, Mead admitted: "From such an *Hypothesis* as this (and, it may be, not very easily from any other) we may account for many of the surprizing Phenomena in the Fermentations of Liquors; and as precarious as it seems, its Simplicity, and Plainness, and agreement with the aforementioned Doctrine, will, I believe, recommend it before any other to those who are not unacquainted with Geometrical *Reasonings."*[25] Mead here implies uniqueness and certainty for his hypothesis, but even he dares not claim to have demonstrated so much. Like other hypotheses of the epoch, his offers simplicity, easy comprehension and self-consistency. The poison theory, moreover, by no means defies the phenomena so blatantly as did the fancy of the medical implications of atmospheric tides. Where, then, is the true role of "Geometrical Reasonings"? It is just as we might expect, a gloss disguising reasoning of another and more accustomed kind, that of the hypothetical physics.[26]

Naïve in his mathematical pretensions, Mead was distinctly more certain of utterance when treating of hypothesis in general, his own hypotheses, of course, always excepted. Mead turned to "Reasons of Numbers . . . *lest it be thought that* [he] *vent* fictitious Hypotheses for mechanical Causes, *and* vain Figments for the *Laws of Nature."* This statement, published in 1712 (in Latin in 1704), may have some bearing on the tangled history of Newton's business with "feigned Hypotheses."[27] No English natural philosopher or physiologist, particularly one so close to and adulatory of the master as was Mead, could escape conquest by Newton's mathematical successes. But this often meant no more, and no less, than a recognition that in mathematics was a way and perhaps the way to certainty in philosophical matters. Not all were competent to follow Newton on his own grounds and, more importantly, not all problems were so readily subject to a precise instrument of analysis as were the celestial and terrestrial phenomena united by gravitation. Mead was certainly a mathematical incompetent, but physiology itself, as even Keill and Cheyne painfully learned, was still far removed from that narrow dependence on physics and chemistry which has since helped make it a more exact science.

An important revision of the poison theory was made in the 1740s. Critics who had spoken unkindly of Mead's mechanical bias were answered in a most revealing manner. Mead first of all transferred allegiance from the mechanical theory to a new fashion, electrical fluids.[28] Gray, du Fay, and Newton (now the "Queries") are duly cited and a new physiological basis for poisoning propounded. From the new edition of *Poisons* was banished all reference to mechanical speculation. A novel philosopher's fluid had been discovered; it lay within the nerve fibers and mediated nervous action; it was exceedingly like, if not the same as, the true "electrical fluid." The discovery was indeed fortunate, for recent experimental work seemed to show that the rapidity of poison action was inconsistent with the lazy circuit of the blood. Obviously, poisons must work directly upon the nerves and ignore the blood.

Such a conclusion admirably illuminates the career of the hypothetical philosopher. With regard to physiological matters one hypothesis was potentially as good as another. Mead with no reluctance virtually revolutionized the explanatory premises of his physiological system, and then interpreted his previous medical data in terms of the new system. There was no inconsistency and little difficulty in this remarkable transformation, for Mead merely continued his allegiance to accepted (but already dated) hypothetical principles. To pretend to certainty Mead could not avoid, and he knew he should find it alone in mathematical demonstration. But between the mechanical and electrical theories, certainly, the mathematical ideal could hardly be decisive. Other factors must enter into the decision. It was their general coherence, neatness, and plausibility which secured Mead's arguments. This the physician fully conceded in 1744: "And if, in a matter so abstruse and difficult, what I have advanced has more in it of conjecture than of demonstration, it may be allowed to be something. . . . Whoever will pass judgment on such nice speculations, must take the whole together. Truth is always a connected scheme; and inferences justly drawn not only illustrate, but confirm one another."[29] From a small number of essential postulates could be derived the large and complex physiological edifice whose internal consistency assured not only its splendor but its truth, truth happily burdened by the hypothetical physiologist with no absolute connotations.

To the writings of Newton Mead remained loyal. In 1704 it was the *Principia* and in 1744 the *Opticks*. While Mead's loyalty was well nigh absolute it was nevertheless more verbal than real. Mead lacked mathematical training and ability; he also lacked methodological discrimination.[30] Mead's Newtonianism was spurious. It was the name and not the substance which he adopted. Vigorous testing of the presumed congruence between hypothesis and phenomena by means of intelligently conceived experiment—the surest mark of Newton's nonmathematical style—Mead ignored. In neither mathematical generalization nor experimental practice did Mead therefore

WILLIAM COLEMAN

follow Newton. Mead's course had begun and remained, despite his frequent protest, that of the hypothetical physicist.[31]

NOTES

[1] My investigation and conclusions owe much to conversations with Robert H. Kargon, Audrey B. Davis, and Theodore M. Brown. I have followed closely various arguments, particularly the delineation of hypothetical physics, in Kargon's *Atomism in England from Hariot to Newton* (Oxford, 1966); see also H. Guerlac, "Where the statue stood: Divergent loyalties to Newton in the eighteenth century," *Aspects of the eighteenth century*, ed. E. R. Wasserman (Baltimore, 1965), 317–334.

[2] Said Hobbes of physical causation: ". . . seeing I have assumed no hypothesis, which is not both possible and easy to be comprehended; and seeing also that I have reasoned aright from those assumptions, I have withal sufficiently demonstrated that they may be the true causes; which is the end of physical contemplation." T. Hobbes, "Elements of philosophy. The first section, concerning body," *Works* (1839, reprinted 1962), I, 531.

[3] Boyle prepared a number of variant drafts of tables of "good" and "excellent" hypotheses. Two versions are published by M. B. Hall, *Robert Boyle on natural philosophy* (Bloomington, Indiana, 1965), 134–135; and R. S. Westfall, "Unpublished Boyle papers relating to scientific method, II," *Ann. science 12* (1956) 116–117. I cite the Westfall version in the text.

[4] R. Boyle, "A proemial essay etc.," *Certain physiological essays and other tracts* etc., *The Works of the Honourable Robert Boyle* ed. T. Birch (London, 1744), I, 194.

[5] R. Boyle, "On the excellency and grounds of the corpuscular or mechanical philosophy," Hall, *Robert Boyle on natural philosophy*, 206–207.

[6] Newton to Pardies (1672), "Mr. Newton's answer to the foregoing letter," *Isaac Newton's papers and letters on natural philosophy*, ed. I. B. Cohen (Cambridge, Mass. 1958), 106. See Kargon, *Atomism in England*, 125 ff.

[7] A constant tension existed in Boyle's writings. Methodology told him that all hypotheses were to be doubted or at least held contingently and until determinative experimental testing. Nevertheless, the corpuscularian philosophy, so closely associated with his name, he regarded as physically true, particularly when contrasted with the older system of Aristotelian forms and qualities. See R. S. Westfall, "Unpublished Boyle papers relating to scientific method, II," 107–108.

[8] The definition of "matter" was consequently of fundamental concern to the seventeenth-century natural philosopher. See M. Boas, "The establishment of the mechanical philosophy," *Osiris 10* (1952), 412–541; T. S. Kuhn, "Robert Boyle and structural chemistry in the seventeenth century," *Isis 43* (1952), 12–36. Newton's speculations on the aether may also form part of this tradition; see A. R. and M. B. Hall, "Newton's theory of matter," *Isis 51* (1960), 131–144, but cf. Kargon, *Atomism in England*, 118–132.

[9] In the narrowest sense corpuscular philosophy and the iatromechanical school are closely associated, but iatromathematicians also made no little use of particulate matter and its movements. See K. Sprengel, *Histoire de la médicine depuis son origine jusqu'au dixneuvième siècle*, trans. A.-J. Jourdan (Paris, 1815), V, 131–194; C. Daremberg, *Histoire des sciences médicales* (Paris, 1870), II, 750–887.

[10] On Pitcairne (1652–1713), see "P." [Henry Pemberton?], "Pitcairne, Archibald," *Biographia britannia* (London, 1760), V, 3359–3366; G. A. Lindeboom, "Pitcairne's Leyden interlude described from the documents," *Ann. science 19* (1963): 273–284.

[11] A. Pitcairne, "Inaugural Oration [Leyden, 1691]," *The works of Dr. Archibald Pitcairne* (London, 1704), 10.

[12] Pitcairne was particularly disturbed that Harvey's discovery of the circulation of the blood had long been obscured by mad speculation. In consequence of this neglect physicians, with the exception of Lorenzo Bellini, had failed to understand that most diseases arose from errors or impediments in the flow of blood: see L. Bellini, *A Mechanical account of fevers* (London,

1720), Propositions I–II, XIX–XX. Pitcairne's views, with emphasis on capillary circulation, are best expressed in his "A dissertation upon the circulation of the blood through the minutest vessels of the body," *Works*, 29–61.

13 *Ibid.*, 52–53.

14 On Mead (1673–1754) see Anon., *Authentic memoirs of the life of Richard Mead* (London, 1755). Subsequent biographical accounts of Mead—(*Biographia britannia* [London, 1760], V, 3077–3086; Anon., "Memoirs of the life and writings of the author," *The Works of Richard Mead* [Edinburgh, 1763], I, 5–16)—differ only in brevity from these *Memoirs*. See also V. A. Ferguson, *A bibliography of the works of Richard Mead* (Librarian's Diploma, Univ. of London, London 1959: unpubl.).

15 R. Boyle, *Some considerations touching the usefulness of natural philosophy. Part II. Essay II. Offering some particulars relating to the pathological part of Physick, Works*, I, 471–480.

16 R. Mead, *A mechanical account of poisons, in several essays* (London, 1702), 21–23. On theories of poison action see M. P. Earles, "Early theories of the mode of action of drugs and poisons," *Ann. science 17* (1961), 97–110.

17 R. Mead, *Medical precepts and cautions, Works*, II, 5, 10.

18 Mead, *Poisons*, 9–13.

19 *Ibid.*, 14–16. Mead, following contemporary usage, designates as "fermentation" the effect of the general disjunction of particles carried in the blood. He also touches upon certain presumed chemical aspects of venom action. These effects, nevertheless, and all others depend upon the blood's "different degrees of *Fluidity* and *Impulse* towards the Parts," that is, upon basic geometrico-mechanical phenomena (*ibid.*, 9–13).

20 R. Mead, *On the power and influence of the sun and moon on humane bodies, and the diseases that rise from thence* (London, 1712). This is a translation, perhaps by Mead, of his *De imperio solis ac lunae in corpora humana, et morbis inde oriundis* (London, 1704).

21 The figures and procedure of this calculation are impossibly obscure in the first edition of *Power and influence* (7–12). They were largely reworked for the revised edition (*Works*, I, 173–174); this edition is cited here in the text.

22 Mead, *Power and influence* (1712), 7. Halley's paper (published in the *Philosophical Transactions* for 1697, No. 226) was but a short and wholly nonmathematical notice of the *Principia*. It was prepared for James II and is as much a witness to that prince's, and indirectly Mead's, mathematical incomprehension as it is a deliberately insubstantial appreciation of Newton's mathematical genius. See R. Schofield, "Halley and the *Principia*," *Newton's papers and letters on natural philosophy*, 397–404.

23 Mead, *Power and influence* (1712), 16–21.

24 Traditional medical concern with "airs" and "places" found theoretical explanation in Mead's conception of atmospheric tides (*ibid.*, 16, 22–25). Mead's speculation did induce F. A. Mesmer to develop (1766) the atmospheric tides into a scheme of genuine "animal gravitation"; only later (1775–1779) did he convert to animal magnetism. See F. A. Pattie, "Mesmer's medical dissertation and its debt to Mead's *De imperio solis ac lunae*," *Journ. hist. med. 11* (1956), 275–287.

25 Mead, *Poisons*, 15–16.

26 One must partially exclude from this judgment mathematico-experimental "Newtonian" physiologists such as Keill, the later Cheyne, John Freind, and Colin Maclaurin. Maclaurin expresses well the increased methodological caution to be encountered in the 1720's: "The only remedy against this Inconvenience [the too free use of "hypothesis"] is the same here [physiology], as in the other Parts of Philosophy; to lay aside all mysterious and unintelligible forms of Speech, nor any longer to be employed in determining the Operations of Beings, to whose very existence we are altogether Strangers; but to enquire after such real Causes, as the Phaenomena necessarily imply, and to endeavor by a further search to discover the degree and manner of the Action of those Causes; pursuing these ends by the proper Means of attaining them, which are only Experiments and just Reasonings drawn from the Mathematical

WILLIAM COLEMAN

Principles." C. Maclaurin, "Introduction" to the posthumous publication of W. Cowper, *Myotomia reformata* (London, 1723), ii. On this matter see the study in preparation by T. M. Brown (Princeton University).

Neither Pitcairne's nor Mead's excesses fared well with their biographers. Of Pitcairne's allegiance to mechanical hypothesis "P." objected that "it has happened very unfortunately for physic, that the warm imaginings of theorists and anatomists, have represented to them many things in themselves extremely precarious, as certain truths; and these have been warmly embraced, as contributing to the confirmation of some favourite system, which their authors were determined to establish at any rate, right or wrong; whence the misapplication of mechanics to medicine, has perhaps done the art of healing more prejudice, than a proper use of them has done it service. The abuse therefore of mechanical learning in physic is highly to be condemned, as the tinsel of the art which makes a noise and shew without contributing any real value." "Pitcairne," *Biog. brit.* (1760), V, 3362, note [D]. Mead's hapless mathematical adventures are understandable in light of the fashion *ca.* 1700 for quantitative results but, regretted his anonymous biographer, "It was very unlucky for the doctor, that the geometrical way of handling physical subjects happened to be the vogue at his first setting out in the world, a method which he was not at all qualified to support, much less to make a figure in. His talents lay neither to mathematics nor mathematical philosophy. Of this he was very sensible . . . ." "Mead,"*Biog. brit.* (1760), V, 3080, note [G]; *Power and influence* permits one to question the magnitude of Mead's sensibility. At least by mid-eighteenth century "mechanical" physiological systems seem on the wane in Britain. They prospered, however, on the Continent and appear to perpetuate the basic themes of the stricter Cartesian corpuscularianism. See L. S. King's account of Friedrich Hoffmann, *The growth of medical thought* (Chicago, 1963), 164 ff.

[27] Mead, *Power and influence* 1712, v–vi. The statement appeared in *De imperio solis ac lunae* (1704), iv, as ". . . et ne quis fortasse putet nos pro *Causis Mechanicis* fictas Hypotheses, pro ipsis *Naturae Legibus* mania *Commenta* venditare." Although Mead seems quite cognizant of the perils of the hypothetical method, I have argued that in practice his preaching had little consequence. Mathematics gave certainty, but corpuscularianism and the hypothetical physics were his science. Newton explicitly rejected the hypothetical method. "Hypotheses non fingo" first appeared in 1713 and in English in 1729. Newton, it is urged (see I. B. Cohen, "The first English version of Newton's *Hypotheses non fingo,*" *Isis 53* [1962]: 379–388), rather "feigned" than "framed" no hypotheses. In the confusion of alternative translations by Clarke and Newton (?) and recorded by Cohen uncertainties often appear compounded and the central issue—why, conceptually, is "feign" preferable to "frame"?—retains its obscurity. Mead's simple language and doctrinaire position reaffirms the ascendency of "feign." Mead, like Newton, knew that hypothetical physics thrived on "feigned" hypotheses; unlike Newton, this was just the physics which Mead thought to be best, that is, that which he followed. Of Mead's methodological position and its public expression Newton was doubtlessly aware. The men were close friends during the whole of Newton's London years and were active together at the Royal Society (Mead became FRS and Newton PRS in 1703; at Newton's behest Mead became VPRS in 1717).

[28] Mead, *Poisons, Works,* I, 1–21. See Earles, "Early theories of the mode of action of drugs and poisons," 100–102.

[29] Mead, *Poisons, Works,* I, 3.

[30] Newton, for example, cast his "Queries" in the negative and thereby implied a greater likelihood for their truth than falsity. But where Newton leaves no more than implication Mead (and many others) immediately leaped from possibility to reality. "Whoever," he suggested, "thoroughly comprehends and considers what is delivered in these pieces, under the form of queries and suppositions, will be let into some knowledge of the secret springs of nature. . . ." One need, therefore, only extend Newton's suggestions to the animate realm to find that physiology is "of a piece with the known system of the universe" and that it studies with natural philosophy the very same "laws of nature." Mead, *Poisons, Works,* I, 16.

31 Mead's dubious Newtonianism opens larger questions which I am unable to pursue. If not Mead, then who were the true Newtonians in biology? Indeed, may we legitimately speak at all of biological Newtonianism? Our sense of symmetry demands that biology find its place in the scientific revolution of the seventeenth century and Newton stands conspicuously at the culmination of this revolution. Nevertheless, seventeenth-century biology is, among other things, significantly more Cartesian than Newtonian. The same situation probably obtained in the eighteenth century, particularly when apologiae by biological Newtonians are discounted and their practice examined. In short, skepticism is in order. The general question of Newtonian influences in biology depends as much open our understanding of what is specifically Newtonian in science as upon what we may subsequently learn about the development of physiological thought. Common accord has by no means been reached on the first point while studies concerning the latter are still rare. We know astonishingly little about the ways of eighteenth-century biological thought and much of what we do know, once we leave England, escapes our Newtonian net.

WILLIAM COLEMAN

JOHN HERMAN RANDALL, JR.

The Religious Consequences of Newton's Thought

E VER SINCE THE DAYS OF THE GREEKS, THE WESTERN TRADITION HAS BEEN
distinguished from other cultures by the possession of intellectual interests
that have grown into what we would recognize today as science and philosophy. From the time of the early Milesian pioneers, we can trace a genuine continuity
of scientific questioning, of concern with finding out what the world really is, as
contrasted with the fanciful and imaginative cosmologies of the Mesopotamians.
And Western philosophizing, as distinguished from the wisdom attained by other
cultures and traditions, has usually faced the ultimate issues of human living and
destiny, with their decisions and commitments to certain values, with an equal concern that such choices be made in the light of the best knowledge available of the
situation that confronts man in his world.

This preoccupation with science and rational, critical vision has developed within
a culture with strong religious traditions. The intellectual leaders of that culture have
normally been powerfully attracted to both sets of values, scientific and religious. Indeed, Western philosophy began and has continued—where its problems have not
become merely "academic" and inherited, as so often today—with the impingement
of new scientific ideas on religious beliefs. Hence those religious beliefs have normally and inevitably been construed and interpreted in the light of the reigning way
of understanding the world. At times the impact of novel scientific ideas has seemed
too revolutionary for religious leaders to accept. More often, scientific and religious
beliefs have been carefully set apart from each other, and taken as dealing with two
quite distinct realms. But in the end Western thinkers have never been willing to
live long with their religious and scientific ideas at variance. From Empedocles on,
at least, they have tried to give their religious beliefs a "scientific" interpretation.
They have tried to "harmonize" their religion and their science; intellectually, they
have been committed to "reconciling" the two.

Hence the great minds who have created the schemes of understanding by which
Western culture has lived have ultimately furnished the intellectual framework
within which religious experience of the world, the play of feeling and action which
is the essence of the religious life, have been understood to occur. Plato, as interpreted
by Plotinus, furnished the concepts by which the Christian vision and commitment
were given intellectual substance. Traditional Christian theology was formulated by
the Church Fathers in terms of what we conventionally call the philosophy of Neo-
platonism. Its technical concepts and distinctions are scarcely intelligible without
an understanding of how that philosophy expressed its vision of the world, and of
man's traffic with and in it. When a millennium later historical circumstances power-

fully attracted Western European thinkers to the comprehensive science of Aristotle, that body of intellectual tools was used to reinterpret this Platonic theology. What Aristotle could explain was "rational" or "natural" theology. Men worked out a new synthesis and a new framework within which the medieval mind could feel at home in the confidence of understanding what is.

In the modern world, the greatest intellectual influence on the understanding of the religious life and its setting has been Isaac Newton. Newton came in the eighteenth century to serve as the symbol of "modern science," and despite the deepening and even transformation of the Newtonian world-picture in our century, there is a sense in which, especially for the popular mind, so influential in determining attitudes toward religion, he still so serves. Newton had predecessors in furnishing new scientific ideas for religious reinterpretation, the Copernicus who inspired isolated thinkers like Bruno and some of the followers of Cusanus; the Descartes who for half a century dominated religious thinkers in France and Holland. He has had no real successor, despite the tremendous influence on religious thinking of the symbols of men like Darwin and Freud. Men still assume that to our knowledge—whatever be our hopes and faith—the world that confronts us is a great machine, even if it be a more intricate and more electrical machine than Newton himself suspected. With this machine-world religious thought must still set out, however far it may advance "beyond" it, or whatever further dimensions it may flatter itself it can discover. The Divine may be remote, and "up there," as the eighteenth century concluded; or it may work through the machine that is its incarnation, as on the whole the nineteenth century decided. But the world we encounter as there for us, or the one whose resources we must use in all our activities, is still the very one the scientist is concerned to explore. In desperation—and crisis—many recent thinkers have followed Heidegger in abandoning the attempt to find any satisfying what-is in the world in which man lives. Alienated from that world, they have sought what "really is" in man himself, in man's own "existence."

This forceful presentation of a world from which man cannot but feel himself alienated has without doubt been the greatest and most enduring consequence of Newton's thought for religion. It is the consequence of that vision of the world for which Newton became the symbol, rather than of the more original suggestions of Newton's own thought. It was after all Descartes, not Newton, who first held that man is a bodily machine that incomprehensibly can "think." Newton himself carefully distinguished between "experimental philosophy"—what we have come to call "natural science"—and those further suggestions which, in the form of queries, he included in a more speculative "philosophy of nature." There are few educated men today who would view the universe in other terms than those of our own proliferating "experimental philosophy"—though what its terms will become tomorrow is still by no means certain. For a century, after their initial enthusiasm had faded, that

JOHN HERMAN RANDALL, JR.

Nature and Nature's laws lay hid in night;
God said, let Newton be, and all was light,

men inclined to think that they must go beyond Nature to its Source, best reached through the soul of man. Experimental philosophy was for them "mere science," and man fortunately had more powerful intellectual resources. This "philosophic Idealism," in the broadest sense, was rooted in Newton's own speculations; it was first forcefully enunciated by Berkeley, who followed up Newton's own views on "spirit," and emphasized one of Newton's own two interpretations of his "experimental philosophy." It culminated in the comprehensive Idealism of Hegel, who identified man —or at least Hegel himself—with God, and made Nature a rather minor part of God. But then Darwin made man inescapably a part of Nature; in their enthusiasm his first readers, forgetting that if man be a part of Nature, he is still a rather distinctive and indeed unique part of it, found Nature once more all that is, and found it an "alien world."

In our own Age of Anxiety, man can scarcely claim to have become less alienated than his late nineteenth-century forebears. But this alienation is now primarily from a technological society, and it is due to the forces for which Arkwright, Ricardo, and indeed Karl Marx—with an assist from Lenin and his successors—must serve as symbols. This burgeoning technology keeps us from worrying too much today about the alienness of Nature; we have more immediate worries. But it would be inconceivable for a contemporary to feel that sympathetic bond with Nature that came naturally to Wordsworth or Emerson. Newton's world, taken seriously once more—as it has had to be for a century—precludes that possibility. The Divine is no longer "up there," as our "God is dead" theologians have belatedly discovered, and as the Soviet cosmonaut ironically reported. Nor is the Divine to be found in the "vernal wood," as the Romantic poets addicted to the pathetic fallacy maintained. If anywhere, the Divine must be found in Man himself—in man's vision of what might be. But, then—where is "what might be" to be located? Surely it is to be found among Nature's possibilities. But how are "possibilities" to be discovered, let alone realized? Not by Newton's "experimental philosophy," which proceeds by "deduction from phenomena." Possibilities are found only by genuinely experimental activity and manipulation—by human "Art." They can be "seen" or discerned only in the artist's or the prophet's vision.

Newton's machine-world, we have said, has been the greatest and the most enduring consequence of Newton's thought for religion. In our own century we have escaped that world of Newton only by abandoning the "realistic" view of science on which it was founded, for other interpretations of what the scientist is really doing. Newton himself started by thinking, and he was traditionally held to have shown, that he was giving a literal description of "what is"—whatever that might mean; or better, that he was seizing directly the intelligible structure of the universe, the Order of Nature. The engraver well expressed this view, in placing below a depiction of Newton as a star of the first magnitude, surrounded by twinkles, the lines:

> See the great Newton, he who first surveyed
> The plan by which the universe was made;
> Saw Nature's simple yet stupendous laws,
> And proved th' effects, though not explained the cause.

Recent philosophies of science, in all their varieties, view the enterprise of the scientist not as "seeing the plan by which the universe was made," but as both *selective,* of certain distinctive features of the world encountered—certain structural features of the way its processes take place—and as intellectually *manipulative,* formulating in symbolic systems the principles that can unite these selected structures into a consistent system of statement. But the world exhibits not only the ways in which events take place—which are the proper objects of the scientist's inquiry—but also the wealth of the many other features which these ways make possible—which the scientist with his concentrated aim properly disregards. Thus even the "science of Man" concentrates on causes and their consequences, and their relations, but leaves out most of the important further features which what we have come to call a "phenomenological" description and analysis of human nature exhibits. The psychologist hardly considers the powers and possibilities of human thinking, feeling, and action to which human artistic, ethical, and religious vision point. What can man do and become in his world? Vision affirms what only the effort of manipulation, of art, can make actual. Newton, and the science or "experimental philosophy deduced from phenomena" he practiced and symbolized, observed only the ways in which nature was doing what it was doing when observed by a *passive spectator.* He did not observe what Nature can do when cooperating with the human part of Nature, with man's additional determinations. We can put this simply by saying that Newtonian science articulates what Nature *is doing*; it fails to state the powers and possibilities of what Nature and man together *might* and *can* do. It is a *passive* report of what is happening, not, like our own science, a *manipulative* effort to find out what can happen or be made to happen.

The human part of Nature can *make* things happen; this we know from direct experience. Can Nature, apart from man, or anything in it, likewise be properly said to *make* things happen? At this point Newton's own thought divides; and as men followed one or the other of its two branches, they worked out one or the other of the two major philosophies of science that have come down through the nineteenth century to our own day. Newton set out, as himself a "realist," as he put it, "from the phenomena of motions to investigate the forces of nature." From these forces, once discovered, their effects could then be deduced in demonstrative form. This was the traditional, ultimately Aristotelian notion of science as demonstration of effects from their causes. Newton started with the notion of "force," that which *makes* things happen; for him all causes were *efficient* causes. Now he was convinced he had indeed deduced from phenomena the force that makes motion take place

JOHN HERMAN RANDALL, JR.

and accelerates it. This was the force of inertia to be found in all masses, and the force of impact—what the Cartesians called *"choque."* But Newton was equally convinced he had *not* found what makes gravitation take place. And what the "force" of gravitation might be he left undetermined to the end of his life—despite the effort of his editor, Roger Cotes, to identify it with a presumed force of "attraction."

Hence when he was thinking of the laws of motion, Newton was led back to the traditional "realistic" view of science as demonstration from causes—efficient causes; to the view that his dynamics deduced the effects discovered in phenomena from discovered causes, the forces of inertia in masses. But when he was thinking of the law of gravitation, he was led on to a novel conception of the nature of science: that it merely described what was observed to take place—the "cause," the so-called "force" of gravitation, had so far eluded experimental philosophy. Newton himself remained convinced that these forces had been placed in masses by God as their Creator or ultimate Efficient Cause, so that in the end what made everything happen was, as tradition had had it, the will of God.

This novel notion of a *descriptive* or *observational* science was worked out with great acuteness by Berkeley, who merely dispensed with the intermediate "forces of masses" and made the cause of all happening the immediate force or will of God. But Hume pointed out that we could never *observe* anything making anything else happen, any "force" in things; the path to a *causing* God was both inscrutable and unnecessary. For Hume, man was left with the pure world-machine, from which all religious values had evaporated.

On the other hand, Newton's notion of a science of motions caused by forces was complicated by his insistence that forces, and the other necessary concepts of his dynamics, like space and time, and indeed the "hard massy particles" that were the ultimate masses, ought to be given directly to *observation* in phenomena—ought to be "simple ideas," as Locke was putting it at the same time. This view, that concepts must be "seen" in facts, goes back in the tradition stretching to fourteenth-century William of Ockham, which had become strongly entrenched in British thought. But *in fact* these concepts or principles were all unobservable: they could *not* be "deduced from phenomena," despite Newton's attempt to *"see"* them directly, in his pail experiment; they could only be taken as assumptions or presuppositions of phenomena. This realization, when developed by the left-wing Newtonians, by Keill, Friend, and the German Newtonian physicists like Leonhard Euler, led straight to the Kantian conception of science as an *interpretation* of what was observed in terms of presupposed principles or assumptions. This view likewise left no room for a causing God, and Kant had to turn to man and man's experience to find God there as a moral ideal.

Thus the religious consequences of *both* of Newton's own two interpretations or philosophies of his science, were to destroy any scientific demonstration of the "existence" of God. God ceased to be a necessary concept of physics. Hence Laplace is reported to have replied to Napoleon's question about the place of God in his celestial mechanics, "Sire, I have no need of that hypothesis." Laplace was expressing the conclusions of Enlightenment science.

Force, and with it God's Will and Providence, vanished from the two technical philosophies of science stemming from Newton. But before God was thus murdered, his character had been already ruined. In Newton's theological thought, God had become the Original Force or Creator, the First Efficient Cause, who made the world-machine and then left its devices to the subordinate forces he had inserted in its masses. Even in Berkeley's version, God, though not remote, remained the causal force making events happen. To view God as solely the remote Creator and Law-giver was, from the standpoint of the warm and humanly accessible God of the long Christian tradition, bad enough. But it was soon observed that if God directly or indirectly "caused" everything, he could scarcely be a moral personality: the old Problem of Evil broke out with renewed force, and was underlined in Hume and in Voltaire's *Candide*. In other words, the Newtonian rational theology, which identified God with the ultimate concepts of mechanics, turned out to have no religious value, because mechanics and its concepts are morally neutral. A science that is to be "harmonized" with religious beliefs must at least explain Man, as both Plotinus and Aristotle had measurably done. But Newtonian mechanics quite failed to understand Man and his vision of powers and possibilities.

Thus one consequence of Newton's thought for religion was to make clear *how not* to harmonize religion and science: by identifying religious ideas with the concepts of a "value-free" science. For however "rationalized," the ideas of a rational theology, in which religious beliefs are given an interpretation in terms of scientific concepts, must explain not just nature apart from Man; indeed, they need not explain Nature at all. What they must make intelligible is human experience, man's experience of what Edmund Husserl came to call his *Lebenswelt*. And this experience of Man's "lived world" is shot through and through with values and ends, which must be intelligibly included if there is to be any explanation of Man at all. The Divine must be taken as at least a valid human ideal. God may or may not be taken as a mythical Efficient Cause, as a causal or creative force—"mythical" because none of our interpretations of science can find sufficient evidence for the presence of such an efficient force. But God must be seen as a Final Cause—as St. Thomas wisely argued—as the goal of human activity. In the rational theologies of both Plato-Plotinus and of Aristotle, the Divine was a Final Cause, a goal or ideal, however mythically unified. But now Newtonian mechanics, when its ultimate categories were identified with theological concepts, had eliminated all idea of final cause—such a concept had no place in dynamics. God was reduced to power or "Force" alone. Traditionally, the Christian God has possessed the attributes of both Power and Goodness. Newtonian rational religion abandoned the goodness, and left Power alone. As J. S. Mill remarked of a later similar reduction, Dean Henry L. Mansel's, to

JOHN HERMAN RANDALL, JR.

replace the Divine Goodness with Power alone is intellectually preposterous, morally damnable, and theologically blasphemous.

We have been emphasizing that the machine-world of Newton's experimental philosophy has been of greatest moment for religious thought: here it is *Newton the symbol* rather than *Newton the original thinker* who is responsible, though Newton's own method of the detached observer deducing his conclusions from phenomena lent powerful support to the conception of the scientist as a passive spectator, who naturally misses in the world all that such a mere spectator cannot discover—the deliverances of artistic imagination, of moral commitment, of religious vision. For a century it was the Newtonian rational theologians, beginning with Samuel Clarke, who in turning the assumptions of mechanics into religious principles, as a result squeezed out all religious values from what ended as a mere rational foundation for physics. Both the philosophies of science initiated by Newton himself—as apart from the "plan by which the universe was made" view for which he served in the popular mind as a symbol—when worked out consistently, in Berkeley and Hume, and in Euler and Kant, respectively, came to deny the need or the possibility for any such rational foundation for physics; and eighteenth-century Rational Theology now lost its scientific function, as it had already lost its religious function. By 1781 the collapse was complete.

This left the machine-world as something which must indeed be accepted as the *starting point* of the effort to understand what is, but must also be *transcended* or passed beyond—escaped from—in the interest of religious beliefs and values. For another century religion and science functioned as two rival cognitive enterprises, two different ways of understanding the world. Either the *religious way* was true, and the scientific way merely provisional; or the *scientific way* was true, and the religious way at best poetry, symbol, and myth, and at worst superstition or even meaningless. For all this conflict, which reached heroic heights when Darwin came in the eighteen sixties to reinforce the supremacy of the Newtonian world, Newton the symbol must accept responsibility. Even when Marx came to set up a new social religion, his faith had, like all nineteenth-century bodies of religious ideas, to be construed as in opposition to and transcending the developing sciences of Man and Society—mere "bourgeois social science," the faithful dubbed them. And even today we still talk seriously, with Rudolf Bultmann, about "demythologizing" religion, as though religious "myth" were a decrepit rival of science that must be allowed to die quietly. Or we find it news that "God is dead," a discovery scarcely novel in Nietzsche himself—for the God who is "dead" is merely the God of Newtonian thought. Indeed even with our more sophisticated conceptions of the nature and function of religion, and of the nature and function of science, it remains hard for us not to see *intellectual rivalry* in what is *really a difference of function*. We find even Paul Tillich setting the "calculating reason" of science over against the "participating reason" of religion—in a "system" that displays little of science and seems to some—though

The Religious Consequences of Newton's Thought

wrongly, I should myself judge—to exhibit little enough of religion. The claims, combined with the inadequacy, of the Newtonian world are still generating this supposed rivalry between two different ways of understanding.

So far, in attempting to trace the religious consequences of Newton's thought, we have been dealing primarily with *Newton the symbol,* rather than with his own *original speculative suggestions*—which he himself always kept carefully distinct from his "experimental philosophy." But these speculations, which contributed powerfully to the current of philosophical Idealism that came to dominate a century of religious thinking after the collapse of Newtonian Rational Theology, had their own consequences in fostering the emphasis on the "immanence" of God, on what may even be called a form of religious pantheism, which was perhaps a natural reaction when the lack of religious value in the wholly transcendent God of Rational Theology had once been revealed. One suspects that this Newtonian conception of the Divine as the Immanent Structure of the world and as the Force that sustains it, was a major factor that made it possible for the late eighteenth-century thinkers like Lessing and Herder to begin to understand Spinoza at last. Newton was henceforth joined with Spinoza as the bulwark of the nineteenth-century renewed attempt at harmonizing religious and scientific thought, at the erection of a new and, it was hoped, more adequate natural theology. When Darwin burst in, it was the continuance of this strain in Newton that led religious thinkers to proclaim,

Some call it Evolution, but others call it God.

And one finds this Newtonian strain still persisting in the physicist Alfred North Whitehead, who could find God as the "principle of concretion" in all concrescent events.

Newton's Philosophy of Nature ultimately purported to describe a world, every element in which, in accordance with his Ockhamism, ought to be directly observable, and yet was quite inaccessible to observation. All the ultimate concepts of his physics ought to be "deducible from phenomena," and would be so observable to a perfect mind. Such an observing mind was a necessity for Newton. Hence it is not surprising that he should have given all his absolutes a home in the mind of God. Absolute time and space are God's "sensorium": by existing God constitutes them, as the ultimate container wherein all motions take place. This Divine Sensorium or Mind sustains the entire field of physics, just as the Divine Will, or ether, the vehicle of force, holds the system of moving masses together. God is for Newton's thought not only the great Observer; he is also the great Conserver. He is exercising ceaseless vigilance to maintain his Law and Order against the subversive forces in the universe. He keeps the stars from bumping together, and gathering in an inert cluster in the center of space, as they otherwise would through the operation of universal gravitation. He also corrects the irregularities which Newton's equations had been unable to banish from the cosmic machine: from time to time he repairs and winds up the clock, and adjusts its operations. For this work "force" is needed, and is supplied through

JOHN HERMAN RANDALL, JR.

the ether that is the vehicle of God's will. Thus physics itself demands the exercise of God's care, and his Providence is rooted in the structure of the universe.

The notion of God as the very *constitutive structure* of the universe of moving masses came to Newton from the Platonic tradition to which the first English harmonizers of religion and science in the seventeenth century had appealed. Here Newton is remembering Henry More, whose ideas he learned first from his mathematics teacher at Cambridge, Isaac Barrow, and then from Lady Masham and her circle at Conway. For More absolute space and God possessed twenty attributes in common: God was identical with the "plastic nature' of the Platonic tradition. Both God and Space are: "one, simple, immobile, eternal, perfect, independent, existing by itself, subsisting through itself, incorruptible, necessary, immense, uncreated, uncircumscribed, incomprehensible, omnipresent, incorporeal, permeating and embracing all things, essential being, actual being, pure actuality."[1]

As Newton interpreted it, the world of nature needs a Supreme Observer to constitute it and hold it together, and to direct and sustain its order. The consequences of the necessity of such a constitutive and sustaining mind have been momentous for the subsequent philosophy of physical science. In Kant's version, "pure reason," a generalized form of the human mind, has replaced the mind of God. But the Divine Mind returned with the idealists seeking escape from the Newtonian machine, and throughout the nineteenth century down to our present day efforts to understand, the world of physics—the so-called "physical world"—when conceived in Newtonian terms as existing in sharp contrast to the world of human experience—the *Lebenswelt*—has always craved a Supreme Mind to lend it structure and permanence. Despite all the drive towards positivism, such a Mind, whether taken as God or objective Reason or Logos, has persisted in some form as an ultimate physical concept. Where such a constitutive objective mind has been wholly lacking, as in the empiricist tradition, natural science has had little structure or permanence; and empiricists have always been committed to trying to persuade physicists that their science ought to be a far different kind of thing, and ought to have a far different kind of structure, from what it in fact is and has. In our own day empiricists have had to remedy the traditional defect in their vision by finding that structure in language; and our own philosophies of science are disputing primarily over how far that language is itself the structure of things—is itself the articulation of what Newton would have called the Divine Sensorium.

These consequences of the Platonic strain in Newton's thought have been momentous for the philosophy of science. But here we can only emphasize their import for religious thought. Berkeley was resolutely opposed to Locke's acceptance of the Newtonian machine of masses, and to his consequent Newtonian theology. But he was trying to work out the religious implications of this other strain in Newton, which in the end became for him a full-fledged Platonism. One of the most interesting and attractive of the early developments of what we can call Newton's "physical pantheism" is the philosophy of Jonathan Edwards, for whom God was all in all, and its parallel in Columbia's Samuel Johnson. For Edwards' Newtonian pantheism, "Certainly the Universe exists no where but in the Divine mind. . . . Space is necessary, eternal, infinite, and omnipresent. But I had as good speak plain: I have already said as much as, that Space is God. . . . To find out the Reasons of things, in Natural Philosophy, is only to find out the proportion of God acting. . . . All is constantly proceeding from God, as light from the sun. In Him we live, and move, and have our being."[2]

For a century, we have seen, Newton the symbol drove thinkers with religious interests to some form of philosophic Idealism as their instrument for rationalizing—and modernizing, reconstructing, and secularizing—the religious tradition. Most of the structure and the details of this idealism came from the post-Kantian Germans, and naturally reflect the Leibnizian idealism of the German tradition and Kant. But in England and America the persisting strain of Newton the speculative thinker, of what we may call "Newtonian Idealism," or "Immaterialism," prepared the ground and often influenced the form which the imported German idealism assumed. From Coleridge on it is not hard to discern in Anglo-American versions of philosophic Idealism the persisting core of English Platonism—and of Newton's version of it.

Newton the symbol has had pervasive consequences for all subsequent religious thought. The ideas he stood for first formed the structure of the reinterpretation of the religious tradition that eventuated in eighteenth-century liberal religion—the rational theology that tried to harmonize religion and science by reducing it to a set of supposedly scientific ideas, which then speedily collapsed under criticism. They then proceeded to convince religious thinkers that religion must offer a way of understanding the world that will oppose, supplement, and transcend the way offered by science. Newton the thinker himself transmitted and set forth the main outlines of what this opposing way of understanding must consist of.

But whether Newton's ideas be taken as the discovery of what religious concepts really mean, or as a set of inadequate conceptions that constitute a "mere science" that must be transcended by a more adequate intellectual method and an enlarged conception of reason, or as going on to suggest what that better way of understanding should undertake, Newton has remained the symbol and the suggestion of something religious thinking must take account of, and somehow come to terms with. It will come to terms with Newton only at its peril—for if Newtonian Rational Theology taught that religion and science could not be harmonized by identifying their ultimate concepts, Newtonian Idealism likewise showed that the two were not to be reconciled by identifying their function—as offering rival bodies of what Hegel called "absolute knowledge" of the world. Religion is not to be "demythologized" by identifying it with Newton's way of understanding the world, or with that of any later physicist. But neither is it to be demythologized by identifying it with Heidegger's and Bultmann's. The twentieth century has still to work out, on the basis of a closer analysis of the distinctive functions of science and of religion, how both can be entertained by the modern mind.

JOHN HERMAN RANDALL, JR.

Our present-day philosophies of Nature agree that Newton is now dead. They vie in pointing out just where he went wrong or stopped short. And present-day religion would be surprised to learn it still had any traffic with what Newton stood for or with what he actually thought. But for religion, we have tried to point out, Newton may be dead, but he certainly is not buried. And his mighty ghost is busily engaged in haunting our own attempts to deal with his problem—the eternal problem of thinking and sensitive men—of uniting knowledge with aspiration and commitment. I suspect that like God himself, Newton is no deader than he ever was.

NOTES

[1] Henry More, *Enchiridion metaphysicum,* Part I, chapter viii, sec. 8.

[2] See Herbert W. Schneider, *A History of American Philosophy,* 2nd ed. (1963), Chapter 3, "Immaterialism."

Contributors

Asger Aaboe is Professor of Mathematics and the History of Science and Chairman of the Department of History of Science and Medicine, Yale University.

J. Morton Briggs, Jr. is Associate Professor of History, University of Rhode Island.

Gerd Buchdahl is Reader in History and Philosophy of Science, University of Cambridge.

I. Bernard Cohen is Professor of History of Science, Harvard University.

William Coleman is Associate Professor of History of Science, Johns Hopkins University.

Pierre Costabel is Directeur d'Études, École Pratique des Hautes Études, Paris.

Jürgen Ehlers is Professor of Physics and Research Physicist, Center for Relativity Theory, University of Texas at Austin.

David Hakes is Associate Professor of Psychology, The University of Texas at Austin.

A. Rupert Hall is Professor of History of Science and Technology, Imperial College, London.

Marie Boas Hall is Reader in History of Science and Technology, Imperial College, London.

Francis Haskell is Professor of History of Art, University of Oxford.

John W. Herivel heads the Department of History and Philosophy of Science, Queen's University of Belfast.

Christopher Hill is Master of Balliol College, University of Oxford.

Thomas S. Kuhn is M. Taylor Pyne Professor of the History of Science and Director of the Program in History and Philosophy of Science, Princeton University.

Frank E. Manuel is Professor of History, New York University.

James E. McGuire is Lecturer in the History and Philosophy of Science, University of Leeds.

Robert Palter is Professor of Philosophy and History, University of Texas at Austin.

John H. Randall, Jr. is F.J.E. Woodbridge Professor of Philosophy, Columbia University.

E. L. Schücking is Professor of Physics, New York University.

Dudley Shapere is Professor of Philosophy, University of Chicago.

Howard Stein is Professor of Philosophy, Case Western Reserve University.

Lawrence Stone is Dodge Professor of History and Director of the Shelley Cullom Davis Center for Historical Studies, Princeton University.

C. Truesdell is Professor of Rational Mechanics, Johns Hopkins University.

Richard S. Westfall is Professor of the History of Science, Indiana University.

D. T. Whiteside is Assistant Director of Research, Department of Pure Mathematics, and Senior Research Fellow, Churchill College, University of Cambridge.

A. E. Woodruff is Associate Professor, Belfer Graduate School of Sciences, Yeshiva University.

Index